# ROCK:
## POSTMODERNISM IN ACTION

FIRST EDITION

## MICHAEL BARNETT

Bassim Hamadeh, CEO and Publisher
Kassie Graves, Director of Acquisitions
Jamie Giganti, Senior Managing Editor
Miguel Macias, Senior Graphic Designer
Mark Combes, Senior Field Acquisitions Editor
Sean Adams, Project Editor
Luiz Ferreira, Senior Licensing Specialist
Christian Berk, Associate Editor
Joyce Lue, Interior Designer

# CONTENTS

**UNIT 2: THE SIXTIES AND SEVENTIES**

# UNIT 3: THE EIGHTIES AND NINETIES

# PREFACE

It could easily be argued that no other type of music is more entrenched in American culture than rock. For many people, myself included, rock music provided the soundtrack to our lives. The songs, the artists, the feeling of freedom and rebelliousness, even the look and the lingo that pervaded rock was a constant presence, a given. In other words, I have much more than an academic interest in rock music. My own relationship with rock goes as far back as anything I can remember in my life and has developed into three distinct yet overlapping roles: first (and always) as a fan, then as a practitioner (particularly a heavy metal drummer), and lastly as a scholar (which I just conceptualize as a fan who has done a lot of research). It is as all three that I offer you the material contained in these pages.

Some years ago when I decided to attend college to study music composition, my nontraditional background as a heavy metal musician caused me many uncomfortable and challenging moments. Most of my professors looked down their nose at me because I was a heavy metal musician. (What business did I have trying to be a "serious" composer!?) Back then, those staunchly conventional academics simply didn't realize what I and so many others already knew: rock is a multifaceted and deeply artistic form of expression, abounding with its own musical syntax and vibrant musicality. Thankfully, in the past couple of decades, rock has gained a secure foothold in academia as a "legitimate" form of musical expression as well as a significant cultural force. As such, its history, music, and artists are topics of classroom study, primarily as elective "appreciation" courses. In the early twentieth century, jazz music met with similar narrow-mindedness from academics but eventually came to be deeply appreciated for its musical sophistication. Jazz and jazz studies are now fixtures in nearly every college-level music program at the professional level. I suspect that in years to come, mainstream universities everywhere will have their own performing rock ensembles, if not full-fledged rock music study programs for aspiring music professionals.

Having taught rock history to many hundreds of college students, I was at first surprised—and now continuously delighted—by the numbers of rock fans among them. That the music of previous generations can still hold so much of its meaning and energy for today's youth speaks volumes. If you consider yourself among those ranks, this book will likely introduce you to many facts—and much music—of which you are not yet aware. If you are not an ardent fan of rock music, it is my sincere hope that by the end of your studies, you will be.

## About the Text and Companion Website

Many textbooks that deal with rock-era music also provide in-depth diversions into other contemporaneous styles such as disco, reggae, rap, and Motown pop that, on one hand, serve some purpose in understanding the interconnectedness of these styles, but on the other hand, devour much of the semester and draw the focus away from rock itself. This also typically results in a breadth of material that cannot be reasonably ingested in the course of a single semester. I have chosen to maintain the focus of this study more or less squarely on rock and heavily rock-based styles, without giving short shrift to the concurrent developments in other popular music styles. I hope my efforts in this will prove successful and provide a rewarding experience to the reader.

The website will enhance the overall course experience primarily through the listening examples but also through discussion group topics, assignment/exam/event calendars, instructor announcements, study and listening guides, and a gradebook that calculates a running percentage score as the semester progresses.

**To the Instructor:** This study is designed to provide the liberal arts, non-music major with insights into the world of rock music and culture but will also be meaningful to the music major who wishes to gain a deeper appreciation of the musical and cultural context of rock; there are numerous examples of musical sophistication and virtuosity on a par with the great works of history of which he or she may not be aware. While there is naturally some overlap, the general discussion of rock can be fairly neatly divided into decades. Given that, the text is arranged into three units: The first unit serves as an introduction to the defining features and historical development of rock; subsequent units each cover rock music and culture by decade from the 1960s through the 1990s; there are some concluding thoughts dealing with rock and popular music culture in the twenty-first century. Within each decade division, chapters are dedicated to various flavors of rock, cultural developments, and central artists and events. In some cases there will be a focus on the lyrics as well as the music, given that lyrics often convey as much or more emotional power and cultural relevance as the music itself. Select examples are accompanied by charts to guide students in understanding form and sectional relationships, which they can then be taught to apply in recognizing similar or varied structures in other examples and in their own pursuits as informed listeners.

There are also easy to follow charts that map common rock rhythms in a manner designed for the musically non-literate, but which will not insult the intelligence of the musically literate.

The entire textbook is designed to correspond to the standard fifteen-week academic semester, allowing instructors to devote roughly one week to each chapter, with one week left over for student presentations, review, or other activities. There are ideas at the end of each chapter for student work on musical concepts/practices, critical thinking and discussion on cultural/social matters that were/are central to rock, and thought-provoking questions on specific topic areas that remain relevant in modern times. There are also suggestions for more in-depth study of specific artists.

The primary function of the website is to provide audio, and for later chapters, embedded video examples for study and analysis. The audio examples are accessible via a Spotify playlist in order to keep student costs as low as possible while providing a consistent resource for music listening. Thanks to the ease and economy of the playlists, I have included copious examples of rock music in each chapter. This will allow instructors many options in selecting songs/videos for further study, and for customizing listening exams. The site also provides PowerPoint slides which can be used in lecture presentations as well as options for online discussion groups.

**To the Student:** A quality liberal arts education can equip one to solve problems, think creatively and critically, and engage with the relevant issues one encounters in personal, professional, and social life. When taken as a part of such an education, a course in rock music can have the effect of enriching one's music-listening experience as well as enhancing one's appreciation for the contributions, musical and otherwise, that the artists who grace these pages have made. But rock goes much deeper than that.

This text and the accompanying website are meant to serve as a musical and cultural guide through the years that helped define much about who we are today. Many of the norms and freedoms we enjoy as a society were, in part, shaped by the musical culture of the rock era. Rock musicians sang out against engrained societal conventions, encouraged alternative worldviews, promoted freedom of thought and expression, championed underdog causes, and eroded or completely erased cultural, racial, and sexual taboos. Even as we ebb and flow in our progress as a species, it is no exaggeration to say that without rock music and the impact it has had on modern culture we would be living in a profoundly different world today.

The fact that you've chosen to take a course in rock music says something about you: At the very least you love music; and you'll probably discover that you know more about music than you might have imagined; perhaps you are an amateur musician seeking to learn more about rock, or possibly a music major who would like to enhance your understanding of a style that has been comparatively overlooked in the traditional music curriculum. In any case, this text will introduce you to many fascinating musicians, as well as encourage you to listen to and think critically about the music and lyrics we study while hopefully strengthening your understanding of the world in which we currently live.

Musical concepts are presented in a way that can be understood by everyone and units are arranged in a roughly decade-based chronology. Chapters within each unit focus on the developments in rock and rock culture, technology, fusions of rock with other styles, and the important artists who made it all happen. The website features Spotify-based playlists for each chapter as well as embedded music videos beginning as early as Chapter 7 and increasing from Chapter 10 on. Your instructor may choose a variety of activities related to the material in the textbook and the audio and video examples on the website.

The most effective way for you to experience this textbook is, as you begin each chapter, go to the course website and open the corresponding Spotify chapter playlist. As you read, take the time to stop and listen to each musical example where it is indicated. Although it will take more time, by proceeding in this way you will have immediate musical reinforcement of the written material and you will likely have a much easier time associating each artist with their music.

Let's rock!

# UNIT ONE
# DEFINITION AND PREHISTORY OF ROCK

1.1: Paul McCartney's bass and George Harrison's guitar

# CHAPTER 1
# Basics of Rock

*Call it what you want, it's all music to me.*
-Jeff Keith of the band Tesla

## The Golden Age of Rock (1960-1999)

To the initiate of music history, the periodization of music can be misleading. We can certainly talk about the "classical period" or the "jazz age" or the "rock era" with a reasonable amount of historical precision, although a more accurate way of understanding the development of music would be to say that as an art form it is in a nearly constant state of evolution with intermittent periods of relative stability, thus giving meaning to the idea of *periods* or *ages* or *eras* in music history. Additionally, contemporaneous styles exert an influence on each other often blurring lines and making it difficult to precisely trace stylistic evolutions within a given time period. At this juncture in human history we can roughly define the rock era to be the period between around 1960 and the turn of the century. I am reluctant to declare wholeheartedly that the rock era has indeed ended as this is a matter that is still open to debate. It may be more accurate to think of the period in question as the "Golden Age of Rock."

A preliminary step in our discussion is to establish an understanding of just what "rock" is, at least in the most basic sense. Labeling music can often prove problematic in that it can be restrictive, vague, contradictory, and even insulting. For example, the term "alternative" was abuzz in the late 1980s and early 1990s. At the time the term was coined it was being used to describe commercially oriented music that was outside of the popular mainstream. However, many so-called "alternative" bands ended up gaining enough popularity to be technically classified as mainstream. What then? The term seems to lose its meaning at that point. Another example from a different corner of the music world is the term "serious music," which in a general sense is associated with contemporary concert hall music—music created by trained composers, without commercial goals in mind and appealing to a relatively limited, usually academic audience (some call this "art" music). Go ask just about any musician if they are "serious" about their music or if they consider what they do to be "art." It is safe to say that the reactions you will get will range from the indignant to the openly hostile.

The term *rock*, although seemingly more descriptive of the music itself than labels like "alternative" or "serious music," is no less problematic. "Rock" is really a subjective label that has come to mean many things to many people: rock is young, rock is old; it is energetic, it is reflective; it is elaborate, it is simple. Rock ranges from the garage band to the grandiose, from the comforting to the disturbing, from the beautiful to the grotesque, from the most light-hearted party music to the most serious social critique. From Aerosmith to ZZ Top, rock is a style that has undergone a nearly continuous evolution over a long period of time with many subgenres emerging in the process (that is, hard rock, pop rock, acid rock, country rock, Southern rock, and so on). It can be said that rock has become a *shared understanding* among a large group of people from a variety of socioeconomic backgrounds, cultural spheres, age groups, and so on.

Moreover, the blurring of genre boundaries and musical cross-pollination over the decades have greatly transformed and expanded what is accepted into the realm of rock music. We need not look far to find examples of this: Led Zeppelin is one of the quintessential rock bands of the era. I know of no one who would argue this point. Yet, a song like "Going to California," a ballad for vocal, acoustic guitar, and mandolin—a traditional bluegrass instrument—was a prominent track on the band's wildly successful 1971 album *Led Zeppelin IV* and is a staple on classic rock radio stations today. The Beatles, arguably the greatest rock band of all time, recorded songs like "Eleanor Rigby," "When I'm Sixty-Four" and many others that have traditional classical or jazz instruments as their core instrumental sound. There are also countless instances of rock musicians writing and recording songs with musicians of vastly different stylistic backgrounds. Case in point: both Paul McCartney and Eddie Van Halen appear on Michael Jackson's *Thriller* album. Another prime example of stylistic merging is the interweaving of traditional classical instrumental and compositional techniques, which abound in certain types of heavy metal music. I could easily go on, but I think the point is clear.

Given these apparent complexities, it would seem wise to abandon the idea of a *static* definition of rock. Instead we will develop a *point of entry* in understanding rock's most basic characteristics, and from that point favor a *dynamic* approach to rock that is shaped by how the style evolved, expanded, and interacted with other musical styles that were either previously developed or developing contemporaneously with rock.

A practical path toward establishing our point of entry will be to divide our view of rock into two distinct components: 1) **musical characteristics** and 2) **cultural contexts**. As we move through the development of rock music and culture we will examine how each component has evolved, and the overall effect that evolution has had on the whole. To be sure, each component is thoroughly entangled with the other; however, clarity in understanding each component will help us build a comprehensive view of rock.

*Musical characteristics* are those elements with which we most closely associate how rock *sounds* and perhaps more importantly, how it *feels*. Defining this aspect will require some basic understanding of the elements of music in general and of rock specifically. Throughout the course of this textbook we will examine how the music changes, adapts, expands, and coalesces with other styles to ultimately become the pluralistic style it is today.

Because no art form exists in a vacuum, it is useful to shed light on the *cultural contexts* that surrounded and in many cases were either generated or supported by rock music. The interaction of rock with the world around it will be central here. It is important to realize that rock was more than just pop culture; rock was at the heart of a *cultural revolution* in the United States and around the world. Rock dominated the music world on a global scale and had an unprecedented cultural impact. Simultaneously there were numerous and varied forces acting in the world at large without which rock may never have come into existence.

## Musical Characteristics

We start by defining the most basic musical content from the earliest moments of what is generally considered to be rock's emergence (this emergence and its historical context will be discussed in Chapter 2). As we move through the decades of the rock era some of these musical characteristics will necessarily expand. But for the moment we will begin by unpacking some "nuts and bolts" questions about what rock music is in its most basic form.

1.  What are the fundamental musical elements of rock?

2.  What instruments do we typically find in a rock band?

3.  How is a basic rock song put together?

What are the fundamental musical elements of rock? To answer this we should first examine what is arguably rock's most defining musical element: rhythm. In the simplest terms, *rhythm* is organized movement through time. In rock music we understand and feel this movement primarily as the *beat*. A beat has several components: **meter** or **time signature**, **tempo**, and **beat subdivision**. A rock beat also employs various types of **syncopation**, including the type most central to rock, the **backbeat**.

**Meter or Time Signature:** This is the primary level at which musicians organize rhythm into units called measures, or bars. The meter defines how many beats are in each measure and what unit of musical rhythm constitutes each beat. These rhythmic beat units (most commonly the quarter note) are fractional divisions of time defined by the **tempo**, or the pace at which we feel the beat. Tempo is usually defined in beats per minute (BPM). So, if we have a piece that is said to be in 4/4 meter (pronounced "four-four") that means that there are four beats per measure (the first "four" in "four-four"), and that the quarter note is the unit that gets the beat (the second "four" in "four-four" and an abbreviation for the quarter note). Thus, if we choose a tempo of say, 120 BPM in 4/4, the beat would express 120 quarter notes per minute. This is a fairly simple concept which your instructor can demonstrate by setting a metronome to 120 BPM (or any tempo for that matter) and clapping the beat while counting to four.

> **Note:** 4/4 meter is far and away the most common meter in rock. In fact, it is the most common meter in Western music, so common that another name for 4/4 is *common time*, a term that dates back centuries.

There are three basic and distinct **beat subdivisions** found in rock music: **eighth note, sixteenth note** and **triplet** subdivision. We will start with eighth note subdivision, the most common in rock and probably the easiest to understand. Any beat subdivision requires us to do a bit of simple musical math. If we take our example of 4/4 meter where the quarter note is our beat and we divide the amount of time it takes to express one quarter note into two equal parts, we are then expressing *eighth* notes. A practical way to realize this concept is to begin by counting out loud "1, 2, 3, 4" several times at a steady pace or tempo. Once you've established this you can then insert the word "and" exactly halfway between each number and, voila, you're counting the eighth note subdivision. ("1 and, 2 and, 3 and, 4 and"). In other words, the eighth note moves exactly twice as fast the quarter note, or the beat in 4/4.

Let's practice eighth note subdivision by counting along with AC/DC's iconic rock song "Back in Black."

Before the song actually begins there are two measures of countoff in which the tempo is established. Over the first measure and a half of countoff (counted "1, 2, 3, 4, 1, 2") you hear the hi-hat cymbal and a muted guitar string expressing the beat together. Over the last half of the second measure ("3, 4") the guitar drops out leaving only the hi-hat. The band then comes in at the beginning (beat 1) of what amounts to be the third measure you hear.

To find the eighth note subdivision being expressed you can listen to the hi-hat cymbal. Once the full ensemble enters after the countoff, the hi-hat cymbal keeps a virtually steady eighth note subdivision moving throughout the entire song. You can count "1 and, 2 and, 3 and, 4 and" along with the hi-hat and you will feel the eighth note subdivision. We will discuss and practice the sixteenth note and triplet subdivisions momentarily, but at this point it is necessary to clarify the meaning and effects of syncopation.

**Go to chapter 1 playlist example "Back in Black" AC/DC, 1980**

Syncopation, while certainly not exclusive to rock music, is one of the key musical devices that makes rock music "rock." All metered music (there are pieces of music that do not employ a meter, but these will not be of concern to us) has an inherent feeling of "downbeats" and "upbeats." Put another way, musical rhythm, although it moves linearly through time, tends to have a feeling of moving down and up as well. Different meters have different inherent patterns of down and up. Let's take our 4/4 meter: The natural rhythmic inflection of 4/4 is down on beat 1, up on beat 2, down on beat 3, up on beat 4. Hence, we refer to beats 1 and 3 as "down" or "strong" beats; conversely, beats 2 and 4 are "up" or "weak" beats. Furthermore, any subdivided part of any beat is understood to be rhythmically "weak." The most *basic* type of syncopation involves accenting or emphasizing a weak beat. Using "Back in Black" again, if you count the quarter note beat you will hear a snare drum giving a heavy emphasis to beats 2 and 4. This basic syncopation, a defining characteristic of rock, is what is referred to in rock parlance as the **backbeat**.

Syncopation creates a conflict or tension against the natural inflection of the meter thereby generating rhythmic energy or lift. The simple backbeat syncopation is fundamental to rock but there are more complex and stronger types of syncopation as well. If we listen the drum part in the intro to the Guns N' Roses song "Paradise City" (the drums come in after four measures of guitar) we can hear a deeper type of syncopation, one that emphasizes a *weak part of the beat*, specifically the "and" of beat 3.

Use the lone guitar intro to help you find the beat (1, 2, 3, 4). As soon as you find the beat begin to count eighth notes (1 and, 2 and, 3 and, 4 and). As the bass drum and snare drum enter you will hear the following four-measure rhythmic pattern (bold underscored indicates an attack, or hit, on that part of the measure):

**1** and **2** and 3 **and 4** and **1** and **2** and 3 **and 4** and **1** and **2** and **3** and **4** and **1** and **2** and 3 **and 4** and

**Go to chapter 1 playlist example "Paradise City" Guns N' Roses, 1988**

Note: The snare backbeat emphasis is present on beats 2 and 4 throughout. But notice how the bass drum syncopation glides over beat 3 to come in on the "and" of 3 creating the feeling of momentary "weightlessness" over the beat. This type of syncopation helps to set up a deeper "groove" than we would feel with an attack on beat 3. A summary definition of *syncopation* would thus be an emphasis or accent on a weak beat or a weak part of the beat.

The second type of rhythmic subdivision we commonly encounter is the sixteenth note subdivision. In the same way that the eighth note divides the quarter note in half, or moves twice as fast, the sixteenth note divides the eighth into two equal portions of time. Just as we inserted the word "and" in between the numbered beats to find the eighth notes, we insert the syllables "e" and "ah" (a soft "a" sound closer to "uh") between the "ands." So in 4/4 we count "**1 e and ah, 2 e and**

**ah, 3 e and ah, 4 e and ah"** for each full measure. Just as the eighth note moves twice as fast as the beat, the sixteenth note moves twice as fast as the eighth, or four times faster than the beat.

To practice this, begin by counting four steady beats: "1, 2, 3, 4" (you might want to take a fairly slow tempo). Next, insert your eighth note "ands" exactly halfway between each beat: "1 and, 2 and, 3 and, 4 and." As you begin to feel comfortable with this, insert the "e" and "ah" exactly halfway between each "and." You may not be able to do this right away but keep practicing. If you're particularly coordinated, try snapping your fingers or clapping along with the numbered beats as you begin. As you work up to the sixteenth note subdivision you'll notice more clearly how the sixteenth note moves four times faster than your snap or clap.

By way of a musical example we can use The Beatles' 1969 hit "Get Back" to demonstrate the sixteenth note subdivision. The "marching" snare drum part that pervades most of the song is particularly easy to follow as you listen and count along. Be aware that the snare drum is not articulating *every* sixteenth note, but enough of them to establish the sixteenth note subdivision as the primary feel of the song.

**Go to chapter 1 playlist example "Get Back" Lennon/McCartney, 1969**

The third type of subdivision common to rock, and probably the most difficult for the non-musician to grasp, is the triplet subdivision. The triplet subdivision divides the beat into three equal parts and is counted thusly:

1 ta ta, 2 ta ta, 3 ta ta, 4 ta ta

In many rock songs this subdivision is expressed by primarily attacking the numbered beats and the second "ta" after each beat. This results in a pattern of "long-short, long-short" and is derived from blues and swing **shuffle** rhythms (more on this in Chapter 2). The attacks in this pattern are shown in bold underscored type:

**1** ta **ta**, **2** ta **ta**, **3** ta **ta**, **4** ta **ta**

An excellent example of the expression of both straight triplet subdivision and the "long-short" blues pattern can be heard in the Beatles' song "Revolution." In the opening bars, the lone guitar sets up the pattern by articulating all of the triplets. When the full band enters, the drums come in with a blues beat emphasizing the numbered beats and the second "ta" after each beat.

**Go to chapter 1 playlist example "Revolution" Lennon/McCartney, 1968**

Developing your counting skills will take a little practice but will become easier the more you do it. You can work on this outside of class while listening to music on your own. Your instructor can also help you find creative ways to practice.

Another musical element fundamental to rock is the **riff**. Riffs are short, repeated musical statements that give a rock song much of its identity. Many riffs focus as much or more on rhythmic repetition than they do on melodic contour, although taken together, this repetition can also form what might be considered the *tune* or *melody* in a rock song. Making a distinction between a riff and a melody is not always clear cut. Perhaps the best way is to list some general comparisons:

The melodic range (highest and lowest notes) is usually wider in a melody than in a riff.

A riff is commonly associated with a frequently repeated rhythmic pattern or patterns whereas a melody often features more rhythmic variety.

Riffs are generally only one or two measures long (or less), whereas a melody tends to unfold over a longer musical space.

Melodies have a greater capacity to stand alone (unaccompanied by other instruments or voices) than riffs.

A melody generally works its way to a specific climax before a release is felt; a riff, because of its brevity, generally does not build up in this way.

Riffs are often fairly simple and the most effective riffs (called "hooks") are easily retained in the memory. Riffs are common to both instrumental and vocal parts in a rock song and often permeate the musical texture. Many rock songs feature a prominent riff in the vocal and/or guitar part accompanied and sometimes answered by riffs in other instruments. (This "answering" technique is what we refer to as "call and response" and will be addressed later in the text).

Eric Clapton's 1977 hit "Cocaine" offers a great example this multi-riffed texture:

**Go to chapter 1 playlist example "Cocaine" Eric Clapton, 1976**

The lead vocal riff in "My Generation" by The Who (1965) is answered by the backing vocal riff:

Lead: "People try to put us down" Backing: "Talkin' 'bout my generation"

**Go to chapter 1 playlist example "My Generation" The Who, 1965**

The three-note pattern in the main riff of Led Zeppelin's "Kashmir" (1975) illustrates just how powerful and effective utter simplicity can be.

**Go to chapter 1 playlist example "Kashmir" Page/Plant/Bonham, 1975**

**Note:** There were rock bands and musicians who wrote more traditional tuneful melodies that are not riff based, but these are clearly the exception rather than the rule.

What instruments do we typically find in a rock band? A quick look at the makeup of the classic rock acts mentioned above, as well as other classics like The Rolling Stones, Pink Floyd, The Jimi Hendrix Experience, The Beach Boys and Black Sabbath, to name but a few, will reveal a basic instrumentation that is universally understood as the *rock band*: guitars, bass, and drums. In subsequent chapters we will uncover how this basic ensemble became the standard in rock, and how its expansion, contraction, and even complete absence helped to shape what we understand to be rock music.

Image 1.2: AC/DC in a recent performance

For most listeners, the vocal part in a rock song is central; it is the element in a song with which most people identify. The reasons for this are not terribly mysterious. Song lyrics, and by extension vocals, give a rock song much of its meaning. While rhythms, riffs, instrumental solos, and the like "speak" to listeners, they do so in a much more abstract way than do the vocals. (Both music and vocals, however, can be quite visceral). Whether a song is about love, partying, social issues, politics, and so on, the vocal part is the conduit through which we grasp its meaning.

On subjective and technical levels, a rock singer need not have a "pretty" or "smooth" voice, nor does that singer need to undergo an enormous amount of training as does the typical opera or jazz singer. This is not to say that there aren't a number of technically proficient and even highly trained rock singers, but it is not a requisite and certainly not the norm. Take Bob Dylan, for example. Most people would not claim that Dylan has a "pretty" voice, nor does he, in fact, possess a very wide vocal range. What he does have is an undeniable skill of *delivery*. On the other hand, a singer like Freddie Mercury of Queen was endowed with a colossal amount of technical vocal prowess. Even though a gulf of technical ability exists between the two, both are considered to be rock singers of the highest order.

The fact is that in our journey through rock music we will encounter singers like Dylan, Mercury, and everything in between. Perhaps more importantly we will explore *what* it was that these singers had to say and the myriad ways in which they said it.

How is a basic rock song put together? The overall structure or layout of a piece of music is what musicians refer to as **form**. As all music is artifice, all music has form. Composers have dabbled in "formlessness" but that too, ironically, is in and of itself a form. Form is as much about the psychology of a piece as it is about the musical goings-on. Form creates understanding, musical logic, and cohesion in a musical work, whether it's a rock song, a classical symphony, or a jazz tune.

We can think of form as a kind of musical *architecture* and it is easily understood through a comparison with actual architecture. Let's say you're walking through a suburban community. You will see many structures that you identify as houses. Although each house may differ somewhat in shape, color, and other basic features, the form that we recognize as a house is evident. In other words, there is an enormous amount of potential for variety and individual expression even when those traits are contained within the same or similar form.

In rock music, an exceedingly common type of musical architecture is what we call **verse/chorus** form. We will explore other forms and expansions of the basic layout below, although none are more prevalent than this standard type. Here is a basic diagram:

Table 1.1: Verse/Chorus Form

Intro: (optional) can be instrumental or vocal or even "extramusical" (for example, the cash register in Pink Floyd's "Money")

Verse 1: the main subject, story, or scene invoking section of the song

Chorus: the "catchy" oft-repeated part of the song; typically calls up the song's title

Verse 2: continues the subject/story/scene set up in verse 1 with identical or very similar musical background

Chorus: repeat of chorus 1, usually verbatim but occasionally with subtle differences

Interlude or Solo: often a guitar solo but can be other instruments or vocals; the background music in the solo part sometimes comes from a verse or a chorus but can be entirely new as well

Verse 3: optional

Chorus: repeat, sometimes varied in key or other ways to lend a feeling of climax or resolution

Outro: (optional; may be supplanted by the classic "fade out" over a repeated chorus)

Queen's 1980 hit "Another One Bites the Dust" perfectly illustrates verse/chorus form:

**Go to chapter 1 playlist example "Another One Bites the Dust" John Deacon, 1980**

Table 1.2: Verse/Chorus Form in "Another One Bites the Dust"

Intro (:00–:22)

Verse 1 (:22–:42) "Steve walks wearily down the street..."

Chorus (:42–:57) "Another bites the dust, another one bites the dust..."

Verse 2 (1:06–1:26) "How do you think I'm gonna get along? ..."

Chorus (1:06–1:41) "Another bites the dust, another one bites the dust..."

Interlude (1:41–2:29)

Verse 3 (2:38–2:57) There are plenty of ways that you can hurt a man..."

Chorus (2:57–3:12) "Another bites the dust, another one bites the dust..."

Outro (3:12–end)

Just like the houses in our walk through suburbia, songs using this basic structure have the potential for enormous variety and individuality within a common formal orientation.

## Cultural Context

A number of social factors and emerging belief systems contributed to the rise of rock as a cultural movement. These include, but are not limited to, the post-WWII economic boom and the growth of the middle class; postmodernism; the Cold War (particularly intensified during the Vietnam Era); the dawn of the television and technological ages; the birth and subsequent commercialization of rock 'n' roll in the mid–late 1950s and early 1960s; the Civil Rights and other human rights movements; and the growing dissent towards government, authority, and cultural norms, particularly in the minds of young people. Each of these factors and their relevance to rock culture will be introduced here and further explored throughout our journey through the rock era.

### The Post-WWII Economic Boom and the Growth of the Middle Class

World War II was arguably the most profoundly transformative event in modern history and it is not an exaggeration to say that the trickle-down effects of that war will be felt for many decades to come. In the immediate aftermath of the war, substantial and often permanent changes could be seen in nearly every aspect of American society. One of these aspects was the American economy. For all of the damage caused by the war, the post-WWII economy in America entered into a robust and prosperous state. Although there was a very brief postwar economic slump, essentially from 1946 until the early 1970s American economic growth spawned extensive changes including urban and suburban expansion and the creation of a large middle class. It was a time when the average American worker, possessing little or no training, could find a good-paying job with the potential for long-term employment, a reasonable degree of financial stability, home ownership, and a comfortable pension for the years following one's retirement—in other words, the "American Dream."

Part and parcel to this economic growth was that more Americans than ever before were able to send their children to college. This massive unprecedented influx of students into American universities meant that a growing number of young people than were being introduced to literature, art, philosophy, critical thinking, and all of the other various benefits of higher education. It was many of these same people who became the earliest fans and supporters of rock music. The economic boom also meant allowances and more jobs for young people thereby providing many with disposable income which could be used to buy music, attend concerts, and plug jukeboxes. These trends were critical to the rise of rock culture. We will also examine how the various economic ups and downs that followed helped to shape the world of rock.

Image 1.3: A typical 1950s middle-class suburb

## Postmodernism

Postmodernism was an intellectual and philosophical movement which developed during the post-WWII era. Growing out of the *existentialist* worldview put forth by some of the great thinkers of the late nineteenth and early twentieth centuries (such as Kierkegaard, Nietzsche, and Sartre)—that finding any meaning in a confusing and absurd world is solely the responsibility of the individual—and as a reaction to *modernism*—the view that objective knowledge dictates the universe—postmodernism was, in essence, a challenge to the "truth claims" or "big story" that sought to "totalize" all human knowledge. Put another way, postmodernist philosophy purports the notion that reality is based on *subjective individual interpretation*. It upheld the view that science and technology had failed to deliver true social progress. This belief was substantiated by the two World Wars and the ensuing Cold War and its constant threat of nuclear annihilation.

Rock music and culture represent what could be termed as "postmodernism for the masses." This began organically and somewhat naively at first with the rock 'n' roll of the late 1950s, though not as any clearly articulated artistic ideology but rather conveyed as an intrinsic attitude; antiauthoritarian, antiestablishment, nonconformist, rebellious, self-deterministic and free thinking. Mainstream American society in the 1950s was mired in social conservatism, conformity, and sexual repression. Elvis, Little Richard, Chuck Berry, and the other early rock 'n' roll stars were the embodiment of all that challenged these social conditions. In the early 1960s, The Beatles epitomized a flippant yet intelligent youthful audacity and laid the groundwork for the rock musician as a social critic; Bob Dylan sang of social unrest and high-minded humanist philosophies; The Rolling Stones, with their sneering antagonism toward conventional social norms, cemented the role of the rock musician as the postmodernist rebel. By the late 1960s the postmodern comes to full self-awareness in the utopian ideals of the counterculture, the ironic self-awareness of Frank Zappa, and the powerfully individualistic music and personae of Jimi Hendrix and Jim Morrison. Postmodernist philosophy will continue to reassert itself throughout the rock era.

## The Cold War

The Cold War, which is generally considered to be the years between 1947 and 1991, was a period unlike any other in human history. The effects of living in a world that had gained sufficient technology to destroy itself, and could do so at any given moment, were confusing and demoralizing. The promise of mutually assured destruction (aptly referred to as "MAD") informed and influenced virtually every aspect of daily life. The psychological impact on the younger population during the early years of the period was profound: American schoolchildren were regularly subjected to "air raid drills" during which they would be made to hide under their desks, and were periodically shown films in which cartoon animals would instruct them in what to do in the event of a nuclear attack.

These efforts were ostensibly to foster "preparedness" but all they really managed to do was instill terror in the minds of the young. Many of these same youngsters were among the first generation of rock fans.

We will come to understand how events either directly or indirectly related to the Cold War helped to shape the music and culture of the rock era. From political calamities like the McCarthy "Witch Hunt" hearings to the Cuban missile crisis to major upheavals like the Vietnam War to seemingly innocuous events like the 1980 Olympic hockey match between the US and Russian teams, the Cold War, the constant threat of communism, nuclear annihilation, and all of the attendant propaganda were omnipresent. The life-altering effects of this period and the threat of human extinction by our own design provided the inspiration for many rock songs, the protest movement, and other movements for peace and political change spearheaded or endorsed by rock musicians.

Image 1.4: A 1950s cartoon mascot for youth preparedness

## The Dawn of the Television and Technological Ages

To a generation that has come of age in the "modern" world, with the ubiquity of mobile devices, the heavy presence of social media, and the rapid advances in day-to-day consumer-level technology (some see these advances as planned obsolescence for the sake of more and bigger corporate profits), there exists a common misconception that high technology is a relatively recent development. In reality, the dawn of the present age of electronic computing can be traced back to the 1930s and 1940s. Advances in other related forms of circuitry vital to the early culture of rock, namely television and the transistor radio, which was for all practical purposes the first iPod, date back as far as the late 1920s. These technologies would not become widely available until the 1950s, but the seeds of technology had been planted and were bearing powerful fruits.

The birth and advancement of rock culture was heavily reliant on many forms of technology; musical instruments, recording technologies and techniques, live sound reinforcement and stage production, media (that is, radio, MTV, Internet), and modes of consumption (that is, vinyl records, CDs, mp3s) all played a fundamental role. Many rock musicians and other industry adjuncts were quick to utilize emerging technologies in order to advance the state of the art of rock. We will see how the results of this practice helped to keep rock music relevant and "fresh" in a constantly changing world.

## The Birth and Subsequent Commercialization of Rock 'n' Roll in the Mid–Late 1950s and Early 1960s

The so-called "British Invasion" of 1964, led by The Beatles, is considered by most to be the dawn of the rock era. Although a more detailed prehistory of rock will be given in Chapters 2 and 3, let it be said here that it was largely due to the heavily commercialized, diluted, prepackaged pap that was passing itself off as "rock 'n' roll" in the early 1960s, most particularly in the United States, that the arrival of the Beatles and the other British Invasion bands that followed on their heels had such a massive impact. American youth had been introduced to *real* rock 'n' roll via Chuck Berry, Little Richard, and Elvis in the 1950s. Late in the decade, Buddy Holly, who represents the major transition between rock 'n' roll and rock, was also a significant force. The various events that led to the disappearance of these early luminaries from the rock 'n' roll scene, along with many nuanced social factors also discussed in Chapters 2 and 3, saw the introduction of a wholly different, now largely forgotten type of nonthreatening, homogenized, rock 'n' roll–based pop music for teens. One could accurately refer to the music of this period as "rock 'n' roll lite." Had the cultural void created during this period not existed, the British Invasion may not have had the steamroller effect that it did.

## The Civil Rights and Subsequent Human Rights Movements

The African American Civil Rights Movement of the 1950s and 1960s was a diverse effort put forth by various factions of society in order to eliminate segregation and end racial discrimination. The movement involved civic and religious leaders, politicians, labor unions, students, and other groups interested in a more unified American society. Music and musicians were a galvanizing force throughout these tumultuous years. Rock music, as well as soul, gospel, folk, blues, and jazz played a significant role in unifying the movement, providing momentum, solace, common ground, and encouragement to all involved. In the following chapter we will see how early rock 'n' roll helps to introduce young white Americans to black culture and throughout our journey we will see how the pluralistic nature of rock music helped to create an enduring sense of equality and belonging to the disenfranchised in American society.

Image 1.5: Bob Dylan and Joan Baez perform at a civil rights march in 1963

## The Growing Dissent Toward Authority in the Minds of the Young

The climate of social conformity and political conservatism that followed WWII can be at least partially attributed to the need for psychological comfort that naturally follows a profoundly traumatic event, as well as the sense of social stability needed to face the new and growing challenges brought on by the Cold War. To be sure, the "age of conformity," as it is known, was as nuanced and uncertain a time as any in America's history, but the perception being put forth by the government and the mass media, which now included television for most families, was that of a society unified through American military might, strong leadership, "morality," "family values," economic prosperity, mass production, and the modernist philosophy.

As the 1950s wore on, the popular belief in these perceptions began to seriously erode, most conspicuously in the minds of the youth culture. This was a generation attracted to rock 'n' roll, Beat poetry, and Hollywood rebels like James Dean and Marlon Brando; a generation with free time, mobility, and the wherewithal to enjoy it. They tolerated, but were not terribly interested in the culture of their parents, nor were they stifled by the narrow views of mainstream society when it came to sex, race, and individuality. They were a kind of prerevolutionary resistance to authority in a quietly turbulent time and whose actions and attitudes would help to plant the seeds for the openly turbulent and revolutionary 1960s; the revolution that would have rock music at its core.

## Suggested Chapter Related Activities

- Get together with a classmate(s) and practice counting through each type of rhythmic subdivision discussed above. One person can keep the beat while others articulate subdivisions. Once a successful result is achieved, try switching roles.

- As your group becomes more facile at understanding and articulating rhythm, try experimenting with articulating various types of syncopation. This can involve hand claps, finger snapping or even percussion instruments, if available.

- Locate examples of "rock" songs that do not use a 4 beat per measure. Determine what beat structure(s) are being used instead.

- Locate modern (post-2000) examples of verse/chorus form as well as songs that employ other formal structures.

- Find a rock era song that does not feature the guitar as its central instrument sound, then discuss *why* it is understood as a "rock" song.

- Find examples of each type of rhythmic subdivision in rock songs from 1964-2000 and from 2001 to the present.

- Locate several rock songs that espouse postmodernist ideals in the lyrics and discuss these.

## Suggested Discussion Topics

- Does the idea of youth oriented dissent play a significant role in modern music?

- Are postmodern ideals still relevant in cultural discourse?

- What role, if any, do modern musicians play in the struggle for progress and equality for all?

- What is considered "taboo" in modern music and how do musicians address these taboos?

- Rock musicians like David Byrne of Talking Heads and Gene Simmons of Kiss have declared that rock is dead, citing various reasons: Byrne believes the style to have lost its vitality, while Simmons claims that file sharing killed rock. Is rock dead? Is it just lying dormant? Has something else taken is place? Where does popular culture go from here? Explore, discuss and write down your thoughts on these and other issues that arise and then compare them to how you feel at the end of the semester.

## Image Credits

# CHAPTER 2

# American Music Before Rock: A Brief History

---

*I sing my song to the free.*

-Roger Daltrey of The Who

---

While music is a universal human form of expression it is not a universal *language*; the musics of different cultures can vary greatly in terms of content, technique, purpose, form, instrumentation, etc. Music that is generally considered to be of "American" culture is really the product of the integration of musical characteristics of two primary cultures: African (black) and European (white). Both African and European musical cultures are richly diverse in and of themselves and each feature distinct characteristics which contribute to American music in general, as well as rock music specifically. Below is a brief description of distinguishing characteristics of the music of each culture. As we progress through the text, and as your listening skills improve, you will begin to recognize these basic characteristics in the myriad ways they surface in rock and other seemingly unrelated contemporary American styles, such as jazz, blues, gospel, doo-wop, funk, rap, and disco.

## Basic African Musical Characteristics

Call and Response Forms: A musical form in which a leader sings or chants a part which is then answered by a chorus. The leader's call is typically more elaborate than the chorus' response.

Polyrhythmic Textures and Strong Beat Keeping: This involves multiple rhythmic patterns occurring simultaneously. Much of the musical complexity in African music lies in dense, interlocking, and highly syncopated rhythmic textures over a strong beat.

Riffs: As mentioned in Chapter 1, riffs are short, repeated melodic patterns, usually involving a narrow range and contour.

Pentatonic Scales: Pentatonic scales appear in many musical cultures, including European music. It is simply a scale containing five distinct pitches. The pitches vary across cultures although the concept is very similar. The African pentatonic scale is particularly important to American music as it is considered by many scholars to be the basis for the blues scale. This scale will be discussed in greater detail later in the chapter.

Multiple Percussion Instruments: Much of the expressive power in African music lies in its complex treatment of rhythm through the use of various percussion instruments. These included both pitched percussion, such as marimbas, as well as an array of nonpitched instruments such as drums, shakers, rattles, and metallic instruments. Instruments were handmade, often by the musicians themselves.

Oral Tradition: African musical traditions were passed down from generation to generation in an unwritten form. This is not unique to African music but the survival of this among African Americans is extremely remarkable when one considers the conditions they faced during their enslavement in the United States and other parts of the western hemisphere. Between the seventeenth and nineteenth centuries, Africans were enslaved in the United States, Haiti, Jamaica, Brazil, and Cuba. Moreover, African people were kidnapped from many regions of western and central Africa, each bearing their own distinct languages, culture, and musical traditions. The intermingling of these diverse African musical traditions with the music of various Western and Latin cultures produced many well-defined hybrid forms which were shaped by various factors: local traditions, social climate, religious practices, accessibility of instruments, and so on.

The survival of African musical traditions under the conditions of slavery is a testament not only to the strength of a people but also to the strength of music itself. In the southern United States, slaves were forbidden from making instruments. (Plantation owners feared that slaves would use drums to communicate with slaves residing on neighboring plantations and form an uprising.) Ironically, the common European practice of converting slaves to Christianity afforded slaves the opportunity to regularly congregate apart from the plantation owners and thus provided a venue for unsupervised music making. Workers most certainly sang in the fields as they worked as well. These situations offered an outlet for expression and the opportunity to preserve the African musical heritage.

Slaves residing in the islands and in South America were not as limited when it came to crafting instruments and music making. This led to hybrid styles that are heavily percussion based such as Afro-Cuban music, salsa, samba, and others. In addition to these styles, we have the music of *Santeria*, a syncretic religion of the Caribbean slave populations which fuses the religious and musical practices of West African descendants with those of their Spanish captors (Catholicism). The music of Santeria is believed to have retained much of the authenticity of the musical traditions of Africa.

The Santeria piece "Song for Odudua" clearly demonstrates all of the musical characteristics listed above.

**Go to chapter 2 playlist example "Song for Odudua" Traditional**

## Basic European Musical Characteristics

Chords or Harmony: A chord is two or more distinct pitches heard simultaneously and consciously treated as a sonic entity. In the European tradition, the triad—a three-note chord,—is the basis for the harmonic language of music. Moreover, *chord progressions*—that is, chords purposefully moving from one to the other—are fundamental to almost all European music.

Ballad and Strophic Forms: A ballad is a song form which typically tells a story, often a historical event, through a series of repeated verses. Each verse uses the same musical accompaniment as the story unfolds. This is also known as *strophic* form and is a predecessor to *verse/chorus* form.

Major, Minor, and Pentatonic Scales: The melodic material in most European music is based on the major/minor system. (The major scale should be familiar to most students as the "Do-Re-Mi" scale that is commonly sung in elementary school music classes). A type of pentatonic scale used in much European folk music is a subset of the major scale as well.

Multiple Melodic and Chord Instruments: The instruments associated with European music are generally divided into families: woodwinds, brass, strings, and percussion. The diversity and range of these instruments is enormous. Many are single-line melodic instruments, such as the flute, and others, such as the piano and guitar, are capable of expressing chords and melodies simultaneously.

Oral and Written Traditions: European music was preserved in both oral and written forms. In general, *folk* or *rural* music, music of the peasantry, was created and passed down orally while *urban* music, music of the middle and upper classes, was preserved through the use of musical notation. A large body of written *sacred* music exists as well, as musical literacy was a luxury common to religious institutions. Eventually, many folk tunes were written down for the sake of accurate preservation and for marketing through the sheet music publishing business, but the origins of these tunes are firmly grounded in oral tradition.

The written form of music, although not a perfect system of preservation, provides a more precise record of a composer's ideas and musical intentions than does oral transmission. The body of notated Western music that exists from the centuries preceding the invention of sound recording is vast beyond imagination and has provided music scholars with a virtually endless resource for accurately interpreting music of the past. This is just simply not the case with music of oral origin.

The European folk ballad is epitomized in the famous example "Greensleeves."

**Go to chapter 2 playlist example "Greensleeves" Traditional**

From our vantage point in the twenty-first century it is difficult to imagine a time when the music of blacks and whites was not fully integrated. Black and white stylistic crossovers are commonplace in today's popular music; many artists from vastly different stylistic backgrounds regularly perform, record, and compose music with and for each other. Fortunately, we take this for granted. In fact, the evolution of popular music in the United States is profoundly connected to the often strained relationship between black and white cultures and their struggles to understand and accept one another. In American popular music, the integration of African and European musical traditions was a process that unfolded by fits and starts since around the time of the American Civil War.

## The Parlor Song

In the eighteenth and nineteenth centuries, the "entertainment center" in many middle- and upper-class American homes was a room called a parlor; its essential fixture was the piano. The industrial revolution facilitated the mass production of affordable upright pianos, while the growth of music education in public schools equipped many more people to perform written music. This in turn led to the increased production of simple printed piano arrangements of popular music; well-known European folk tunes were often set to a modest piano accompaniment. This mode of music making eventually gave rise to the **parlor song**. These were genteel songs featuring simple right-hand melodies and basic left-hand chordal accompaniment patterns, written specifically for home performance by amateur musicians. The lyrics of these songs often dealt with sentimental subjects such as romance and courtship. Parlor music remained at the center of musical life in the home until the 1920s and the advent of radio.

Stephen Foster (1826–1864) was an extremely popular and successful nineteenth-century songwriter who helped bring the parlor song into prominence. He was also the first American to earn a living as a professional songwriter.

**Go to chapter 2 playlist example "Beautiful Dreamer" Stephen Foster, 1864**

## The Minstrel Show

In the 1830s, a form of musical entertainment known as the **minstrel show** came into being, appearing most notably in the urban working-class districts of New York City. These shows featured primarily young white male performers in "blackface" makeup performing Anglo-American folk music in a manner which mimicked the stereotyped speech, singing, dance, and dress patterns of blacks. Minstrel songs were infused with dance rhythms taken from European jigs and reels, and strophic forms were expanded to include a recurring chorus. By the 1840s, these shows had grown considerably in popularity; many minstrel troupes toured the country and a plethora of minstrel tunes became available in sheet music form. Although the overlay of African musical *style* was superficial, the main expression of African influence rested primarily in the employment of African images and musical instruments, minstrelsy is generally regarded by scholars as the first synthesis of African and European musical elements and thus, the first truly American popular music form.

**Go to chapter 2 playlist example "Dixie" Dan Emmett, circa 1850**

The popularity of the minstrel show appeared to peak around and just after the Civil War and played a significant role in the formation of the United States' popular music industry, though in the course of rising to mainstream popularity the minstrel show became a predictable and highly commercialized affair. There is a great deal of irony in this process in that we see a style which emerged on the fringes of society, with a considerable amount of rebellious energy directed at the mainstream—in this case, genteel white European music—but as the minstrel show grows in popularity and *becomes* the mainstream much of its original meaning and rebellious spirit is lost. There is a parallel here which will see with mainstream rock of the 1970s and hard rock of the 1980s.

Through our modern lens, minstrelsy justifiably appears hideously racist and is often viewed with anger and shame. However, on another level it does reflect an attempt by whites—albeit a crude one—to understand and emulate black culture; imitation, it is said, is the most sincere form of flattery. It is also asserted by many scholars that minstrelsy represented white urban youth culture struggling to exert its independence by adopting elements of black style. It is precisely this phenomenon which gives rise to jazz and rock 'n' roll and what we have been experiencing in recent decades with white appropriation of elements of rap, "gangsta" rap, and hip-hop. Furthermore, minstrelsy is the direct predecessor to *vaudeville* (see below) and the touring tent shows, which in the late nineteenth and early twentieth centuries were significant in providing a mobile music culture for important early African American blues and jazz musicians.

As was stated earlier, the fusion of black and white elements in American popular music oc-curred in a kind of two-steps-up-one-step-back fashion from the time of the minstrel show, though once American music begins to move toward a cultural fusion, the changes in pop music and music culture gradually become fixed and permanent. In the years shortly after the Civil War, things take a step back for a time; although the influence of the minstrel show has had lasting effects. Unlike popular music prior to minstrelsy, the vast majority of pop music between the 1870s and the early twentieth century commonly featured dance rhythms, stronger dance beats, and something much closer to the verse/chorus form that becomes such a major factor in rock.

## Brass Bands

From the 1870s to around 1900 two types of popular music prevailed in the United States: the waltz and the patriotic march. Waltzes were popular, commonly lighthearted dance pieces which often employed a verse/chorus form, while the march/brass band sensation was brought on by the growing sense of nationalism and as a symbol of national unity following the Civil War. Brass bands originally existed as military units but after the Civil War civilian commercial groups began to appear in droves. Most US cities, as well as scores of small towns, had a local brass band and a bandstand, or band shell, where these groups would regularly perform. Many brass bands, in addition to playing patriotic marches, frequently performed arrangements of popular waltzes, polkas, adaptations of classical works, and cakewalks—a dance form that was introduced during the height of minstrelsy. The brass band itself was derived from military marching bands and included not only brass instruments (that is, trumpets, trombones, tubas), but could include woodwinds (that is flutes and clarinets) and percussion (that is, bass and snare drums, and cymbals) as well. Brass band music and concerts were a staple of post–Civil War era musical life in America. Brass band instrumentation plays a role in the development of jazz and big band swing in the early twentieth century which in turn, play a part in the development of rock.

Image 2.2: John Philip Sousa and the US Marine Corps Band

The most prominent composer and conductor of brass band music was John Philip Sousa (1854–1932) so much so that he came to be known as America's "March King." Sousa toured extensively with both military and commercial bands and employed the finest band musicians of his day. He also exploited the relatively new medium of the phonograph record (see below), invented by Thomas Edison in 1877, to capture and disseminate his music. Sousa was important in establishing the modern music business model as well in that he was one of the pioneers in establishing royalty payments to musicians by music publishers.

**Go to chapter 2 playlist example "Stars and Stripes Forever" John Philip Sousa, 1897**

## Recording Technology and the Development of the Phonograph Record

Perhaps the most profound development in the history of music is the ability to record sound. Until this technology was developed, music was transmitted either orally or in sheet music form, both of which were highly problematic. Oral transmission had the obvious problems of inconsistency and variance as music was passed down from generation to generation, and although notated music is much more consistent and precise, it is far from a perfect system of preservation. Recorded audio was the game changer. All subsequent advances in the recording arts are merely improvements to this fundamental technological development.

Although recording technology was not developed by a single inventor (two other lesser-known figures, Edouard-Leon Scott de Martinville and Charles Cros were essential to the process) the *phonograph* was patented by Thomas Edison in 1877. These early recording devices captured the air pressure changes produced by sound as grooves imprinted on wax or tin foil cylinders. These cylinders were then read by means of a stylus, or needle, running over the grooves and transmitting the vibrations through a mechanical amplifying device. The cylinders were effective but bulky and not easily mass produced. However, in 1887, and inventor named Emile Berliner developed the *gramophone* record, a flat disc that was much more portable and far easier to store than Edison's bulky cylinders. The flat discs were also easy to mass produce using a molding process. The record disc had arrived and it would reign for nearly a century.

As early as the 1890s, the first jukeboxes, then known as "nickelodeons," were showing up in many public places. For a nickel consumers could listen to the newest recorded music. The commercial standardization of the 78 rpm, double-sided record disc occurred in 1904. These discs held about four minutes of music per side, were made of shellac, and were relatively fragile compared to vinyl discs which first appeared in the early 1930s, became commonplace after World War II, and with which we are familiar today. Consumer-grade record players, popularly known as the "Victrola" (actually a brand name), became a fixture in the early twentieth century American home as well. In the early 1900s, two companies, Columbia Records and Victor, grew to dominate the burgeoning record industry. Still, it would not be until 1920s and 1930s that records begin to overtake the firmly entrenched sheet music business as the primary mode of music consumption.

## Ragtime

In the 1890s a new original black style of highly syncopated music known as **ragtime** began its ascension to popular music status. The term ragtime, believed to be coined by a composer named Ernest Hogan (1865–1909) describes a style whose central musical trait is a syncopated or "ragged" rhythm. Early rags were commonly written for the piano and presented a fusion of energetic, syncopated melodies in the pianist's right hand, accompanied by a fairly straightforward rhythmic and chord pattern, based directly on the march rhythm and European harmonies, in the pianist's left hand. Rags fuse black and white musical elements with a truly African sensibility towards rhythm and syncopation, unlike white minstrel music, which lacked the authentic African rhythmic feel. This fusion of authentic African rhythms into pop music was an essential step in the evolution of American music; it gave white America a genuine taste of an authentic black rhythmic style. During the ragtime era, many rags by both black and white composers appeared and the genre expanded to include instruments and ensembles beyond the piano. Ragtime music took such a strong hold of popular tastes that during the era that nearly any pop tune with an energetic rhythm and even a mild degree of syncopation was labeled as a rag.

Scott Joplin (1867/1868?–1917), also known as the "King of Ragtime" was its most famous and influential composer. Although Joplin was not the progenitor of the style, his 1899 publication of "Maple Leaf Rag" achieved massive success in the United States and Europe and established Joplin as ragtime's central figure. Joplin published forty-four rags over the course of his career but was never able to repeat the success he had with "Maple Leaf Rag." Nonetheless, his name remains synonymous with ragtime. In 1916 Joplin was admitted to a mental institution due to dementia brought on by syphilis. His death the following year is considered by many to signify the end of the ragtime era. It is in and around this same time that blues and jazz, two styles which are musical descendants of ragtime, begin to rise in popularity.

The web examples "Maple Leaf Rag" and "The Entertainer" exemplify Joplin's work and piano rags as a whole.

**Go to chapter 2 playlist examples "Maple Leaf Rag" and "The Entertainer" Scott Joplin**

Note: Joplin's music experienced a revival in the 1970s with the release of a million-selling album of his music, recorded by pianist Joshua Rifkin, and the placement of his rag "The Entertainer" as the theme music to the 1973 Academy Award–winning Newman/Redford film *The Sting*.

## Radio

The importance of radio in the dissemination and evolution of American music cannot be over-stated. From the 1920s until the early 1950s, the radio was the recreational centerpiece of the American home and family, providing a source of news and entertainment, including sports, serials, and both live and recorded music. The first commercial radio stations appeared in 1920 and by 1927 there were over one thousand commercial radio stations operating in the United States. The first nationwide commercial broadcast network—NBC—was established in 1926. Throughout the 1920s as radios became more affordable, family ownership of a radio was commonplace.

## Billboard Magazine

*Billboard* is a music and entertainment industry trade magazine that began to track the popularity of recorded music in the 1930s through the use of various means of calculation. This first focused on the jukebox industry, then record sales and radio plays but has expanded in recent years to calculate all manner of digital download and streaming. Music is categorized and rated by stylistic/genre "charts" with a "crossover" being a song or album that ranks on multiple charts. In 1940 the first chart, Pop, was introduced and by the 1949 had expanded to three charts: Pop, Rhythm & Blues, and Country & Western. For many years, the weekly syndicated radio show "American Top 40" counted down the top forty Pop hits of the week in reverse order.

Current chart designations are in the dozens and include virtually every type of modern media: physical sales, digital downloads, radio, ringtones, video placement, even the "Social 50" chart which tracks plays on social media sites like Facebook, YouTube, Twitter and others. Moreover, *chart performance*, sometimes as much or more than actual *musical characteristics*, can exert an influence on how the public perceives the stylistic orientation of a band, album or song. The various methods by which Billboard calculates its data is bafflingly complex and, thankfully, not relevant to this text.

### Tin Pan Alley, Vaudeville, Broadway, Movies, and the Reinvention of the Pop Song

In the 1890s, the modern American popular music industry began to take shape. The landscape of the sheet music publishing business was being reshaped by urban expansion, immigration, and the changing tastes of the mainstream music-buying public. Energetic and industrious new publishing firms, many of them established by Jewish immigrants living in New York City, were outstripping the established publishers whose focus had been mainly classical music and genteel parlor songs. Mass markets were helping to generate million-plus sales of sheet music hits and publishers became increasingly concerned with producing these hits.

The majority of these upstart, hit-producing publishers had their offices and studios on a stretch of 28th Street in lower Manhattan. On warm days, a cacophonous mix of pianos and singers working to churn out the newest hit could be heard drifting through the open windows of these studios. In 1899, songwriter Monroe Rosenfeld, while ambling along this stretch of 28th Street, quipped that the sound reminded him of tin pans clanging together. Thus the name "Tin Pan Alley" was born. Over the next several decades the name Tin Pan Alley became synonymous with the mainstream style of hit songs being produced there. Tin Pan Alley songs represented an evolution of the sentimental parlor song with innovations in form and instrumentation and would evolve to include the **fox-trot** (see below), a stylized dance piece which was enormously popular in the 1920s and 30s.

Tin Pan Alley songs and style came to dominate the popular mainstream for most of the first half of the twentieth century. This was achieved through particular songwriting strategies, vigorous promotion, and the development of new marketing techniques and emerging technologies.

Tin Pan Alley lyrics typically dealt with subjects of love, nostalgia, idealized romantic relationships and family life, and generally lighthearted subjects; the songs were an escape into an untroubled world. On a musical level there was an approach toward memorable simplicity and common connection. One early Tin Pan Alley composer, Harry Von Tilzer (1872–1946) composed with the philosophy of keeping the tunes so simple that "even a baby could hum them" and Irving Berlin (1888–1989) the most prolific of all Tin Pan Alley composers, once said "My ambition is to reach the heart of the average American, not the highbrow nor the lowbrow but that vast intermediate crew which is the real soul of the country."

Standard Tin Pan Alley forms are not unlike the verse/chorus form we will see in so many rock songs in that they are calculated to create a framework that is coherent and psychologically pleasing. For example, one extremely common Tin Pan Alley form is what we call AABA. This form is based on introducing an idea (A), reinforcing it (A), departing from the original idea to create contrast and interest (B), and then returning to the original point of familiarity to create a sense of resolution or completion of a musical journey (A). To be sure, there are many variations on and expansions of this basic form, as there are with verse/chorus form, but the basic foundation is present.

Irving Berlin's "Blue Skies" is a perfect illustration of this tried and true approach to song form and, in part, accounts for the song's popularity and longevity. Since its composition in 1926, "Blue Skies" has been recorded by literally hundreds of artists including Bing Crosby, Judy Garland, Ella Fitzgerald, Mel Tormé, Frank Sinatra, Willie Nelson and Rod Stewart. Below is a diagram of the form:

Table 2.1: Form of "Blue Skies"

Intro (instrumental)

A: "Blue skies smiling at me…"

A: "Bluebirds singing their song…"

B: "Never saw the sun shining so bright…"

A: "Blue days all of them gone…"

A: (instrumental solo)

A: (instrumental solo)

B: "Never saw the sun shining so bright…"

A: "Blue days all of them gone…"

Outro

**Go to chapter 2 playlist example "Blue Skies" Irving Berlin (Rod Stewart), 1926**

Street-level promotion of early Tin Pan Alley songs was the work of "song pluggers." These were professional musicians who were paid to perform music for potential customers in public places such as department stores, beer gardens, and specialty music shops. Many song pluggers became well-known songwriters and performers in the own right.

**Vaudeville** was another medium through which Tin Pan Alley publishers could promote the latest work of their songwriters. These theater-style shows were a direct descendant of the minstrel show and an important source of popular entertainment in the late nineteenth and early twentieth centuries. A typical vaudeville show might feature singers, dancers, comedians, acrobats, jugglers, and even trained animal acts. Vaudeville shows became so popular that by the turn of the twentieth century nearly every reasonably sized town in the United States boasted a vaudeville theater, with multiple theaters operating in metropolitan areas. It was common business practice for Tin Pan Alley publishers to contract with vaudeville theaters to promote and perform their songs.

Broadway musicals, which became incredibly popular in the years following World War I, also provided an important commercial medium for Tin Pan Alley music. These and productions called *revues*, which were akin to vaudeville shows, provided a mutually beneficial business arrangement between music publishers and theater companies. Broadway musicals and Tin Pan Alley seemed to be made for one another. Broadway helped to bolster the careers of composers and composer/lyricist teams such as Cole Porter, Jerome Kern, the Gershwin brothers, Rodgers and Hart, and Rodgers and Hammerstein.

**Go to chapter 2 playlist example "Night and Day" (from the musical *Gay Divorce*) Cole Porter, 1932**

Hollywood films from the late 1920s into the early 1950s also played a significant role in the promotion of Tin Pan Alley music. In fact, the first "talkie" (a nickname for early sound films) was *The Jazz Singer* (1927) starring Al Jolson. The film featured Jolson singing Irving Berlin's "Blue Skies" and Paul Dresser's "My Gal Sal," both Tin Pan Alley songs. In the following decades many Tin Pan Alley–based Broadway musicals were adapted into Hollywood films as well.

> **Note:** The relationship of Tin Pan Alley to rock is not so much one of musical influence, but rather that it evolves into the music against which the early appearance of rock 'n' roll in the 1950s seemed so radical. However, Tin Pan Alley *forms* persist and are often used to great effect in rock and popular music. We will note significant examples of this in subsequent chapters.

## Blues

Very little is known about the true origins of blues except that it emerged out of the Deep South from rural African American communities in the early nineteenth century. What is abundantly clear is that blues has had more to do with informing rock than any other earlier American style. Before we discuss exactly what musical elements define blues as a form and as a genre, or become familiar with its earliest stars, we will begin by considering what characteristics converged to shape blues. Its influence on subsequent styles, including jazz, swing, country and honky-tonk, rhythm & blues, and rock 'n' roll will become apparent as we make our through the early/mld twentieth century.

Blues is a combination of traditional African call and response forms, specific chord progressions (based on European harmonic practice), African American field songs carried down from the years of African enslavement, the blues scale, shuffle rhythms based on triple beat subdivision, heavy syncopation, and perhaps most importantly, the raw, deeply emotional style of delivery that gives the genre its enormous power. Early blues exposed the underbelly of life in way that no other previous American style had. Blues lyrics might describe the hardships of life and work, struggles with money and inequality, alcohol, and the topic of sex and relationships. Sexual references in the early twentieth century were quite a different matter than they are today; sex had to be hidden in euphemism, veiled reference, and innuendo. As we will see, many blues songwriters were adroit at imagining clever and often amusing ways of accomplishing this.

Thus far we have heard the call and response technique and highly syncopated style of African folk music, as well as simple chord progression in European parlor songs which are all fundamental to blues. Here we turn to the African American field songs which were also central to its formation. It is in these pieces that we can clearly hear the deep expression of emotion, particularly through the use of "blue" notes (see below), that is so essential blues and blues style.

The field song tradition is most often associated with the years of African enslavement but extended into the post-emancipation years, most notably in African American agricultural and railroad labor crews working in the south. These songs very often originated as an **improvisation**, that is, they were created spontaneously. These were sung in a variety of ways and would have been performed *a cappella* (vocally with no instrumental accompaniment): as solo, chants, in a group chorus fashion, or as a call and response between a leader and a group. Field songs existed as an oral tradition for many decades but began to appear in written transcriptions shortly after the Civil War. In a practical sense they served several purposes: boosting worker morale; coordinating rhythmic, team-related work; communicating coded messages not understood by overseers; and as a means of expressing sorrow, venting frustration, and withstanding the hardships of heavy labor. In these early recorded examples collected by folklorist Alan Lomax in the 1930s, we can hear the roots of blues singing.

**Go to chapter 2 playlist examples "Arwhoolie" and "Calling Trains" Traditional**

## Blues Basics

As a form and a genre, blues is marked by specific musical elements which serve as the raw materials for blues songs. These include **12-bar blues** form, the **blues scale**, and the **shuffle** rhythm.

The shuffle rhythm was discussed in Chapter 1. Here we discuss 12-bar form and the blues scale in turn:

> Note: For the sake of clarity and aural understanding, your instructor can demonstrate these concepts at the piano or with a guitar.

12-bar blues form is essentially a **chord progression** that is drawn directly from European music, but with a twist: standard, traditional chords are ordered in a completely nonstandard way. The chords which musicians refer to as the I (one), the IV (four), and the V (five), also known as "primary" chords, are a basic building block of the European harmonic and melodic language. In fact, it would be virtually impossible to find a European musical composition from around 1600–1900 and beyond that does not express these chords in some way. Traditionally, when dealing with just with these primary chords, we will encounter the following chord progressions or sequences:

> I-V-I

> I-IV-V-I

or occasionally

> I-IV-I

Although this may seem quite simple, composers and songwriters have gotten an enormous amount of mileage out of these basic progressions!

The blues pattern is built on this difference:

> I-IV-I-V-IV-I (note the V moving "backwards" to the IV)

In the 12-bar blues pattern the chords appear thusly (each chord numeral represents one 4-beat bar or measure):

> I-I-I-I

> IV-IV-I-I

> V-IV-I-I

> Note: There is typically a corresponding phrase structure in blues lyrics in which there is a line of text stated with the first four bars, repeated (or slightly varied) over the next four bars and then answered or "resolved" with the final four bars. We call this **AAB** phrase structure. Furthermore, the 12-bar pattern, although exceedingly common, is occasionally adjusted in length but retains the basic progression.

The blues scale is another fundamental component, and that which lends most to the intense expression of emotion in blues. Although the earliest appearance of the scale is unknown, some scholars speculate that the blues scale is derived from a hybridization of the West African pentatonic scale and the European natural minor scale (also called Aeolian mode). Whatever the true origin, it is the so-called "blue notes" (E-flat, G-flat, and B-flat) which give the blues much of its feeling. The "flatting" of the notes creates a "sagging" or "mellow" quality which carries enormous potential for the expression of sadness, sorrow, and general sense of woe.

African Pentatonic: **C**, D-flat, **E-flat**, **G**, A-flat

European Minor: **C**, D, **E-flat**, **F**, **G**, A-flat, **B-flat**

Blues Scale: C, E-flat, F, G-flat, G, B-flat

*Classic and Country Blues*

Many blues artists had been performing "real" blues in traveling tent shows and other obscure venues since the early twentieth century but the blues came to mainstream America in stages.

The first known published blues in sheet music form appeared around 1912 and was popularized by W.C. Handy (1873–1958), the self-styled "Father of the Blues." Handy achieved popular hits with "Memphis Blues" in 1912 and "St. Louis Blues" in 1914. Although Handy employed basic blues elements, his compositions owe much to the popular song structures which were characteristic of the Tin Pan Alley styles of the time as well as Latin rhythms. In other words, this wasn't "real" blues but rather a blues-infused form of early twentieth-century popular music. Still, "St. Louis Blues" remains one of the most recorded blues songs of all time and earned Handy millions in royalties during his lifetime. Handy was an important music business figure as well as the cofounder of the first African American–owned music publishing company.

**Go to chapter 2 playlist example "St. Louis Blues" (W.C. Handy version), 1914**

One of Handy's contemporaries, an African American songwriter/pianist named Perry Bradford (1893–1970), believed that there was a market for recorded blues music and in 1920 convinced executives at Okeh Records to record blues singer Mamie Smith (1883–1946) performing his (Bradford's) song "Crazy Blues." Within the first month of its release, the record sold over seventy thousand copies and it has been estimated that sales eventually topped the 1 million mark. "Crazy Blues," although it is more of a popular-style song with blues elements than a true blues piece, demonstrated that there was largely untapped market for black music marketed to black audiences. (The broad appeal of this music to white audiences was likely unforeseen by either Bradford or Okeh Records.)

Ralph Peer (1892–1960), a talent scout at Okeh Records and assistant in the Smith recording sessions, coined the term "race music" as a promotional catchphrase for the recording. This marked the birth of the so-called **race records**, music recorded by black artists and marketed primarily to a black audience, and the creation of a new and hugely important segment of the American recording industry.

Other record labels were quick to cash in on the race record market and a profusion of recorded blues music followed. In fact, most race records were blues and blues-based pieces. The music captured in these recordings is now widely referred to as **classic blues** and its biggest stars were Mamie Smith, Bessie Smith ("Empress of the Blues") (1894–1937), Gertrude "Ma" Rainey ("Mother of the Blues") (1886–1939), Ethel Waters (1896–1977), and Alberta Hunter (1895–1984). Ensembles commonly consisted of a female vocalist accompanied by small, varied combos (piano, horns, bass, and drums). Classic blues music was regularly performed in nightclubs in northern cities like Chicago and New York and the recordings sold well to both black and white audiences clearly demonstrating the expanding white fascination with music that featured deeply African characteristics.

Bessie Smith's 1925 recording of W.C. Handy's "St. Louis Blues" is a prime example of the hybrid blues-pop that introduced much of white America to the blues performance style. In this piece we hear all of the elements which are associated with blues: 12-bar pattern, blues scale and blues vocal inflection, shuffle rhythm, and call and response. Although the piece is somewhat removed from the authentic, earthy flavor and more traditional forms of the so-called **country blues** (see below) all of the constituent elements are present. Smith's rough yet expressive delivery and first-person lyric perspective are also fundamental to blues. Notice too, the phrase structure (AAB) which is common to blues as it lines up quite well with the 12-bar forms.

**Bars 1–4**: I hate to see the evenin' sun go' down (cornet response)

**Bars 5–8**: I hate to see the evenin' sun go' down (cornet response)

**Bars 9–12**: It makes me think I'm on my last go 'round (cornet response)

**Go to web audio example 2.13 "St Louis Blues" W.C. Handy (Bessie Smith version), 1925**

**Note**: The cornet part in this recording is handled by the then future jazz legend Louis "Satchmo" Armstrong (1901–1971).

**Country blues,** a more authentic form of roots blues, also called "rural," "folk," or "old-fashioned" blues, is actually the music that originally inspired Handy and is the style of blues that most informs the rock music of the 1960s and beyond. This music is regarded as the "real" blues of the Mississippi Delta and other regions of the rural South and Southwest, as opposed to the classic blues songs popularized by Handy and his contemporaries. Ironically, it was because of the popularity of classic blues that country blues begins to appear on recordings in the 1920s. This music had existed for decades as an oral tradition, largely among the rural black work force in post-emancipation southern regions, and had only begun to be recorded commercially in 1926 when Paramount Records released the music of Blind Lemon Jefferson (1897–1929). Even then

Jefferson's recordings were marketed as "real old-fashioned blues by a real old-fashioned blues singer" (Starr and Waterman 2010).

In Jefferson's 1926 recording of his piece "That Black Snake Moan" we encounter all of the genuine blues elements which are so spellbinding: deeply expressive vocals with a wide variety of shading and inflection; a capricious conception of timing and phrasing based on an underlying shuffle rhythm; and the sparse, "lonesome" sounding guitar which peppers the texture with a mix of chords and licks that serve as the response to the vocal call. What's more is the lyric is gritty and full of sexual innuendo; it is quite obvious that the "black snake" is a phallic reference. As stated earlier, this type of euphemistic expression of sex and sexual imagery was commonplace in blues.

**Go to chapter 2 playlist example "That Black Snake Moan" Blind Lemon Jefferson, 1926**

Other country "bluesmen" that followed on the heels of Jefferson's recordings were Charley Patton (1881–1934), Huddie Ledbetter (Leadbelly) (1888–1949), Blind Willie McTell (1898–1959), Son House (1902–1988) and perhaps the most influential bluesman of all, Robert Johnson (1911–1938).

Robert Johnson's life and music have become the stuff of myth, legend, and poignant irony. Not much is known about his early life or his mysterious and untimely death at the age of twenty-seven; little more than anecdotal evidence regarding his travels, performance practices, and professional career exist. Furthermore, Johnson achieved only modest regional fame during his lifetime. The combination of his sparse historical record and the enigmatic nature of his music have surrounded him in a powerful mystique. Tales abound regarding deals with the devil; furtive movements while performing; whiskey, women, and jealous husbands; extensive travels; and a private, sometimes sulky-natured man who was known to disappear for weeks at a time. What has endured are his recordings, twenty-nine in all, and these stand out as some of the most original and expressive in the blues repertoire.

Johnson's guitar technique is extremely advanced; the complex textures he creates and the kind of sonic acrobatics he performs have inspired many of rock's most legendary guitarists. Jimi Hendrix, Keith Richards, Eric Clapton, Jimmy Page, Pete Townshend, Alex Lifeson, and dozens of others have cited Johnson as a major—if not primary—influence. Moreover, a host of modern guitar industry experts have ranked Johnson at or near the top of extensive lists of the greatest guitar players of all time. Johnson's singing has informed many great rock singers as well; the unencumbered vocal style with which he delivers his often sexual and sometimes cryptic lyrics demonstrate the finest kind of natural musicianship. He has inspired the singing of Bob Dylan, Robert Plant, Mick Jagger, and on and on. Perhaps the most remarkable quality in Johnson's music is his approach to rhythm. His timekeeping is totally liberated from any kind of metronomic pulse yet the flow of time is organic and instinctive. His rhythms are primal and sophisticated at the same time. Johnson's impact on rock is inestimable. It is no exaggeration to say that without Robert Johnson, rock music today would be an entirely different matter.

**Note**: Robert Johnson is considered to be the original member of the "27 Club," an assemblage of musicians, most of them rock musicians, who died at the age of twenty-seven. The most famous of these include Jimi Hendrix, Janis Joplin, Jim Morrison, Brian Jones, Ron "Pigpen" McKernan, and more recently Kurt Cobain and Amy Winehouse.

Johnson's "Cross Road Blues" offers a shining example of his genius. His energetic guitar playing here demonstrates the aggression and uninhibited feeling that finds its way into rock through players like Clapton, Page, and Townshend as well as the kind of sonic exploration of the instrument's expressive range and color which comes to full flower in the music of Jimi Hendrix. Johnson's singing reciprocates with his guitar playing, also ranging from impassioned highs to throaty lows which are often connected by sliding and bending notes.

**Go to chapter 2 playlist example "Cross Road Blues" Robert Johnson, 1936**

## Hillbilly and Early Country Music

In 1923, Ralph Peer of Okeh Records, the label that had pioneered the so-called race record market, was on a talent scouting trip in the rural south seeking fresh African-American musicians to record. After several prospects had fallen through, a local record store owner in Atlanta with whom

Peer was working suggested that they record a local musician by the name of Fiddlin' John Carson (1868–1949). Peer was reluctant but apparently, having nothing more pressing at the moment, agreed. Following the session, Peer had little hope or regard for the music he had captured. The record store owner, a man by the name of Polk Brockman, had a different sense of the rural white market in the south and ordered five hundred copies. The recordings sold out in less than a month without any promotion or advertising on the part of Okeh Records. It didn't take long for Peer and Okeh Records to realize that there was an untapped market here as well and they were quick to act.

These early recordings, which were originally dubbed **hillbilly records**, would come to be known as **country and western** and eventually just **country music**. It is important to understand that the music on these recordings was not *new* music; it was rooted in Anglo-American folk song and had existed among white musicians in the rural south for several generations as an oral tradition. In fact, prior to the time of his first recordings Carson had been performing all over the south for several decades and had built a strong regional reputation. Carson and other stylistically similar musicians had also been receiving support from the Atlanta radio station WSB through a series of live-broadcast performances from around 1922.

Indeed it was southern, white-owned radio stations that would become a decisive factor in the growth of hillbilly music. By 1922 there were more than eighty radio stations operating in the south, many of which began to specialize in hillbilly and country music as the decade wore on. Radio, more so than any other medium, was responsible for the rapid growth of country music. By contrast, race records relied heavily on phonograph sales as their main source of dissemination. The ownership of radios, to say nothing of radio *stations*, was largely a white privilege in the 1920s and 1930s. Radio served almost no purpose in the popularization of race music. This fact will become even more significant in shaping the landscape of American music as radio began to erode record sales in the late 1920s, and during the years of the Great Depression when the record industry suffered a precipitous decline.

On an August day in 1927, Peer's tireless efforts to scour the south in search of new and potentially lucrative talent paid off in a most remarkable way. Peer had arranged and advertised an open recording session in Bristol, Tennessee, which drew in a number of country musicians from all over the region. Among these musicians were two acts, the Carter Family and Jimmie Rodgers, who would change the course of country music and serve as inspiration to many diverse musicians for generations to come. What is perhaps most extraordinary about that summer day and the subsequent success of both acts (their recordings transformed country into a major national segment of the music business) is the stark contrast between their respective music and the values that each represented.

The Carters were made of the stuff of tradition, simplicity, and quiet introspection, while Rodgers was a beacon pointing the way to the future of country music through the innovative weaving of elements of blues, jazz, and the free-spirited romance of the open road. These two factions of country music represent a long-standing dichotomy that exists within the style even to this day.

The Carter Family hailed from an isolated region of Virginia in the foothills of the Clinch Mountains. The trio was comprised of A.P. "Doc" Carter (1891–1960), vocals; his wife Sara Carter (1899–1979), vocals and autoharp; and Doc's sister Maybelle Carter (1909–1978), vocals, guitar, and autoharp. The music they recorded between 1927 and 1941, over three hundred singles in all, was a combination of adaptations of traditional Anglo-American folk songs, sacred hymn songs and quasi-original sentimental songs in the vein of the earliest Tin Pan Alley song. All of their music was simply but skillfully arranged for the group by Doc Carter. He would periodically travel around regions in the south collecting material from both white and black musicians, which he would then arrange to suit his group's vocals and instrumentation. This practice of working with existing folk tunes as a basis of commercial songwriting would become a longstanding tradition among country and folk musicians alike.

The most influential component of the Carter Family's music was the guitar playing of Maybelle Carter. An instinctively adept and gifted musician, she developed a style of guitar voicing known as "thumb and brush" picking in which she would pluck out a melodic line on the low strings of the guitar while brushing out a chordal accompaniment on the higher strings. In essence she was playing two parts at once. This approach to the instrument was (consciously and unconsciously) adapted by generations of future guitarists in many different styles and genres ranging from country and folk to rock and pop.

**Go to chapter 2 playlist example "Wildwood Flower" Carter Family**

Image 2.6: Jimmie Rodgers

The music and persona of Jimmie Rodgers exerted a profound influence on the future of country music. Hank Williams, Willie Nelson, Waylon Jennings, and Merle Haggard, to name but a few, have all cited Rodgers as a fundamental force in shaping their music and careers. Rodgers captured the essence of the traveling musician who in his ramblings is willing to absorb the sights and sounds of the world around him and express them through his music. He successfully employed traditional elements alongside those of blues, African-American work songs—which he encountered in his early life working on railroads—and jazz. He even made a recording with African-American jazz cornetist Louis Armstrong and Louis' wife Lil Hardin Armstrong on piano; white and black musical collaborations were virtually unheard of at the time. Rodgers was progressive and innovative. He preceded Elvis Presley in that he was a "white man with a black sound."

In "Blue Yodel No. 9" recorded in 1930, we hear the strong blues components and the blurred genre lines which were a feature of Rodgers' work.

**Go to chapter 2 playlist example "Blue Yodel No. 9" Jimmie Rodgers (Louis Armstrong, cornet), 1930**

Country music would continue to thrive during the Depression and during and after World War II. In addition to radio, country music did well in Hollywood with the so-called Singing Cowboys (Gene Autry, Roy Rogers, and others), and as increasing numbers of white southern country fans migrated to northern cities in search of work, they brought their music with them. In Chapter 3 we will see how a new manifestation of blues-influenced, amplified country music called **honky-tonk** came of age in the early 1950s and exerted its influence on the musical world around it.

## Early Jazz and the Jazz Age

In the first two decades of the twentieth century and around the same time that country blues was circulating in the rural south, musicians working primarily in New Orleans were developing their own take on blues, a form of mostly instrumental, highly syncopated, richly textured music known as "hot" music or **jazz**. New Orleans was—and is—a hotbed of musical and cultural activity. In addition to African American work song traditions, including improvisation and blues, the jazz music which originated there was touched by ragtime, marching band music, French and Italian opera, Caribbean and Mexican music, Latin rhythms, Tin Pan Alley, and even music related to funeral processions. A good deal of early jazz was danceable music but it was not purely dance music like rags or waltzes.

> **Note:** The word "jazz" carried several meanings at the time in New Orleans: there were musical connotations which referred to speeding up the tempo and/or increased musical complexity, but there was also a heavy reference to sexual intercourse. We will see a similar etymology in the term "rock 'n' roll."

The so-called "Jazz Age" occupies the period from around 1917–1935. (Although jazz would develop down its own artistic path throughout the twentieth century, our concerns here are with jazz as a popular music form). Jazz exploded into the American consciousness in 1917 when the Original Dixieland Jazz Band (ODJB), a group from New Orleans working in New York, released a recording on Victor Records. Within a matter of weeks the recording had created a national interest in this "new" style of music. It is ironic that the ODJB were white musicians when one considers that jazz originated as a black style. Given the racial climate of the time, it is also likely that if black musicians had been the first to release a jazz recording it would not have been so well received by the white market. We will see this phenomenon again in a major way with Elvis Presley in the 1950s. In any case, the ODJB recordings introduced white, middle-class American youth to jazz and a significant expression of African American musical culture … and they were hooked.

**Go to chapter 2 playlist example "Livery Stable Blues" Original Dixieland Jazz Band, 1917**

A more authentic African American flavor of early jazz can be heard in the recordings of King Oliver's Creole Jazz Band, led by jazz cornetist, bandleader, and pioneer Joseph Oliver (1881–1938). The 1923 recording of "Canal Street Blues" is representative of the blues-influenced, improvisational jazz that came out of New Orleans. From 1908 to 1917 Oliver achieved great success in New Orleans and was popular with both black and white audiences. In 1918 he relocated to Chicago, solidifying the Creole Jazz Band in 1922. The recordings that followed garnered acclaim from a national audience.

**Go to chapter 2 playlist example "Canal Street Blues" King Joe Oliver (with Louis Armstrong), 1923**

Other factors played a major role in the growth of jazz music and culture throughout the 1920s: World War I provided a major stimulation to the national economy fueling the "roaring twenties." With this came the expansion of transportation, mass migration from country to city, an abundance of jobs, the growth of the urban middle class, and more and better access to music and the technologies that supported it. Mass media in the form of talking films and radio and the expanding diversity of the record industry contributed to the growth of jazz and helped to shape a more interconnected culture.

The **fox-trot**, a style of syncopated, danceable jazz-oriented song, came to be the most common form of popular dance song during the 1920s and 1930s. The fox-trot beat, a two-beat pattern in which a bass note alternates with a snappy backbeat, forms the rhythmic foundation over which dance orchestras and jazz bands would play and sing syncopated riff-based melodies. All of these musical characteristics grew out of black styles (ragtime, blues, and jazz) and clearly demonstrate the extent of black influence on the white mainstream. The fox-trot and its beat became the most common foundation for the popular dance music of the 1920s and early 1930s (as mentioned above, many Tin Pan Alley hits of this era were fox-trots). The George Olsen Orchestra's 1927 hit "Varsity Drag" exemplifies the fox-trot rhythm.

**Go to chapter 2 playlist example "Varsity Drag" Ray Henderson/George Olsen, 1927**

The jazz culture of the 1920s presages both the rock 'n' roll culture of the 1950s and the rock culture of the late 1960s: The ascension of jazz as a social movement represents the first distinct American youth culture defined by and situated around a popular music style. The young men and women who were drawn to the jazz clubs, dance halls, and speakeasies—lawless establishments that served alcohol during the years of prohibition (1919–1933)—adopted their own fashion, lingo, dances (often considered to be immoral), and attitude. These were young middle- and upper-class whites striving to assert their independence by adopting elements of black music and style, and the beginning of a trend which would intensify, particularly after World War II, helping to shape American music throughout the twentieth century. Jazz was music for the young and the wild, but because the youth market was not considered to be significant to the major labels and publishers the bulk of the popular mainstream belonged to the exceedingly white world of Tin Pan Alley song and style.

## Boogie-Woogie

Boogie-woogie is a blues-based, piano-centric style that captivated audiences in rowdy urban night-clubs in cities like Chicago, Memphis, and New Orleans throughout the 1920s and appeared on the popular radar late in the decade in the form of the first commercial boogie-woogie hit recordings (although emerging scholarship traces the style to Texas as far back as the late 1870s). Unlike classic blues with its emotional heaviness and country blues with its free conception of rhythm, boogie-woogie is almost exclusively related to high-energy dancing; tempos are brisk with strong backbeats and melodies and lyrics are commonly lighthearted and playful. Basic piano boogie-woogie is characterized by a heavy-handed left-hand part which outlines a 12-bar blues over a strong shuffle rhythm (long-short pattern based on triple subdivision) with syncopated, riff-based melodies played in the right-hand part. Strong and steady beat keeping in basic 4/4 time is also a defining characteristic.

Although early boogie-woogie was conceived as solo piano dance music, it could expand to accompany vocals. Clarence "Pine Top" Smith (1904–1929) recorded the first boogie-woogie cross-over hit, "Pine Top's Boogie-Woogie" in 1928. In this song, Smith gives the audience instructions on how to dance to his boogie-woogie. In a sense, he is basically "rapping" over the piano part. He also employs a variety of techniques such as tremolo (rapid alternation between notes) and a kind of "stop time" that lends to the feeling of rhythmic freedom at those moments.

**Go to chapter 2 playlist example "Pine Top's Boogie-Woogie" Pine Top Smith, 1928**

As we will soon discover, boogie-woogie blues style played a significant role in the musical conception of a great deal of important music and musical developments that followed. Big bands coming out of the Kansas City, Missouri, region in the 1930s used the boogie-woogie rhythm and riff style as a foundation for many successful compositions; swing music would be based on the idea of riff-based melody and four-beat rhythms; and boogie-woogie would become a fad during World War II with hits like "Boogie Woogie," "Boogie Woogie Bugle Boy," and "The Booglie Wooglie Piggy."

Boogie-woogie concepts would form the basis of much rhythm and blues, rockabilly, and would facilitate the transition to the early rock 'n' roll styles of Little Richard, Chuck Berry, Fats Domino, Jerry Lee Lewis, and a host of others.

## Black Gospel Music

The African American **spiritual** had been a central component of black Christian worship since well before the Civil War. Spirituals emerged as black interpretations of the congregational **hymn** singing practice common to white churches, though this music was infused with a fervor that expressed the religious experiences unique to African Americans. **Gospel** song, as a distinct style of sacred music, began to take shape in the late 1920s when a successful blues musician named Thomas A. Dorsey (also known as "Georgia Tom") decided to leave the world of secular commercial music and devote his efforts to what he coined "gospel songs." Dorsey's experience with and affinity for blues stylings found its way into his original pieces and reworking of traditional spirituals. Dorsey's defining moment came in 1930 at a black Baptist convention in Chicago when he performed "If You See My Savior, Tell Him That You Saw Me." From that point, gospel songs rapidly grew into a staple of black musical worship.

Early black gospel music was not intended as a commercial style, nor did it have much of a presence outside of the black community, except among some southern whites. Efforts were made by Dorsey and others to spread the music through publishing and recording but it would be some time before gospel would become widespread. By the latter part of the twentieth century, countless tunes penned by Dorsey and his contemporaries had become standard fare in the hymnals and songbooks of many denominations of Christianity. Still, the purpose and purity of gospel as a tool of worship placed it, at least conceptually, above the toil for commercial gain.

Gospel exerted a powerful influence on many young singers whose earliest exposure to music came in the form of gospel singing; singers ranging from Aretha Franklin to Elvis Presley and Little Richard to Johnny Cash all had roots in gospel singing, and it resonated in their own music. Many commercial musicians have recorded gospel standards which they first encountered in their youth; Elvis Presley recorded dozens of gospel tunes. Even modern pop stars like Mariah Carey and the late Whitney Houston have cited gospel music as having a profound effect on their development and style.

In the gospel recordings of 1930s and 1940s there were two common performance traditions: the male quartet and the female soloist. Male vocal quartets such as The Mills Brothers and The Ink Spots were popular in the early 1930s and may have been an impetus for the formation of gospel quartets; however, most male gospel groups sang *a cappella*, that is, without instrumental accompaniment. Gospel quartets were often quite innovative in their approach. In "The Golden Gate Gospel Train" performed by the Golden Gate Jubilee Quartet in 1937, we hear the use of special vocal effects that simulate the sound of a train along with the rich harmony and strong beat keeping. The percussive vocal "special" effects are a predecessor of doo-wop (see Chapter 3), as well as an ancestor of modern "beatboxing" and other techniques used in contemporary hip-hop and funk.

**Go to chapter 2 playlist example "Golden Gate Gospel Train" The Golden Gate Quartet, 1938**

Female solo singers were a major force in gospel music as well; these were powerhouse singers who employed an arsenal of impressive techniques. Melismatic passages (emblematic melodic flourishes on a single syllable) along with blue notes, bent notes, syncopated phrasings, and other highly stylized techniques infused gospel music with a wealth of musicality and sincerity. Instrumental accompaniment in the form of piano or organ was common with female soloists and occasionally backup singers or choirs enhanced the musical texture. Singers like Sallie Martin, Marion Williams, Clara Ward, Shirley Caesar, and the brightest star of them all, Mahalia Jackson, sang with an infectious passion that would prove to be enormously influential not only musically, but in raising the stature of women in American music.

Image 2.7: Mahalia Jackson

**Go to chapter 2 playlist example "Take My Hand Precious Lord" Mahalia Jackson, 1956**

## Symphonic Jazz, the Great Depression and the Big Band Swing Era

In the 1920s and early 1930s, the most commercially successful dance bandleader was Paul Whiteman. Although Whiteman proclaimed himself the "King of Jazz" and his recordings sold millions, the music Whiteman offered up could best be described as a "whitewashed" form of symphonic, jazz-influenced dance music. To be sure, this was high-quality music played by fine musicians, but it lacked the energy and edge of authentic jazz. Whiteman did, however, build his brand into a mighty music industry force. He franchised his name and image and sanctioned official "P.W." bands around the country, some touring and many more playing steady engagements in hotels and dance clubs all over the United States. Whiteman's overwhelming commercial presence served two important purposes: it brought jazz-based dance music to a broader audience and, as we will soon discover, helped to set the stage for the Big Band Swing Era.

**Go to chapter 2 playlist example "Whispering" Paul Whiteman, 1920**

The Great Depression of 1929 had a profound effect on the record business. Through the 1920s, record sales had been generating hundreds of millions of dollars (there was a decline in the late 1920s because of radio) but by 1933 that number had decreased dramatically; Americans, by and large, simply did not have the extra income to spend on the luxury of recorded music. Many small record labels tanked and race record production suffered accordingly. The labels that did survive did so by relying heavily on well-established artists, like Whiteman, to generate sales. The days of heavy experimentation and field expeditions in search of the next big thing ground to a halt. To a great extent, radio and movies stepped in to fill the void as they both provided a relatively inexpensive form of entertainment. Nevertheless, musicians in every style struggled to remain creative and productive during the years between 1929 and 1935. Swing music, which exploded in 1935 helped to pull the American music industry out of the Great Depression.

In the late 1920s and early 1930s, around the same time that Paul Whiteman was enjoying his success, a host of syncopated dance orchestras were taking shape in Northern cities like New York and Chicago, and notably in Kansas City, initially through the work of jazz-oriented African American bands/bandleaders such as "Duke" Ellington (1899–1974), Fletcher Henderson (1897–1952), Count Basie (1904–1984) and Bennie Moten (1894–1935) and later by white groups and their leaders, including Benny Goodman (1909–1986), Tommy Dorsey (1905–1956) and Artie Shaw (1910–2004). These bandleaders and their ensembles offered an exciting new kind of dance music with a distinctly "uptown" feel; the aesthetic was one of polish and urban sophistication with music centered on four-beat rhythms, complex textures, call and response techniques, and riff-based melodies (all of which are found in rock). Ensembles gradually grew in size and moved out of the intimate lounges to grand ballrooms. The images of musicians striking carefree poses and mugging for the cameras were supplanted by those of neatly arranged and well-groomed groups in matching evening wear.

The term "swing" originally referred to the fluid motion created by the music itself but as the style grew it came to embody states of freedom and good times; in the context of the Great Depression, the music and dancing no doubt represented an escape. The repeal of Prohibition in 1933 assuredly contributed to the party culture of swing as well. Musicians used the word in song titles like Duke Ellington's "It Don't Mean a Thing If It Ain't Got That Swing" and Bennie Moten's "Moten Swing," both recorded in 1932. The use of swing as a stylistic designation caught on in the music industry around 1935. It was also in 1935 that swing had its breakout moment.

The birth of swing as a national sensation occurred virtually overnight following a 1935 appearance by the Benny Goodman Band at the Palomar Ballroom in Hollywood. The group had been on tour that summer performing a number of "hot" syncopated arrangements, many of which Goodman had purchased from bandleader Fletcher Henderson; however, these arrangements were performed in Goodman's inimitably precise and controlled way. Although the music had failed to captivate Midwestern audiences, the group was received with overwhelming enthusiasm on the West Coast and the massive publicity surrounding the show and the music garnered national attention. The Swing Era had arrived.

Image 2.8: Count Basie and Members of His Orchestra circa 1938

Within a short time swing bands sprang up all over the country and the ensuing race to cash in on the craze began in earnest. Over the next decade swing music would became a cultural movement of unprecedented scope and popularity. The swing craze included Latin swing, a swing style based on Latin dance rhythms (see below); and western swing, a fusion of country music and swing elements. Solo crooners like Frank Sinatra and Nat "King" Cole had their popular origins singing with swing bands before embarking on substantial careers of their own.

The success of Goodman and other white bandleaders helped to broaden the audience for black bandleaders, like Duke Ellington and Count Basie, although musical differences between black and white groups were often fairly well pronounced; blues and boogie-woogie were often at the core of the rhythmic and formal conception of the black bandleaders and there was a tendency to favor a more intense swing rhythm with a "looser," more improvised feel that carries over from jazz. A sampling of Benny Goodman alongside Count Basie will reveal these fundamental differences.

**Go to chapter 2 playlist example "King Porter Stomp" Jelly Roll Morton; Benny Goodman, arranged by Fletcher Henderson, 1935**

**Go to chapter 2 playlist example "Jumpin' at the Woodside" Count Basie**

Perhaps the most innovative and versatile of the Swing Era big bandleaders was composer/pianist Edward Kennedy "Duke" Ellington. Although he began his career as primarily a jazz musician and moved into swing in the late 1920s, his music really transcends jazz and swing. In speaking of his own music he said it was "beyond category." Duke was a master of the three-minute gem suited for 78 rpm records as well as longer, more elaborate works based on classical music forms. He also composed musicals which highlighted themes of the African experience and enjoyed long runs in Los Angeles and New York. If Duke's music epitomized his consummate artistry, his philosophy "jazz is music, swing is business" highlighted his understanding of the music industry. His career spanned more than half a century and his name is synonymous with music of the highest order.

Duke's big band music is noted for its unusual treatment of instrumental color combinations, richly dissonant harmonies, thick textures, and infectiously catchy riffs.

**Go to chapter 2 playlist example "Koko" Duke Ellington**

It was during the latter part of World War II that swing music began to decline. Many musicians were drafted to the military and touring became less feasible due to the wartime economy (fuel and vehicle shortages and so on). To hasten the decline of swing even further, musician's union strikes in 1942 and 1948 shut union instrumentalists out of recording studios or banned them from making records entirely. By the time the 1948 strike had ended, crooner-heavy Tin Pan Alley pop had taken over the mainstream and jump bands along with other R&B styles had filled the void for energetic, youthful dance music (see below). As singers were not considered by the union at that time to be "musicians" and therefore denied admission, they escaped the recording bans. Likewise, many R&B musicians simply did not belong to the union and were thus free to do as they pleased.

While swing music captivated millions of Americans, not everyone was attracted to the hard-swinging, energetic style. Another big band style that came to be known as **sweet** music was drawing in its own fans and selling millions of recordings. This music was essentially an outgrowth of the society dance orchestras of the late 1920s, and was considerably closer to what musicians like Paul Whiteman were doing. Highly skilled groups like Guy Lombardo and His Royal Canadians, Les Brown and His Band of Renown, and the most famous of all, Glenn Miller and His Orchestra produced silky smooth, tuneful big band music with gentler beats (usually fox-trots) and far less syncopation than swing. A characteristic Glenn Miller piece demonstrates the much milder nature of sweet music.

Go to chapter 2 playlist example "Moonlight Serenade" Glenn Miller, 1939

Another important subgenre of swing music that emerged during the era was **Latin** swing. The Latin contribution to American music came mainly in the form of dance rhythms (discussed later in the text) incorporated in various ways and in the percussion instruments associated with **Afro-Cuban** styles. These are a wide range of styles which developed through the intermingling of Caribbean, South American, and Mexican styles with African and European styles. These influences came to the United States through immigration and found a voice in the early jazz of New Orleans (a gateway from the Caribbean) and other forms of dance music in urban areas like New York and Los Angeles in the early twentieth century.

Latin swing's biggest star was Xavier Cugat (1900–1990), a gifted violinist and bandleader who was born in Spain, spent his early childhood in Cuba, and migrated to the United States around 1915. He played in tango bands in in New York and moved to Los Angeles in 1920 where he led a dance band called the Gigolos. His eventual return to New York in the early 1930s culminated in a steady engagement at Manhattan's Waldorf–Astoria Hotel where he and his Waldorf–Astoria Orchestra would remain for nearly three decades. Cugat introduced many Americans to authentic Latin rhythms and instruments through his arrangements and recordings. "Brazil," written by Brazilian composer Ary Barroso and recorded by Cugat in 1943, was Cugat's most successful release, reaching the number two position on the Pop charts that year.

Go to chapter 2 playlist example "Brazil" Xavier Cugat, 1943

**Note:** Latin music and musicians helped to shape the musical landscape of the Swing Era and would continue to exert a powerful influence on dance music in particular throughout the decades that followed. We will discuss the Latin influence as it pertains to rock in subsequent chapters.

## Socially Conscious Folk Music

Anglo-American folk music has, for many decades, served as a vehicle for expressing the experiences of the peasant class. Its persistence into the twentieth century was evident in the success of musicians like the Carter Family. In the 1930s, a folk musician named Woodrow Wilson "Woody" Guthrie (1912–1967) would elevate folk music to the level of serious social commentary, which eventually had a massive impact on rock. In essence, Guthrie was the first "protest" singer. He was a prolific songwriter, having written or adapted more than one thousand songs during his career and was considered to be the quintessential "rambling musician." During the 1930s and 1940s Guthrie moved in radical political circles, sang in marches and on picket lines, and was deeply and personally concerned with the plight of the economically and politically disenfranchised.

Image 2.9: Woody Guthrie (note the sticker on his guitar reads "This Machine Kills Fascists")

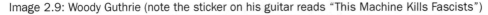

Guthrie's musical style was one of unadorned simplicity and placed no emphasis on innovation. Instead, his music is simply a backdrop for his powerful, heartfelt messages. He sang of personal experiences as a migrant worker in the "Dust Bowl" era of the Great Depression, of corruption in government, of economic inequality, of communal living, and of brotherly love. Through his music he championed the causes of the extreme political left, of union organizers, and human rights activists. He was also a prolific writer, having penned thousands of pages of unpublished poetry and prose, as well as an autobiography.

Although Guthrie always wished to be considered a member of the working class, and not as an intellectual, his music, politics, and attitudes directly influenced a wave of future urban intellectual folk musicians like Pete Seeger and the Weavers, as well as Bob Dylan.

**Go to chapter 2 playlist example "The Jolly Banker" Woody Guthrie, 1940**

## American Music in the Wake of World War II

The years following World War II were marked by an increased sense of political and social conservatism. Years of uncertainty and personal sacrifice on the part of millions of Americans had understandably had profound psychological and emotional effects. On one hand, Americans were exhilarated to have achieved victory in a long and costly war, and on the other, most people simply wanted their lives to return to a state of peace and stability. With millions returning home from overseas, the lifting of wartime restrictions on the production of domestic goods, and industry in full swing, the economy boomed; urban areas expanded rapidly and the suburban middle class exploded in size. By and large, Americans had an abiding trust in the institutions and leadership of government. With the atrocities of war still very fresh in their minds, people were eager to settle down, buy a home and start families, and put the whole mess behind them. This was an age of conformity, at least on the surface.

The war had subsurface effects as well. The United States' global role had ostensibly become that of defender of the oppressed and protector of democracy. Millions of lives, both white and black, had been sacrificed in the fight against inequality, yet the inequality that existed within American borders had not changed in any substantial way for many decades. To many Americans, and to the rest of the world, this appalling truth became uncomfortably evident. The blatant hypocrisy of the racial situation in America began to erode long-standing attitudes of prejudice. Change, however, doesn't always happen overnight, yet the seeds had been planted and music helped them to grow.

Changing attitudes and tastes, along with the downsizing of big bands during the war, helped to pave the way for a new and significantly popular form of black music called **jump band blues**. The musical outcome of paring a big band down to its essential **rhythm section** (piano, bass, drums, and sometimes guitar), and retaining one or two saxophones and a cornet or trumpet is the emergence of a leaner, tighter, more agile ensemble. Toward the end of and after WWII, jump bands surpassed big bands as young America's dance music of choice. Jump bands proffered a brand of hard-swinging, up-tempo, boogie-woogie style blues that featured a strong backbeat, a party attitude, and often a sense of humor and playfulness. Like jazz and the "hot" brand of swing, this was a youth-oriented style.

No jump band was more popular in the 1940s than Louis Jordan and His Tympany Five. Jordan (1908–1975) was a gifted saxophonist as well as the band's lead singer. He was a consummate showman with a skill for comedic interjection. Jordan and the Tympany Five's recording of Johnny Mercer's song "G.I. Jive" was their first crossover hit, reaching number one on *Billboard's* "Harlem Hit Parade" and its Pop chart in 1944. It held the number one position for two weeks and eventually sold more than a million copies. A string of crossover hits such as "Caldonia," "Stone Cold Dead in the Market," "Choo-Choo-Ch-Boogie," and "Ain't Nobody Here But Us Chickens" followed along with successful tours and sold-out performances.

**Go to chapter 2 playlist example "Caldonia" Louis Jordan, 1945**

**Note**: Although Jordan and other black recording artists did much to bring black music and culture to a young white audience in the late 1940s, entrenched racial attitudes persisted; as, on many occasions, there was particularly high demand for tickets by both black and white patrons when Jordan and other popular black stars performed, concert organizers would commonly hold two separate shows, one for white audiences and one for black. When this wasn't possible, white and black audience members were kept apart by various means of dividing the hall.

Image 2.10: Louis Jordan circa 1946

Youth culture in post-WWII America played an increasingly significant role in the development of music and music markets. The economic boom in the United States trickled down to teenagers and young adults in the form of job availability and allowances. Young people had unprecedented spending power which in turn opened up new markets for the products they were demanding. By some estimates in the late 1940s, the under–twenty-one market accounted for a full third of record sales in the United States. Still, not all of these record-buying youth were spending their money on race records and the big record companies were apparently inclined to view fringe styles as passing fads. Much of the music being produced by the major labels was still marketed to a more conservative and typically older audience.

The predominantly conservative attitudes of the mainstream were most evident in the music of artists like Frank Sinatra (1915–1998), Perry Como (1912–2001), Doris Day (b. 1922), Peggy Lee (1920–2002), and others. Many of these singers had made names for themselves by appearing with big bands during the swing era, as mentioned earlier. Their singing styles expressed sentimentality, gentility, and a suave, urban sensibility that was often associated with the so-called "sweet" music of the era. Several of these singing stars appeared regularly in films and on television in the 1950s. This was essentially a kind of updated Tin Pan Alley music and would be, most directly, the music against which rock 'n' roll would rebel in the mid-1950s.

**Go to chapter 2 playlist example "They Say It's Wonderful" Irving Berlin (Frank Sinatra)**

That the major labels showed little interest in performers outside of the mainstream was central to the reappearance of independent labels in the years following the war. These "indies" also benefitted from advances in recording technology that facilitated cheaper studio and production costs. In the late 1940s independent record labels were popping up all over the country and would come to play a pivotal role in the popularization of rhythm & blues and eventually the rise of rock. There was still some distance to go but the dedication and persistence of the "little guy" would ultimately prevail.

Throughout the 1940s, *Billboard's* chart designations for music other than Pop shifted from "race" and "hillbilly" to "Western and Race" to "American Folk Records" and other categories like "Harlem Hit Parade." In 1949 *Billboard* magazine officially consolidated its chart categories into three overarching designations: Pop, Country & Western, and Rhythm & Blues. Rhythm & Blues, like Pop and Country, was not one particular style but rather a conglomerate of styles or genres. R&B, as it came to be known, included—but was not limited to—jump bands, boogie-woogie, urban blues, gospel-influenced vocal groups, black crooners, and **electric blues** (discussed in detail in Chapter 3); in other words, the music of black artists which was primarily aimed at a black audience.

As we will see in Chapter 3, the middle-class white youth audience for R&B would continue to grow through the 1950s and R&B would become the impetus for the emergence of rock 'n' roll, the "generation gap," the polarization of the music business, and the eventual erosion of the conservative mentality that dominated the popular music industry.

## Suggested Chapter Related Activities

- Try to identify the individual instruments you hear in each piece in this chapter.
- Try counting along with each piece in the chapter to determine rhythmic subdivision, number of beats, etc.
- Locate several post-2000 songs that use AABA form either as a complete form or as a starting point (i.e. AABABA).
- Locate several post-2000 songs that use a twelve-bar blues or twelve-bar blues derived structure. Are there other blues-derived characteristics in each song? If so, what are they?
- Find examples of jazz and big band influenced pop or rock music from the 21st century.
- Can you locate examples of new types of stylistic fusion that clearly derive/incorporate one or some of the elements from other styles discussed in this chapter? If so, please share them with the class.
- See if you can find a post-2000 electronic song that incorporates "old-fashioned" elements.
- Try to identify the individual instruments you hear in each piece in this chapter.

## Suggested Discussion Topics

- What challenges do modern "indie" musicians face?
- What role does race, gender, sexuality play in modern music?
- Do you feel that modern white musicians who co-opt contemporary black musical forms of expression (i.e. rap/hip hop/R&B) represent a contemporary parallel to minstrelsy?
- We will discuss socially conscious music throughout the semester. What are your initial thoughts on the current state of affairs in the expression of social concerns in music? Does it matter?
- Should popular artists feel obligated to address social concerns?

## Image Credits

Image 2.1: The Celebrated Negro Melodies, as Sung by the Virginia Minstrel, 1843. Copyright in the Public Domain.
Image 2.2: http://www.loc.gov/pictures/item/2004682117/. U.S. Department of Defense, 1891. Copyright in the Public Domain.
Image 2.3: St. Louis Globe-Democrat, 1903. Copyright in the Public Domain.

# CHAPTER 3

# The Fifties, R&B, and Rock 'n' Roll

*I've been getting some bad publicity-but you got to expect that.*
-Elvis Presley

## Cultural Context

By 1950, the effects of the postwar economic boom in America were apparent: middle-class suburbs had expanded into vast tracts of "cookie cutter" homes; the automobile and other consumer goods industries were experiencing vigorous expansion; television sets became increasingly common-place (replacing radio as the dominant form of in-home family entertainment); urban infrastructure and highways expanded to meet the needs of commuters and travelers; and the population was expanding rapidly due to the "baby boom." This was an age of unprecedented materialism and to the vast majority of Americans it seemed that the world's problems could be solved through science and technology.

This was also an age of conspicuous dichotomies. While economic prosperity and modern conveniences created a world of heretofore unknown affluence and leisure, the tension of the Cold War and the constant threat of nuclear annihilation loomed large. Conservative values were put forth by the Republican-dominated government in the form of anti-Communist and homophobic "educational" films and literature, as well as in the mainstream media through television sitcoms like *Father Knows Best* and *Leave It To Beaver* and music-based variety shows such as *The Perry Como Show*. Simultaneously, "Beat Generation" writers like Jack Kerouac, Allan Ginsberg, and Gregory Corso challenged the academic establishment, runaway capitalism, and widely accepted social norms, including the prudish attitudes toward sex held by their parents' generation; sex, if discussed at all, was referred to in vague, euphemistic terms like "the birds and the bees." Even as

America held itself up to the world as a stronghold of freedom and equality, within American society entrenched bigotry and sexist attitudes toward minorities and women prevailed. And although opportunities for higher education and individual growth expanded like never before, psychologically driven advertising and television encouraged a "keeping up with the Joneses" type of mass conformity.

The common misconception of the 1950s being a time of placid, easy-paced serenity—where Mom, surrounded by modern domestic conveniences, minded the home in her neatly pressed apron; Dad, donning his flannel suit, drove happily to the office in the family sedan; and the kids, maybe just a bit grudgingly, went off to school and did their best to learn the lessons of the day—is largely a product of the popular television shows, movies, and advertisements of the time. The reality is that the 1950s were a turbulent and transformative decade marked by the Korean War, the McCarthy "witch hunt" Communist hearings, the birth of the Civil Rights Movement, a dramatic increase in the consumption of alcohol and prescription antidepressants largely attributed to disillusionment with modern life (men who felt pressured by the "rat race" of corporate life and women suffering from feelings of isolation and so-called "Housewife Syndrome"), and a rebellious, mobile youth culture with a fair amount of free time and wherewithal who were increasingly less willing to adopt the worldview of their parents.

This was a time of rapid technological innovation as well. The development and deployment of the first nuclear weapons by the United States in 1945 marked the dawn of a new age: the age of modern technology. Advances in electronic circuitry during World War II and the ensuing Cold War race for technological superiority over the Soviet Union necessarily meant substantial advantages for private-sector consumer electronics. As new technologies trickled down into everyday life, the ways in which people encountered music began to change dramatically. Most cars came with built-in AM radios and the advent of the transistor radio made broadcast music portable and accessible from nearly anywhere. Many teens now had the luxury of listening to music of their own choosing, on their own time, and their own terms. As we will soon see, this accessibility will have a profound effect on middle-class white youth culture as rhythm & blues and rock 'n' roll take to the airwaves.

## Multitrack Recording and New Record Formats

Thanks in part to advances in electronics, the quality of recorded music and the recording arts progressed significantly. Magnetic tape recording had been developed in Germany and Japan in the 1930s. This allowed for vast improvements in recorded sound, as tape was better suited to capture the full range and dimension of musical sounds than the earlier process of recording directly onto a phonograph disc. Tape machines also became more affordable, allowing greater access to those with fewer financial resources. This access made it possible for independent record labels to produce quality audio recordings without a huge budget.

By the late 1940s, eminent pioneers in the recording arts, most notably **Les Paul** (1915–2009), had developed techniques and technologies to produce **multitrack** recordings. This innovation, also known as "sound on sound" or "overdubbing," afforded recording artists the luxury of layering multiple vocal and/or instrumental parts asynchronously; that is, a musician could record a part and then go back and record additional parts alongside the original. This opened the door for many advances in the recording process, including better sound quality through the separation and manipulation of individual tracks and greater levels of experimentation in the creative process. For example, a singer could now harmonize multiple parts along with her *own* lead vocal line. This process could be applied to other instruments as well. **Stereo** recording, another important development in recording technology, also evolved from Paul's pioneering efforts.

> **Note:** Les Paul is perhaps best known for helping to develop the solid-body Gibson electric guitar that bears his name. The solid body guitar is essential to the sound of rock.

In the late 1940s, the long-used 78 rpm shellac record disc was upgraded in both storage capacity and material quality. Two new formats, the 12-inch 33 1/3 rpm LP (long-play) disc and the 7-inch 45 rpm single were introduced in 1948 and 1949, respectively. The benefits of these new formats were several: First, the maximum amount of music storage capacity increased from around four minutes per side (on 12-inch 78 rpm discs) to roughly thirty minutes per side on an LP. (This would have much greater significance in the 1960s when the LP album became the dominant commercial format.) Secondly, the vinyl material used was less brittle than shellac and tended to produce better audio playback quality. Thirdly, the 7-inch 45 rpm format was hugely successful in the 1950s as **singles** were the dominant unit of currency for pop, R&B, and country in the 1950s. Singles were also reasonably priced, making them very appealing to the teen market; the more compact size of the 45 made it the prime choice for jukeboxes as well.

> **Note:** The LP has made a surprising comeback in recent years. Many attribute this to the millennial generation's desire for a more "tangible" music experience in a world now dominated by digital downloads and streaming music services. How long this trend will continue remains to be seen.

## The Recording Industry Association of America (RIAA)

The RIAA was formed in 1952 and is made up of a variety of record label officials and distributors. It was originally founded to deal with copyright issues, union issues, and to do research into the recording industry and monitor laws and government regulations. They have also presided over issues of standardization within the record industry, such as the dimensions and revolution speeds of record discs. Since 1958, part of the RIAA's mission has been to keep track of record sales and issue awards based on high volume distribution and sales. Until 1975, the "Gold" record award was based on a dollar amount in sales exceeding $1 million. In 1975 the criteria were changed to units sold, with a "Gold" record earned at five hundred thousand units and a "Platinum" award with 1 million units. In 1999, the "Diamond" record was introduced and is awarded to recordings reaching sales of 10 million units.

Since the late 1990s, the RIAA has been involved in a staggering array of lawsuits and other types of litigation to protect the intellectual property rights of its artists due to the rise of music piracy and peer-to-peer file-sharing websites.

## The Changing Role of Radio and the Birth of the Disc Jockey

As the age of television as the dominant form of home entertainment dawned, radio underwent significant changes. From its earliest days, radio provided an assortment of news and entertainment including variety shows (many with live music), comedic and dramatic serials, and mystery shows. As TV took over, the majority of these shows were relocated to the new medium, creating a considerable gap in radio programming. For most radio stations, music, particularly recorded music, quite naturally became the mainstay of their broadcasts.

This shift also gave rise to a new type of celebrity: the "radio personality" or "disc jockey" (DJ). Many DJs became leading media personalities in their own right and garnered their own devoted followings: fans tuned in as much for the DJ as for the music he was playing. Alan "Moondog" Freed, "Jocko" Henderson, Casey Kasem, Tommy "Dr. Jive" Smalls, and Bill Randle were among the most popular 1950s DJs. Their celebrity also gave them an enormous amount of influence. DJs in those days had more or less *carte blanche* to play the music that they chose. As a result, the more popular DJs became "kingmakers" by choosing to heavily promote a specific artist or artists; many careers were profoundly impacted, both positively and negatively, by the radio DJ. Along with this power there were also alleged instances of its abuse which culminated in the so-called **payola** scandal (Radio, Freed, and payola are discussed in detail later in this chapter).

## 1950s Popular Music

The conservative politics and values of mainstream society in 1950s America were clearly reflected in the prevailing popular music styles. This era in music, so far as the most visible forms, was marked by a periodic regression away from the infusion of African musical elements into popular styles (we saw this in the latter part of the nineteenth century with march music and in the 1920s with symphonic jazz) and an intensified "whitewashing" of the musical elements of the Swing Era. A generally "sweet" musical accompaniment, which leaned much more heavily on melody than on rhythmic energy, supported established popular crooners such as Frank Sinatra, Perry Como (1912–2001), and Nat "King" Cole (1919–1965). Soundtracks to Hollywood film adaptations of Broadway musicals were enormously popular as were young pop singers like Pat Boone (b. 1934), Eddie Fisher (1928–2010), Tony Bennett (b. 1926), and Patti Page (1927–2013). The goal of much of 1950s major-label pop was a smooth, inoffensive sound which placed the focus on vocalists and the ensembles in a supportive role. Lyrics were G-rated and avoided any topics considered to be incompatible with a family audience. In short, big record labels set their sights on reaching the broadest possible audience, and young audiences were generally expected to listen to the music that their parents enjoyed.

To say that the popular music of the 1950s is "conservative" is not to make any negative value judgments of the music or the performers. In fact, the pop music of the era, for what it was, was extremely well executed and well produced, often employing emerging technologies such as multitrack recording and the latest studio techniques. However, because of its general lack of rhythmic energy and raw emotion, and the largely innocuous lyric content, rhythm and blues and rock 'n' roll would, by contrast, come across as that much more radical and threatening. A cross-section sampling of early 1950s popular music will help to better illustrate the nature of the major label mainstream.

## Crooners, Pop Stars, and Musicals

Crooning is a vocal style that became a common pop staple in the 1920s following the advent of the electric microphone and was closely associated with Tin Pan Alley music. A crooner is a male singer who typically delivers a sentimental or romantic lyric in a smooth, intimate manner. The microphone made it possible and practical for crooning to be heard over large orchestras, big bands, and other ensembles; and since its rise in the 1920s it has never gone out of style. Traditional crooning has merged with many other styles, including rock; Elvis crooned in songs like "Love Me Tender" in the 1950s, Jim Morrison crooned in the 1960s in songs like "The Crystal Ship" and "Indian Summer" and pop rock stars such as Elton John and Billy Joel kept crooning alive through the 1970s, 1980s, and 1990s. In fact, contemporary pop singers such as Michael Bublé and Frank Ocean are fine examples of modern-day crooners connected to a long-standing American musical heritage.

In the 1950s, Perry Como was one of the most popular and visible crooners. From 1949 to 1963 he was seen weekly on television primarily as host of the *Perry Como Chesterfield Show* and helped to pioneer the TV genre of the musical variety show. He was unique among his crooning contemporaries in the way that he took full advantage of the new medium of television. His image both on and off screen was one of gentility, even temperament, wholesomeness, and "good taste" (although Chesterfield, the show's sponsor, was ironically a cigarette company!). Como also enjoyed a fruitful recording and performing career which lasted for more than fifty years. In the following audio example we get a sense of the genteel, polished sound of 1950s pop as well as the regression toward a musical expression with little rhythmic energy—but rather with the focus placed squarely on the melody.

**Go to Chapter 3 playlist example "Wanted" Perry Como, 1954**

One of the most successful pop singles stars of the first half of the 1950s was singer Eddie Fisher (1928–2010). Fisher, like Como and Sinatra, was essentially a romantic crooner but presented a morc youthful image and appeal. He sold millions of records and, like many of his contemporaries, took advantage of film and the emerging television market, hosting two separate shows from 1953 to 1957 (*Coke Time with Eddie Fisher*) and from 1957 to 1959 (*The Eddie Fisher Show*). He was married to movie star Debbie Reynolds, with whom he costarred in the 1956 musical comedy *Bundle of Joy*. The couple split in 1958 following a scandalous affair Fisher had with film icon Elizabeth Taylor, whom he subsequently married. Prior to his affair and divorce, Fisher epitomized the clean-cut early 1950s pop star image. He was drafted to the US Army in 1951 and served as an entertainer in Korea from 1952 to 1953. During his active service he occasionally made guest appearances on television dressed in his uniform and was billed as PFC Eddie Fisher. Fisher's smooth tenor and nonthreatening look was geared toward the majority tastes of the early 1950s pre rock 'n' roll teenager and at the same time offered a "safe" style and image that was palatable to parents.

**Go to Chapter 3 playlist example "Wish You Were Here" Eddie Fisher, 1952**

Image 3.1: A newspaper advertisement for Eddie Fisher's Radio Show on the Mutual Broadcasting System

Although the entertainment world was clearly a male-dominated industry, female pop stars maintained a relatively strong presence in the 1950s and were responsible for generating hundreds of millions of dollars in record sales. Patti Page (1927–2013) was among the top-selling female artists of the decade. A good deal of her music was a skillful blend of pop, Tin Pan Alley, and country elements. In 1950 she recorded a rendition of Redd Stewart and Pee Wee King's country song "The Tennessee Waltz" with which she scored a major hit. The song reached number one on the *Billboard* pop chart for thirteen weeks. The stylized 1950s pop elements are evident in the delicate instrumental accompaniment. Page was also the first female pop singer to overdub her own vocals, making use of the new technology as early as 1947. We hear her harmonizing with herself in "The Tennessee Waltz" as well.

**Go to Chapter 3 playlist example "The Tennessee Waltz" Stewart/King arr. Patti Page, 1950**

Another important source of 1950s pop music was singles from Hollywood musical films (a genre which had become popular in the 1930s), many of which were adaptations of Broadway productions. This film genre produced many of the classic pop hits of the era and even took advantage of the popularity of early rock 'n' roll stars like Elvis Presley later in the decade. The popularity of the Hollywood musical had kept alive the vaudevillian tradition of the "song and dance man" (a phenomenon which will reemerge with a vengeance during the golden age of 1980s MTV). Among the decade's biggest hits was the 1952 production *Singin' in the Rain* which starred Gene Kelly and featured song and dance numbers which are now considered to be among the Hollywood classics. Although the film's plot necessarily involves Tin Pan Alley era music, that genre maintained a foothold in much of the music of Hollywood and Broadway in the 1950s.

**Go to Chapter 3 playlist example "Singin' in the Rain" from *Singin' in the Rain*, 1952 (performed by Gene Kelly)**

This overview of mainstream popular music of the 1950s will help to shed light on why rock 'n' roll seemed so revolutionary by comparison as it emerged mid-decade. The fact is that rock 'n' roll was an amalgamation of rhythm & blues, country, and pop, blending elements of all three in a way that created something different. We turn now to the developments in the fringe styles of country and rhythm & blues which were crucial to the emergence of rock 'n' roll.

## Honky-Tonk

As we have seen, country music had become popular in the 1930s, mostly among southern whites and largely through its dissemination on radio. By 1950 regularly broadcast radio shows like the *Grand Ole Opry* and *Louisiana Hayride*, along with the mass migration of rural southern populations to major northern urban centers had created a national audience for the style. A genre of country known as **honky-tonk** experienced its own golden age in the early 1950s. The style draws its name from honky-tonk bars, which date back to the early twentieth century. These were hard-edged, working-class bars where people came to drink and dance. In an effort to be heard over the din of large, noisy crowds, honky-tonk bands in the late 1940s and early 1950s often added a drum kit and amplified string instruments such as the pedal steel guitar (an electric version of the Dobro) and electric guitars.

Honky-tonk lyrics dealt in subjects that communicated to its working-class audience. Songs about the ups and downs of romantic relationships were common, as were songs about drinking, vehicles (particularly trains and trucks), work, and the hardships of day-to-day blue-collar existence. The music itself had a relationship to the blues in the sense that much of it was basically a white man's interpretation of blues style, vocal inflection, and backbeat rhythm; honky-tonk musicians grew up with the blues and often learned from blues musicians. The music reflected the earthy simplicity of the blues as well as its intense emotion, and combined these characteristics with those of country and pop; later in the decade musicians like Bill Haley, Carl Perkins and, most notably, Elvis Presley would fuse honky-tonk elements with those of R&B to form a new style known as **rockabilly** (discussed below).

**Image 3.2: Hank Williams, Sr. in a 1952 live performance**

In the 1950s, honky-tonk music reached its zenith through artists like Webb Pierce, Hank Locklin, Lefty Frizzell, and George Jones, but its biggest star, then and now, was Hank Williams, Sr. (1923–1953). Williams is one of the most influential figures in the history of honky-tonk and progressive country music. He grew up in Georgiana, Alabama and as a youngster there received his earliest musical training from a black blues musician named Rufus Payne. Williams would reputedly give Payne money or food in exchange for guitar lessons. The blues had a great deal to do with Williams' mature style, which he himself called "moanin' the blues." Williams also embodied the "live fast, die young" lifestyle that so many rock musicians would emulate. His tragic early death at the age of twenty-nine brought on by alcohol and prescription painkillers catapulted him into the realm of myth and legend.

Williams' 1950 hit song, the aptly named "Moanin' the Blues," epitomizes honky-tonk style. A sharp backbeat, the use of traditional and popular instruments, and verse/chorus form are all present in a manner that moves progressive country much closer to early rock 'n' roll.

**Go to Chapter 3 playlist example "Moanin' the Blues" Hank Williams, Sr., 1950**

**Note:** The Williams family music dynasty has extended for three generations. Williams' son, Hank "Bocephus" Williams, Jr. and his grandson, Shelton Hank Williams, also known as "Hank 3", both currently enjoy prosperous careers in country music.

## Perception, Reality, and the Mass Media

America in 1950 was still a very segregated nation and the *Billboard* charts were not exempt: R&B was used to designate black music while country and pop, for the most part, signified white music. There was not yet a musical style known as rock 'n' roll, much less a chart designation for it. Yet in less than a decade, rock 'n' roll would emerge as a distinct style with its own musical characteristics and major stars. As it has been noted, rock 'n' roll was a fusion of R&B, country, and pop, but its earliest incarnation is far more closely related to R&B than country or pop.

The separation of rhythm & blues into rock 'n' roll as a distinct style was essentially a three-stage process: nominal, reinterpretive, and stylistic transformation.

- The nominal stage began around 1950 when DIs, most notably Alan Freed, started to use the term rock 'n' roll to describe what was really black R&B.

- The reinterpretive stage unfolded as white groups begin to record **cover versions** of R&B hits, as well as with the emergence of **rockabilly**.

- The stylistic transformation happened as artists like Chuck Berry, Little Richard, and Jerry Lee Lewis introduced fundamental shifts in rhythmic conception.

**Stage 1**: Alan Freed (1921–1965) was the first white DJ to play black R&B exclusively during his broadcasts and is widely recognized as the first media personality to use the term "rock 'n' roll" when describing music. Prior to this, the term was actually a euphemism for sex and had been used in a number of R&B songs in that context ("rocking and rolling"). Freed began calling R&B rock 'n' roll in 1951 on his show, "The Moondog Rock 'n' Roll Party," on WJM in Cleveland, suggesting that the term described the "rolling, surging" beat of the music. His motives may have been commercially driven as well; black music and the designation R&B were still stigmatized in those days. Calling it rock 'n' roll may have gone a long way to broaden Freed's audience. After all, in the media, perception can create its own reality.

Freed's on-air enthusiasm and "hipster" style of patter set him apart from his contemporaries and built him a large regional following. In 1952 he decided to venture into concert promotion. He put together what is now heralded as the first rock 'n' roll concert in history: "The Moondog Coronation Ball." It turned out to be quite a fiasco, though, as twenty-five thousand people showed up to a venue that only seated ten thousand. Not deterred by this, Freed continued promoting shows in Cleveland before moving to WINS in New York City in 1954. There he reached a national audience and his fame, along with the term rock 'n' roll grew substantially. He was featured in four films about rock 'n' roll in 1956 and 1957 while he continued his broadcasts and concert promotion in New York.

Freed's career and life both ended badly, however. For years in the 1950s, it was a quietly understood and fairly common practice for DJs to take **payola**—monetary and other favors in exchange for airplay—from record labels and distributors. In 1960, payola was deemed illegal and in 1962 Freed and several other prominent DJs were convicted of commercial bribery and subsequently blackballed from the industry. Freed in particular had been persecuted by major label interests as well as politicians who resented his efforts to champion R&B and rock 'n' roll. Unable to find work and distraught, he spiraled into alcoholism and died a penniless, broken man in 1965.

Freed was a media king who might be thought of as the Howard Stern of his day. His efforts in championing black music changed history. He belongs to a very small group of nonmusicians to be inducted into the Rock and Roll Hall of Fame, of which he was the first.

**Stage 2**: As black R&B songs gained popularity and crossed over onto the pop charts, many major-label white artists and groups began releasing **cover versions** of these songs, that is, re-recorded, often "whitewashed" renditions which, in many cases, sold better than the original. This widespread practice was a double-edged sword in the 1950s. On one hand, it shows the inequality within the music industry as well as the racial bias among the music-buying public: Because of the greater distribution mechanisms of the major labels whites simply had a much better chance of hitting the pop charts and garnering media exposure. Moreover, many whites were more likely to buy music recorded by white musicians. On the other hand, covers went a long way in drawing attention to and generating sales for the original, as well as introducing droves of white listeners to music they may not have heard otherwise. The situation is compounded even further when one considers that many of these R&B hits were themselves remakes or covers of standards from earlier eras.

The very idea of originals and covers was also in flux during the 1950s. By the end of the decade, popular culture began to form a new conception in understanding a *specific* recording as a recognizable piece of intellectual property and thus the "original." This concept would solidify in the 1960s.

**Rockabilly** also marks a significant step in the white reinterpretation of R&B as it fused traits of that music with elements of honky-tonk and traditional country. The term itself is a portmanteau of "rock" and "hillbilly" which first came into use around 1956 and was not an altogether flattering term. The genre is characterized by 12-bar blues structures (or variations on these) and lighter textures than most R&B. Sonorities focus more on the upper musical ranges giving it a "twangier" flavor that is more akin to country. Brisk shuffle rhythms are standard but usually with less gravity on the backbeats. Rockabilly's ultra-specific traits have proven rather limiting in terms of its overall expressive quality, and though the genre has never truly disappeared, it sounds very dated even when produced in a modern context. The real importance of rockabilly is its function as a musical link between R&B and rock 'n' roll. We will discuss specific rockabilly artists and important developments later in this chapter.

**Stage 3**: In the mid 1950s, the real point of musical separation between R&B and rock 'n' roll had to do almost entirely with a shift in the fundamental rhythmic conception of the music. In Chapter 1 you were introduced to the fundamental rhythms of rock, including its most common type, the eighth note subdivision. Rock 'n' roll truly takes on its own *musical* identity when the shuffle rhythms of the swing era (dividing the beat into three parts, or two unequal parts—long-short, long-short) are replaced by this equal two-part beat subdivision (1 and 2 and 3 and 4 and). The first notable instances of this are Little Richard's "Tutti Frutti" and the Chuck Berry song "Roll Over Beethoven" from 1955 and 1956, respectively. Berry also brings the electric guitar front and center in rock 'n' roll helping to establish it as the quintessential rock instrument. His work will also be discussed in depth later in this chapter.

Underlying, and on some levels motivating each of these three stages was the need for adolescents, particularly the white middle class, to establish their own distinct cultural identity. Rock 'n' roll provided that: Beyond the music itself, it was a nearly self-contained culture with its own dances, fashion, and lingo. This transformation required a widespread interaction of black and white musical cultures. This was not the first time this happened; recall minstrelsy, ragtime, and jazz, but the difference with rock 'n' roll (and by extension, rock) was the sheer scope of its impact and the long-term cultural and social influence it would exert over the rest of the twentieth century.

There were massive commercial ramifications as well. As Larry Starr and Christopher Waterman point out:

> What resulted was an increasingly volatile give-and-take between, on the one hand, products and trends that were prefabricated for teens by the adult commercial culture, and on the other hand, products and trends chosen and developed unpredictably by the members of the new generation themselves. (p. 199)

The major record labels, in other words, had expected teenagers to consume the same music that their parents did; though what many label executives saw as a passing fad turned out to be much more. This facilitated the rise and substantial success of many independent labels or "indies."

## Rhythm & Blues, Rock 'n' Roll, and the "Indies"

Even with the new *Billboard* chart designation for R&B in 1949, the early 1950s business model for black music styles remained fairly unchanged; that is, R&B was performed by and marketed to black Americans. However, as millions of those same black Americans migrated to major cities like New York, Chicago, Detroit, and Los Angeles and to smaller southern cities like Memphis and New Orleans after WWII, the support mechanisms for R&B expanded dramatically. Simply put, the southern folk traditions of the rural south which had shaped R&B (gospel, blues, boogie-woogie, and so on) moved out of the country and into the city, and in the process became more urbanized and up to date. Moreover, the postwar economic boom was not exclusive to white Americans; black Americans enjoyed more and better-paying jobs as well and also had more disposable income to spend on entertainment. Dance clubs and lounges provided an outlet for live performances of R&B; but more importantly, independent record labels and radio increasingly began to compete for a share of the growing urban market, a market which would soon expand to include white middle-class youth.

The conglomeration of early 1950s styles that fell under the R&B umbrella and the independent record labels that were successful in their production and distribution were more or less connected to specific geographical areas and local talent. These were relatively small operations commonly staffed by just a few individuals for whom scouting talent locally was often necessity based. For example, in New York, Atlantic Records handled the early careers of solo artists like Ray Charles, Big Joe Turner, and Ruth Brown as well as doo-wop groups The Clovers and The Chords; in Los Angeles, Imperial Records helped to establish Fats Domino and T-Bone Walker; also in Los Angeles, Specialty Records supported Guitar Slim and the inimitable Little Richard; in Chicago, Chess Records was producing the electric blues of Muddy Waters, the unique work of Bo Diddley, and the earliest rock 'n' roll of Chuck Berry; in Memphis, Sam Phillips of Sun Records was responsible for the budding careers of Jackie Brenston and Little Junior Parker as well as extremely important white artists like Elvis Presley, Jerry Lee Lewis, Johnny Cash, Carl Perkins, and Roy Orbison.

A sampling of early 1950s R&B clearly demonstrates the sharp musical contrasts to the pop mainstream as well as the characteristics of R&B which were assimilated into rock 'n' roll:

## Atlantic Records

As **Ray Charles** (1930–2004) was beginning to emerge on the R&B charts in 1951 and 1952 with Swing Time Records in Los Angeles, that label went bankrupt. In 1953, he signed with Atlantic Records and scored a hit that year with a recording of the boogie-woogie style song "Mess Around," a song written by one of Atlantic's founders, Turkish immigrant Ahmet Ertegün. Charles had his first number one R&B hit in 1955 with a composition of his own called "I Got a Woman." In "Mess Around" Charles' blues and boogie-woogie roots are evident: 12-bar blues over a boogie-woogie bass line form the basis of the song and we clearly hear the call and response technique between the vocal and saxophone as well as the high energy backbeat and syncopation that so deeply influenced rock 'n' roll.

**Go to Chapter 3 playlist example "Mess Around" Ray Charles, 1953**

In his breakout 1955 hit "I Got a Woman" Charles employs elements of gospel, blues, and jazz in a way that move this song even closer to rock 'n' roll as well as creating a prototype for Charles' work in soul music.

**Go to Chapter 3 playlist example "I Got a Woman" Ray Charles, 1955**

Image 3.3: Ray Charles performs at the Montreal Jazz Festival in 2003 (his last performance ever)

Known as "The Genius of Soul" or simply "The Genius," Ray Charles built one of the most eclectic and significant careers of any musician of the modern era. His work would expand to include nearly every modern popular style including country, pop, rock, jazz, and gospel as well as various fusions of all of these. Charles recorded duets with everyone from Willie Nelson to Billy Joel and was featured in the 1985 *USA for Africa* charity video of the song "We Are the World" which boasted a laundry list of some of the biggest music stars of all time. With a career that spanned more than half a century, he won numerous honors and awards including the Grammy Lifetime Achievement Award and Kennedy Center Honors. Charles is truly a national treasure whose influence on modern music is incalculable.

**"Big" Joe Turner** (1911–1985) began his career, a career which would move through the transitional periods of big bands to jump bands to R&B and finally to early rock 'n' roll, in the clubs of Kansas City singing boogie-woogie blues with his pianist partner Pete Johnson in the mid-1930s. Through the 1940s he made a name for himself as a "blues shouter," recording with such greats as Art Tatum and Duke Ellington. Following a performance at the famed Apollo Theater in 1951, at which Ertegün was in attendance, Turner was signed to Atlantic Records. He recorded a string of successful blues standards for Atlantic and although his recordings were frequently on the R&B charts in the early 1950s, his lyrics were often peppered with sexual innuendo which were too audacious for many radio stations.

Turner's most important 1950s recording was a 1954 single called "Shake, Rattle and Roll." The song reached number one on the R&B charts and number twenty-two on the pop charts and made Turner a national celebrity. Lighter, quicker-paced cover versions of the song by Bill Haley 1954 and Elvis Presley in 1955—both of which placed the electric guitar at the forefront—would enhance Turner's celebrity while hastening the transition between R&B and rock 'n' roll (white cover versions of black R&B songs are discussed later in the chapter). Perhaps the most noteworthy aspect of Turner's original version was its sexual lyrics. In it he sings:

*I've been holdin' it in way down underneath/you make me roll my eyes, baby make me grit my teeth*

*I'm like a one-eyed cat peepin' in a seafood store/well I can look at you, tell you ain't a child no more*

The sexual references contained in the song are fairly obvious and seem relatively mild when viewed through our modern lens. However, to 1950s America this was quite shocking. Turner's lyrics though, are in keeping with a long tradition of blues lyrics which allude to sex—that is, wrapping sexual subjects in euphemism and innuendo.

In both covers by Haley and Presley the lyrics were cleaned up somewhat (bowdlerized), most likely in order to garner more airplay. The "one-eyed cat" line must have been vague enough to elude most people, or at least the censors, for it remains in all three versions of the song.

**Go to Chapter 3 playlist example "Shake, Rattle and Roll" Big Joe Turner, 1954**

**Note**: 1950s gender bias against women was so ensconced that the line "Get out in that kitchen and rattle those pots and pans/well roll my breakfast 'cause I'm a hungry man" in Haley's version as well as similar blatantly sexist lyrics in Turner's and Presley's versions didn't seem to bother anyone!

Image 3.4: Big Joe Turner at the Apollo Theater in 1955

Ruth Brown (1928–2006) was known for bringing a pop sensibility to R&B through a blending of blues and Tin Pan Alley forms. She recorded a string of R&B hits with Atlantic Records and in 1953 she scored a crossover hit with "Mama, He Treats Your Daughter Mean" (number one on the R&B charts, number twenty-three on the pop charts). This song uses a 16-bar blues form to create an AAAB lyric structure within each section (similar to standard Tin Pan Alley AABA form), and overall approaches something closer to verse/chorus form. Brown's vocal style is a mixture of a warm but edgy tone with occasional upward wailing inflections that add a bluesy tinge (the likes of which we will hear in the vocals of Little Richard).

**Go to Chapter 3 playlist example "Mama, He Treats Your Daughter Mean" Ruth Brown, 1953**

Although Brown played a major role in establishing Atlantic Records, she received little of the money her music earned and, sadly, was forced to leave the music business to earn a living for herself and her two children. After a comeback in the 1970s she became an advocate for musician's rights in royalty collection and contracts and later won a Tony Award for her performance in the Broadway musical *Black and Blue*.

The genre known as **doo-wop** denotes a musical style that was the most popular form of R&B in the 1950s, although the name doo-wop only begins to be applied around 1961. In the 1950s, it was simply a very popular type of vocal-based R&B. Doo-wop emerged in the post-WWII era in urban neighborhoods and typically consisted of a solo singer backed by three or four accompanying vocalists who would fill out the musical range from soprano to bass. As the majority of doo-wop groups were entirely male, singers utilized the "falsetto" voice to cover the higher ranges. Street corner groups performed *a cappella* (without instrumental accompaniment) often because they simply could not afford instruments, and through the use of creative vocal techniques were capable of executing effects that could simulate the sounds of instruments. The primary characteristics of the music were its rich harmonization of the tune and its percussive effects through the use of "nonsense" syllables (a practice derived from a jazz style of vocalization called **scat** singing).

Independent label talent scouts frequently "discovered" these groups busking in the streets for tips or putting on street concerts with other neighborhood groups. Recording the groups in the studio often involved adding instrumental accompaniment, which professional house musicians could build from the vocal arrangements. The most successful doo-wop groups cast many of their songs in Tin Pan Alley forms which leant an air of familiarity to mainstream audiences; there were also elements of the vocal harmony groups of the 1930s and 1940s like The Ink Spots and The Mills Brothers, gospel style (recall The Golden Gate Jubilee Quartet from the previous chapter), G-rated lyrics primarily dealing with romantic relationships, and novel, even humorous effects which gave this music its broad appeal.

Atlantic Records was the home to two of the era's most successful doo-wop groups: **The Clovers** and **The Chords**. We'll discuss each in turn.

The Clovers' lineup in 1951, at the time of their first recording sessions at Atlantic, consisted of Harold Lucas, Buddy Bailey, Matthew McQuater, Harold Winley, and Bill Harris, who had recently been added on guitar. The group scored their first number one R&B hit later that same year with "Fool, Fool, Fool." Their success in the R&B charts continued throughout the decade with their first pop crossover hit coming in 1956 with "Love, Love, Love" and their second in 1959 with "Love Potion No. 9."

**Go to Chapter 3 playlist example "Fool, Fool, Fool" The Clovers, 1951**

The song that really introduced the white mainstream audience to doo-wop was "Sh-Boom" by The Chords. "Sh-Boom" hit number three on the R&B charts and number nine on the pop charts in 1954 making it the first doo-wop tune to reach the Pop top 10. The Chords' members included Carl and Claude Feaster, Jimmy Keyes, Floyd McRae, and William Edwards. They were signed to Atlantic when someone scouting for that label heard them singing in a subway station. The success of "Sh-Boom" spawned several covers, some of which sold better than the original; regardless, The Chords hold their place in history as helping to build the bridge between doo-wop and rock 'n' roll. Although The Chords were never able to repeat the success they had with "Sh-Boom," the song holds a unique place in the repertoire.

"Sh-Boom" more or less follows a typical AABA Tin Pan Alley–like form but also synthesizes elements that were not typical for an up-tempo R&B song in the mid-1950s: the *a cappella* introduction would have been something that listeners expected to hear in a slow ballad; the saxophone solo in the middle of the song is accompanied by a scat vocal background on the word "sh-boom;" the song ends in an unconventional way with the group intoning the word "sh-boom" over a rich, jazz-like harmony. A diagram of the form illustrates:

Table 3.1: Form of "Sh-Boom"

:00–:07 *a cappella introduction*

**A** :08–:22 *"Life could be a dream…"*

:23–:28 *(scat interlude)*

**A** :29–:42 *"Life could be a dream…"*

**B** :43–:56 *"Every time I look at you…"*

**A** :57–1:11 *"Life could be a dream…"*

1:12–1:22 *(scat interlude)*

1:23–1:52 *(saxophone solo accompanied by "sh-boom" vocal)*

**A** 1:53–2:07 *"Life could be a dream…"*

2:08–end *(scat interlude with sudden ending on "sh-boom")*

**Go to Chapter 3 playlist example "Sh-Boom" The Chords, 1954**

## Imperial Records

One of the most important crossover artists of the decade was **Antoine "Fats" Domino** (b. 1928). His music and career are an indication of the blurred lines between R&B and rock 'n' roll. Between 1950 and 1963 he sold over 65 million records, a feat unmatched by any other artist of the era save Elvis Presley. His overwhelming pop and R&B chart presence after 1955 (sixty-three pop chart hits; fifty-nine R&B chart hits) is a clear testament to the expanding mainstream white audience for R&B and rock 'n' roll. Nationwide recognition first came to Domino in 1950 with his R&B chart topper "The Fat Man." Some historians consider this to be the first rock 'n' roll song but it would be more accurate to view it as an important early transitional moment in popular music of the 1950s and the harbinger for what was to transpire mid-decade. In any case, the song put Domino and Imperial Records on the R&B map.

Go to Chapter 3 playlist example "The Fat Man" Fats Domino, 1950

Domino grew up in New Orleans, assimilating the richly diverse musical styles that were part of that city's heritage, jazz, Latin, boogie-woogie, and blues, to create his own sound. He was also no stranger to the music of Tin Pan Alley and, in fact, recorded a number of Tin Pan Alley **standards** (songs with enduring popular appeal) with which he had much success: the most notable of these was his biggest selling single "Blueberry Hill," a 1956 remake of a Rose/Stock/Lewis tune first made famous in the 1940s by Glenn Miller. It should be clearly understood though, that Domino recorded these songs in his own distinct style, preserving his characteristic New Orleans drawl and rhythmic vitality, and in doing so brought the mainstream spotlight to a new kind of musical fusion. In a 1956 interview in *Downbeat* magazine Domino said "The rhythm we play is from Dixieland-New Orleans" and in the liner notes of his 1991 box set, *They Call Me the Fat Man*, he states: "Everybody started callin' my music rock and roll, but it wasn't anything but the same rhythm and blues I'd been playin' down in New Orleans." This statement further illustrates the often indistinguishable line between R&B and rock 'n' roll (Rock & Roll Hall of Fame 2015).

Go to Chapter 3 playlist example "Blueberry Hill" Rose/Stock/Lewis arr. Fats Domino, 1956

In 1950, Imperial Records signed a blues guitarist named **Aaron Thibeaux "T-Bone" Walker** (1910–1975). Walker came to music at an early age and was heavily influenced by Blind Lemon Jefferson, with whom he had a close personal association: The teenaged Walker became Jefferson's "lead boy" in Texas in the early 1920s; that is, he would lead Jefferson around the streets in Texas where he (Jefferson) performed. Walker's own recording career began in 1929 in the acoustic country blues style of Jefferson and in 1934 he moved to Los Angeles. Shortly after relocating Walker began playing the electric guitar and in doing so became the earliest of the country bluesmen to go electric. Throughout the late 1930s and 1940s he recorded and toured with both big bands and smaller combos making earning a reputation as a formidable blues guitarist.

Walker's stint with Imperial Records lasted until 1954 during which time he recorded a handful of singles. Although he was not enormously successful in his lifetime, Walker's electric blues stylings would play an influential role in the music of legendary bluesman B.B. King; rockers Chuck

Berry, Eric Clapton, Jimi Hendrix, and Stevie Ray Vaughan; and a host of other major rock guitarists of the 1960s and beyond. T-Bone Walker is now widely recognized as one of the major forces in the urbanization of the blues. He was posthumously inducted into the Rock and Roll Hall of Fame in 1987.

**Go to Chapter 3 playlist example "The Hustle Is On" T-Bone Walker, 1950**

## Specialty Records

Eddie Jones (1926–1959), better known as **Guitar Slim**, would find a brief but influential career at Specialty Records beginning in 1951. After some mild success in the R&B charts he scored his biggest hit in 1954 with the song "The Things That I Used to Do," a 12-bar blues tune which highlights the electric guitar. The song reached number one on the R&B charts and sold more than 1 million copies. Slim had built a reputation as an over-the-top performer who was known to move about the audience while playing through the use of very long guitar cords. He was also fascinated by the newly developed sound of distorted guitar (discussed in more detail later in this chapter). Guitar Slim's commercial success was rather limited, and after fading from popularity he descended into alcoholism and died at the age of thirty-two. His work would later influence such important guitarists as Jimi Hendrix, Stevie Ray Vaughan, John Mayer and, Dan Auerbach, who all recorded and released their own renditions of "The Things That I Used to Do." Other noteworthy artists who cite Guitar Slim as an influence include Frank Zappa, Billy Gibbons of ZZ Top, and Buddy Guy.

Slim's recording was arranged and produced by Ray Charles, who also plays piano on the track. The song is listed in the Rock and Roll Hall of Fame's "500 Songs That Shaped Rock and Roll."

**Go to Chapter 3 playlist example "The Things That I Used to Do" Guitar Slim arr. Ray Charles, 1954**

Like many musicians who grew up in the south in the first part of the twentieth century, Richard Penniman aka **Little Richard** (b. 1932) had his earliest experiences with music through singing gospel in church. He began his professional career performing as a boogie-woogie singer and pianist in tent shows and clubs while still in his teens. Exposure to the often raucous performances of R&B musicians in these environs inspired Little Richard in developing the flamboyant stage antics for which he would become well known. Early demo recordings landed Little Richard a contract with major record label RCA in 1951, although he left the label in 1952 after his recordings failed to catch on. Peacock Records in Texas signed Little Richard in 1953 but a contentious relationship with the label's owner led Little Richard to leave in search of better circumstances. In 1955 he signed with Specialty Records and that same year had his first major hit with a song called "Tutti Frutti." It made Little Richard a star overnight. More importantly, the rhythmic foundation of the piano part (played by Little Richard) establishes the eighth note rock n' roll rhythm.

**Go to Chapter 3 playlist example "Tutti Frutti" Little Richard, 1956**

In addition to the aggressive rhythms, raspy vocals, wild stage antics, flamboyant dress (which often included eyeliner and lipstick), and overt sexuality that would inspire generations of rock performers, Little Richard was a key figure in the rhythmic transformation of R&B to rock 'n' roll. His song "Lucille" from 1956 represents his final step in the reconception of the boogie-woogie shuffle pattern to the essential rock 'n' roll eighth note subdivision as it involves the entire ensemble.

**Go to Chapter 3 playlist example "Lucille" Little Richard, 1956**

It is virtually impossible to overstate the importance of Little Richard as one of American music's most influential pioneers; he can claim direct responsibility for shaping the music and careers of Elvis, Buddy Holly, The Beatles, The Rolling Stones, Bob Dylan, Jimi Hendrix (who apprenticed in Little Richard's backup band), David Bowie, Freddie Mercury, Prince, Michael Jackson, James Brown, Elton John, AC/DC, Deep Purple, Motörhead, and on and on.

Image 3.5: Little Richard performing in 2007

It is important to recognize Little Richard's contributions to society as a whole. His concerts were among the first public events to bring white and black audiences together (not cordoned off from each other or separated according to balcony or floor), despite such efforts to segregate the two groups; he shattered color lines. And although Little Richard's own descriptions of his sexual orientation vary—he has referred to himself as gay, bisexual, and even "omnisexual"—his openly sexual persona and stage performances helped to pave the way for the freedom of sexual expression which is taken for granted in modern society. It may be difficult for us to understand the courage it took be a pioneer for not only the black community but the LGBT community as well.

## Chess Records

The artist roster of Chess Records in Chicago boasted a list of musicians who are now recognized as central to the development of rock 'n' roll. The label was formed in 1950 when Polish immigrant brothers Phil and Leonard Chess essentially bought out and renamed a company called Aristocrat Records of which Leonard had been part owner. The brothers had a keen sense of the music business and an ear for R&B. Throughout the 1950s they built what has been called "America's greatest blues label."

In 1954, one of the most significant Chess artists, **Muddy Waters**, born McKinley Morganfield (1913–1983), released his most identifiable recording "Hoochie Coochie Man." The song was composed by Waters' bassist, **Willie Dixon** (1915–1992) and essentially perfected the so-called **Chicago blues**, more commonly known as **electric blues**. Electric blues had come about in much the same way as honky-tonk: out of the sheer necessity of being heard over noisy crowds. The blues began to be amplified in the late 1940s by artists like T-Bone Walker, John Lee Williamson, and Johnny Shines and was first recorded by Johnny Young, Floyd Jones, and Snooky Pryor. Muddy Waters brought the style to full flower through a series of genre-defining recordings beginning in 1948 with "I Can't Be Satisfied" while working with Leonard Chess at Aristocrat. In 1950 he recorded the song "Rollin' Stone" on Chess Records, which eventually reached number nine on the R&B charts and was famously the song that inspired Keith Richards and Mick Jagger to name their band The Rolling Stones.

Muddy Waters and the electric blues formed the bridge between Delta blues and rock 'n' roll. As a young guitarist growing up in the rural south, Waters cut his teeth on the music of Robert Johnson, Son House, and Blind Lemon Jefferson, all of which he would emulate in his updated, amplified musical environment. Electric blues *is* Delta blues. The addition of amplified guitar, bass, and drums gives the music an edge that seems to be the logical next step. It also infused the blues with an almost supernatural power that reverberated through the next several decades and formed the basis for much of the British Invasion, hard rock, and heavy metal.

Lyrically, Waters/Dixon tie into the well-established blues tradition of overt male sexual bravado but also invoke elements of superstition, occult iconography, fortune telling, and good fortune through the aid of "hoodoo", a type of African folk spirituality that evolved in the black culture of the Mississippi Delta region during the slave era and beyond. We will encounter the concept of sexual bravado in the lyrics of countless rock songs but also references to occult/superstitious imagery and concepts with bands like The Doors, Led Zeppelin, and Black Sabbath.

Verse 2:

*I got a black cat bone/I got a mojo too*

*I got the Johnny Conkeroo/I'm gonna mess wit' you*

*I'm gonna make you girls/lead me by my hand*

*Then the world gonna know/the Hoochie Coochie Man*

**Go to Chapter 3 playlist example "Hoochie Coochie Man" Muddy Waters, 1954**

The enigmatic **Bo Diddley**, born Elias Otha Bates (1928–2008) was an early rock 'n' roll era artist who defied categorization. Born in Mississippi but relocating to Chicago at an early age, he studied the violin and subsequently played in his church orchestra until the age of eighteen; however, the fervent rhythms of R&B would spark his interest in the guitar. He plied his trade by playing on street corners and eventually formed his own bands, with whom he began performing regularly in the clubs of Chicago's predominantly black South Side. He caught the attention of the Chess brothers and was signed to their label in late 1954. Early in 1955 Chess released the single "Bo Diddley" which climbed to the number one spot on the R&B chart.

Bo Diddley developed a fascination with rhythm in general, and specifically with a rhythmic pattern known variously as the "clave" pattern, which is associated with Latin dance, or "hambone" rhythm commonly connected to the "Juba" dance, a West African traditional dance that made its way to the plantations of the slave era. This pattern was so pervasive in Diddley's early hits that it also came to be known as the "Bo Diddley Beat." Diddley claimed to have come up with the idea entirely independently of either tradition. In any case, the pattern itself maps perfectly onto the eighth note subdivision but regroups the overall structure to create an asymmetrical feel that is quite energetic.

Normal eighth note subdivision over two measures compared to "Bo Diddley Beat":

1 & 2 & 3 & 4 & 1 & 2 & 3 & 4 &

<u>1</u> 2 3 <u>1</u> 2 3 <u>1</u> 2 3 4 <u>1</u> 2 <u>1</u> 2 3 4

The accented notes in the "Bo Diddley Beat" line up at various points along the eighth note pattern to create tension against the beat (first measure: 1, the "and" of 2, 4; second measure: 2, 3). This rhythmic structure has been used extensively in rock, pop, funk, and rap. We hear the pattern dominating Diddley's earliest R&B chart hits:

**Go to Chapter 3 playlist example "Bo Diddley" Bo Diddley, 1955**

**Go to Chapter 3 playlist example "Pretty Thing" Bo Diddley, 1956**

Another noteworthy and influential aspect of these Bo Diddley songs is the nearly **static harmony**, or absence of any chord movement, we encounter. This idea pervades the 1960s work of James Brown, funk of the 1970s and 1980s, and rap. In other words, the influence of Bo Diddley goes far beyond the rock 'n' roll of the 1950s and the rock that would follow. Bo Diddley may not have achieved multiplatinum superstar status in his lifetime but the impact of his work is still being felt today.

> **Note**: Bo Diddley experienced a resurgence in popularity when he was part of the late-1980s/early-1990s "Bo Knows" Nike ad campaign. The ads featured multisport athlete Bo Jackson trying his hand at the guitar, and failing miserably, at which point Bo Diddley would appear to tell him "Bo, you don't know diddley." The music for the ads was written and performed by Diddley.

Image 3.6: Bo Diddley's trademark rectangular guitar at the Rock and Roll Hall of Fame

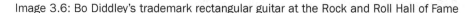

Charles Edward Anderson Berry (b. 1926), better known as **Chuck Berry**, is perhaps the single most important musician involved in the final transformation of R&B to rock 'n' roll. His biography on the Rock and Roll Hall of Fame web site states: "While no individual can be said to have invented rock and roll, Chuck Berry comes the closest of any single figure to being the one who put all the essential pieces together. On 'Maybellene'—Berry's first single, released in 1955—he played country & western guitar licks over a base of rhythm & blues. The distorted sound of Berry's guitar captured the rough, untamed spirit of rock and roll. The song included a brief but scorching solo built around his trademark double-string guitar licks" (Rock and Roll Hall of Fame 2015).

**Go to Chapter 3 playlist example "Maybellene" Chuck Berry, 1955**

"Maybellene" was Berry's first hit, and despite its considerably brisk tempo, guitar solo, and heavy backbeat, Berry still hadn't made the crucial rhythmic transformation from the R&B swing pattern to the eighth note rock 'n' roll pattern. However, the song is a clear indication of the growing racial ambiguities between the old and the new: Berry, a black man, sounded white (in contrast to Elvis, who sounded black). Berry's rhythms and vocal delivery at this stage were still akin to rockabilly. Although rockabilly will be discussed in more detail later in the chapter, it will be prudent here to draw some comparisons between "Maybellene" and a 1952 rockabilly recording by Bill Haley called "Rock the Joint."

**Go to Chapter 3 playlist example "Rock the Joint" Bill Haley and His Comets, 1952**

To be sure, there are some noticeable differences in the production and the distorted guitar tone in "Maybellene" but these are more superficial than stylistic. The most significant *musical* difference between the two is the form: rather than the more or less standard 12-bar blues strophic form that we hear in "Rock the Joint," and that, in fact, many rockabilly songs that follow, Berry's work is structured with the **verses** over a static chord and the **choruses** over the 12-bar blues structure. The overall effect of this is a more dynamic formal design that allows for Berry to relate the tale of "Maybellene" in a much more dramatic way. It also offers a form that is ever closer to rock.

Berry's first real rock 'n' roll moment occurred with the song "Roll Over Beethoven" in 1956. In a song that has been hailed by critics and scholars alike as a defining moment in rock 'n' roll, Berry brings the new rhythmic conception into very clear focus: the eighth note drives the entire ensemble (with the possible exception of the drummer, who seems to be unsure as to whether to swing or rock at various points in the song). The title of the song attests to Berry's awareness of just what he had concocted as it suggests that Beethoven and Tchaikovsky would "roll over in their graves" with the birth of rock 'n' roll. It is also possible to interpret the lyric as a double entendre, implying that Beethoven himself is "rolling" to the music. There are also lyrics in the song that refer variously to "rhythm and blues", rockin', rollin', reelin', and even fiddling. In short, the lyrics seem to be a celebration of his new rock 'n' roll sound.

**Go to Chapter 3 playlist example "Roll Over Beethoven" Chuck Berry, 1956**

History is not always fair in its assessment of the truth. If one examines the plain facts, Chuck Berry, not Elvis, should be recognized as the "King of Rock 'n' Roll" (this is not to deny Elvis' contributions to American music). Berry brought everything that epitomizes rock 'n' roll into sharp focus: he puts the guitar at the front of the ensemble, he places the rhythmic emphasis squarely on the eighth note, his lyrics embody early rock 'n' roll in every way (cars, sex, dancing, having fun, etc.) and because Berry wrote almost all of his own music he also is a primary figure in ushering in the age of *specific* recordings standing as *original* versions (an important rock era concept). His work would be covered extensively over the next several decades, yet in every instance Berry's versions are clearly understood as the originals.

**Go to Chapter 3 playlist example "Sweet Little Sixteen" Chuck Berry, 1958**

**Go to Chapter 3 playlist example "Johnny B. Goode" Chuck Berry, 1958**

## Sun Records

Visionary producer and recording engineer **Sam Phillips**, like DJ Alan Freed, wanted to bring black R&B to a white audience. From 1950, Phillips struggled to find his niche. Sun Records began variously as the Memphis Recording Service and Phillips Records. These early incarnations failed to achieve financial stability but they nurtured two fundamental business practices that would eventually prove to be the cornerstones of success: The first was a mission to record black artists of the south who had no other place to go, and the second was an open-door policy which afforded anyone the opportunity to make a record for a small fee. The former practice led to what has been often, if erroneously, hailed as the "first rock 'n' roll record" and the latter to the discovery of none other than Elvis Presley.

In 1951, the struggling Phillips Records formed an association with Chess Records providing that label with demos to potentially build their roster. It was during this time that one of the most "happy accidents" in rock history occurred: the birth of **distorted guitar**, as recorded in the **Jackie Brenston** song "Rocket 88."

As the story goes, Brenston and his band the **Delta Cats** had traveled from Mississippi to Memphis with their gear in the car for a recording session at Sun. Upon arriving and getting set up they discovered that the amplifier of guitarist **Willie Kizart** had suffered some accidental damage. Reports vary from water damage to the amp being dropped. In any case, when Kizart played through the amp it produced a fuzzy, distorted tone. Phillips heard the sound and decided that he could make it work. He brought the guitar out in the overall mix and in doing so gave the recording a rough, edgy sound which was quite different from contemporaneous R&B recordings. That year the track was licensed to Chess Records and became the second best–selling R&B single of 1951.

Although the song is not rock 'n' roll by stylistic definition—rather, it fits better into the jump band genre of R&B—it introduced the sound of distorted guitar. This was enormously significant in the development of rock 'n' roll and rock; distorted guitars are ubiquitous in rock. After the release and subsequent popularity of "Rocket 88," guitarists began to find ways of "doctoring" their amps to produce distorted tones; the technology was eventually developed to distort the guitar tone without actually damaging the amplifier. Distorted tones may or may not have been developed intentionally but nobody can say for sure. Either way, Kizart's was the first.

**Go to Chapter 3 playlist example "Rocket 88" Jackie Brenston and His Delta Cats, 1951**

**Herman "Little Junior" Parker** (1932-71) was an R&B singer/harmonica player who, with his group the **Blue Flames**, was signed to Sun Records in 1953. Their work stands as evidence of both the similarities and the differences between R&B and rockabilly. Parker and the Blue Flames enjoyed only limited success with their singles "Feelin' Good," "Love My Baby," and "Mystery Train" but some of their music exerted considerable influence on the rockabilly sound that was emerging in Memphis and beyond. In 1955, Elvis, along with guitarist Scotty Moore and bassist Bill Black, remade "Mystery Train." In their rendition, Moore actually recycles the guitar riff from Parker's "Love My Baby," demonstrating just how ambiguous categorization, genre lines, and stylistic reinterpretation were in the early 1950s. It is also evidence of the transitional moments that were occurring.

**Go to Chapter 3 playlist example "Love My Baby" Little Junior's Blue Flames, 1953**

**Go to Chapter 3 playlist example "Mystery Train" arr. Elvis Presley, 1955**

While the intermingling of musical characteristics was essential to the eventual stylistic divergence, clear contrasts between R&B and rockabilly can be heard if we compare Junior Parker's "Mystery Train" to Elvis' version above:

**Go to Chapter 3 playlist example "Mystery Train" Little Junior's Blue Flames, 1953**

In 1953, an eighteen-year-old southern boy named **Elvis Presley** (1935–1977) walked into Sun Studios ostensibly with the intention of making a record as gift for his mother; there is good reason to believe that he was hoping to get into the music business. The young singer/guitarist made two recordings, "My Happiness" and "That's When Your Heartaches Begin" as well as a minor impression on Sam Phillips. Phillips asked his receptionist Marion Keisker to keep Elvis' name on file for future reference. Phillips had a sense of the expanding teen market for R&B but understood the stigma that the white market attached to black music. He also sensed that a way around this problem would be to find a white singer that sounded black and had made somewhat of a quest of this in the early 1950s. Presley persisted in returning to Sun to record again in January of 1954; still, nothing came of it.

In June of that year, Phillips obtained a demo of a song called "Without You" and feeling that it was a good fit for the young Presley, contacted him to come in. During the ensuing recording session Phillips began experimenting with Elvis, asking him to sing anything he knew. The results excited Phillips enough for him to arrange to have local professional musicians **Scotty Moore** (guitar) and **Bill Black** (upright bass) come in to work out some tunes with Presley. The session that followed on July 5 extended late into the night but was not producing anything of real musical worth; the musicians were ready to pack it in and go home. It was at this moment that Elvis picked up his guitar and began an impromptu rendition of bluesman Arthur Crudup's "That's All Right." With Moore and Black joining in, Phillips was taken aback by what he heard. The trio quickly worked out and recorded an arrangement of the song. This was the "white man with a black sound" Phillips had been seeking.

Phillips delivered the single to his friend, the popular Memphis DJ Dewey Phillips (no relation), who played it on his Memphis radio show *Red, Hot and Blue*; it was a runaway hit with listeners. The phones went crazy with callers wanting to know who this singer was. Shortly thereafter, Elvis was interviewed on the air during which time the DJ pointedly asked Elvis what high school he attended, a subtle way of clarifying to listeners that Elvis was white, as schools were still segregated then. On hearing "That's All Right," many listeners had likely assumed that he was black. Elvis' style was as ambiguous as it was fresh: the B side of "That's All Right" featured a rockabilly rendition of the bluegrass song "Blue Moon of Kentucky." Rockabilly was not new but seemed to crystallize in a new way with Elvis.

**Go to Chapter 3 playlist example "That's All Right" Crudup arr. Elvis Presley, 1954**

From that point, the trio took to the road and stage. Moore and Black soon quit their other engagements to work exclusively with Elvis while DJ/promoter Bob Neal was hired to manage the group. During this time Elvis developed the energetic and sexually charged performance style that would draw so much controversy and help to make him the first international music superstar. In late 1954 after a successful debut on the Shreveport-based radio program, *Louisiana Hayride*, Elvis and his group were booked there for a year of Saturday night appearances. The show was broadcast to 198 radio stations in 28 states. The band soon extended their live engagements into Texas and Arkansas.

By early 1955 Elvis had recorded ten more sides with Sun, and through touring and airplay had built a considerable regional reputation. Presley and his group drew the attention of **Colonel Tom Parker,** a well-known manager and promoter who had helped to build the careers of several major country stars. Parker signed on as the group's official adviser while Neal continued to manage. Around this time, drummer **D.J. Fontana**, who was working as the house drummer on *Louisiana Hayride*, was made a full member of the group.

Performances in support of national acts such as rockabilly band Bill Haley and His Comets, who had topped the pop charts earlier that year with "Rock Around the Clock," exposed the group to much larger live audiences and in late 1955 Presley began attracting the attention of several major record labels. Three major labels had offered Sun Records up to $25,000 to buy out Elvis' contract. Phillips held out but Elvis was growing beyond Sun's capacity, and Phillips was in financial straits due to an unrelated lawsuit. In November, Parker and Phillips negotiated a deal with RCA Victor to release Elvis' contract for $40,000, an absolutely unheard-of sum in those days for an artist who had not yet proven his viability in a national market.

In January of 1956, Elvis began recording for RCA in Nashville and later that month released "Heartbreak Hotel" which landed on the pop, R&B, *and* country charts, adding to the uncertainty of just exactly what kind of musician Elvis was. In March of 1956, Elvis signed with Parker exclusively whose management led to several major network television appearances. There began the meteoric rise of arguably the most significant individual in international pop culture and a firestorm that rapidly grew into an unprecedented inferno of controversy. Elvis' massive media presence met with extreme reactions; there seemed to be no middle ground where he was concerned. He was idolized by some and demonized by others; his sexuality and dangerous abandon represented freedom to young people and frankly, terrified many adults.

**Go to Chapter 3 playlist example "Heartbreak Hotel" Durden/Axton arr. Elvis Presley, 1956**

Between 1956 and 1958, Elvis had a string of number one hits and sold many millions of records. He also began to star in Hollywood movies. 1958 saw a major disruption in Elvis' performance career when he was drafted into the army. He was offered the chance to enter the Special Forces entertainment branch; by then he was one of the biggest stars on the planet. Instead, he chose to enter as a regular soldier, a decision that earned him great respect from his fellow soldiers. RCA prepared for Elvis' absence by holding back a cache of unreleased material. Elvis scored no less than ten top 40 hits between his induction and his discharge. Among these was 1959's number one hit "A Big Hunk O' Love."

**Go to Chapter 3 playlist example "A Big Hunk O' Love" Schroeder/Wyche arr. Elvis Presley, 1959**

Elvis almost singlehandedly brought rock 'n' roll to the mainstream. He deftly expressed a broad stylistic range that was unmatched by his peers; whether he was wailing or crooning, shouting or whispering, it was all sincere. The truth of late 1950s R&B, rockabilly, and rock 'n' roll is that all three had precipitated a cultural phenomenon. Elvis was certainly in the right place at the right time but he had the charm, looks, and musical ability to bring this phenomenon to mainstream middle-class teens. It is undeniable that Elvis became an icon because he was white; it is also impossible to deny that he helped to build a bridge between two cultures: By performing black R&B hits on national network TV shows like the Ed Sullivan and Milton Berle shows, Elvis destroyed racial barriers and paved the way for those who would come after. That he was a threat to so many most certainly reflected the racial antagonism that polluted 1950s mainstream culture.

While Elvis' career extended into the 1960s and 1970s it should be understood that his most important period was between 1955 and 1958.

In the wake of Elvis' success, Sun Records helped to launch the stellar, but very brief career of **Jerry Lee Lewis** (b. 1935). His biggest recording, a Blackwell/Hammer song called "Great Balls of Fire" helped to solidify the rock 'n' roll rhythm that Little Richard and Chuck Berry had introduced as it catapulted Lewis to international renown. Lewis' two-fisted piano style and a strong rock 'n' roll beat propel the song, but the overtly sexual lyrics of "Great Balls of Fire" pushed it over the top. The song sold 1 million copies within ten days of its release and more than 5 million in total, making it one of the best-selling singles ever.

**Go to Chapter 3 playlist example "Great Balls of Fire" Blackwell/Hammer arr. Jerry Lee Lewis, 1957**

It seemed that Lewis was on the fast track to stardom when in 1958, at the age of twenty-two, he made the unfortunate decision to marry his thirteen-year-old cousin. The ensuing scandal proved to be Lewis' undoing. Show dates were cancelled and his music was blackballed from nearly every radio station in the country (surprisingly, Alan Freed continued to play Lewis' records until his own career fell apart). Lewis continued to record and release music at Sun but the scandal and negative publicity had done its damage. Lewis eventually made comebacks with rock 'n' roll and country recordings and is still held up as one of the progenitors of rock 'n' roll piano. He was among the first group of inductees to the Rock and Roll Hall of Fame in 1986.

## Buddy Holly and the Future of Rock

**Buddy Holly** (1936–1959) with his band the **Crickets**, came on with a second wave of rock 'n' rollers in the late 1950s, a wave that had benefitted from the significant influence of the indie rock 'n' roll emerging from 1955. Like Chuck Berry, Holly wrote most of his own music; and like Elvis, Holly demonstrated a remarkable stylistic range (although he didn't have Elvis' vocal chops). Where Holly rose above Berry was in his treatment of form; he variously employed everything from standard 12-bar blues to AABA, to simple verse/chorus and contrasting verse/chorus forms (discussed below) and more. The results of this approach took his music far beyond a feeling of "painting by the numbers" and into a mode that would set the standard for the next several decades of rock. Holly equaled—if not surpassed—Elvis in the way he fused country & western, R&B, rock 'n' roll, and pop elements into his music. Additionally, some of his very last recordings show a foray into quasi-experimental, orchestra-laden pop. The most remarkable thing about Buddy Holly is that his professional career lasted only a year and a half. He died at the age of twenty-two in a tragic plane crash. In that time, he recorded over fifty singles.

Buddy Holly's hit single, "That'll Be the Day," shows his innovative use of contrasting verse/chorus form: he leads into the song with the chorus (the hook), rather than a verse. This modification was relatively original in its time and was adopted in many rock songs of the 1960s and beyond: The Beatles, The Beach Boys, Jimi Hendrix, and others used this form to write hit songs. In fact, this technique is quite common in modern pop.

Table 3.2: Form of "That'll Be the Day"

Negligible Guitar Intro (:00–:03)

Chorus (:04–:17) *"That'll be the day when you say goodbye..."*

Verse 1 (:18–:33) *"You give me all your lovin'..."*

Chorus (:34–:47) *"That'll be the day..."*

Interlude (:48–1:11) *(guitar solo)*

Chorus: (1:12–1:26) *"That'll be the day..."*

Verse: 2 (1:27–1:41) *"When Cupid shot his dart..."*

Chorus (1:42–1:57) *"That'll be the day..."*

Outro (1:58–end) *(fragment of chorus)*

**Go to Chapter 3 playlist example "That'll Be the Day" Buddy Holly, 1957**

Whereas musicians like Elvis and Little Richard displayed wild, larger-than-life stage personae, replete with makeup, hairdos, upturned collars, and flashy clothing and dance moves, Buddy Holly presented a much more down-to-earth image; he looked like the boy next door. He proved that one didn't need to be a matinee idol or an over-the-top showman to make serious statement in rock 'n' roll. His lyrics projected vulnerability. Countless teenaged males took Holly's success as evidence that rock 'n' roll was as accessible to them as it was to anyone. As Michael Campbell and James Brody put it, "Male teens may have wanted to be another Elvis, but they could put themselves in Buddy Holly's shoes much more easily. Many did, in garages around the United States and in England" (p. 122).

Buddy Holly and the Crickets did more than any other 1950s rock 'n' rollers to shape the future of rock: They set the standard for the two guitar, bass, and drum configuration found in innumerable rock bands; The Beatles cite Holly as their main influence, as is evidenced not only in their insect-themed name but in their early music and image; Bob Dylan saw Holly perform two nights before his (Holly's) death and often spoke of the lasting impression he made; Keith Richards mentions Holly's guitar playing as an early model for his own; Eric Clapton recalls seeing Holly perform and feeling that it was the "future'" Bruce Springsteen has said he listens Holly every night before going to bed; and the Grateful Dead famously performed the Holly song "Not Fade Away" countless times in live performance.

Image 3.10: Buddy Holly publicity photo

**Go to Chapter 3 playlist example "Words of Love" Buddy Holly, 1957**

**Go to Chapter 3 playlist example "Not Fade Away" Buddy Holly, 1958**

Buddy Holly's music, image, and influence arguably establish him as the earliest example of "rock 'n' roll" becoming simply "rock." He pointed the way to the future in a way that no other 1950s musician had. Although rock will truly solidify with The Beatles and the British Invasion, Buddy Holly laid the foundation for the future.

## A Changing Society

The Supreme Court ruling in the *Brown v. Board of Education* case in 1954 determined that public school segregation was unconstitutional, overturning the longstanding policy of "separate but equal" established in the late nineteenth century, and the following year the Court ordered that school segregation be phased out with "all deliberate speed." The decision was met with both praise and scorn from white civic leaders and leaders in education. In 1955 in Montgomery, Alabama, a woman named Rosa Parks was arrested when she refused to give up her seat to a white passenger on a public bus. The resulting publicity led to citywide bus boycott by most of Montgomery's nearly fifty thousand black citizens. The boycott lasted for 381 days until the ordinance segregating blacks on public buses was overturned.

These were some of the earliest rumblings of the **Civil Rights Movement** in the United States which began in earnest in 1954 with the *Brown* decision and tapered off sharply in 1968 with the April 4 assassination of Dr. Martin Luther King, Jr. and the riots that ensued. On April 10, the movement culminated in Lyndon Johnson's signing of the Civil Rights Act of 1968, prohibiting discrimination based on race, religion, and national origin. The era was marked by organized civil disobedience and the nonviolent, peaceful protest espoused by King and other black leaders.

That rock 'n' roll emerged around the beginning of this era and developed fully into rock by the end of it is no coincidence. In some ways, musicians and young fans—black and white—were fully participating in, if not leading the charge toward integration and the rejection of the entrenched worldview held by most adults and the put forth in the mainstream media. Rock 'n' roll was its own kind of nonviolent resistance and it was becoming self-aware. Millions of young white people were forming their own identity and it had little to do with who their parents were. This came to be called the "generation gap."

Deena Weinstein states:

> Middle-class parents were horrified that their children, brought up in post-war affluence, should be attracted to performers who were not their betters and were clearly of a lower status. It was a slap in the face...

> The major labels were not fans of rock 'n' roll either. They had lost their dominance in the market because of the new music. Both their economic interests and the moral panic among adults were strong motivations to fight to change the music. From the end of the 1950s to 1963, it would seem that these anti-rock forces would prevail. (p. 71)

The early 1960s, as we will see, are just the calm before the storm. The fact is that in 1959 many had begun to feel that rock 'n' roll had just been a flash-in-the-pan. This belief had been substantiated by a chain of events that removed the first wave of rock 'n' roll's biggest stars from the spotlight: In 1957 Little Richard made the sudden decision to leave secular music and pursue his gospel interests (he would vacillate between the two throughout his career); Elvis was in the army in 1958 and was, for all intents and purposes, removed from public performances and TV appearances; Jerry Lee Lewis was scandalized by his marital issue; in 1959 Chuck Berry was arrested in connection with transporting a teenager across state lines (a conviction put him behind bars for two years); Buddy Holly was dead and it seemed to many that rock 'n' roll had died with him. In reality, it only lay dormant.

Campbell and Brody write:

> In spite of the death or decline of its first heroes, rock and roll helped engineer a major cultural shift—first in the generation that listened to it and ultimately in the English-speaking world. Like the civil rights movement, rock and roll entered mainstream consciousness slowly, often through disruptive events. (pp. 126–127)

The mainstream attack on rock 'n' roll and the rebellious youth culture supporting it was blatant in some ways, subtle in others: the emergence of rock 'n' roll and the heavy commercialization of Elvis brought scathing criticism from politicians, PTA groups, established media personalities and even other popular musicians (Frank Sinatra called rock 'n' roll "brutal" and "ugly"). American culture—even as the 1960s dawned—was mired in racism, sexual repression, and class separation. Corporate music culture was heavily invested in these dogmata as well. However, the major labels found a way to cash in on the market for rock 'n' roll without alienating the adult market. They began to manufacture and promote rock 'n' roll–*based* pop which aimed to be both appealing to young people and inoffensive to adults.

The music that resulted was neither remarkable nor enduring. Pale imitations of the early Elvis in the form of pinup teen idols produced a body of insipid pop tunes that were ultimately ineffective in turning the tide. Rock 'n' roll had changed things forever, and ambitious prodigies were coming together in garages, dive bars, and a small British city called Liverpool.

## Suggested Chapter Related Activities

- Practice the "Bo Diddley" beat until you are comfortable with it. Then locate several post-2000 songs that are based on that rhythmic structure.

- Locate several examples of doo-wop influence in post-2000 songs.

- Find examples of "male bravado" in several post-2000 song lyrics and compare it to the kind we hear in Muddy Waters' music and the like. Can you find other connections to the blues in these songs? As an added challenge, locate similarly self-aggrandizing lyrics by female artists and consider these as well. If the references are sexual in nature, are the explicit or implicit?

## Suggested Discussion Topics

- If you are a fan of modern country music, you may have noticed that many contemporary country artists have pulled rock elements into their music, either in the recording studio, in live performance or both. Why do you think it is that these artists retain their identity as country musicians rather than rock musicians? Consider this with other styles as well.

- How does mass media influence our perception of popular music?

- Elvis destroyed racial barriers in the 1950s. What barriers do modern artists face and how are they choosing to deal with these?

- Many students enjoy listening to the music of their parents (i.e rock, metal, grunge, etc.) in a way that the first generation of rock 'n' roll fans did not. Does this change or erode the idea of a "generation gap?" What does this say about modern popular music?

## Image Credits

# UNIT TWO
# THE SIXTIES AND SEVENTIES

4.1: Vietnam War protestors march in Washington, 1967

# CHAPTER 4

# American Rock Before 1964

---

*The times they are a-changin'.*
-Bob Dylan

---

## Cultural Context

While it is important not to romanticize the 1960s it is equally important to realize the profound degree to which our modern culture was shaped by the events and shifting attitudes of that decade. Put another way, if a typical college student were to travel back in time to 1959, she would encounter cultural and social constructs that appear utterly foreign. If that same student were to travel to 1969, the behavioral norms of society would be far closer to what she understands today. The 1960s mark the time when American popular culture and society "grew up;" however, growing up often involves a great deal of turmoil.

On the geopolitical front, the 1960s witnessed the Vietnam War along with the escalation of the Cold War, the ongoing arms race, the space race, and the political assassinations of John Kennedy, Malcom X, Martin Luther King, and Robert Kennedy. On the social front there was the expansion of the Civil Rights and Black Power Movements, the so-called "Second Wave" of feminism, emergence of the counterculture, the drug and sexual revolutions, the Gay Rights Movement, and the most widespread social unrest (much of it connected to antiwar protests) in American history. Societal taboos regarding individual and sexual expression were virtually erased by the end of the decade. America in 1969 bore little resemblance to America just a decade earlier.

Rock music would come to be inextricably connected with—and in some cases at least partially responsible for—many of the important social, cultural, and even political developments of the decade, and through the work of a number of significant artists would become a voice of unity and liberty for multiple generations. Moreover, the music itself experienced prodigious expansion even as it was realizing its own identity. This came about through innovative production techniques and technological advances, to be sure—but more substantially through sheer artistic genius and the spirit of defiant self-expression that came to dominate popular culture. American music between 1960 and 1963, however, was only just beginning to show signs of the intense stirrings that would come later.

Rock 'n' roll had made an indelible mark on the musical landscape by the end of the 1950s. However, the dictates of commercialism and an increasingly outmoded sense of "morality" dominated the big label mainstream mentality as well as the world of television. For many artists and music businesspeople, it seemed pragmatic to cash in on the rock 'n' roll market (which now spanned across two distinct age groups: teens and young adults) but at the same time fulfill long-standing cultural expectations of "decency" and "good taste." Both markets were targeted using specific business models which looked to the past, and in doing so created a body of music that has been largely forgotten.

## Teen Idols

The massive success of Elvis Presley was the impetus for the so-called **teen idol**. In the 1950s Elvis was highly controversial due in large part to the sensual nature of his performance style. His post-military/Hollywood image had been carefully reinvented to cast him as a more clean-cut, much less rebellious figure. Teen idols of the early 1960s were essentially consciously crafted hybrids of these two images: they were attractive without being overly sensual. All were pale imitations of Elvis, musically and otherwise. While some teen idols wrote or cowrote their own music, most teen idols sang songs written by professional songwriters and were backed by experienced studio musicians. Many had only marginal musical abilities but they were good looking, accessible, and highly marketable.

**Go to Chapter 4 playlist example "Wild One" Appel/Mann/Lowe arr. Bobby Rydell, 1960**

**Go to Chapter 4 playlist example "Runaway" Del Shannon/Max Crook, 1961**

**Note**: Although the teen idols of the early 1960s were awash in mediocrity and have been lost to history, parallel marketing tactics have survived to the present day. The so-called "boy bands" of subsequent decades (for example, Backstreet Boys and One Direction) and teen idols such as Justin Bieber and Miley Cyrus tap into this dubious institution of mass marketing to teens. Some commentators have referred to this pejoratively as "Happy Meal Music."

## Girl Groups and Phil Spector

Fashionable among the early 1960s rock-oriented pop music was that of the **girl groups**. Although most of these performers were actually young *women*, the moniker likely derived from a combination of 1960s sexism and the type of lyrics common to this specific category, which most often dealt with teen-esque relationships and the ups and downs of adolescent love. The music was a vocal-driven amalgamation of doo-wop, rock 'n' roll, and pop elements. As such, girl group performers were necessarily skilled in singing rich harmonies and often performed choreographed moves while sporting elegant evening wear, stylish hairdos, and professionally applied makeup. In other words, girl groups presented a style of pop music that was completely and consciously packaged for mass market appeal.

Like the teen idols, the girl groups affected a softening of the image of rock 'n' roll through pop hybridization; though in doing so they unwittingly served a higher purpose: expanding the feminine presence in rock 'n' roll-based pop music; rock 'n' roll had been a primarily male-dominated style up to that point. The girl groups helped to clear away some of the early barriers for women in rock and rock-oriented styles.

There were roughly 750 distinct girl groups charting between 1960 and 1966, although among the most popular and best remembered were those several groups associated with and working under the tutelage of producer **Phil Spector** (b. 1939). Spector began his career as a singer and guitarist for a group called the Teddy Bears and enjoyed a million-selling single in 1958 with "To Know Him Is to Love Him." He moved into production in the late 1950s and early 1960s and earned accolades for his pioneering technique in the recording process, the end result of which came to be known as the **wall of sound**.

In 1961 Spector formed his own label, Philles Records, where his recording and production techniques were perfected. Spector's approach involved recording large ensembles, often doubling and even tripling certain instruments, to create a mass of recorded sound. The use of a reverberation chamber was also central to the process. This involved running microphones, which were picking up the instrumental performance, to speakers in a large separate room where the reverberating sound would then be captured and channeled onto the tape track. On another track he would use the same technique with vocals. The outcome is an extremely dense sound with almost no "space" between any of the elements or musical events. (Contrast this to the electric blues aesthetic, for example, which makes great dramatic use of the space between the notes).

Spector's recordings were calculated to sound their best on the most common medium of the time—monaural AM radio—and the techniques he pioneered made him quite famous. In fact, his recordings were the very first to bear the *producer's* signature sound in a way that was instantly recognizable to many. That sound was often more important to the success of the recording than the actual song. Spector himself said he was looking for a sound so strong that if the material was not the greatest, the sound would carry the record.

Although his wall of sound technique is today most often connected to the girl groups, Spector applied it to many other famous hits, most notably The Righteous Brothers' "You've Lost That Lovin' Feelin'," the song that is said to have had more US airplay than any other single in the twentieth century. Spector also worked on some of the post-production elements of the Beatles' *Let It Be* album and he produced John Lennon's 1971 classic "Imagine." His techniques exerted a huge influence on artists ranging from The Beach Boys to Queen to Bruce Springsteen and truly helped to evolve record production to a higher art form. The following are fine examples of Spector's wall of sound recordings:

**Go to Chapter 4 playlist example "He Kissed Me" Spector/The Crystals, 1962**

**Go to Chapter 4 playlist example "Be My Baby" Spector/The Ronettes, 1963**

Phil Spector is widely regarded as one of rock music's most bizarre personalities: He was extremely temperamental, infamously reclusive, and in 2008 he was convicted of second-degree murder in the 2003 shooting death of actress Lana Clarkson. He is currently serving a nineteen-year-to-life prison sentence.

## A Producer's Role

As we have discussed some important producers thus far and will learn of numerous others throughout the course this book, it will be helpful at this juncture to clarify the role a producer plays in making a recording. In a very general way, it could be said that a producer, through a variety of means, helps to shape the vision of a composer or songwriter and bring his or her artistic intentions into focus before, during, and after the recording process. Quality record production helps to capture the full meaning and potential of the music, whether it involves the nuances of a performance like timing, intonation, precision, conviction, or general execution; the orchestration of a piece; or even the subtleties of the sonic atmosphere suggested by the lyric. A skilled producer can bring out the best in a performer through coaching, consulting, collaborating, or controlling the individual and collective elements of the record.

A producer may also be responsible for practical matters such as booking studio time, hiring session musicians, managing recording budgets, and acting as an intermediary between the artist and the record label, to name a few.

The extent to which a producer is involved in the recording process varies dramatically. Phil Spector exerted total control over his productions in everything from writing the songs to orchestrating to arranging to engineering, thereby leaving *his* unique sonic stamp on his work. George Martin, on the other hand, played a more *collaborative* role with The Beatles; he didn't write any of the music or lyrics but he made some major artistic decisions regarding orchestration. In *The Art of Music Production: The Theory and Practice*, Richard James Burgess outlines no less than six basic types of producers all with contrasting styles, backgrounds, and levels of musical/technical expertise; and ranging in involvement from wielding almost total artistic control to performing purely administrative functions.

One final type of producer bears mentioning: the self or artist producer. Historically this had been a relatively rare occurrence simply because it requires a level of objectivity which most artists find too challenging. Some famously successful self-producing artists of times past include Jimmy Page of Led Zeppelin, Prince, and Stevie Wonder. Self-production has been on the rise in recent times, though; primarily because of the increased access to high-level digital recording and dissemination technologies, home recording studios, and the rise of the new Internet "indie" or "DIY" musician.

## The Brill Building and Remnants of Tin Pan Alley

You may recall from Chapter 1 that Tin Pan Alley is a term used not only to describe specific location also a musical style and a business model. In that way, the **Brill Building** can be thought of as an early 1960s analogue to Tin Pan Alley. Like Tin Pan Alley the "Brill Building Sound" in the late 1950s and early 1960s came to encompass more than one specific building, although professional music businesses which were housed in the actual building carried a certain prestige.

The Brill Building itself is located at 1619 Broadway in the New York City borough of Manhattan. Many publishers had established offices and studios there from around the early 1940s at the tail end of the Swing Era. Through the late 1950s and early 1960s, songwriters working for these publishers in the Brill Building had enjoyed a great deal of commercial success writing music that blended elements of pop, R&B, gospel, and Latin specifically tailored to appeal to a late teen/young adult audience. They capitalized on the void left in the youth market just after the first wave of rock 'n' roll but moved the emphasis and control away from the individual performer or performance and back to the songwriters and publishers. In fact, performers were virtually interchangeable. This was fundamentally identical to the business model of the Tin Pan Alley publishers.

There were quite literally hundreds of songwriters working to create the next hit, either directly from within the Brill Building or with the "Brill Building Approach," many of whom became famous names in the rock-oriented pop music of the early 1960s. Several went on to have significant performance/recording careers of their own, including Carole King, Paul Simon, Neil Diamond, Neil Sedaka, and Burt Bacharach.

This method of producing highly commercialized, nonthreatening music was decidedly successful, albeit safe and fairly methodical. In an era of relatively unremarkable mainstream popular music, Brill Building pop easily stands out in stark contrast as some of the most memorable music of its time.

**Go to Chapter 4 playlist example "Any Day Now" Bacharach/Hilliard arr. Chuck Jackson, 1962**

## The Twist: A Rock-Oriented Dance Craze

The taming and mass commercialization of American rock 'n' roll in the early 1960s was repre-sented in perhaps no finer fashion than by a song called "The Twist." Written and originally released by Hank Ballard on the independent King label in 1959, it is basically a 12-bar blues progression over a rock 'n' roll beat with a teen-oriented lyric about a dance known as the twist. It was cho-sen for a B-side and met with rather modest success in the R&B charts. In 1960, executives at Philadelphia's Parkway Records arranged to have one of their rostered singers, a young man called **Ernest Evans** (b. 1941), record the song, believing it had greater commercial potential than had been realized by Ballard's original.

Fortuitously for Parkway Records, Philadelphia was also the home of a nationally broadcast teen-oriented show called *American Bandstand* hosted by **Dick Clark** (1929–2012). The show, loosely modeled after *The Ed Sullivan Show*, had become famous for featuring studio-audience teens enjoying and dancing to the latest rock 'n' roll records. The close physical proximity aided Parkway Records in developing a mutually beneficial relationship with Clark's team: The label often provided music and musicians to perform on the air. "The Twist" seemed a perfect fit for *American Bandstand*. Clark's wife suggested that Evans change his name to **Chubby Checker**, no doubt as a play on the popularity of Fats Domino, and an instant runaway dance hit was born.

The dance itself was something that virtually anyone could do. It only involved one basic move (twisting) and could be done in pairs, groups, or even alone. There was also no physical contact, so the dance was not viewed as unseemly or sexual to parents and chaperones.

The song *and* the dance caught like wildfire among teens, both black and white, but in fairly short order something unexpected transpired. Joseph G. Schloss, Larry Starr, and Christopher Waterman write:

> Soon adults of all ages and classes and races were doing the twist, along with the teenagers. In turn, the popularity and wide social acceptance of this free-form dancing brought rock 'n' roll music to a significantly broader audience than ever before: It was no longer just music for teenagers but an accepted fact of American social life. (p. 91)

The popularity of Chubby Checker's recording of "The Twist" was evident in its chart success: After reaching number one on the pop charts in 1960, it resurfaced in 1962 to reach number one for a second time. The only other song in pop chart history to achieve this was Bing Crosby's perennial classic "White Christmas."

Many rock 'n' roll dance hits, replete with their own moves and trendy titles, began to crop up almost overnight. The watusi, the swim, the mashed potato, and the monkey are but a few. In keep-ing with dance trends, performing musicians would frequently include stage dancers (sometimes called "go-go" dancers) in their live shows.

## Activist Folk Music

Folk music extends back many centuries and is found in every culture on earth. The implication is music by, of, and for "common" people. As such, folk music is intrinsically rooted in technical simplicity and accessibility to untrained musicians. The melodies, harmonies, and forms of folk are most frequently not the *point*, but rather a *vehicle* for telling a tale or delivering a message. The activist folk music of twentieth-century America is deeply associated with the struggles of the working class and politically and socially oppressed people, both black and white, as well as antiwar/antigovernment sentiment.

Folk music entered 1960s consciousness on what is often referred to as the "second wave" of the folk revival, chiefly through the music of Tom Paxton, Phil Ochs, Joan Baez, and Bob Dylan. Folk music is decidedly low tech; the instrument of choice was (and is) the acoustic guitar, which is highly portable and allows for an intimate, informal musical environment and clear delivery of the lyrics. (Folk rock, a hugely important genre of rock will come to the forefront later in the 1960s on the heels of the British Invasion).

The beginnings of the twentieth-century American folk revival can be traced back to Woody Guthrie and his leftist political folk music of the 1930s and 1940s. As discussed in Chapter 2, Guthrie championed causes related to the labor movement and the American Communist Party and exerted a powerful influence on the growth of folk music as a vehicle for social and political expression. Pete Seeger, a disciple of Guthrie's, formed the folk group The Weavers in the late 1940s. The group had a commercial presence but faced serious professional and political backlash during the "Red Scare" and the resulting communist paranoia of the 1950s. Seeger was even subpoenaed to testify before the House Un-American Activities Committee in 1955 and was indicted for contempt of Congress for refusing to name those with whom he was politically and personally associated.

Because of its strong association with political dissent, most folk music had been marginalized by the mainstream in the 1950s; it existed in its own sphere under a virtual media blackout. Coffeehouses, college campuses, and open-air festivals became the hotbeds of folk music; as did many of the distinctly bohemian communities of major cities, like New York's Greenwich Village, San Francisco's North Beach, Cambridge, Massachusetts, and Boulder, Colorado. In this climate of dissent we hear the whisperings of rock's incipient postmodernism and witness an inchoate counterculture.

As the fans of the first wave of rock 'n' roll moved into early adulthood, and particularly as greater and greater numbers of them were attending college, songs like "The Twist" and "He Kissed Me" offered this group little that was relevant to the changing world around them, nor did it resonate with their growing awareness of sophisticated political ideologies and philosophical concepts. The music that had given them a sense of identity and self-expression had been co-opted and watered down by the very establishment from which it sought liberation. Folk music represented a mature expression of the issues that mattered most to them. Moreover, even many younger teenagers were becoming disillusioned with the music that was passing itself off as rock 'n' roll.

Grace Elizabeth Hale writes:

> If early rock and roll had given many white middle-class teenagers a taste of what rebellion in the form of playing black could feel like, by the late 1950s the liberating force of music seemed spent, buried under derivative product and an outpouring of criticism from politicians, ministers and parents, as well as the growing force of the segregationists. Folk music filled in the gap. It gave these white middle-class teenagers a seemingly pure and noncommercial version of the last decade's teenage rock rebellion. It gave them a music they could grow up into but still signaled their opposition to their parents' culture. It offered a rich and serious story, locating the outsider in a specific place and time, a pre-modern, pre-capitalist historical moment when people made music for the pleasure of expression rather than for cash. (pp. 86–87)

Folk music in the early 1960s embodied contempt for the paradigms of corporate America, mainstream popular culture, political conservatism, social oppression, and the expanding military industrial complex. America's deepening involvement in the Vietnam War as well as the growing Civil Rights Movement fueled a wave of youth-driven, antiestablishment sentiment and was given voice by idealistic folk musicians. Their lyrics echoed the cries that originated with the Beat poets: an outright denunciation of the standard cultural narrative.

**Tom Paxton** (b. 1937) became a fixture in the Greenwich Village coffeehouse folk music scene around 1962 playing, as many others did, a blend of traditional folk favorites alongside his own original songs. In 1963 he made his debut appearance at the Newport Folk Festival, an annual major open-air event which featured the most important folk musicians on the scene. During the 1960s and beyond he was involved with numerous human rights causes including civil and labor rights as well as voter registration drives, singing his songs at events and rallies to raise support and awareness.

Paxton's career has endured for more than fifty years and his songs have addressed a wide range of topics; from racial injustice in the 1960s to 9/11; and from the Holocaust to hot-button contemporary political issues like the government bailout of the financial system in 2008. His 1963 recording "What Did You Learn in School Today?" shines a sadly humorous light on the way schoolchildren are indoctrinated in the mythology of "American" ideals as opposed to being told the truth of the situation.

**Go to Chapter 4 playlist example "What Did You Learn in School Today?" Tom Paxton, 1963**

Although **Phil Ochs** (1940–1976) was often described as a "protest" singer, he preferred the term "topical" singer. He developed interests in music, politics, and journalism at a young age and was particularly intrigued with the Cuban Revolution of 1959. As a journalism student at Ohio State University, Ochs penned articles for the school newspaper which often reflected his radical politics. He eventually dropped out of college and moved to New York in 1962 to pursue folk singing. Like Paxton, Ochs was invited to the Newport Folk Festival in 1963 and made an enormous impression with songs like "Too Many Martyrs," "Take Birmingham Jam," and "Power and the Glory." He remained active as an antiwar and human rights advocate throughout his career.

In the latter part of the 1960s, Ochs experimented in the recording studio with more elaborate instrumentation and often met with harsh criticism. The turbulent political climate of the late 1960s and early 1970s, compounded by Ochs's alcohol use and bipolar disorder, led to a steady decline in his mental health through the 1970s. Ochs took his own life in 1976.

**Go to Chapter 4 playlist example "Draft Dodger Rag" Phil Ochs, 1965**

**Joan Baez** (b. 1941) is another musician who has enjoyed a career spanning more than fifty years. Her work since the end of the 1960s has expanded to include everything from rock to country to gospel. During the early 1960s she was an important and influential figure who sang songs about social injustice, poverty, war protest, and human rights. She had been a regular at the Newport Folk Festival since 1959 where her haunting voice and unpretentious beauty earned her such various titles as "barefoot Madonna" and "Earth Mother." By 1961, she was quite well known in the folk scene. She also played a significant role in introducing to that scene a then-unknown singer named Bob Dylan by covering his music and performing live duets with him. The two were also romantically involved for a time.

**Go to Chapter 4 playlist example "There But for Fortune" Phil Ochs arr. Joan Baez, 1964**

Baez has been involved with many important social causes over the course of her career. She has written and performed music opposing the death penalty and has been active in the fight for everything from gay and lesbian rights to environmental causes to the Occupy movement of recent times.

**Bob Dylan** (b. Robert Zimmerman, 1941) has been called one of the most influential musical and cultural figures of the twentieth century. His music and lyrics helped to define an entire era of American and world cultural history. He has won countless awards, including a special citation from the Pulitzer Prize jury and the Presidential Medal of Freedom, and has been inducted into no less than four major halls of fame. Dylan was a fundamental influence on many of rock's greatest luminaries like The Beatles, The Who, The Rolling Stones, Bruce Springsteen, and David Bowie, to name but a few. His poetry has been placed in the company of Eliot, Keats, and Tennyson. His

1965 rock hit, "Like a Rolling Stone," is ranked by *Rolling Stone* magazine as the "Greatest Song of All Time." It is frankly impossible to exaggerate the consequence of Bob Dylan.

Robert Zimmerman grew up in Minnesota and, like many teens, became a fan of R&B and rock 'n' roll—as well as country music—in the 1950s. As he grew into a young man and budding musician, he realized that if he wanted to say something serious, he had to do it through folk songs. His career in folk music began in Minnesota in 1959 where he was enrolled as a student at the University of Minnesota. He played at local coffeehouses where he first introduced himself to audiences as "Bob Dylan," an acknowledgment to the influence of poet Dylan Thomas. Bob Dylan dropped out of college in 1960 and relocated to New York City in 1961. There he sought out Woody Guthrie, whom he had come to idolize by this time. Guthrie had been suffering from a debilitating illness and was confined to a hospital, though Dylan spent time with him and performed for him. Dylan spoke of Guthrie as the "true voice of the American spirit."

Within a short time Dylan was appearing in clubs and coffeehouses in Greenwich Village and making a name for himself in the local folk scene. His talents came to the attention of John Hammond, an important producer, civil rights activist, and talent scout for Columbia Records. In 1962, Columbia released *Bob Dylan*, an album consisting of familiar folk, blues, and gospel music along with two of Dylan's own songs. The album barely made enough in its first year to cover recording expenses. Columbia wanted to drop Dylan but Hammond's staunch support stayed their hand.

In 1963, Dylan released his second album, *The Freewheelin' Bob Dylan* which included one of his most celebrated songs, "Blowin' in the Wind," a song which implores the listener to examine his humanity through a series of philosophical questions about peace, war, and personal freedom. The powerfully ambiguous answer comes in the chorus: "the answer my friend is blowin' in the wind." Other album highlights include "Masters of War," a caustic indictment of the military industrial complex as well as "Oxford Town," Dylan's response to the 1962 segregation battle at the University of Mississippi. As a collection of nearly all original material, it showcased Dylan's songwriting as well as his capability as a lyricist, but many began to see him as something more than that; he articulated the views of his folk music peers as well as the way that many young people all over the country felt about serious issues like nuclear proliferation and civil rights, and he did so in a musically and poetically potent way.

Other artists began to cover Dylan's songs around this time as well, ultimately helping to increase his reputation and reach. Peter, Paul and Mary, a pop-oriented folk trio scored a hit with their version of "Blowin' in the Wind," which was released just a few weeks after Dylan's original, and the song so impressed soul singer Sam Cooke that he began to sing it in his live act. It was eventually covered hundreds of times, most notably by Stevie Wonder and Dolly Parton.

The form of "Blowin' in the Wind" is a 16-measure strophic macrostructure—traditional folk— with an AAAB inner structure that gives the *sense* of a chorus during the last four measures of each strophe. Moreover, this is where he sings the title phrase. Dylan interjects the harmonica solos between each strophe as well creating more interest:

Table 4.1: Form of "Blowin' in the Wind"

**A:** *How many roads? …*

**A:** Yes and *how many seas? …*

**A:** Yes and *how many times? …*

**B:** *The answer my friend is blowin' in the wind…*

*Harmonica interlude*

**A:** *How many years? …*

**A:** Yes and *how many years? …*

**A:** Yes and *how many times? …*

**B:** *The answer my friend is blowin' in the wind…*

*Harmonica interlude*

**A:** *How many times? …*

**A:** Yes and *how many ears? …*

**A:** Yes and *how many deaths? …*

**B:** *The answer my friend is blowin' in the wind…*

*Harmonica outro*

**Go to Chapter 4 playlist example "Blowin' in the Wind" Bob Dylan, 1962**

**Go to Chapter 4 playlist example "Blowin' in the Wind" Peter, Paul and Mary cover, 1962**

By 1963, Bob Dylan was participating in the Civil Rights Movement and performed together with Joan Baez that summer at the **March on Washington**, the enormous rally in Washington, D.C. where Martin Luther King, Jr. delivered his legendary "I have a dream" speech (discussed below). Dylan was not insensitive to the reality, though, that as a white man, he may not have been the best choice as a public image for the event.

In spite of Dylan's apparent sense of awkwardness at being a face person for the March on Washington, the fact remains that folk music was an important factor in recruiting white supporters to the Civil Rights Movement.

Hale states:

> The association between folk music and the civil rights movement made support for civil rights in the South popular among many middle-class white kids—another way for them to express their rebellion against the world of their parents. *Time* explored the rising popularity of "integration songs" among folk music fans: "In a cocktail lounge in Ogunquit, Maine," *Time* reported, "a college girl shouts out 'Sing something about integration.'" The fact that folksingers supported the civil rights movement helped turn many folk fans into movement supporters too. Some of those college girls asking for integration songs would go hear the Freedom Singers. Some would send money. Some would join northern friends of SNCC [Student Nonviolent Coordinating Committee] support groups. Some might even go south themselves. (p. 115)

1963 also saw the release of Dylan's third album *The Times They Are a-Changin'*. It was his first effort containing all original material and dealt with themes of social change, poverty, and racism. By this time, Dylan had come to be somewhat of a rarity in the folk community, even though he was its brightest young star. As Schloss, Starr, and Waterman point out:

> Bob Dylan was important to the folk movement for many reasons. He was one of a relatively small number of folk singers that wrote their own songs, and one of an even smaller number that performed them in a style intended to make them feel as deeply authentic as the centuries-old ballads, blues songs and spirituals that made up much of the folk repertoire. In this way, he offered the best of both worlds: the legitimacy and power of the ancient folk tradition combined with the topicality of current music.[1]
> (p. 115)

They go on:

---

1 Joseph G. Schloss, Larry Starr, and Christopher Waterman, Rock: Music, Culture, and Business, pp. 91, 115, 131, 106. Copyright © 2012 by Oxford University Press. Reprinted with permission.

When Dylan became famous, many people in the folk scene saw him as one of their own friends—and for many, he was! Even for those who did not know him personally, his creativity was seen as representing the creativity and sincerity of the entire community, as a way of showing an older generation that—despite what rock 'n' roll may have led them to believe—the youth were capable of making great artistic and political statements in their music. (p. 131)

Dylan though, seems to have begun to show signs of cynicism toward the role of political spokesperson that had been thrust upon him. In 1964, he would release what would be his last all-acoustic folk album, *Another Side of Bob Dylan*. This recording marks the real beginning of his departure from folk music through a deepening exploration of the possibilities of complex language and the use of highly impressionistic imagery and sophisticated metaphor. One track on the album, "It Ain't Me Babe," ostensibly a love song, has been interpreted as Dylan's response to being exalted by his peers as the champion of the folk music world. An excerpt from the first verse:

*I'm not the one you need*

*You say you're lookin' for someone*

*Who's never weak but always strong*

*To protect you an' defend you*

The song "My Back Pages" from the same album, with its refrain "ah-but I was so much older then/I'm younger than that now" has been also been interpreted as representing Dylan's growing disillusionment with the folk movement and his desire to explore other musical and philosophical horizons. Whether one interprets these lyrics prophetically or not, Dylan will make the transformation to rock musician in 1965 and never look back. This transformation will be discussed in Chapter 6.

## Brian Wilson, The Beach Boys, and Surf Rock

**Brian Wilson** (b. 1942), his two younger brothers, Dennis (1944–1983) and Carl (1946–1998), their cousin Mike Love (b. 1941), and friend Al Jardine (b. 1942) comprised the original lineup of **The Beach Boys**, though it is Brian Wilson's creative vision in the areas of songwriting, arranging and production that we are really talking about when we discuss The Beach Boys; he was the guiding force behind their most significant work.

Brian Wilson and The Beach Boys represent the union of Chuck Berry's driving rock 'n' roll rhythms, Buddy Holly's core rock instrumentation and proto-rock forms, Phil Spector's masterful production techniques, and a measure of doo-wop and pop sensibility. The result is the earliest subgenre of *rock*: **surf rock**. As Dylan was signaling a new direction for what rock music would *say* later in the 1960s, The Beach Boys were fundamentally defining—and continually redefining—how rock music would *sound*. Moreover, The Beach Boys were the first major American band to begin their career with rock 'n' roll as their *model* and create their own style by moving outward from there.

By 1966, The Beach Boys would become one of the most innovative and influential bands of the twentieth century. In reference to Brian Wilson and his particular importance, Schloss, Starr, and Waterman have this to say:

> In a sense, Brian Wilson represented a new generation of rock 'n' rollers. By this we mean two things. First, that Wilson explicitly acknowledged his reliance on, and reverence for, his predecessors in the rock 'n' roll field—by covering, and quoting from, their records. In other words, he did not begin with musical material from other genres like rhythm & blues or country. Musically and culturally, rock itself was his starting point and his ongoing touchstone. Second, that at the same time, Wilson carved out distinctive new ground—by deliberately moving the lyrics, and eventually the music, of his own songs beyond the territory carved out by his predecessors, into novel areas that were of particular meaning to him, to his time and his place in America. (The Beatles, the Rolling Stones and other bands were also self-conscious new-generation rock 'n' rollers in this sense, but it is important to realize that Brian Wilson was, in all essential respects, the first fully realized representative of this type of pop musician.) (p. 106)

In 1962, within a year of the band's formation, they found success in the *Billboard* charts with the single "Surfin' Safari." After signing with Capitol Records that year, a steady stream of exceedingly well-crafted hits—lyrically focused on the glorification of the Southern California youth lifestyle (surfing, hot rod cars, bikini-clad girls, and the occasional love ballad)—followed. The lyrics and image of the band would stay along this commercial line until 1964 when Brian Wilson stopped touring to become a full-time studio musician.

The early Beach Boys' lyrics and image were a substantial part of their market appeal but their real significance—then and throughout the 1960s—lies squarely in the sophistication of the music. Even as early as their first hit, "Surfin' Safari," Wilson's gifts as a songwriter were obvious, and although Nick Venet is officially listed with production credits, Wilson had begun to take substantial control of this aspect as well. Beginning with their third album, 1963's *Surfer Girl*, Wilson would assume full responsibilities and album credits for production. With chord progressions, riffs, and rhythms that show rock 'n' roll as the starting point, its use of verse/chorus form and core instrumentation "Surfin' Safari" exemplifies of all of rock's essential musical elements.

Table 4.2: Verse/Chorus Form in "Surfin' Safari"

Intro (based on chorus) (:00–:08) *"Let's go surfin' now, everybody's learnin' how…"*

Verse 1 (:09–:20) *"Early in the mornin' we'll be startin' out…"*

Chorus (:21–:40) *"C'mon baby, wait and see…"*

Verse 2 (:41–:52) *"Huntington to Malibu they're shootin' the pier…"*

Chorus (:53–1:12) *"C'mon baby, wait and see…"*

Interlude (1:13–1:24) *Guitar Solo*

Verse 3 (1:25–1:36) *"They're anglin' in Laguna and Cerro Azul…"*

Chorus (1:37–1:57) *"C'mon baby, wait and see…"*

Outro (1:58–end) *"Yeah me, with me…"*

**Go to Chapter 4 playlist example "Surfin' Safari" Brian Wilson and Mike Love, 1962**

Wilson's obsession with detail and his inclination toward innovative structures and novel sounds brought the band to the forefront of pre–British Invasion American rock. The deceptively simple doo-wop style ballad "In My Room" from the album *Surfer Girl* demonstrates the use of complex vocal arrangement and production, as well as the use of harp and electric organ to create a subtle but extremely effective sonic "atmosphere." Lyrically, the song suspends the band's standard themes of girls, cars, and surf for a more inward-looking perspective. In terms of form, the song has an AABA overall pattern. This is not by any means an innovation but is a testament to the tried-and-true design of countless Tin Pan Alley classics. This highly effective formal design persists in popular music.

**Go to Chapter 4 playlist example "In My Room" Brian Wilson and Gary Usher, 1963**

Even as The Beatles and other British Invasion bands were taking America by storm in 1964, the Beach Boys scored their first number one hit, "I Get Around," a track featured on *All Summer Long*, which would prove to be Wilson's last beach-themed album. According to Brian Wilson himself, The Beatles' immediate and overwhelming success in the United States forced The Beach Boys to "get off their asses in the studio." The song "I Get Around" shows not only the impeccable production that, by this time, had become a hallmark of The Beach Boys, but an inventive reworking of verse/chorus form.

The song opens with an elaborate vocal hook on the title phrase accompanied with only a single sustained guitar chord (the perceived effect is really *a cappella*). After four measures the entire ensemble enters with a full chorus section. The first verse follows with four measures of singing, interrupted by a 2-measure "bridge" which leads to the second half of the first verse. This opens up into the full chorus. However, rather than going directly to the second verse, we get another 2-measure vocal-based bridge of sorts leading to an 8-measure guitar solo which is supported by thick vocal harmonies using doo-wop–style syllables (ooh-wah-wah-ooh). This segues into the second verse which has the same 10-measure structure as the first verse. A full chorus follows, as we should expect, but then rather than riding the chorus out to the end, we hear the same big vocal hook from the beginning of the song, this time truly *a cappella*, which only then shifts back to the chorus fading to the end of the song.

Table 4.3: Form of "I Get Around"

Vocal Intro (:00–:07) *"Round, round get around, I get around…"*

Chorus (:08–:19) *"I get around…"*

Verse 1 (:20–:36) *"I'm getting' bugged drivin' up and down the same old strip…"*

Chorus (:37–:49) *"I get around…"*

Bridge (:50–:53)

Interlude (:54–1:05) *Guitar Solo*

Verse 2 (1:06–1:22) *"We always take my car 'cause it's never been beat…"*

Chorus (1:23–1:39) *"I get around…"*

Restatement of Vocal Intro (1:40–1:46) *"Round, round get around, I get around…"*

Chorus to fade out

**Go to Chapter 4 playlist example "I Get Around" Brian Wilson and Mike Love, 1964**

Although the beach-themed image of the band in their first few years had in no small way contributed to their commercial success, shedding that image in favor of a more artistically and personally mature one did nothing to diminish their momentum. On the contrary, the period from just after the British Invasion through the end of the 1960s marked the most intensely creative and artistically significant period in Brian Wilson's already brilliant career. Wilson's contributions to rock after 1964 are considerable and will be discussed in greater detail in Chapter 6.

Image 4.3: Brian Wilson behind a mixing console in 1976

## Roy Orbison

In 1957 **Roy Orbison** (1936–1988) relocated from his native Texas to Memphis with his band, the Teen Kings. Although the group signed with Sam Phillips' Sun label, they and Orbison were unable to find any real success, in spite of their best efforts. Orbison spent the late 1950s either touring in support of bigger artists, trying his hand at country music, or simply in a state of musical inactivity. By 1960, Orbison had managed to capture the attention of a producer at Monument Records named Fred Foster. During his early days at Monument, working with Foster and an engineer named Bill Porter, Orbison began to develop his own distinct vocal sound.

Their first sessions together produced a modestly successful song called "Uptown" that—along with a core of guitars, piano, bass, and drums—featured doo-wop style backup singers and orchestral strings (at Orbison's own request). Although the song failed to achieve significant commercial success, it seemed to Orbison and his production team that they were moving in the right direction. Working with these elements, Orbison recorded a single which he had cowritten with songwriter Joe Melson. "Only the Lonely," a doo-wop–flavored song with a combination of rock and orchestral instruments was released in May of 1960. It soared up the charts to reach the number two spot in the United States and number one in the United Kingdom and Australia. Suddenly, Roy Orbison found himself rather in demand.

Orbison followed up with "Blue Angel" and "I'm Hurtin'" and had begun to develop a distinct sound. The rock band base with orchestral accompaniment, along with Orbison's evocative tenor voice created an edgy yet elegant sound heretofore unknown in popular music. In an attempt to break away from doo-wop and pop elements, he wrote and recorded "Running Scared" in early 1961. The song features an incessant rhythmic pattern that builds to a climactic ending; in essence, it is just one long crescendo. "Running Scared" was an international hit, reaching number one on the US pop charts and number nine in the United Kingdom.

**Go to Chapter 4 playlist example "Running Scared" Roy Orbison and Joe Melson, 1961**

Orbison scored a string of hits through 1962 and in 1963 was invited to tour the United Kingdom with The Beatles, who had been making quite a name for themselves in the European club circuit. The Beatles were known to have deeply admired Orbison's music. He formed friendships with all of them and especially George Harrison with whom he would record toward the end of his life.

In 1964, Orbison would write his two most successful songs, "It's Over" and "Oh, Pretty Woman" with friend and collaborator Bill Dees. Both songs sold many millions of copies and cemented Orbison as an icon of early 1960s rock. As did many American pop and rock musicians of the early 1960s, Orbison struggled to stay relevant through the British Invasion with little success. Sadly, he was beset by a series of personal tragedies beginning in 1966 when his wife was killed in a motorcycle accident and in 1968, while on tour in England, he received news that his two eldest sons had died in a house fire in Tennessee.

Although he worked through the 1970s, he had no significant commercial presence of his own. In the late 1970s, however, prominent artists of that era found success in remaking Orbison classics, thus helping to make his name and music relevant to a new generation. Rock artists like

Gram Parsons, Nazareth, and Linda Ronstadt re-recorded his music with great success. In 1980, Don McClean (most famous for his hit "American Pie") remade Orbison's "Crying" and in 1982, hard rock giants Van Halen scored a huge hit with their hot-rodded version of "Oh, Pretty Woman," clearly demonstrating that Orbison was a kind of prophet in early rock. A side-by-side comparison of the two versions is confirmation of Orbison's visionary music.

**Go to Chapter 4 playlist example "Oh, Pretty Woman" Roy Orbison and Bill Dees, 1964**

**Go to Chapter 4 playlist example "Oh, Pretty Woman" Van Halen Remake, 1982**

Roy Orbison would rise to prominence again shortly before his untimely death at the age of fifty-two. In 1987, Orbison was working with Jeff Lynne of Electric Light Orchestra (ELO) fame to put a new album together. During this time, Orbison and Lynne happened to have lunch one day with their mutual friend George Harrison, who invited Orbison to sing on a new album he was making. Plans were made to work in Bob Dylan's home recording studio and on the way to the first session, Harrison stopped by Tom Petty's house to pick up a guitar he had left there. All five musicians ended up getting together that evening at Dylan's studio and writing a song called "Handle with Care." This fortuitous turn of events culminated in the **supergroup** The Traveling Wilburys. The groups released one album with Orbison, *The Traveling Wilburys Vol. 1*, in October of 1988 which was an enormous success. Orbison, however, died of a heart attack in December that year.

> **Note**: "Supergroup" was a term that was used beginning in the 1970s and described the relatively common occurrence of well-established major stars, known as solo artists or members of other bands, forming new bands together to record and tour. The Traveling Wilburys exemplify this practice.

Orbison's lasting contributions to rock can be seen clearly in several aspects of his music. His addition of orchestral elements in a rock context significantly challenged the norms of early rock and his richly expressive, multiple-octave voice brought an operatic quality to his music, but his most notable contribution may be in the varied and sometimes very complex ways he handled song structure. For example, typical pop rock verse/chorus structures of the time, diagrammed using letters, as A-B-A-B-C-A-B with the "A" representing the verse, the "B" representing the chorus and "C" standing for the interlude. In Orbison's song "In Dreams" from 1963, we see a structure that can only be described as A-B-C-D-E-F; seven distinct parts with none of them repeating. Not only is this an extremely advanced compositional technique but also a very unlikely formula for a pop hit. Yet the song charted as high as number seven on US charts in 1963. He was also quite capable of dealing in utterly simple forms as we heard in "Running Scared," which can be shown as A-A-A-A-B.

**Go to Chapter 4 playlist example "In Dreams" Roy Orbison, 1963**

Roy Orbison's music can perhaps best be described as a world unto itself. He was remarkably influential to rockers of future generations including Robert Plant, Billy Joel, Elton John, Bruce Springsteen, and countless others. His diversions from contemporaneous standards verge on eccentric, yet there is a nameless magnetic quality in his sound that cannot be ignored. One might think of Roy Orbison as rock's first great nonconformist.

## Garage Bands

The Pacific Northwest is the unofficial home to another uniquely American form of early rock 'n' roll–inspired ensemble: the **garage band**. Although the phenomenon existed around the country, the earliest garage band hit came from a Portland, Oregon, band called The Kingsmen in 1963 (discussed below), thus creating the perception that the Pacific Northwest was its region of origin. In truth, there were noteworthy regional scenes in California, Texas, and throughout the Midwest. It is also important to note that during the 1960s, garage bands and/or garage rock, as it was later called, was not a named genre but rather, a rudimentary form of rock that had a growing commercial presence after 1963.

A typical garage band was made up of middle-class teenagers, often with little or no musical training and playing on inexpensive instruments—usually core rock instruments—in their parents' garage or basement. Many early 1960s garage bands learned to play late 1950s rock 'n' roll or R&B covers, with possibly an occasional original, and perhaps played at local dances, parties, or bars. Bands playing in regional scenes would often organize a "battle of the bands" in which judges or fans could elect their favorite. Many garage bands became local celebrities and many musicians who would rise to prominence in the 1960s and beyond had their start in garage bands.

The appeal of the garage band was the raw, unrefined sound which was reminiscent of the early days of rock 'n' roll, when it lacked studio polish and high-end production. The over-commercialization of rock 'n' roll, more often than not meant big studio budgets, trained studio musicians, and an overall removal of the rough edges that leant a certain energy and vitality to the independent music of the previous decade. Garage bands rekindled that raw energy. Ironically, garage bands that enjoyed any success beyond a lone independently produced hit were often dragged into the same environment of studio refinement, and in the process lost the allure that earned them recognition in the first place. Not surprisingly, we will see what could be called the "garage band effect" occur in several extremely significant movements: in the 1970s with punk and new wave; the 1980s with underground metal; and in the 1990s with grunge.

The band that first brought the garage band sound to the national and international audience was **The Kingsmen** (Jack Ely, vocals; Lynn Easton, drums; Don Gallucci, keyboards; Mike Mitchell, guitar; and Bob Nordby, bass) though their remake of a 1957 Richard Berry tune called "Louie, Louie" becoming a major hit could easily be described as a fluke. Although there are various versions of the story behind the recording, the most consistently related is this: The band was making a demo of "Louie, Louie" at the behest of their manager, Ken Chase, who was also a local DJ in the Portland area and wanted to play it on his show to promote the band. Chase had noticed several other local bands performing the song to great reception and The Kingsmen had, in fact, added it to their own live set. Chase wanted the recording to sound raw and arranged that the band record "live" (no multi-tracking) into just three microphones. Ely basically had to shout, rather than sing, into a microphone that was suspended from the ceiling. The band had less time to prepare than they would have liked and were unhappy with the take (Ely actually comes in early on the third verse and has to wait for the rest of the band to catch up). This, however, ended up being the finished take upon which Chase demanded.

Chase promoted and distributed the recording and in an odd twist, a rumor began to circulate that Ely had injected several obscenities into parts of the song (his vocals throughout are indeed garbled and virtually unintelligible). The rumor apparently reached the governor of Indiana, Matthew Welsh, who put a ban on the song. Welsh's ban prompted an FBI investigation and drew the song into the national media spotlight. Rather than discouraging listeners, the negative attention had exactly the opposite effect: the single raced up the charts. The FBI eventually concluded that they were unable to interpret the lyrics and the case was closed. Drummer Lynn Easton would later claim he yelled "fuck" after dropping a drumstick. In any case, the success of the song demonstrated widespread validation for the garage band phenomenon.

### The Social Climate on the Eve of the British Invasion

The March on Washington of August 27 and 28, 1963, was one of the largest political rallies for human rights ever held in the United States. Over a quarter of a million people—both black and white—participated. The March was organized by civil rights and religious leaders and is credited with helping to pass the Civil Rights Act of 1964 as well as the Voting Rights Act of 1965. Earlier that year, on June 11, President Kennedy gave his famous civil rights address on national TV and radio, announcing that he would push for civil rights legislation. Although there was pushback from white supremacist groups against civil rights progress, particularly in the South, there was also a pronounced feeling of promise that the social situation in the United States was changing for the better. Young people had been given cause to believe that the world they were inheriting would be a more peaceful and tolerant one.

Less than three months later, on November 22, 1963, President Kennedy was assassinated in Dallas, Texas.

To be sure, the gravity of the Kennedy assassination and the attendant feeling that the vision of a more equitable world put forth by Dr. King was slipping away, weighed heavily on the minds of all concerned. Young people were no exception. It has been suggested by many commentators that there was a strong connection to the powerful events of the period and the wild reception of The Beatles and other British Invasion bands. There is also good reason to speculate that The Beatles would have been a hit regardless, but it seems safe to say that the band provided some cultural balm for the deep wounds inflicted on the collective youth psyche. At any rate, it cannot be denied that after The Beatles appeared on the *Ed Sullivan Show* on February 9, 1964, popular culture—and indeed society as a whole—would never be the same.

## Suggested Chapter Related Activities

- Locate several examples of post-2000 **acoustic folk music**. Do the lyrics address social issues?

- Find examples of modern "dance instruction" songs. Do these songs have any musical similarities to "The Twist" in either form or instrumentation?

- Find at least one example of a post-2000 song in any style that uses metaphor to convey a message related to a contemporary social issue, such as Dylan's "Blowin' in the Wind" does.

- Locate a contemporary remake of an early 1960s song. In your opinion, does the remake improve on or diminish from the original? How?

## Suggested Discussion Topics

- Discuss contemporary social issues with which musicians are involved. Does commercialization help or hinder music with a serious message?

- Discuss your perspective on so-called "Happy Meal Music." Why is it so popular? Who is making it so? How does it relate to the commercialization of rock 'n' roll in the early '60s?

## Image Credits

# CHAPTER 5

# The Beatles and the British Invasion

---

*We're more popular than Jesus now.*

-John Lennon

---

## The Beatles' Formation

In June of 1962, The Beatles began a recording career that, in just eight short years, would not simply change the course of rock history but—in nearly every way—*determine* it. Their output from 1962 to 1970 can be characterized as a continuously advancing process of musical evolution, innovation, and expansion during which the band—both collectively and individually—showed a virtually boundless ability to reach unprecedented heights of rock artistry. Through their unique gifts of musical expression, they broke through the barriers of their time and rose, almost heroically, to meet the occasion of their own moment in history. The Beatles, supported by a small cast of talented production, management, and engineering personnel, and appearing at their specific juncture in history, formed what could easily be called "Rock's Perfect Storm." We begin by examining the British music scene in the 1950s from which the band emerged.

American music and culture had a marked influence on Great Britain in the post-WWII period. Mass media, recorded music, a common language, and the stationing of US troops in the country had fostered a great deal of cultural cross-pollination. As a result, Britain experienced some of the same social developments, particularly the emergence of well-defined youth cultures which were often situated around music. Two youth-oriented styles, **trad** and **skiffle**, became popular there in the late 1940s and early 1950s. Trad, short for traditional, was influenced by early American jazz, boogie-woogie, jump bands, and blues. Skiffle emerged as an often amateurish, folk music–based offshoot of trad and commonly employed acoustic guitars, banjos, and even homemade instruments like jugs and washboard basses. Skiffle might be thought of as some-thing of a British counterpart to the American garage band: Only basic musical skill was needed; instruments were relatively inexpensive; and local groups—which numbered in the thousands countrywide—were afforded the opportunity to perform in a variety of small venues like dance halls, coffeehouses, and nightspots.

In the mid-1950s, American rock 'n' roll began to establish a substantial presence in Britain. Artists like Bill Haley, Elvis, Little Richard, Chuck Berry, and Buddy Holly not only appeared frequently in the British charts and on British radio but also toured in the United Kingdom and Europe and appeared on British TV shows. As American rock 'n' roll established a significant presence on the British scene, many British artists began to emulate their favorite American rock 'n' roll musicians. Among the first successful British rock 'n' rollers were Tommy Steele, Wee Willie Harris, and most notably Cliff Richard, whose 1958 hit "Move It" is widely considered to be Britain's first authentic rock 'n' roll record.

**Go to Chapter 5 playlist example "Move It" Ian Samwell arr. Cliff Richard and The Drifters, 1958**

It was in this musical climate that, in March, 1957, a sixteen-year-old **John Lennon** (1940–1980) formed a skiffle group called the Quarrymen with the help of some friends from his Liverpool high school, Quarry Bank. In July of that year, Lennon met **Paul McCartney** (b. 1942) who was fifteen at the time, and enlisted him to play guitar. In February of 1958, McCartney introduced Lennon to his guitarist friend, **George Harrison** (1943–2001) who, at just fourteen years of age, struck Lennon as being too young for the group. Harrison persisted in hanging around with the group and proving his musical worth, however, and within a month Lennon ceded. After about a year of playing locally at small parties and dances, Lennon's original Quarry Bank friends eventually went their separate ways leaving Lennon, McCartney, and Harrison, all playing guitar, as the remaining members. By this time, rock 'n' roll had become the musical focus of the band: they built an extensive repertoire by learning a wide variety of music by American artists. The three guitarists, whenever they could find a drummer to sit in, performed as Johnny and The Moondogs (a name no doubt inspired by Alan Freed). Lennon, also talented in the visual arts, upon graduating high school, enrolled as a student at the nearby Liverpool College of Art. There he befriended fellow artist and bassist **Stu Sutcliffe** (1940–1962), whom he asked to join the band. Now a quartet, in 1960 they changed their name to The Silver Beetles for several months before finally settling on The Beatles.

Their unofficial manager at the time, Allan Williams, succeeded in booking the band for a several month engagement in Hamburg, Germany. Still in need of a full-time drummer, they held auditions and hired **Pete Best** (b. 1941) in August of 1960 and left for Germany several days later. The Beatles' first engagement in Hamburg did not go particularly well: The club owner with whom they were contracted learned that the band had been performing side gigs at a rival club. Upon this discovery he gave the band a termination notice and promptly reported to authorities that George Harrison was underage. This resulted in Harrison's deportation back to England. The following week, McCartney and Best were arrested for attempted arson after the same club owner accused them of setting a small fire in a concrete hallway in the back of his building. They too were deported shortly thereafter. They all soon regrouped in Liverpool and, retaining Best as their permanent drummer, continued to play in and around the area.

The burgeoning music scene in Liverpool in the early 1960s afforded The Beatles many performance opportunities in local clubs and coffeehouses. The terms "Beat" and "British Beat" music began to be used to describe the musical style of bands that were working in the local and regional scene. That, along with the insect theme derived from Buddy Holly and the Crickets, is considered to be the inspiration for the band's "misspelled" name. Beat music was primarily a merging of the rock 'n' roll of Chuck Berry and Buddy Holly, based on the eighth note subdivision, doo-wop, skiffle, and R&B. (The fusion of these styles is clearly evidenced in The Beatles' early original music, which began to constitute an increasing portion of their live repertoire.) Eventually the term "Merseybeat" was applied to this genre in connection with the Mersey River which runs along the city of Liverpool. Although the Merseybeat scene would produce many important British Invasion musicians, the term became more or less synonymous with The Beatles by 1963.

In March of 1961, The Beatles would return to Hamburg under a new contract for their second extended engagement there, although Sutcliffe would leave the band that July to pursue his studies in visual arts (sadly, he would die suddenly the following year of a brain hemorrhage). Following Sutcliffe's departure from the band, McCartney switched to bass guitar. They finished their engagement in Hamburg successfully as a quartet and returned to Liverpool where their popularity continued to grow. In November, 1961, they met **Brian Epstein** (1934–1967) while performing at the Cavern Club. Epstein, a local record store owner and music journalist was immediately taken with the band, citing what he called a "fresh" sound and "star quality." Over the next couple of months he persuaded the band to hire him as their manager. As his first order of business, Epstein freed the band from some minor contractual obligations and began seeking a recording contract. In May of 1962, following several unsuccessful auditions for other labels, the band auditioned for producer **George Martin** (1926–2016), who signed The Beatles to London's EMI Records. Thus began the most important recording career in rock music.

For our purposes, we will divide The Beatles' career into two distinct phases: the years during which they were a touring band and the years after they stopped touring to become a "studio" band.

## Beatlemania and Touring Years: 1962–1966

The Beatles' recording career and collaboration with Martin began in London's **Abbey Road Studios** on June 6, 1962. During the first sessions, Martin expressed his dissatisfaction with Best's drumming and strongly suggested to Epstein that he be replaced. The other band members had already been considering the dismissal of Best in favor of **Ringo Starr** (b. Richard Starkey, 1940), a drummer whom they had known from the Merseybeat scene band Rory Storm and the Hurricanes. Epstein was tasked with firing Best, and Ringo Starr officially became a Beatle in August, finalizing the lineup the world would soon come to know. On September 4, the band was back at Abbey Road and recorded "Love Me Do," with Starr on drums. Still not quite satisfied with the drumming, however, Martin hired session drummer Andy White to record the track the following week. This third session yielded several songs, including "Love Me Do" with White on drums, and "Please Please Me" and "P.S. I Love You" with Starr playing. Martin would eventually opt for Starr's version of "Love Me Do" for the band's debut single as well, although the White version was released in subsequent pressings.

"Love Me Do" was released in October and reached number seventeen in the UK charts. At a subsequent studio session in November, Martin suggested increasing the tempo of "Please Please Me" and it was re-recorded. Released in January, 1963, it became The Beatles' first British number one hit.

**Go to Chapter 5 playlist example "Love Me Do" Lennon/McCartney, 1962**

**Go to Chapter 5 playlist example "Please Please Me" Lennon/McCartney, 1963**

While The Beatles would go on to help establish verse/chorus form as a standard in rock as well as help to develop many innovative and expanded song structures, they also had an innate understanding of how to make use of the effective song structures that had come before them, such as Tin Pan Alley AABA form. They would begin with this basic form as a foundation for some of their most powerful songs like "Yesterday," "Hey Jude," and "The Long and Winding Road." In the song "Love Me Do," Lennon and McCartney not only build outward from a standard AABA form, they introduce out-of-the-ordinary phrase structures: typical AABA forms are based on a 32-measure pattern (eight measures for each phrase). Notice Lennon and McCartney's unusual, but nonetheless pleasing treatment of the phrasing.

Table 5.1: Expanded AABA Form in "Love Me Do"

*Harmonica Intro* (8 measures)

**A:** *"Love, love me do. You know I love you..."* (9 measures)

*Harmonica Break* (4 measures)

**A:** *"Love, love me do. You know I love you..."* (9 measures)

*Harmonica Break* (4 measures)

**B:** *"Someone to love, somebody new..."* (8 measures)

**A:** *"Love, love me do. You know I love you..."* (9 measures)

**B:** *(same music as first B section with harmonica solo)* (8 measures)

*Half of Harmonica Intro from the beginning* (4 measures)

**A:** *"Love, love me do. You know I love you..."* (9 measures)

*Harmonica Break to fade...*

In December of 1962, the band was wrapping up what would be their last extended club engagement in Hamburg. With their commercial potential becoming more evident, Epstein sought to give the band a more polished and professional image. Up to this point, The Beatles had been little concerned with their dress and comportment on stage: They dressed very casually (usually in jeans), smoked cigarettes, swore, and even ate while performing. Epstein suggested that they cultivate an image befitting their growing stature. The Beatles began appearing in sharp, modern clothing and developed a more calculated performance style. It was also around this time that the band collectively decided to relegate vocal duties to Harrison and Starr on occasion, giving them a greater sense of validation as full-fledged collaborative members, even though the songwriting partnership of Lennon and McCartney was the prevailing creative force.

In February of 1963, The Beatles were back at Abbey Road to record their first full-length LP, *Please Please Me*. The album included ten new tracks, captured in a single laborious session, as well as the four they had already released as singles. Of the fourteen total songs on the album, eight were written by Lennon and McCartney and six were covers. The band, riding the wave of their initial success in January, were in somewhat of a rush to release new material and maintain their momentum. The intensity of the marathon session as well as the innate musical craftsmanship comes through in the recording despite Lennon's assertion that they put very little thought into the compositions themselves. His characterization of the music he and McCartney wrote for the album was recounted later as "… Buddy Holly pop songs, with no more thought of them than that—to create a sound. And the words were almost irrelevant" (Sheff 1981).

The album was an enormous success in the United Kingdom and features some Beatles classics. The Beatles, even then, were beginning to set the trend of what one commentator would later refer to as the "self-contained rock band—" a band that wrote their own material and played their own instruments. They followed up their debut album with two more enormously successful hit singles, "From Me to You" and "She Loves You" in April and August of 1963, respectively.

**Go to Chapter 5 playlist example "From Me to You" Lennon/McCartney, 1963**

**Go to Chapter 5 playlist example "She Loves You" Lennon/McCartney, 1963**

**Note**: "She Loves You" is a contrasting verse/chorus form based on Buddy Holly's model.

Image 5.1: The legendary Abbey Road Studio in London

The overwhelming demand for The Beatles led to three successive UK tours—one of them with American musician Roy Orbison—as well as a tour of Sweden. The attendant media exposure and fan frenzy led to the coining of the term **Beatlemania**, which would follow them through their arrival in the states until the end of 1964. The British media loved the band almost as much as the audiences. Upon their return from Sweden, they were greeted at the airport by hundreds of screaming fans and a veritable media circus consisting of nearly one hundred reporters and photographers as well as representatives from the British Broadcasting Corporation (BBC), the nation's dominant TV network.

The follow-up album, *With the Beatles* was released in the United Kingdom on November 22, 1963, and featured eight original songs with six covers—one of them a Chuck Berry song, "Roll Over Beethoven." Among the originals was George Harrison's first recorded solo composition, "Don't Bother Me," which, with its brooding lyrics ("... So go away, leave me alone, don't bother me..."), stood in contrast to the Lennon/McCartney compositions and their innocuous yet classic expressions of young love like "All My Loving" and "It Won't Be Long." The album was also released in Canada with the expanded title *Beatlemania! Meet the Beatles* marking the band's first official North American release. Unlike their first album, which had been recorded very quickly by any standard, the follow-up was recorded with the luxury of more time and better production techniques. As such, it met with critical acclaim not just in its own right but as an improved sequel to *Please Please Me*. There was even a series of newspaper articles written by composer turned critic, William Mann, in which he gave a detailed musical analysis, a rather unheard-of occurrence, but one that gave The Beatles that much more musical credibility.

The Lennon/McCartney–composed single "I Want to Hold Your Hand" was released on November 29 in the United Kingdom and reached the number two chart position on the day of its release—only to be held off of number one by "She Loves You." It would become The Beatles' first number one hit in the United States two weeks after its release there in the final days of 1963.

**Go to Chapter 5 playlist example "I Want to Hold Your Hand" Lennon/McCartney, 1963**

"I Want to Hold Your Hand" is another example of The Beatles' early use of expanded AABA form. The form is AABABA but with a clever twist: The A sections are twelve measures long, the last four of which feel almost like a chorus, creating an illusory sense of verse/chorus form. Another oddity is the B section, which is eleven measures long. Moreover, there is a 3-measure outro that echoes the 4-measure *chorus-like* part. All in all, a rather uncommon treatment of a traditional form:

Table 5.2: Expanded AABA Form in "I Want to Hold Your Hand"

*Intro* (4 measures)

**A:** *"Oh yeah I tell you somethin'..."* (8 measures) *"I want to hold..."* (4 measures)

**A***: "Oh please say to me..."* (8 measures) *"I want to hold..."* (4 measures)

**B:** *"And when I touch you..."* (11 measures)

**A:** *"Yeah you got that..."* (8 measures) *"I want to hold..."* (4 measures)

**B:** *"And when I touch you..."* (11 measures)

**A:** *"Yeah you got that..."* (8 measures) *"I want to hold..."* (4 measures)

*Outro* (3 measures)

## Landing in America

Management issues and complex legal hang-ups with EMI's American subsidiary, Capitol Records, had prevented any Beatles recordings from being released in the United States until the last days of December 1963. Given the widespread assertion that the band's arrival in New York in early 1964 and their subsequent television and concert appearances helped to pull many Americans out of the deep sadness brought on by the Kennedy assassination, the timing may have been serendipitous for all concerned. In any case, The Beatles' immediate impact on the American music scene was staggering.

On February 7, 1964, The Beatles left for America from London's Heathrow Airport where they were seen off by over four thousand ardent fans. A crowd nearly as large and every bit as enthusiastic greeted them at JFK International Airport in New York. Brian Epstein had orchestrated several mass marketing campaigns around the country which heralded the band's arrival and primed American audiences. Their February 9 performance on *The Ed Sullivan Show* was seen by a record-setting viewing audience of approximately 73 million Americans, over one-third of the national population.

Image 5.2: The Beatles are greeted by fans at JFK Airport in February 1964

Don J. Hibbard and Carol Kaleialoha write:

Incredibly impossible adulating inundation summed up the beginning of nineteen-sixty-Beatle-four. During the first three months of the year, The Beatles, stars gone supernovae, single-handedly rescued the record industry from its era of "profitless prosperity" and produced approximately sixty percent of the industry's single sales. Their first American hit, "I Want to Hold Your Hand," moved from number forty-five on January 18, 1964, to number one in a matter of two weeks, and remained at the top of the charts until March 21, only to be replaced by "She Loves You," which was followed by "Can't Buy Me Love." On April 4, 1964, the first of five weeks to herald "Can't Buy Me Love" as America's top tune, the group claimed the initial five spots on the singles charts with "Can't Buy Me Love," "Twist and Shout," "She Loves You," "I Want to Hold Your Hand," and "Please Please Me," *plus* the top two albums, *The Beatles' Second Album* which climbed to number position just two weeks after its release, and *Meet the Beatles*, the best-selling album in music history up to that time. A week later, fourteen Beatles songs appeared in *Billboard's* "Hot 100." An astounding record, a phenomenal phenomenon, such figures only begin to tell the story of the frenzied fanaticism with which post-Kennedy America greeted the British singing sensations. (pp. 26–27)

**Note**: The US release of *Meet the Beatles* on the American Capitol label was in essence an enhanced repackaging of the original music featured on their British debut, *With the Beatles*. *The Beatles' Second Album* contained the five cover songs originally released on *Meet the Beatles* plus new originals and a cover of Little Richard's "Long Tall Sally." However, an album made up primarily of tracks from *Please Please Me* was released on the independent Vee-Jay Records ten days prior to the first Capitol release, making it the official US debut. Labels and legal issues notwithstanding, all three albums sold millions of copies and held top chart positions.

Although the critical reception following the band's *Ed Sullivan Show* debut was lukewarm, the popular reception was unmistakably fervent. Several live concert performances followed including a show at the Washington Coliseum and two shows at New York's Carnegie Hall. Their second appearance on *Ed Sullivan* the following week garnered more than 70 million viewers and made it clear that Beatlemania had taken America. The Beatles gained a grip on the American public not only through their music, but in interviews through their impish charm and their good-natured irreverence. Their on-air personae, which prompted the nickname **The Fab Four**, displayed a confidence and charisma that defied the commercially established conventions of the teen idol. They were as quick-witted and impudent as they were musical. They seemed to reawaken and update the rebellious nature of early rock 'n' roll and in doing so they touched the latent nonconformist aspirations in youth culture; even then, they began to build a foundation for the idea of the rock musician as social commentator.

The Beatles were promptly offered a three-movie deal through United Artist Records film division, the first of which, *A Hard Day's Night* was filmed in March and April of 1964. Like Elvis' movies, it was generally assumed that rather than being high-level pieces of cinematic art, the film would serve primarily as a vehicle for selling the music in the soundtrack. It was also a given that, like Elvis' films, The Beatles' movies would be financially successful. What few expected was that their first film would win the praise of critics as well. *A Hard Day's Night*, a clever satire on the Beatlemania phenomenon, did just that. It was lauded by top film critics around the world and still stands today as one of the most highly influential musical films of all time. Of course, the soundtrack did quite well, too. The band would make five films over the next five years, although none would win the critical acclaim of their first.

The album *A Hard Day's Night* featured only original music and showcases the development of Lennon and McCartney's songwriting talents which were already blossoming dramatically:

**Go to Chapter 5 playlist example "And I Love Her" Lennon/McCartney, 1964**

**Go to Chapter 5 playlist example "Can't Buy Me Love" Lennon/McCartney, 1964**

"Can't Buy Me Love" is an excellent early example of something that would characterize The Beatles throughout their career: Even as they establish conventions of form they expand upon them through innovative and original techniques. These techniques range from subtle expansions or reconfigurations to the outright reinvention of popular song form. "Can't Buy Me Love" is based on a contrasting verse/chorus form which uses a 12-bar blues progression as a basis for the verse. Both the intro and outro material draw on the chorus: the former foreshadows the chorus while the latter echoes it. The full chorus is delayed by a second verse, creating a sense of anticipation and thus greater satisfaction when it finally arrives. Oddly enough, the third verse before the guitar solo has one extra measure in which Paul screams "ooooww!"

Table 5.3: Verse/Chorus Form in "Can't Buy Me Love"

> Intro (:00–:08) (foreshadows the chorus)
>
> Verse 1 (:09–:25) *"I'll buy you a diamond ring my friend…"*
>
> Verse 2 (:26–:41) *"I'll give you all I got to give…"*
>
> Chorus (:42–:53) *"Can't buy me love…"*
>
> Verse 3 (:54–1:11) *"Say you don't need no diamond rings…"* +1: *"ooooww!"*
>
> Interlude (1:12–1:28) *guitar solo*
>
> Chorus (1:29–1:39) *"Can't buy me love…"*
>
> Verse 4 (1:40–1:55) *"Say you don't need no diamond rings…"*
>
> Outro (1:56–end) (echoes the chorus)

Upon completion of filming *A Hard Day's Night*, The Beatles embarked on a world tour in the summer of 1964 with engagements in Denmark, the Netherlands, France, Australia, New Zealand, Hong Kong, and finally the United States in August. Beatlemania was rapidly becoming a global phenomenon. It was during the band's tour of France that they happened upon Bob Dylan's 1963 album *The Freewheelin' Bob Dylan*. Although The Beatles were known to keep up with current trends in music, Dylan was still in the commercially obscure world of folk music. He simply hadn't been known to them. Immediately upon their discovery of the album, the whole band, and Lennon most particularly, became enamored with Dylan. They virtually wore the record out. Lennon would later say "For three weeks in Paris, we didn't stop playing it." While The Beatles had been growing steadily more musically sophisticated, lyrically their songs had been clearly aimed at a teenage audience who were vastly more interested in dancing to rock than engaging with intellectual poetry accompanied by acoustic guitar. Dylan's potent lyrics carried a depth of meaning that apparently affected Lennon deeply. He admired Dylan's idealism.

Almost immediately, Lennon's lyrics began to assume a more serious cast. While on tour that summer he penned "I'm a Loser," which was recorded in early August. One of its verses:

> *Although I laugh and I act like a clown*
>
> *Beneath this mask I am wearing a frown*
>
> *My tears are falling like rain from the sky*
>
> *Is it for her or myself that I cry*

These are the first Beatles lyrics to reflect the influence of Dylan: they represent Lennon's departure from writing mindless expressions of young love and his first step in an evolution toward a style that demonstrates a more mature, narrative-driven approach in the manner of Dylan. Within roughly a year Lennon will reveal a full mastery of this folk-inspired idiom in "Norwegian Wood" (discussed below).

As the summer of 1964 wore on, Dylan had achieved an almost hero-like status with Lennon and his bandmates. While in New York in late August of 1964, John Lennon learned that Bob Dylan was nearby and asked music journalist Al Aronowitz to try and set up a meeting. Dylan responded by showing up at the Delmonico Hotel where the band was staying. It was during this now legendary encounter that Bob Dylan would turn The Beatles on to pot. The Beatles were not strangers to drugs: in their early days in Hamburg, they were introduced to the drug Preludin, a type of stimulant or "speed" which they used both recreationally and as a tool to help them stay awake during all-night performances. That, along with alcohol, had constituted the band's drug experience; they had not yet been introduced to any psychoactive drugs.

The meeting with Dylan had a profoundly transformative effect on The Beatles in several ways: Their use of marijuana escalated rapidly and would soon expand to include LSD, cocaine, and for John Lennon, even heroin. Ringo Starr would later state that "we were smoking pot for breakfast" in describing the band's drug use after the Dylan encounter. Intense experimentation with drugs was only the beginning. There was also a marked expansion in their songwriting style, and they would soon begin experimenting with their song arrangements while in the recording studio. Of the aftereffects of this famous meeting, Michael Campbell and James Brody write:

> Still, there was more to this meeting than turning The Beatles on. It seemed to fur-
> ther motivate both parties to learn from the other. For The Beatles, Dylan raised the
> bar—the standard to which The Beatles would hold their music. More specifically, his

music occasionally served as a model for their songs, especially those in which Lennon provided significant creative input. Later, in explaining their musical breakthrough in the mid-sixties, McCartney said, "We were only trying to please Dylan." Without question, the music they created after the meeting, especially from *Rubber Soul* on, represents a far more substantial legacy then their earlier work. (p. 162)

The influence that The Beatles exerted on Bob Dylan will be discussed in Chapter 6.

The Beatles' fourth studio album *Beatles for Sale* was released in the United Kingdom in December 1964. Commercial pressure to release a new album, however, was in direct conflict with the band's creative aspirations. They had sought to continue recording only their own original material as they had on *A Hard Day's Night*, but the demands of heavy touring as well as shooting a feature-length film had taken a toll on the band's production of new original songs. As it happened, the album contained eight originals—"I'm a Loser" among them—and six covers from their vast backlog of live repertoire, including Chuck Berry's "Rock and Roll Music" and Buddy Holly's "Words of Love." One of the originals appearing on the album, "Eight Days a Week," represented an important first for the band: The song was not entirely finished before the sessions during which it was recorded began. This is the first situation in which The Beatles experimented in the recording studio with several different arrangements of the song before deciding on the finished version. This would soon become a fairly common practice with the band, and one that no doubt led to the expanded use of studio technology not just as a means of capture, but as an actual tool in their songwriting process. Several different arrangements of the song's introduction during the sessions were done before they came up with the finished version that uses a "fade-in" effect, a relative rarity in recorded music at the time.

**Go to Chapter 5 playlist example "Eight Days a Week" Lennon/McCartney, 1964**

**Note**: The rhythmic basis of the song is not a standard rock rhythm but a long-short shuffle pattern.

As much as The Beatles were inspired lyrically by the work of Bob Dylan, the boldly innovative and exceedingly well-crafted studio productions of Beach Boy Brian Wilson had begun to make a serious impression on them as well. As was discussed in the previous chapter, Wilson had by 1964 devoted his efforts solely to studio work. His projects were a large part of the rapid advances being made in the recording arts. Because of Brian Wilson, The Beatles and George Martin were beginning to more fully consider the potential of the studio as an artistic medium unto itself.

Like the previous Beatles albums on EMI, *Beatles for Sale* was not released in the United States, but a similar counterpart called *Beatles '65* was released in January 1965 and soared into the number one chart position there within its first week.

Early in 1965, John Lennon and George Harrison were introduced to LSD. They were attending a dinner party at the home of John Riley, their dentist, when he surreptitiously laced their after-dinner coffee with the drug. LSD was a little-known drug at the time and was still legal. Its use was becoming fashionable among middle-class London "swingers." In recounting the experience later, Lennon described it as "terrifying but fantastic" while Harrison called it "a very concentrated version of the best feeling I've ever had in my whole life." The two began using LSD regularly. Ringo Starr was known to join them on occasion but Paul McCartney was reluctant and did not have his first LSD experience until late in 1966. As the first Beatle to discuss the drug publicly, McCartney would say of his experiences: "it opened my eyes" and "made me a better, more honest, more tolerant member of society" (Brown and Gaines 2002).

That drugs played a significant role in influencing The Beatles' creative output is undeniable. Though in this regard, they were neither alone, nor were they the first; the intermingling of music and drugs literally dates back centuries. However, because of their massive fame, they would be dogged by the press regarding their drug habits; it became a public affair and in many ways, the band helped to make casual drug use trendy among young people. The Beatles were among the first major rock acts to reference drugs both directly ("With a Little Help from My Friends") and indirectly ("Lucy in the Sky with Diamonds") in their music and lyrics, and in this way, they helped to inspire and define the emerging **hippie** movement and **counterculture** of the later 1960s (this will be discussed in detail in Chapter 6). In public discourse, they were often elusive or reticent on the subject, which many took for an admission of guilt. Later in the decade, Lennon, Harrison, and McCartney would all face drug charges in their own separate run-ins with the law. Specific drug references in both lyrics and music will be discussed below.

The Beatles second film, *Help!*, while not as widely acclaimed as *A Hard Day's Night*, produced an important album of the same name made up of songs from the film as well as additional material. The British release contains fourteen songs, seven from the film comprising side one, and seven additional songs on side two. Of the fourteen total tracks, there are only two cover songs. Moreover, this would be the last time The Beatles include any covers on an album, with the exception of their final album *Let It Be*, which includes a very brief outtake-like excerpt (around forty-five seconds) from a Liverpool folk song called "Maggie Mae," a song the band used to play in their skiffle days. *Help!* Included several important moves forward for The Beatles: They expanded their use of vocal overdubs dramatically; they include classical instruments for the first time on a recording, most notably a string quartet in Paul McCartney's "Yesterday;" John Lennon's "You've Got to Hide Your Love Away" further illustrates his dramatic shift towards lyrics of a much more serious and reflective nature.

**Go to Chapter 5 playlist example "Yesterday" Lennon/McCartney, 1965**

**Go to Chapter 5 playlist example "You've Got to Hide Your Love Away" Lennon/McCartney, 1965**

On August 15, 1965, The Beatles gave what may be their most legendary concert performance at Shea Stadium in New York City in front of a then record-sized crowd of nearly fifty-six thousand (plus approximately two thousand security personnel). Among the many musical frontiers that the band pioneered over the course of their career, the successful "stadium" concert holds particular importance. Although the Shea concert was not the band's first stadium show (they had played at Kansas City's Municipal Stadium and New Orleans' City Park Stadium in 1964) it was by far the largest and most publicized of these. That a concert of such magnitude proved successful both logistically and financially was a great leap forward for live rock performances. In other words, The Beatles proved it could work—and in doing so, they helped to usher in an era of massive arena shows, stadium tours, and outdoor music festivals.

On a technical level, the concert was not such a success story. The noise from the crowd was so deafening that the band could not hear what they were playing, nor could the crowd hear much of the music. It became obvious that large concerts—especially those held outdoors—needed far more powerful sound systems, and that "fold-back" or stage monitor systems were needed so that the musicians could hear what they themselves were doing. The Beatles' Shea Stadium show was the earliest impetus for these technological developments in the field of live sound reinforcement and helped to advance the state-of-the-art for rock concerts as a whole.

Image 5.3: The Beatles at Shea Stadium, 1965

There was a documentary film of the concert produced which first aired in 1966. It shows footage of the performance itself as well as events leading up to it. The audio tracks from the live show underwent heavy post-production processing in order to render them useable. There was a great deal of overdubbing and some were re-recorded entirely. Two songs had to be completely omitted due to technical problems. Overall, though, the film is an important piece of rock concert history.

In October of 1965, The Beatles entered the studio to begin work on what would be their most groundbreaking recording to date, *Rubber Soul*. This was the first time the band had begun recording sessions with the luxury of an extended time period with no other significant commitments. They were thus free to focus their time and creative energies, uninterrupted, on the task of making a record. The resulting album is a masterfully crafted and artistically cohesive blend of rock, soul, folk, vocal pop, and psychedelia. They even introduce exotic sounds and flavors, most notably in the use of the Indian sitar, a characteristic-sounding string instrument, in "Norwegian Wood," and in McCartney's singing of French phrases in the song "Michelle." Unlike the band's earlier albums, which were, according to producer George Martin, "a collection of singles," with *Rubber Soul*, he said "Now we were really beginning to think about albums as a bit of art on their own" (Hertsgaard 1995).

**Go to Chapter 5 playlist example "Norwegian Wood (This Bird Has Flown)" Lennon/ McCartney, 1965**

**Go to Chapter 5 playlist example "Michelle" Lennon/McCartney, 1965**

**Note:** The use of the sitar foreshadows what will become a genre known as **world music**.

It was apparent that The Beatles were evolving both musically and lyrically. Their life experiences and the surreal effects of global fame notwithstanding, the heavy presence of marijuana in their lives undoubtedly played a major role in shaping the album's material. Lennon once famously referred to *Rubber Soul* as the "pot album" while Starr noted that the influence of pot in the writing process had profound effects on the way the band played. Starr also famously called to *Rubber Soul* "our departure record." While the unmistakable signs of artistic and personal growth are present throughout *Rubber Soul*, there are also tracks on the album that reflect the band's centrality in affirming rock's enduring verse/chorus structure. Case in point: the opening track from the British release of *Rubber Soul*, "Drive My Car."

Although in this song we see a near-textbook example of verse/chorus form, it is worth noting that the bass guitar is now functioning as an *independent* voice in the texture, as opposed to much of the band's earlier music in which "walking" bass lines (one bass note per beat) serve in a *supportive* capacity:

Table 5.4: Verse/Chorus Form in "Drive My Car"

Intro *(guitar riff and drum fill)*

Verse 1 *"Asked the girl what she wanted to be..."*

Chorus *"Baby you can drive my car..."*

Verse 2 *"I told that girl that my prospects were good..."*

Chorus *"Baby you can drive my car..."*

Interlude *(guitar solo)*

Chorus *"Baby you can drive my car..."*

Verse *"I told that girl I can start right away..."*

Chorus *"Baby you can drive my car..."*

Outro *"Beep, beep yeah! ...*

## The Final Tour (and Revolver)

By the time The Beatles had entered Abbey Road Studios in April of 1966 to work on what would be their pivotal album *Revolver* they were already growing increasingly disillusioned with touring. As their crowds grew larger and more enthusiastic, it was often difficult—if not impossible—to hear the band. The Beatles were troubled by the reality that their live shows had become events of such pandemonium and concerts were now more about *seeing* them than *hearing* them. That they were contemplating a cessation of touring even as they began the *Revolver* sessions in June is evident in their approach to the recording process. They consciously incorporated cutting-edge studio techniques in the song creation process, which resulted in much of the album being either impractical or impossible to perform live, including the use of tape loops and other special effects in "Tomorrow Never Knows" and orchestral strings as the musical setting in the song "Eleanor Rigby." *Revolver* was completed that June and released in August, just as their final tour was getting underway, yet The Beatles chose not to perform any music from the album, even those songs which would have been workable in a live situation. Such as it is, *Revolver* will be considered later, as part of the band's studio phase.

The inclination to stop touring was solidified by three separate incidents. The summer of 1966 was a tumultuous time for The Beatles: a rather dangerous situation that unfolded while the band was on tour in the Philippines in July was flanked by two major controversies, one in June and the other in August:

**1)** In June, Capitol Records released a compilation album of Beatles music called *Yesterday and Today* which originally featured a cover photo of the band dressed in butcher coats and draped in hunks of raw meat and mutilated baby dolls. The immediate reaction from the media, record distributors, and disc jockeys was quite negative. The album was recalled and repackaged with an alternate cover photo but not before many copies were purchased. The backlash from the original cover was defended by Paul McCartney's statement that it was the band's "comment on the Vietnam War." Not surprisingly, surviving copies of the original issue album cover are extremely valuable and have fetched over $10,000 at auction.

Image 5.4: The controversial "butcher" cover

**2)** While the band was touring in the Philippines in July of 1966, they narrowly escaped the country when their refusal to breakfast with first lady Imelda Marcos resulted in a massive riot outside the band's hotel. The band and their manager Brian Epstein, who issued a polite refusal solely on the basis that the band was not in the habit of accepting such invitations, were unaware that the Marcos regime was not accustomed to taking "no" for an answer. The band and their entourage fled the country amid riotous protests that spread to the airport and very nearly resulted in physical injury.

**3)** In a March 1966 interview for the *London Evening Standard* John Lennon made this now infamous comment:

> "Christianity will go. It will vanish and shrink. I needn't argue about that; I'm right and I'll be proved right. We're more popular than Jesus now; I don't know which will go first, rock 'n' roll or Christianity. Jesus was all right but his disciples were thick and ordinary. It's them twisting it that ruins it for me."

At the time the interview was first published in England, Lennon's comment met with relatively little notice or reaction. However, in August, the interview was reprinted in the US teen magazine *Datebook* where it set off a firestorm of controversy and protest. The reaction was immediate. Radio DJs began to call for boycotts on Beatles music and the *New York Times* reported on the article igniting widespread national criticism. Brian Epstein held a press conference in New York and expressed regret on behalf of the band but it had little impact. Criticism soon spread around the globe; there were anti-Beatles demonstrations in Mexico, South Africa, and Spain; even the Vatican issued a denouncement of Lennon's comments. When the band kicked off their August US tour, various threats ensued and protests led by religious groups, conservative groups, Ku Klux Klan factions, and others—particularly in the South and the Bible Belt—marred concert appearances. There were also public bonfires held in various places where people were encouraged to burn their Beatles records (Gould 2008).

Lennon was not without his supporters and was adamant that his comments were misunderstood. He stated that he was not comparing himself with Christ, expressed his widely shared view that Christianity was on the decline, and that what people call "God" is something in all of us. Despite this, he was pressed to give an apology, which he reluctantly did. The incident would continue to dog Lennon for years. It was even later stated by Mark David Chapman, the man who would murder John Lennon in 1980, that he was infuriated by the remarks, calling them blasphemous; quite a hypocrisy coming from the man who would rob the world of one of its greatest artists and advocates for peace.

From 1962 to 1966 The Beatles toured almost constantly and had given more than fourteen hundred concerts. On August 29, 1966, they played their last commercial concert at Candlestick Park in San Francisco. From then on, The Beatles would become a studio band. The truth is that

The Beatles no longer needed to tour to promote their albums. Their decision to focus solely on their studio work was one of the most important choices in the history of rock. The work they would do between 1966 and 1970, without the burden of touring and, more importantly, not having to record songs that could be played in concert, led to a period of massive experimentation and a fundamental transformation of rock.

## Psychedelia and the Studio Years: 1966–1970

The Beatles' *Revolver* album marked a new era not only for the band but for the very idea of what a rock album could be. It featured highly experimental song structures and recording techniques. For example, the song "Tomorrow Never Knows" was recorded using a sophisticated process of tape looping, artificial double tracking, and tape speed variation, recording while reversing tape direction (a technique known as "backmasking") and recording Lennon's vocals through the rotating horn of a Leslie speaker cabinet. All of these techniques were either invented during the sessions or adapted from contemporaneous experimental techniques being employed in the newly emerging world of electronic music. The effect that Lennon was aiming toward in "Tomorrow Never Knows" was the musical representation of the transcendental state known in eastern mysticism as *samādhi*, a state of being totally aware of the present moment. His inspiration for this came from a book coauthored by 1960s LSD guru Timothy Leary called *The Psychedelic Experience: A Manual Based on the Tibetan Book of the Dead* (MacDonald 2005).

**Go to Chapter 5 playlist example "Tomorrow Never Knows" Lennon/McCartney, 1966**

At the other end of the technological spectrum is the classic McCartney song "Eleanor Rigby" which some commentators have called the first **art rock** song. It is rendered by an all-acoustic **string octet** (4 violins, 2 violas, and 2 cellos). To be sure, producer George Martin played a significant if somewhat behind-the-scenes role in all of The Beatles' recordings; however, in songs like this his contribution rises plainly to the surface. None of The Beatles were musically literate; that is, they had no knowledge of the art of standard musical notation. Martin, a highly trained classical composer, would have been fundamental in transferring McCartney's ideas for the song from notes most likely played to him at the piano to the ensemble that we hear in the finished recording. This is an art form known as **arranging**, and often falls under the duties of a producer. Album credits indicate that Martin also conducted the ensemble. The string octet is a time-honored classical ensemble. What makes "Eleanor Rigby" so revolutionary from a stylistic point of view is that the song comes from a *rock* band. This fundamentally and profoundly expanded the boundaries of the *understanding* of what a rock song could be; The Beatles were walking the line between "popular" culture and "high art" culture.

From a musical standpoint "Eleanor Rigby," like "Tomorrow Never Knows," paints a sonic picture of what the lyric offers in up in relatively plain language. This is a traditional classical technique known as **text painting**. The lyric in "Eleanor Rigby" portrays two characters, Eleanor and Father McKenzie, whose toiling yet meaningless lives are thoroughly represented in the bustling rhythmic activity that sits over a nearly unchanging harmony (moving about but going nowhere); and the melodic yearning we hear in the upper string arrangements effectively indicates the despair that attends such pointless suffering. Where "Tomorrow Never Knows" explores eastern philosophy and states of being through the LSD experience, "Eleanor Rigby" is an intense 2-minute-6-second study of the branch of **existentialist** philosophy known as **Absurdism**. Campbell and Brody describe the song thusly:

> The musical setting is as bleak as the words. A string octet, scored by George Martin from McCartney's instructions, replaces the rock band; there are no other instruments. The string sound is spare, not lush—the chords used throughout emulate a rock accompaniment, not the dense cushions of sound heard in traditional pop. Like Eleanor Rigby herself, the melody of both chorus and verse don't go anywhere. Set over alternating chords, the chorus is just a sigh. The melody of the verse contains longer phrases, but they too mostly progress from higher to lower notes. The harmony shifts between chords; there is no strong sense of movement toward a goal. Lyric, melody and harmony, and the repetitive rhythm of the accompaniment convey the same message: time passes without apparent purpose. (p. 172)

**Go to Chapter 5 playlist example "Eleanor Rigby" Lennon/McCartney, 1966**

George Harrison's creative contributions to *Revolver* were more substantial than they had been up to that point; he had become a nearly equal partner in the songwriting process. Since around 1964, Harrison had become fascinated with Indian classical music and culture and other Eastern philosophical concepts; he found musical inspiration in these. His composition "Love You To" features the sitar and the tabla, a traditional Eastern hand drum used in Hindustani classical music as well as the traditional folk music of Afghanistan, Nepal, and Sri Lanka.

**Go to Chapter 5 playlist example "Love You To" George Harrison, 1966**

The album is not without its rockers: Harrison's song "Taxman," a scathing and cleverly worded denunciation of the high levels of taxation to which the band was subject under the British Labour Party government of Harold Wilson. In fact, he and Conservative Party leader Edward Heath are called out by name in the lyric. The song is a verse/chorus form but with three verses before the interlude (guitar solo) and two after it; however, from the third verse on, the verses are progressively elaborated with backing vocals lending a strong sense of variety and musical evolution within the form itself. Another remarkable musical feature is the totally independent, funky bass line which was thought to be inspired by Motown bassist James Jamerson.

**Go to Chapter 5 playlist example "Taxman" George Harrison, 1966**

*Revolver* also features a horn section ("Got to Get You into My Life"), tape loops of a marching band ("Yellow Submarine"), a variety of percussion and percussive effects, various organs, and the Indian instruments discussed above, as well as piano, guitars, bass, and drums throughout. While its initial critical reception was relatively muted due to the controversies surrounding the band at the time of its release, it has come to be universally regarded as one of the greatest recordings ever made and the moment that The Beatles left everyone else far behind (MacDonald 2005).

> **Note**: Another significant behind-the-scenes person crucial to *Revolver* was recording engineer, **Geoff Emerick** (b. 1946). He first worked as an assistant on earlier Beatles records but was requested as main engineer by Martin for the *Revolver* album. He would continue in this capacity on *Sgt. Pepper's Lonely Hearts Club Band*, *The Beatles* (otherwise known as *The White Album*) and *Abbey Road*. At the time the *Revolver* sessions began, Emerick was a mere nineteen years old.

With the rigors of touring now comfortably behind them, The Beatles officially became a studio band and, as such, adopted an even more experimental approach to their follow-up to *Revolver*, the seminal *Sgt. Pepper's Lonely Hearts Club Band*. "Sgt. Pepper's," as it is familiarly known, is almost universally regarded as the most important rock album ever made. The Beatles were working with an unlimited budget and had the time, talent, and personnel to realize any artistic vision they could conceive. The technology and innovative studio techniques used during the recording process went even further than *Revolver*: The recording employs a wide variety of novel and highly imaginative elements, including random tape splicing, a cutting-edge musical instrument called a Mellotron, direct injection recording, tape speed variation, and an array of advanced signal processing techniques including compression, reverb, signal limiting, and flanging. The methods pioneered in recording Starr's drum kit, including damping and close miking, became common studio practice following the album's release. Producer George Martin and engineer Geoff Emerick contributed heavily to the project.

Following their final tour in August 1966, The Beatles took a well-earned vacation. They began work on *Sgt. Pepper's* in November 1966, a project that would take until April 1967 to complete and would involve over seven hundred hours in recording sessions alone. During a flight to London back from the band's holiday, Paul McCartney was struck with the idea for what would be the title track, a song about a fictional band, which would eventually lead to the overall concept of the album: a record representing a performance of the fictional band, with The Beatles themselves developing alter egos who could experiment musically. George Martin wrote of his reaction to the idea in his autobiography:

> "Sergeant Pepper" itself didn't appear until halfway through making the album. It was Paul's song, just an ordinary rock number … but when we had finished it, Paul said, "Why don't we make the album as though the Pepper band really existed, as though Sergeant Pepper was making the record? We'll dub in effects and things." I loved the idea, and from that moment on it was as though *Pepper* had a life of its own. (p. 202)

On a musical level, the band skillfully weaves elements of many genres—including rock 'n' roll, blues, pop, psychedelic, big band, vaudeville, music hall, piano jazz, circus, avant-garde, chamber, and Western and Indian classical music—into an aesthetically cohesive whole.

Lyrically, *Sgt. Pepper's* is laden with what many have interpreted to be drug references, both blatant and veiled: "I get high with a little help from my friends" in the song "With a Little Help from My Friends;" the song title "Lucy in the Sky with Diamonds" has been widely viewed as a code for LSD; the line "I'd love to turn you on" in the song "A Day in the Life" is thought to refer to being "turned on" to LSD; the title "Fixing a Hole" as well as the mention of "Henry the Horse" in "Being for the Benefit of Mr. Kite!" are both considered to be references to heroin. The Beatles have variously denied and confirmed these suggestions over the years. At the time, these lyrics were enough to cause a variety of radio stations and DJs to ban selected songs from their broadcasts and caused quite a media stir for the band. Many commentators have suggested that *Sgt. Pepper's* contributed greatly to the unification of the revolutionary youth culture movements of the late 1960s.

*Sgt. Pepper's* was an album of many firsts; it was arguably the first—certainly *among* the first—self-conscious "concept" albums in rock; it was the first rock album to win a Grammy for Album of the Year; it was the first major rock album to include the song lyrics on the cover. The album established the LP as the new unit of rock currency and began the erosion of the long-standing format of the single as rock's primary sales medium; it is credited as being the first "art rock" LP as well as aiding in the development of **progressive** rock (discussed later). In a 2003 listing of the "500 Greatest Albums of All Time" compiled by *Rolling Stone* through the polling of selected rock musicians, critics, and music industry figures *Sgt. Pepper's* was named number one. Author and critic Jonathan Gould writes:

> The overwhelming consensus is that the Beatles had created a popular masterpiece: a rich, sustained, and overflowing work of collaborative genius whose bold ambition and startling originality dramatically enlarged the possibilities and raised the expectations of what the experience of listening to popular music on record could be. On the basis of this perception, *Sgt. Pepper* became the catalyst for an explosion of mass enthusiasm for album-formatted rock that would revolutionise [sic] both the aesthetics and the economics of the record business in ways that far outstripped the earlier pop explosions triggered by the Elvis phenomenon of 1956 and the Beatlemania phenomenon of 1963. (p. 418)

Because of the sheer amount of musical diversity on the album, it is difficult to represent an accurate cross-section in two or even three songs. It is strongly suggested that the student experience the album as a whole; however, due to the scope of this book, the following songs are chosen to illustrate at least some of the album's stylistic range:

**Go to Chapter 5 playlist example "Lucy in the Sky with Diamonds" Lennon/McCartney, 1967**

**Go to Chapter 5 playlist example "Within You Without You" George Harrison, 1967**

**Go to Chapter 5 playlist example "A Day in the Life" Lennon/McCartney (w/Martin), 1967**

**Note**: It is important to recognize that there were two albums, both released in 1966, which exerted a heavy influence on The Beatles and George Martin during the making of *Sgt. Pepper's*: Brian Wilson's *Pet Sounds* and Frank Zappa's *Freak Out!* (both of which will be discussed in some detail later in the text). During the *Sgt. Pepper's* sessions, McCartney was known to have repeatedly stated "This is our *Freak Out!*," and George Martin was once quoted as saying "Without *Pet Sounds*, *Sgt. Pepper* never would have happened. ... *Pepper* was an attempt to equal *Pet Sounds*" (Crowe 1997).

In August of 1967, The Beatles were introduced to Maharishi Mahesh Yogi (1918–2008) in London. The Maharishi had developed a school of Transcendental Meditation in India and had become known around the world through his teachings. The Beatles decided to travel to Bangor, Wales for a ten-day meditation retreat, arriving there on August 25. On August 27, the band received a phone call informing them that their manager, Brian Epstein, had died of a drug overdose. This left the band deeply troubled and uncertain of their future. Their initial encounter with Mahesh was thus cut short, and the loss of Epstein as a guiding force in their lives would result in the band traveling to Mahesh's ashram in India for what was to be a three-month meditation retreat in February of 1968 (discussed below).

*Magical Mystery Tour* was released in December 1967 as both a soundtrack EP to the band's film of the same name, and as a compilation LP of the film's songs and nonalbum singles released that year. For our purposes, we will discuss the LP version. Although the film was quite poorly received, the music met with high acclaim. The LP, which was initially released only in the United States, included six new songs from the film, among them "Fool on the Hill" and "I Am the Walrus," and five additional single tracks. Notable among these are "All You Need Is Love," which had been adopted as an unofficial anthem for the Summer of Love's "flower power" movement earlier that year, and "Strawberry Fields Forever," which was actually recorded during the *Sgt. Pepper's* sessions.

**Go to Chapter 5 playlist example "Fool on the Hill" Lennon/McCartney, 1967**

**Go to Chapter 5 playlist example "I Am the Walrus" Lennon/McCartney, 1967**

**Go to Chapter 5 playlist example "All You Need Is Love" Lennon/McCartney, 1967**

**Go to Chapter 5 playlist example "Strawberry Fields Forever" Lennon/McCartney, 1967**

As was mentioned earlier, The Beatles had decided to attend Maharishi Mahesh's three-month guide course to study in depth his methods of Transcendental Meditation. The band and an entourage of wives, girlfriends, assistants, and reporters descended on the Maharishi's ashram in India in February 1968. The Beatles' arrival brought massive media attention and helped to open the Western world to the concept of meditation. Although the period would prove to be one of the most prolific for Lennon, McCartney, and Harrison in terms of songwriting, the retreat itself ended somewhat badly: Starr and his wife would leave after only ten days citing an aversion to insects and food difficulties; McCartney left after one month due to business obligations, although he claimed to have felt renewed by the experience; Lennon and Harrison departed after six weeks disillusioned by reports that the supposedly celibate Maharishi had been making sexual advances to various women at the ashram. Many mixed accounts of the entire affair have surfaced since, and the whole truth of the situation may never be known.

In any case, eighteen of the thirty songs appearing on the band's next recording, the self-titled double length LP *The Beatles*, more commonly known as *The White Album*, were written while in India or in connection with the experience.

The recording sessions for *The White Album* took place from the end of May to mid-October 1968 and were marked by increasing creative and personal tensions among the band and their production crew: Ringo Starr quit the band for about two weeks in August; Martin took a sudden leave of absence; and engineer Geoff Emerick quit the project entirely. This period really was the beginning of the end for The Beatles. Paul McCartney had taken over as the primary creative force and John Lennon seemed to be seriously losing interest in his life as a Beatle: His open disregard for what had been a long-standing band policy of "no girlfriends" in the recording studio was evident as his then-girlfriend Yoko Ono regularly attended the sessions. This created further tensions. Although the album was a commercial success and is widely regarded as a Beatles masterpiece, from this period onward, the band members became increasingly estranged, both creatively and personally.

*The White Album* is arguably the most diverse Beatles album. There are thirty songs which represent the band's enormous musical vocabulary and mastery of the art and craft of songwriting. At the same time the work is much more individualized than any previous recording due to the growing divisions between the band members. The album marks a departure from the highly experimental nature of the three previous albums, possibly reflecting The Beatles' penchant for delivering the unexpected—or possibly showing the fractures within the group. There are, however, songs that are clearly "studio" pieces, and songs that are more traditional rock group pieces, as well as several acoustic ballads. Guest artists on the album include Eric Clapton and Yoko Ono, as well as a host of session musicians. Interestingly, only sixteen of the thirty songs feature all four Beatles performing together.

The following two examples represent two distinct musical styles explored on the album: "Blackbird" is a tender acoustic ballad laden with artful touches such as changing time signatures (a common feature of progressive rock), a gentle percussive sound (reportedly McCartney's foot-tapping) and overdubs of a birdsong. According to McCartney, the music was inspired by J.S. Bach's *Bourrée in E minor*. Lyrically, the song is a metaphor for the civil rights struggles of black Americans in the 1960s. "Revolution 1" is an alternate version of "Revolution," which was released as a single (referenced in Chapter 1). The song is a blues/rock/doo-wop/avant-garde piece laden with a variety of studio effects. Lyrically, it was Lennon's response to several violent political protests that were occurring in various parts of the world in 1968. He appears to have been expressing his uncertainty over the tactics of demonstrators—"but when you talk about destruction, don't you know that you can count me out- in." It also reflects his recent experiences with Transcendental Meditation—"you'd better free your mind instead."

**Go to Chapter 5 playlist example "Blackbird" Paul McCartney, 1968**

**Go to Chapter 5 playlist example "Revolution 1" John Lennon, 1968**

The *Yellow Submarine* album of 1969 was not viewed by the band as an important release, but rather as fulfilling the contractual obligations of providing music for the film of the same name. It includes six Beatles songs, only four of which were new. The remainder of the album consists of orchestral tracks composed by George Martin for the film. While the film itself was a critical and commercial success, the album was generally understood as an accoutrement to the film.

The final two album releases from The Beatles, *Abbey Road* and *Let It Be*, respectively, were not conceived or recorded chronologically. Both albums, although they represent some of the greatest music of the era, were recorded at the lowest point in the band's interpersonal relationships.

*Let It Be*, which was initially titled *Get Back,* was begun in January 1969 and largely finished before *Abbey Road*. The album was originally intended to be performed live with no overdubs and filmed as a television special. McCartney felt that the ill feelings that crept into the *White Album* sessions were due in part to the band's loss of cohesiveness from not rehearsing and performing together as a live act. Hence, the working title *Get Back* signified the band getting back to their roots. The others agreed to this approach. However, as rehearsals and filming began on January 2, 1969, on a sound stage at London's Twickenham Film Studios, the bickering and disagreements soon crept in. The sessions became so unbearable for Harrison that he walked out for five days and upon returning, threatened to leave permanently unless the idea of a live performance was put aside in favor of simply getting the record finished.

At Harrison's behest, the original idea was scrapped and sessions resumed, with subsequent film footage simply documenting the recording process rather than a live performance, at Apple Studios in the Apple Corps building, the location of the recently established headquarters for the band's business operations as well as their own recording facility. The band finally did agree to perform live in order to create a suitable ending for the film. The resulting performance, shot on the rooftop of the Apple Corps building, was the last performance that The Beatles would ever give. The resulting documentary film, more than showcasing the making of a record, effectively shows the band tearing itself apart. The release of the recording went through a period of postponement so that it could coincide with the release of the film, but by then *Abbey Road* had been completed and was released instead. *Get Back* would eventually be remixed by Phil Spector, renamed *Let It Be*, and released as The Beatles' final studio album in May 1970. Less than a month earlier, The Beatles had "officially" broken up when Paul McCartney publicly announced his departure from the band. The break-up had in fact been a gradual process occurring from 1968 to 1970 and involved many factors.

In spite of all of the friction between the band members, whether artistic, personal, or otherwise, their last two albums show no signs of this. Both are cohesive and immaculately produced works of art and have been held up by many critics and publications as ranking among the Beatles' finest works. That these albums demonstrate the full artistic maturity of a band that had repeatedly surpassed their contemporaries is evident.

**Go to Chapter 5 playlist example "Here Comes the Sun" George Harrison, 1969**

**Go to Chapter 5 playlist example "You Never Give Me Your Money" Paul McCartney, 1969**

**Go to Chapter 5 playlist example "The Two of Us" Lennon/McCartney, 1970**

**Go to Chapter 5 playlist example "Across the Universe" John Lennon, 1970**

The Beatles, most notably Lennon and McCartney, would go on to have substantial solo careers. These will be discussed in Chapter 7.

It is nearly impossible to place too much emphasis on the importance of The Beatles. Nearly every development in rock over the next two decades and beyond can be directly or indirectly connected to their work and influence. According to Jonathan Gould:

> The Beatles changed the way people listened to popular music and experienced its role in their lives. From what began as the Beatlemania fad, the group's popularity grew into what was seen as an embodiment of sociocultural movements of the decade. As icons of the 1960s counterculture, they became a catalyst for bohemianism and activism in various social and political arenas, fueling movements such as women's liberation, gay liberation and environmentalism." (pp. 8–9)

## Other Important British Invasion Bands

The runaway popularity of The Beatles in early 1964 fueled American fervor for British music as well as inspiring American bands to adopt the characteristics, musical and otherwise, of their British counterparts. Many British pop bands that followed The Beatles came and went; however, several have had a lasting impact on rock music and culture around the globe. Among the more significant British acts of the 1960s are The Rolling Stones, The Yardbirds, Cream, and The Who. Unlike The Beatles, who evolved from primarily rock 'n' roll and pop roots, these bands were the product of emerging rock sensibilities combined with elements of the blues styles of the Mississippi Delta.

The Merseybeat scene had its counterpart in London, centered in clubs like The London Blues and Barrelhouse Club, The Marquee Club, The Roundhouse Pub, and The Crawdaddy Club. Unlike Merseybeat, the music heard at these spots in London was heavily steeped in the blues of the Mississippi Delta and was nurtured by local blues purists like Alexis Korner and Cyril Davies (who also ran The London Blues and Barrelhouse Club). Having heard Muddy Waters perform in 1958, Korner and Davies formed Blues Incorporated, an electric blues band whose many members would include Jack Bruce and Ginger Baker (Cream) and Charlie Watts (Rolling Stones). Mick Jagger, Keith Richards, and Brian Jones (Rolling Stones), and Jimmy Page (Yardbirds and Led Zeppelin) would also sit in with Blues Incorporated on occasion.

The music that was cultivated in the London blues scene was inspired by not only Muddy Waters' and T-Bone Walker's electric blues style but even more fundamentally by the American bluesmen of an earlier generation, most notably Robert Johnson and Blind Lemon Jefferson. As Campbell and Brody observe:

> The blues revival that paralleled the folk revival of the late fifties and early sixties exposed young rock musicians to the power and emotional depth of **deep blues**. The British musicians who immersed themselves in the blues took from it several of its most distinctive features: the attitude and posturing of the bluesmen, often obvious in its sexual challenge; lyrics that told their stories in plain, direct language, often with a nasty edge (Muddy Water's "I Can't Be Satisfied" and The Rolling Stones' "[I Can't Get No] Satisfaction"); a rough, declamatory vocal style; heavy guitar riffs and string-bending blues-scale guitar solos; a strong beat; and a thick, riff-laden texture. This music is identified variously as **hard rock**, as a hard-rock sub-style, such as **heavy metal** or **southern rock**, or simply as "rock." (p. 201)

## The Rolling Stones

Apart from The Beatles, The Rolling Stones—or The Stones, as they are commonly known—are perhaps the most iconic of the early British Invasion bands, as well as one of the most enduring bands in history. Their career has spanned over half a century and their name has become synonymous with "classic" rock. Originally formed by vocalist **Mick Jagger** (b. 1943), guitarist **Keith Richards** (b. 1943), guitarist **Brian Jones** (1942–1969), and pianist **Ian Stewart** (1938–1985) out of the London blues scene in 1962, the lineup would solidify to include bassist **Bill Wyman** (b. 1936) and drummer **Charlie Watts** (b. 1941) by January 1963. Stewart was removed as a regular member that year but continued to appear on recordings until his death. **Mick Taylor** (b. 1949) would replace Jones from 1969 to 1975 and **Ronnie Wood** (b. 1947) would succeed him.

Originally billed as the "anti-Beatles" in the United Kingdom, The Stones cultivated a "bad boy" image that was in direct contrast to The Beatles. Their look, sound, and demeanor were edgier and grittier than their witty, media-friendly counterparts. International success came for The Stones in 1965 with their hit "(I Can't Get No) Satisfaction," a song which embodies a heavy infusion of the blues as it manifests itself in a rock context.

The song begins with a heavily distorted guitar riff and a free bass line that immediately conveys the sneering bravado of The Stones. The rhythmic texture of the song is dense, complex, and highly syncopated. The drums mark every beat which give the song an intensely aggressive feel, particularly in the context of contemporaneous music. The lyrics are a combination of sexual frustration mixed with a similarly frustrated and cynical view of commercialism. This is angry music.

**Go to Chapter 5 playlist example "(I Can't Get No) Satisfaction" Jagger/Richards, 1965**

Unlike The Beatles, The Stones found their most defining musical characteristics very early in their career. In other words, their signature sound and style was well articulated from 1965 with little attempt at stylistic experimentation. Their single foray into quasi-psychedelia was the 1967 release *Their Satanic Majesties Request*, which came to be regarded by many as a feeble attempt to outdo The Beatles' *Sgt. Pepper's*. Following the negative response, The Stones would return to their blues rock roots with the albums *Beggar's Banquet* in 1968 and *Let It Bleed* in 1969 to finish out the decade on a critical and commercial high note. The Stones would on occasion employ nontraditional or exotic instruments, like dulcimer and marimba in "Under My Thumb" and sitar in "Paint It Black," both from the 1966 album *Aftermath*, though even these songs embody the core elements of rock.

**Go to Chapter 5 playlist example "Under My Thumb" Jagger/Richards, 1966**

**Go to Chapter 5 playlist example "Paint It Black" Jagger/Richards, 1966**

Image 5.6: The Stones in 1967

The Rolling Stones have dealt with more than their fair share of tragedy and controversy: In June of 1969, strained relations with Brian Jones would lead to his departure from the band. He was found dead less than one month later in an apparent drowning. He was 27. In December of 1969, while performing at the now infamous Altamont Free Concert, audience member Meredith Hunter was stabbed to death during a Stones performance. Drugs would haunt the band for decades as well, leading to various arrests, jail sentences, and rehabs. In their career, which has spanned more than fifty years, The Rolling Stones have experienced just about everything a rock band can.

The Stones can claim a virtual catalog of classic rock hits; though arguably, their most important musical work would come between 1968 and 1972 (*Sticky Fingers* in 1971 and *Exile on Main Street* in 1972). They would peak commercially in the late 1970s and early 1980s. Stones concert tours have repeatedly dominated the "highest-grossing" lists thus far in the twenty-first century, often outselling major contemporary stars and large modern festivals.

## The Yardbirds

While The Yardbirds would only achieve modest significance, the group would serve as a training ground for three of Britain's most important and influential guitarists (Eric Clapton, Jeff Beck, and Jimmy Page) and would eventually morph into **Led Zeppelin**, one of the greatest rock acts of all-time. By the time **Eric Clapton** (b. 1945) would join The Yardbirds in 1963, the group had already become the house band at London's Crawdaddy Club where they performed the music of American bluesmen Howlin' Wolf, Muddy Waters, Bo Diddley, Elmore James, and others. Clapton joined vocalist **Keith Relf** (1943–1976), guitarist **Chris Dreja** (b. 1945), bassist **Paul Samwell-Smith** (b. 1943) and drummer **Jim McCarty** (b. 1943). The quintet released two modestly successful blues-influenced singles before scoring a breakthrough hit with their third, the more pop- and British Beat–oriented "For Your Love." Clapton, a blues purist at heart, could not reconcile himself with the new direction the band had taken and left on March 25, 1965, the very same day that the single was released.

Although Clapton would recommend his friend **Jimmy Page** (b. 1944) to serve as his replacement, Page was enjoying a well-paying gig as a studio musician and was disinclined to accept. He in turn recommended **Jeff Beck** (b. 1944), who joined the band and was performing with them within a matter of days. With Beck, The Yardbirds produced a number of hit singles, many of which featured his innovative use of distorted guitar tones and guitar **feedback** as a musical device. (Feedback is the high-pitched squeal that occurs when a sound loop is created between an audio input and an audio output). Beck found that he could control his guitar feedback and use it as a special effect.

In the 1966 Yardbirds hit "Shapes of Things," we hear feedback and distortion effects, lending to its somewhat psychedelic atmosphere, along with several other remarkable characteristics: The song features a lyric that is both pro-environment and antiwar, as well as an early exploration of progressive rock rhythmic structures. The music moves through triplet, eighth note and sixteenth note subdivisions.

**Go to Chapter 5 playlist example "Shapes of Things" The Yardbirds, 1966**

After bassist Paul Samwell-Smith left the band in June 1966, Jimmy Page was asked to replace him until Chris Dreja could comfortably transition to bass. Page would then take Dreja's spot on guitar. This time Page accepted and, in short order, was sharing guitar duties with Jeff Beck. This lineup would only produce a handful of singles as Beck was fired in October for what the other members claimed was his overbearing perfectionism and an unpredictable temperament. The single "Happenings Ten Years Time Ago" is the most substantial product of the short-lived Page–Beck era. This was the first single recorded after Page joined. Dreja appears on the recording as rhythm guitarist, while future Zeppelin bassist John Paul Jones, then a session player, handles the bass part. The composition brings together elements of psychedelic rock and experimental hard rock. The highly dissonant dual guitar solo is its most striking feature.

**Go to Chapter 5 playlist example "Happenings Ten Years Time Ago" The Yardbirds, 1966**

By 1968, The Yardbirds were experiencing a decline in their commercial success as well as a widening gap in the artistic goals of the members. Page wanted to pursue "heavier" music while Keith Relf and Jim McCarty were becoming more interested in classical music and folk. Dreja was more in line with Page's goals but was also developing an interest in photography. The Yardbirds would play their last gig in July 1968. Dreja and Page recruited singer **Robert Plant** (b. 1948) and drummer **John Bonham** (1948–1980) for a project that was to be called The New Yardbirds. Dreja left the band shortly thereafter to pursue photography and was replaced by **John Paul Jones** (b. 1946). The New Yardbirds would change their name to Led Zeppelin before releasing any material. Zeppelin will be discussed in detail in Chapter 7.

## Eric Clapton and Cream

After leaving The Yardbirds, Eric Clapton joined John Mayall & the Bluesbreakers, a band with a constantly evolving lineup that served as a clearinghouse for some of the greatest British musicians of the era, including John McVie, Peter Green, and Mick Fleetwood of Fleetwood Mac; Mick Taylor of The Rolling Stones; and drumming great Aynsley Dunbar. While playing in Mayall's band, Clapton established a reputation as the premier blues guitarist in the British club scene. He left the Bluesbreakers in 1966 to join drummer **Ginger Baker** (b. 1939) and bassist/vocalist **Jack Bruce** (1943–2014) in Baker's newly formed band **Cream**. Baker and Bruce, already well-established musicians themselves, have led many commentators to name Cream as the first supergroup.

The instrumental configuration of Cream formed what came to be known as a **power trio**: guitar, bass, and drums (with one or more of the members assuming vocal duties) which highlight the exceptional skill of the guitarist. In truth, artistically successful power trios also require that the bassist and drummer possess a high level of skill, particularly in a live situation, so that when the guitarist abandons the rhythm part to solo, there is still a substantial musical background to provide support. In studio situations the rhythm guitar is frequently—though not always—dubbed in, creating the illusion of a second guitarist. The fact is that power trios like Cream, and others we will discuss in later chapters, have traditionally showcased some of rock's most virtuosic players.

Cream would go on to record four albums before their breakup in 1969, *Fresh Cream* (1966), *Disraeli Gears* (1967), *Wheels of Fire* (1968), and *Goodbye* (1969). They had a number of radio-friendly studio hits but were best known for their live performances, during which the band would embark upon extended jams which at times exceeded twenty minutes in length and featured Clapton's brilliant soloing. Cream created a successful blend of British psychedelia, American blues, and semiprogressive elements to become one of the most respected bands of the 1960s. Clapton—along with his American counterpart, Jimi Hendrix—were rock's first "guitar gods." Clapton was ever faithful to his blues roots as is evidenced in Cream's remake of the Robert Johnson classic "Crossroads" from *Wheels of Fire*.

**Go to Chapter 5 playlist example "Crossroads" Robert Johnson arr. Cream, 1968**

Eric Clapton went on to play briefly with Blind Faith and Derek and the Dominoes and has since enjoyed a long and varied solo career. He is arguably the "bluesiest" of all of the British blues-based guitarists and is revered for his purity and technical prowess. Clapton is ranked number two on *Rolling Stone* magazine's list of the "100 Greatest Guitarists of All Time" just behind Jimi Hendrix.

Image 5.7: Eric Clapton in 1975

## The Who

The Who were formed in February 1964 by vocalist **Roger Daltrey** (b. 1944), guitarist **Pete Townshend** (b. 1945), and bassist **John Entwistle** (1944–2002) from the ashes of a band called the Detours. They solidified their most classic lineup when they hired drummer **Keith Moon** (1946–1978) later that same year. The band's first hit came in 1965 with the anthemic "My Generation," a song that came to represent the counterculture maxim "don't trust anyone over 30." The lyric is considered to be one of the most concentrated expressions of youthful rebellion in the history of rock. The song reflects a blues sensibility most clearly in the call and response technique of the verse:

People try to put us d-down (Talkin' 'bout my generation)

Just because we g-g-get around (Talkin' 'bout my generation)

Things they do look awful c-c-cold (Talkin' 'bout my generation)

I hope I die before I get old (Talkin' 'bout my generation)

**Go to Chapter 5 playlist example "My Generation" The Who, 1965**

The Who became well known for extremely loud, aggressive live shows during which guitars were smashed and drums were kicked off of the riser. They were also one of the first major rock acts to make use of emerging synthesizer technology, both on recordings and in live performance. The band, particularly Moon, acquired a reputation for debauched off-stage behavior as well, such as destroying hotel rooms, blowing up toilets and embracing a high-paced, drug-fueled lifestyle (sadly, Moon would die of a drug overdose in 1978 at the age of thirty-two).

Released in 1967, the band's third album, *The Who Sell Out*, a concept album on which a collection of unrelated songs are linked together by mock advertisements interspersed throughout the record, met with critical acclaim and commercial success. Up to this point they had been considered a "singles" band. With this release, Townshend declared The Who to be a "pop art" band stating that they therefore viewed advertising as an art form. This was understood by many as an ironic response to the counterculture's anticonsumerist philosophy. In addition to its display of expert musicianship, the album was praised for its exquisite humor, which was based on how "pop" the psychedelic era had become. *The Who Sell Out* has also been viewed as prophetic in light of the massive commercialism that has come to dictate the music industry.

The Who's most significant artistic contribution to rock would come in 1969 with the double-length LP *Tommy*, the first album to be billed as a **rock opera**. While the music is clearly rooted in the rock aesthetic, it is not an "opera" in any strict formal sense; rather, it is an opera in name only. The music connects with the story itself in terms of the structure and pacing of the songs: There is no adherence to standard conventions of form or length; there are songs as brief as twelve seconds and songs that exceed ten minutes in length. Like opera, *Tommy* is designed to be performed live. There is a very limited use of any non-rock instruments, and these are all handled by the band members in performance. Campbell and Brody write:

> Musically, what's remarkable about Tommy is not so much the fact that The Who make an artistic statement but *how* they make it. Unlike The Beatles and so many of those who followed in their footsteps, The Who didn't abandon their rock roots, or at least overlay them with classical music trappings. There are no strings, no synthesizers, and no other classical music features associated with so much of the art rock of the period. (p. 261)

*Tommy* has been hailed by many critics and commentators as one of the most effective artistic endeavors of the 1960s and as one of the first successful extended statements in rock. The work was made into film in 1975 (with appearances by Elton John, Tina Turner, Eric Clapton, and Jack Nicholson) and has been adapted and performed by countless Broadway and off-Broadway companies, orchestras, and other musical theater groups. The following examples demonstrate the contrast between songs of extreme brevity and those of a more epic nature:

**Go to Chapter 5 playlist example "Miracle Cure" The Who, 1969**

**Go to Chapter 5 playlist example "We're Not Gonna Take It/See Me, Feel Me" The Who, 1969**

**Image 5.8: The Who after a 1975 performance**

The impact of the British Invasion on American music was profound and lasting. Many permanent musical changes occurred as a direct result of the artistry and self-expression of The Beatles and the British bands that followed. The cultural interconnections of British and American rock and pop remain strong to this day (Mark Ronson, Adele, Ed Sheeran, and Sam Smith stand as a testament to this). Moreover, the era marked the first truly global music culture, much of it dominated by the ideals of an increasingly aware and educated youth population with a deep commitment to itself and a sturdy resolve to control its own destiny. From 1964, rock became the soundtrack, the common ground, the quintessence of a worldwide cultural revolution.

We now turn to American rock as it evolved after the British Invasion.

## Suggested Chapter Related Activities

- Select several Beatles songs from the chapter that are not analyzed in detail. Look for relationships between the music and lyrics. Analyze the forms, rhythmic structures, instrumentation, etc.

- See if you can find a post-2000 song that employs text painting in the way that "Eleanor Rigby" or "Tomorrow Never Knows" does.

- There are many veiled references to drugs in The Beatles' lyrics. Can you find post-2000 examples of a song(s) that refer to drugs in a similar way?

- Listen to Robert Johnson's "Cross Road Blues" and Clapton's "Crossroads." Make a list of the musical similarities as well as the contrasts.

- Listen to "My Generation" and make a list of all of the song's elements that stem directly from the blues. Also, find a post-2000 song that expresses a similar lyric idea regarding modern youth culture.

## Suggested Discussion Topics

- Discuss Lennon's "Jesus Controversy" and speculate how such a comment might be received today.

- The Beatles music, especially after 1965, was both challenging and entertaining, and pushed the boundaries of rock out in every direction. Much of it was central to the earliest self-conscious expression of postmodern ideals in rock as well. Modern popular music seems to be less challenging, in general, both in musical substance and lyrics. Do you see this as a shortcoming? Does the responsibility for this fall on the listener or the musician? If you disagree with this statement, can you give examples of music/lyrics to disprove it?

## Image Credits

Image 5.1: Mahlum, https://commons.wikimedia.org/wiki/File:Abbey_Road_Studios_London.jpg, 2007. Copyright in the Public Domain.

Image 5.2: https://commons.wikimedia.org/wiki/File:The_Beatles_in_America.JPG, 1964. Copyright in the Public Domain.

Michael Campbell and James Brody, Rock and Roll: An Introduction, pp. 162, 172, 201, 261. Copyright © 2008 by Cengage Learning, Inc. Reprinted with permission.

Image 5.3: Michael Ochs, http://www.gettyimages.com/license/73906750. Copyright © 1965 by Michael Ochs Archives/Getty Images.

Image 5.4: The Beatles/Robert Whitaker, Yesterday and Today. Copyright © 1966 by Apple Corps, Ltd.

Image 5.5: Copyright © Tom Swain (CC BY-SA 3.0) at https://commons.wikimedia.org/wiki/File:Abbeyroadtomswain.jpg.

Image 5.6: Copyright © Ben Merk (CC BY-SA 3.0) at https://commons.wikimedia.org/wiki/File:Stones1967BenMerk_Detail.png.

Image 5.7: Copyright © Matt Gibbons (CC by 2.0) at https://commons.wikimedia.org/wiki/File:Eric-Clapton_1975.jpg.

Image 5.8: Copyright © Jim Summaria (CC BY-SA 3.0) at https://commons.wikimedia.org/wiki/File:Who_-_1975.jpg.

# CHAPTER 6

# American Rock from 1964–1969

*Strange days have found us.*
-Jim Morrison of The Doors

## Cultural Context

Among the most significant cultural developments of the mid- to late 1960s was the so-called **counterculture**, a multifaceted and highly nuanced social phenomenon rooted largely in political and social **activism** as well as the embracing of alternative, "nontraditional" lifestyles. Various social movements began to grow in earnest during the period just after the assassination of John Kennedy, inspired and empowered by the progress of the African-American Civil Rights Movement, sharply at odds with the escalation of the war in Vietnam, and no longer willing to accept the worldview of the "establishment." Within the larger culture were smaller, independent groups who championed a number of causes. These included but were not limited to human rights, free speech, antiwar and antinuclear, feminism, environmentalism, gay rights, sexual liberation (including birth control, sex outside of traditional heterosexual, monogamous relationships and legalized abortion), recreational drug use, and drug use as a consciousness-raising activity.

While it is an oversimplification to think of the counterculture as a specific group of people with a well-organized hierarchy and a clearly articulated agenda, the counterculture was mainly youth driven. The middle-class baby boom generation had come of age; they had more education, more affluence, and more social awareness than the generation of their parents, many of whom by stark contrast had grown up during the Depression Era and WWII. These were the children of rock 'n' roll; many had been steeled by witnessing their older siblings rebel against the values and practices of their parents in the late 1950s. Now, the awareness that their world could be different was more clearly defined; the postmodernist philosophies that had previously been the precinct of academics were filtering into mainstream consciousness, as were the radical notions of the Beat poets. These young people chose creativity over dogma, free thinking over indoctrination, and innovation over tradition; and in the main, rejected corporate capitalism and consumerism.

Organized activities such as rallies, boycotts, marches, sit-ins, and walk-outs, held in the spirit of challenging authority, occurred frequently during the era. These were often countered with arrests and violent opposition from law enforcement and the military; pepper spray and billy clubs were regularly used to intimidate and control protestors. Movements and gatherings, most particularly those in protest of the Vietnam War, were often portrayed in a negative light by the mainstream media. The Johnson administration was known to have deployed undercover agents to infiltrate and surveil activist groups in an effort to gain intelligence that could be used against them. There were even reasonable suspicions that government infiltrators were instructed to commit provocative acts toward security forces in order to justify the use of violence against protestors. In any event, tense situations occasionally erupted into riots or worse.

On May 4, 1970, at Kent State University in Ohio, four college students were killed and nine others wounded—one of whom was left paralyzed—when US Army National Guardsmen opened fire on a group of unarmed protestors. Sixty-seven shots were fired during a thirteen-second period. In the image below, photojournalism student John Filo captured Mary Ann Vecchio as she kneels next to her classmate Jeffrey Miller moments after he was killed. The photograph won a Pulitzer Prize and helped bring attention to the incident. Eleven days later, police at Jackson State University in Jackson, Mississippi, opened fire on a group of unarmed students, killing two and wounding twelve more. Despite a massive public outcry, no criminal convictions were obtained against any of the guardsmen or police involved. Many musicians penned songs in tribute to those killed in the massacre, most notably Neil Young ("Ohio") and Steve Miller ("Jackson-Kent Blues").

Before 1964 activist folk music, most notably that of Bob Dylan, was speaking to the burgeon-ing counterculture mindset; and by 1965 (the year Dylan went electric) rock musicians, primarily influenced by The Beatles, jumped into the fray—acting as a unifying force, lending a strong sense of identity, and emboldening acts of protest and civil disobedience. Music was central to the counterculture. It gave voice to many contemporary concerns and causes. **Psychedelic** or **acid** rock frequently spoke directly to the experimentation with and glorification of drug use while folk rock and other forms of rock often laid bare social problems such as inequality based on class, race, and gender. Much of the music of the period dealt with war and peace, corruption in government and politics, environmental concerns, sexual expression, and antiauthoritarian themes. In addition to music, the counterculture expressed itself through art, literature (both prose and poetry), film, theater, Eastern philosophies, and spiritual practices, dress, hairstyles, jargon, and even alternative forms of sport such as Frisbee.

While many rock musicians acted as unofficial spokespersons for the counterculture, there were also a number of prominent figures who promoted alternative ideas and lifestyles within the larger social context. **Timothy Leary,** a psychologist, author, and Harvard professor advocated the use of

LSD and other psychoactive drugs as therapeutic tools for treating alcoholism and criminal behavior. Leary often appeared as a lecturer and on television. He coined and popularized the counterculture philosophical catchphrases "tune in, turn on and drop out" and "think for yourself and question authority." **Ken Kesey,** an author and activist who had his first exposure to psychoactive drugs as a volunteer test subject in the CIA's MK-ULTRA project, a highly secret series of experiments to test the effects of drugs as a mind-control agent, became the leader of a group called the Merry Pranksters. Kesey and the Pranksters traveled around the United States in a bus making art out of everyday objects and experiencing life on the American road while high on LSD. His experiences as a test subject inspired his famous book *One Flew Over the Cuckoo's Nest.* **Allen Ginsberg,** famed Beat poet and author was involved in countless movements regarding human rights and personal freedoms. His 1955 epic poem "Howl" was the subject of an obscenity trial in 1957. Ginsberg scored a major victory for free speech when the courts ruled in his favor. Throughout the 1960s, he worked with and drew inspiration from Paul McCartney, Bob Dylan, Phil Ochs, and other notable rock and folk musicians. Other prominent figures involved in countercultural activism are too numerous to list but included media personalities, comedians, actors, consumer advocates, professors, and philosophers.

The enduring effects of the counterculture era—both the intended and unintended—are still debated in academia and among social scientists, philosophers, activists, artists, and others. There are various arguments presented in favor of and against the changes in general society since the end of the 1960s. However one chooses to interpret the history, the fact is clear that it was a time of great expansion in terms of social awareness; post-1970 mainstream culture has been profoundly shaped by counterculture ideals, ideals that continue to shape art, music, literature, and film, as well as political and social movements and attitudes toward human rights.

## Folk Rock

The combined force of Bob Dylan's folk music and The Beatles' rock music in the mid-1960s helped to inspire a hybrid genre known as **folk rock**, a stylistic fusion which grew rapidly and exerted an immense influence on rock and popular music for decades. Folk rock would become central in the late 1960s as an expressive vehicle for many countercultural beliefs. In April 1965, a Los Angeles–based rock group called The Byrds recorded and released an electrified cover version of Bob Dylan's folk song "Mr. Tambourine Man." Their version reached number one in both the United States and the United Kingdom and led the music press to coin the term folk rock. The Byrds' version was released amid Dylan's transitional period between folk music and rock music: less than a month earlier Dylan released his pivotal album *Bringing It All Back Home* (discussed below) which contained the acoustic version of "Mr. Tambourine Man."

In Dylan's original version of "Mr. Tambourine Man," the lyrics have been variously interpreted as a reference to drugs (one which Dylan himself denied), transcendental states of consciousness, and as a metaphorical call to the creative muse. In any case, the language evokes impressionistic fantasies and surreal imagery with phrases like "take me on a trip upon your magic swirling ship" and "take me disappearing through the smoke rings of my mind, down the foggy winds of time."

A comparison of both versions reveals The Byrds' more commercial approach in the overall form of the song as well as its more radio-friendly length; Dylan's version is more than five minutes long with four verses, the cover is less than three minutes with only one verse.

**Go to Chapter 6 playlist example "Mr. Tambourine Man" Bob Dylan, 1965**

**Go to Chapter 6 playlist example "Mr. Tambourine Man" arr. The Byrds, 1965**

A profusion of folk rock acts followed in the wake of The Byrds' success: Simon & Garfunkel, The Mamas & the Papas, The Lovin' Spoonful, and The Youngbloods, to name a few. Their lyrics were often humanistic and appealed to the emerging counterculture's ideals of peace, universal love, and global awareness. Many folk rock songs became vehicles for voicing growing concerns over the Vietnam War while others posited "radical" views regarding anti-consumerism and communal living.

**Go to Chapter 6 playlist example "Get Together" The Youngbloods, 1967**

## Dylan Rocks

Moved by his admiration for The Beatles, his apparent disillusionment with the folk scene and the commercial success that more pop/rock oriented musicians had in covering his songs (recall Peter, Paul and Mary), Bob Dylan made a move that would have significant consequences in the world of rock and popular music. He had already begun to shift away from the topical lyrics of his first recordings and into songs of a more personal nature with his 1964 album *Another Side of Bob Dylan*. *Bringing It All Back Home*, released in March, 1965, marks the moment of transition between Bob Dylan the folk singer and Bob Dylan the rock star. The album is half acoustic, half electric. John Covach and Andrew Flory write:

> Dylan's interest in rock instrumentation was also evident on his album *Bringing It All Back Home*, half of which used electric instruments, including his first hit single, "Subterranean Homesick Blues." The folk community did not express an overwhelmingly negative reaction to Dylan's electrified music when the album was released perhaps because of the strong acoustic-based material. However, when he played the Newport Folk Festival in July 1965 an enormous controversy began. As a headliner, Dylan was one of the most sought after artists at the festival. The festival program only allotted Dylan a short set, and he performed three electric numbers ("Maggie's Farm," "Like a Rolling Stone," and "Phantom Engineer") backed by the Paul Butterfield Blues Band. When he left the stage after only a few songs, the crowd heckled Master of Ceremonies Peter Yarrow (of Peter,

Paul and Mary) until Dylan came back out. As an encore, Dylan performed acoustic versions of "Mr. Tambourine Man" and "It's All Over Now Baby Blue." Despite the positive reaction to his acoustic material, Dylan's electric numbers met with resistance among the more traditionally minded folkies in attendance. Many senior members of the folk establishment who had strongly supported Dylan up to this point (including Pete Seeger) felt betrayed by his turn to electric instruments. Dylan's insistence upon performing nontopical material with a rock band made him the target of very strong criticism within folk circles.[1] (p. 195)

**Go to Chapter 6 playlist example "Subterranean Homesick Blues" Bob Dylan, 1965**

Bob Dylan would not return to folk music; from 1965 on he was a rock musician. His next recording effort, *Highway 61 Revisited*, released in the summer of 1965, marked Dylan's full transformation to the world of rock, a seamless transformation which attested to his remarkable skills as a songwriter and lyricist. Dylan's new musical approach included a full rock band with keyboards and harmonica and opened up to include a hearty mix of blues, rock, honky-tonk, garage, and pop, in the matchless and arresting Dylan fashion; the single exception being "Desolation Row," the eleven-and-a-half minute epic acoustic ballad that closes the album. The opening track, "Like a Rolling Stone," became a global hit. In style and structure, it unapologetically cut through the all of the preexisting boundaries of the conventional rock song. Michael Campbell and James Brody describe it thusly:

> Mind-expanding rock: in subject and style, Dylan's lyric obliterated the conventions of pop and rock before June 16, 1965 (the date of the recording). The lyrics were provocative, not pleasant. They challenged the listeners to think, then feel. They were *cinema vérité*, rather than beach movies or James Bond. By integrating such thought-provoking lyrics into a rock song, *and* scoring big with it, Dylan essentially freed rock from its self-imposed limitations. After songs like this, rock could be anything; it could say anything, as The Beatles and others would soon prove.[2] (p. 166)

In 2010, "Like a Rolling Stone" was named number one on *Rolling Stone* magazine's "500 Greatest Songs of All Time" list.

**Go to Chapter 6 playlist example "Like a Rolling Stone" Bob Dylan, 1965**

---

1   John Covach and Andrew Flory, What's That Sound?: An Introduction to Rock and Its History, pp. 195. Copyright © 2012 by W. W. Norton & Company, Inc. Reprinted with permission.
2   Michael Campbell and James Brody, Rock and Roll: An Introduction, pp. 166, 229. Copyright © 2008 by Cengage Learning, Inc. Reprinted with permission.

Although Bob Dylan's career has endured for more than five decades, his most important work would arguably occur before the 1960s ended. The two albums that followed *Highway 61 Revisited*, *Blonde on Blonde* (1966) and *John Wesley Harding* (1967), both represent further dramatic shifts in tone and character. *Blonde on Blonde* has been regarded by many critics and commentators as the last installment in the trilogy of records that started with *Bringing It All Back Home* and Dylan's pinnacle of expression as a visionary rock poet, merging blues and rock roots with postmodernist literary devices. *John Wesley Harding*, with its self-consciously rustic musical approach and enigmatic lyrics, was regarded as reactionary in the midst of the psychedelic era of the late 1960s.

While these recordings only represent a small cross-section of the albums as a whole, each helps to illustrate the points above:

**Go to Chapter 6 playlist example "Desolation Row'" Bob Dylan, 1965**

**Go to Chapter 6 playlist example "Ballad of a Thin Man" Bob Dylan, 1965**

**Go to Chapter 6 playlist example "Rainy Day Women #12 & 35" Bob Dylan, 1966**

**Go to Chapter 6 playlist example "Pledging My Time" Bob Dylan, 1966**

## Brian Wilson's Pet Sounds and Good Vibrations

Released in May 1966, The Beach Boys' album *Pet Sounds* is perhaps best understood as a Brian Wilson solo project. He was the guiding force in virtually every aspect of the album's creation and recording. In every way, Wilson was exploring uncharted territory in rock and pop music. The album has been called the first psychedelic rock masterpiece and is known to have deeply affected the music and recording techniques of The Beatles from *Revolver* on. *Pet Sounds*, along with *Rubber Soul*, *Revolver*, and the folk movement have been credited with generating the greater part of the development of post-1965 rock music. *Pet Sounds* was noted by many critics as the recording that helped rock to snowball into a self-conscious art form. In that the songs are thematically linked, it can be viewed as the first rock concept album although Wilson has repeatedly claimed that it was not meant to be taken as a conceptually linked narrative. Be that as it may, it is clearly one of the earliest, if not *the* earliest example of progressive rock. Innovations in harmony, form, and instrumentation as well as advanced recording techniques are evident throughout.

A sampling of music from *Pet Sounds* demonstrates the radical departure from pre-1965 pop rock:

**Go to Chapter 6 playlist example "Wouldn't It Be Nice" Beach Boys, 1966**

**Go to Chapter 6 playlist example "I Just Wasn't Made for These Times" Beach Boys, 1966**

While *Pet Sounds* was well received in the United Kingdom, it was not nearly as commercially successful in the United States as earlier Beach Boys music had been. The band's shift toward psychedelic sonic landscapes would garner mass praise in October 1966 with the release of the landmark single "Good Vibrations." The song was an immediate commercial and critical success in the United States and abroad and became the band's first million-selling single.

Initially begun as part of the *Pet Sounds* project, "Good Vibrations" was ultimately not included as part of the album. The recording of the song was completed in multiple stages throughout the summer of 1966, involving more than a dozen sessions done in four separate studios. It is considered to be the single most influential recording in establishing the recording studio as an instrument unto itself. The cost of recording the single relative to today would be nearly half a million dollars, an unheard-of amount.

The progressive treatment of form is evident in the six distinct sections of the composition. A verse/chorus opening is followed by two completely contrasting episodic departures which lead back to a restatement of the chorus and finally to an unanticipated coda (closing) section. The instrumentation and texture vary dramatically from section to section. Moreover, the use of standard and nonstandard rock instruments and complex vocal arrangements lend to a richly diverse sound world. The use of the Electro-Theremin pointed the way toward early synthesizers. The song's lyrics, partially written by Beach Boy Mike Love, spoke directly to the "Flower Power" movement within the larger counterculture. In short, this song is the first of its kind, and the antithesis of pop music of the time. It ultimately caused many listeners and critics to reconsider *Pet Sounds*.

**Go to Chapter 6 playlist example "Good Vibrations" Brian Wilson w/Mike Love, 1966**

Table 6.1: Form of "Good Vibrations"

> Verse 1 (:00–:25) "I … I love the colorful clothes she wears…"
>
> Chorus (:26–:50) "I'm pickin' up good vibrations…"
>
> Verse 2 (:51–1:16) "Close my eyes, she's somehow closer now…"
>
> Chorus (1:17–1:41) "I'm pickin' up good vibrations…"
>
> Departure 1 (1:42–2:13) "Exci … tations…"
>
> Departure 2 (2:14–2:56) "Gotta keep those love good vibrations … AAAHHH"
>
> Chorus (2:57–3:12) "Good, good, good, good vibrations…"
>
> Coda (3:13–end) "Na na na na na, na na na…"

## Frank Zappa

No musician we will discuss throughout this book was as diverse or prolific as **Frank Zappa** (1940–1993). He was, in fact, one of the most productive artists of *any* type in the entire twentieth century. In addition to recording and releasing more than sixty albums during his lifetime (plus forty posthumous releases by the Zappa Family Trust) ranging from rock to orchestral to jazz fusion to electronic music to avant-garde and beyond, Zappa acted in and directed films and videos, produced music, and was a successful author and businessman. He was one of the twentieth century's great iconoclasts; he was an active social and political commentator who was fearless in his criticism of mainstream education, organized religion (he described his own religion as "musician"), and in his lifelong fight against censorship. He was passionately antiauthoritarian and a staunch advocate of political participation. Although his commercial success in music was limited, he built a relatively small but devoted following and earned the admiration and respect of musicians to an almost universal degree. Zappa was a brilliant satirist, a gifted guitar virtuoso, an electronics wizard, and a musical pioneer of the highest order.

Zappa's 1966 debut album *Freak Out!* with his band, **The Mothers of Invention**, was a satirical exposition of American pop music and culture. The album was far more experimental than any other rock album of its time. The album was neither commercially nor critically successful in the United States but was well received in Europe; it instantly established Zappa as rock's eccentric genius. It is also considered to be rock's first concept album. A track called "Who Are the Brain Police?" illustrates the highly unusual nature of the record.

**Go to Chapter 6 playlist example "Who Are the Brain Police" Frank Zappa, 1966**

Image 6.2: Zappa performing in Norway, 1977

Zappa's political battles were many. During the 1980s, in performances, on recordings, and in interviews and televised debates, he outwardly opposed the policies of the Republican Party and the Reagan Administration including the War on Drugs (although he actually disapproved of drug use), the Strategic Defense Initiative, and he warned that the US government was at risk of becoming a "fascist theocracy" (an occurrence which many would now argue has come to pass). Along with musicians John Denver and Dee Snider of the band Twisted Sister, Zappa testified in front of the Senate in 1985 in a battle against the Parents Music Resource Center (PMRC) over the application of a proposed rating system for recorded music containing explicitly "sexual" or "satanic" song lyrics. Zappa encouraged his fans and audiences to vote; he went as far as having voter registration booths set up at his concerts. In the late 1980s Zappa even considered a bid for the office of President of the United States.

Although Zappa died of prostate cancer more than two decades ago, his musical legacy is still being sorted out. A diverse array of rock artists (including Zappa's son, Dweezil) classical ensembles, bands, and chamber groups around the world regularly perform his music. Academic music theorists and scholars regularly attempt to define and analyze his works in theses, dissertations, and journal articles and no doubt will continue to do so for some time to come.

It is impossible to even approach a fair representation of Zappa's music in a few samples; students are strongly encouraged to explore his vast output on their own. Zappa's excellent official autobiography *The Real Frank Zappa Book* is also highly recommended reading for the interested fan and/or scholar.

From the 1970 release *Weasels Ripped My Flesh* highlighting Zappa's guitar prowess:

**Go to Chapter 6 playlist example "My Guitar Wants to Kill Your Mama" Frank Zappa, 1970**

From the 1979 live album *Sheik Yerbouti*, this track, recorded live in 1978 in London, is a satirical portrayal of 1970s disco culture:

**Go to Chapter 6 playlist example "Dancin' Fool" Frank Zappa, 1979**

From an album trilogy comprised of *Shut Up 'n Play Yer Guitar*, *Shut Up 'n Play Yer Guitar Some More* and *Return of the Son of Shut Up 'n Play Yer Guitar*, this seven-minute instrumental jam features Zappa at his finest:

**Go to Chapter 6 playlist example "Shut Up 'n Play Yer Guitar Some More" Frank Zappa, 1981**

## Jim Morrison and The Doors

Formed in 1965 in Los Angeles, The Doors represent a unique conception of a counterculture-era rock band. Comprised of a classically trained pianist; a flamenco-style guitarist; a jazz drummer; and a self-styled poet with an explosive personality, a proclivity for obscure literature, an existentialist philosophy, and a voracious appetite for drugs and alcohol, The Doors' music is a concoction of psychedelic art rock, pop, blues, and sophisticated—often very dark—lyrics. The band's name was inspired by the Aldous Huxley novel, *The Doors of Perception*, and the quote by William Blake therein: "When the doors of perception are cleansed, everything will appear to man as it is, infinite."

Vocalist **Jim Morrison** (1943–1971) and keyboardist **Ray Manzarek** (1939–2013) had known each other casually during their time as students at UCLA, where they both majored in film studies. The Doors began after a chance encounter between Morrison and Manzarek occurred on Venice Beach in the summer of 1965. After discussing some lyrics Morrison had been working on, the two decided to form a band and write songs together. By midyear the lineup was completed to include drummer **John Densmore** (b. 1944) and guitarist **Robbie Krieger** (b. 1946). Oddly, The Doors worked without a bass player; in live performance, Manzarek would play "bass lines" in the lower register of the keyboard although the band did hire studio bass players on occasion to record with them.

After a period of honing their skills in lesser venues of Los Angeles club scene, The Doors were hired as the house band at the famous Sunset Strip venue, the Whisky a Go Go in the summer of 1966. It was there that the band was noticed by Elektra Records' president, Jac Holzman, and producer Paul Rothchild and offered a recording contract. Several days after signing, in a now infamous incident, The Doors were fired from the Whisky after Morrison broke into an alcohol-fueled, profanity-laced account of the Greek tale of Oedipus during a performance of the band's song "The End" in which he was reported to have writhed around on the stage repeating the phrase "Mother, I want to fuck you!" This would be the first in a series of on-and-off stage episodes that would cause serious grief for the band, yet would eventually propel Morrison into the realm of rock mythology.

The Doors' self-titled debut album was recorded soon after the incident. Produced by Rothchild, engineered by Bruce Botnick, and released in January 1967, it resulted in the band's commercial breakthrough single "Light My Fire," as well as climbing to number two in the album charts that year. *The Doors* has been lauded as one of the greatest rock albums, and is certainly one of the greatest debut albums of all time. It is an essential fusion of rock, jazz, blues, classical, psychedelia, and stunning poetry. A representative sampling reveals all of these elements as well as the band's capacity for epic, improvisatory forms of musical expression as witnessed in "The End."

**Go to Chapter 6 playlist example "Soul Kitchen" The Doors, 1967**

**Go to Chapter 6 playlist example "The Crystal Ship" The Doors, 1967**

**Go to Chapter 6 playlist example "The End" The Doors, 1967**

Although The Doors' music was embraced by various counterculture groups, Morrison's lyrics often expressed concepts and imagery that were sharply at odds with counterculture ideologies; Morrison harbored a fascination with alienation, violence, insanity, and death which he often expressed in his lyrics and poetry. "The End" is an obvious example of this. However, more subtle references to these recurring themes appear throughout his lyrics. The song "Moonlight Drive" from the band's second album, *Strange Days* (1967), suggests a drowning incident as two young lovers take a nighttime swim in the ocean; while the highly dissonant spoken-word piece "Horse Latitudes" paints a haunting picture of horses being jettisoned to their deaths from a ship at sea in order to lighten the ship's load. Many metaphorical interpretations of this song have been put forth; none were ever confirmed or denied by Morrison or any of the other members of the band.

**Go to Chapter 6 playlist example "Moonlight Drive" The Doors, 1967**

**Go to Chapter 6 playlist example "Horse Latitudes" The Doors, 1967**

Converse to Morrison's darker themes, the counterculture had much to connect to in his lyrics. 1968 saw the release of the band's third LP offering, *Waiting for the Sun*. It featured two songs which tied in strongly to the protest movement, although not without Morrison's characteristic dark edge; "Five to One" and "The Unknown Soldier" are both graphic musical portrayals of antiestablishment, antiwar sentiments that verge on militancy in their intrinsic antagonism and musical aggressiveness.

**Go to Chapter 6 playlist example "Five to One" The Doors, 1968**

**Go to Chapter 6 playlist example "The Unknown Soldier" The Doors, 1968**

The Doors' fourth album, *The Soft Parade*, released in 1969, was the first to meet with tepid reviews from mainstream rock critics; although it received a fair amount of praise from jazz critics for its experimentation and was commercially successful as well. This album marked the first time that individual members were given songwriting credits. This was believed to have stemmed from Morrison's desire to distance himself from Krieger's revolution-themed lyrics in the song "Tell All the People." There was a notable departure from the established Doors sound but it did contain a smattering of the band's more familiar flavors, as evidenced in the track "Wild Child."

**Go to Chapter 6 playlist example "Wild Child" Jim Morrison, 1969**

*Morrison Hotel*, released in 1970, saw The Doors returning to a more hard rock– and blues-based approach. Critical acclaim for the album was immense, with many critics calling it a "comeback" album following the experimental nature and lukewarm reception of *The Soft Parade*. One of the more remarkable songs on the album is "Peace Frog," a funk rock piece which is built of several distinct **sixteenth note layer** riffs piled on top of each other. The music was recorded before Morrison had decided on any lyrics. He eventually chose a piece of poetry from a collection he had written called "Abortion Stories." In the interlude of the song, Morrison reverts to a spoken word approach that describes an experience he claimed to have had as a child; while traveling with his family through the desert, they came upon the scene of an accident involving Native Americans:

"Indians scattered on dawn's highway bleeding … ghosts crowd the young child's fragile eggshell mind." Morrison claims that it was his first real taste of fear. Nearly every line in the song begins with the word "blood."

**Go to Chapter 6 playlist example "Peace Frog" Morrison/Krieger, 1970**

April 1971's *L.A. Woman*, the band's sixth full-length album, would be the last Morrison would record before his death in Paris three months later at the age of twenty-seven. Despite the fact that tensions in the studio reached such a pitch that producer Paul Rothchild quit the project in midsession, the album, along with their 1967 debut, is considered to be the best work the band ever produced. *L.A. Woman* contains rock radio staples including the title track, "Love Her Madly," and one of The Doors' best-loved compositions, "Riders on the Storm." The song is written in **dorian mode** giving it a somber feel and bleak overall character. Manzarek's descending keyboard runs emulate and connect with the sounds of rain and thunder which are dubbed into the song at various points. It is basically a modified verse/chorus form with extended instrumental solos. Even with the extended instrumental sections, Morrison's dark lyrics and haunting delivery dominate the song. The first two verses create a disjointed narrative although each relates its own clear idea:

*Riders on the storm*
*Riders on the storm*
*Into this house we're born*
*Into this world we're thrown*
*Like a dog without a bone*
*An actor out on loan*
*Riders on the storm*
*There's a killer on the road*
*His brain is squirmin' like a toad*
*Take a long holiday*
*Let your children play*
*If you give this man a ride*
*Sweet family will die*
*Killer on the road*

**Go to Chapter 6 playlist example "Riders on the Storm" The Doors, 1971**

The potency of the first verse is in its metaphorical depth, whereas the power of the second verse lies in what is not overtly stated: we never know if the driver stopped or passed the killer by.

On July 3, 1971, Jim Morrison was found dead in the bathtub of his Paris hotel room of what is now generally believed to be a drug and alcohol overdose. No autopsy was ever performed since there was no evidence of foul play. On that day, he became the third major music star to join the ranks of the "27 Club" within a single year; Jimi Hendrix and Janis Joplin both preceded him in 1970 in their own drug- and alcohol-related deaths. It was a dark period for rock music with three of its brightest stars snuffed out in their prime and in rapid succession.

Morrison had in fact been on a long, slow downhill slide since the band's debut. His drug and alcohol consumption had become almost legendary, nearly tearing the band apart several different times. Adding to a generally tense situation, Morrison had a number of run-ins with the law between 1967 and 1969:

Image 6.3: The Doors

In 1967 in New Haven, Connecticut, he was arrested while performing following an incident backstage in which he was attacked with mace by a police officer; the officer came upon Morrison and a female fan, and not realizing Morrison had every right to be in the restricted area, threatened the singer and his companion. When Morrison tried to explain to the officer who he was, it fell on deaf ears and the attack ensued. After recovering from the effects of the mace, Morrison took the stage and began describing what had just occurred as well as taunting the police who were alongside the stage area. After a profanity-laced tirade, Morrison was dragged off the stage by the police and booked on charges of inciting a riot, among others. He was acquitted several weeks later due to lack of evidence. It did not end there. During the band's 1968 tour, Morrison's performances frequently whipped audiences into a frenzy; there were several instances where tensions between fans and police rose to a fever pitch adding to the growing reputation of Morrison's controversial stage antics. In March 1969, he landed in more trouble. During a performance in Florida, Morrison, who had been drinking heavily all day, was accused of and arrested for allegedly exposing himself to the audience after he halted a performance of the song "Touch Me." He had been antagonizing the crowd (many believe as a personal experiment in mass behavior manipulation), when a fan took to the stage and poured champagne on the singer. Morrison removed his wet shirt and yelled to the audience "Let's get naked!" Morrison then allegedly put his shirt in front of his groin and began making gestures that simulated masturbation. Four days later, a warrant was issued for the singer's arrest citing several serious charges relating to the incident including indecent exposure and public drunkenness. He was later tried, convicted, and sentenced to six months' hard labor. He was free, pending an appeal when he died. In 2010, Morrison was posthumously pardoned.

For several years after Morrison's death, the other band members tried to carry on with The Doors, but to little avail. His charisma and towering musical presence were too essential to The Doors' identity.

## Jimi Hendrix

In a professional solo career that spanned only four years, **Jimi Hendrix** (1942–1970) managed to become one of the most influential musicians and showmen of the twentieth century and, along with Eric Clapton, succeeded in establishing the guitar as rock's virtuosic solo instrument.

Acquiring his first guitar at the age of fifteen and ingesting a steady diet of blues, R&B, soul, jazz, and rock 'n' roll, Hendrix formed his first garage band within a year and was playing parties and small clubs in his hometown of Seattle, Washington, by 1960. A naturally talented and passionate musician, he devoted himself to the instrument and grew rapidly in proficiency. Hendrix enlisted in the army in 1961 in which he spent just over a year: He was ultimately discharged on the basis of unsuitability. Soon after leaving the military, he moved to Clarksville, Tennessee, where he formed a band called the King Kasuals and began to develop several of his trademark performance moves, most notably playing the guitar with his teeth and playing with the instrument behind his head. In addition to performing with his own band, Hendrix gained experience backing various established musicians like Sam Cooke, Wilson Pickett, and Jackie Wilson. In 1964, he moved to Harlem and quickly established himself at the Apollo Theater in an amateur guitar contest. As a result, he came to the attention of Ronnie Isley of the Top 40 doo-wop group the Isley Brothers and was hired in their backup band. Several months later he was hired into Little Richard's touring group and spent the next year recording and touring as an R&B sideman. Not fulfilled by this role, Hendrix relocated to New York's Greenwich Village in 1966 and formed the band Jimmy James and the Blue Flames, which he fronted as Jimmy James. Following a May 1966 performance, Hendrix befriended Rolling Stone Keith Richards' girlfriend, Linda Keith, whose connections led Hendrix to **Chas Chandler** (1938–1996), a former bassist of the British band The Animals who had moved into managing and producing. Chandler convinced Hendrix to sign with him and go to London. There, Hendrix formed the band that would rise to global fame, **The Jimi Hendrix Experience**.

Through Chandler, Hendrix met bassist **Noel Redding** (1945–2003) and drummer **Mitch Mitchell** (1947–2008) who were well suited to back him. Following in the footsteps of Cream, The Experience would become one of the earliest bands to popularize the power trio lineup. The formidable rhythm section of Redding and Mitchell provided Hendrix the ideal musical environment in which to develop his unique sonic landscapes. Hendrix's approach to the guitar had by then expanded to employ newly emerging special effects such as the **wah-wah pedal** and an unprecedented use of controlled feedback as a musical device. The band's live performances were a mix of high volume jazz-like improvisation, blues and rhythmic swing, all deeply infused with rock's bravado and power. Donning their trendsetting psychedelic garb and wild hairdos, the band took the London club scene by storm. Other luminaries in the British scene, such as members of The Beatles, Eric Clapton, Pete Townshend, Mick Jagger, and Jeff Beck were often in attendance at Hendrix's early club appearances and have all testified to his brilliance.

In October of 1966, the band began recording their first album, *Are You Experienced*, which would take place over the next several months and in several different studios. Released in the United Kingdom in May 1967, the album was an immediate commercial and critical success there and also produced several hit singles. Though successful in Europe, the pre-album single "Hey Joe" failed to make much of an impression on US audiences. The band's breakthrough in the United States came after a performance at the Monterey Pop Festival in mid-June 1967 at which The Experience played a wildly unpredictable set that reached its climax with Hendrix lighting his guitar on fire. The photograph below, taken by seventeen-year-old audience member Ed Caraeff of Hendrix on his knees, beckoning the flames higher, has become one of rock's most iconic images.

Following the band's triumphant performance at Monterey, Reprise Records agreed to distribute *Are You Experienced* in the United States in August. Its North American release soon established Hendrix as the world's premier rock guitarist. For all of its unbridled energy, *Are You Experienced* is incredibly focused. The following tracks from the album highlight both the raw, riff-driven energy and the hard-edged psychedelia that were uniquely Hendrix.

**Go to Chapter 6 playlist example "Purple Haze" Jimi Hendrix, 1967**

**Go to Chapter 6 playlist example "Fire" Jimi Hendrix, 1967**

The band's second album, *Axis: Bold as Love*, was released in the United Kingdom in December 1967 but would not appear in the United States until early 1968, as Reprise did not want to disrupt the robust sales of the band's debut album. While this album has been called the least impressive of the band's three offerings, it does feature music that shows a more experimental side of Hendrix. The opening track, "EXP," showcases the experimental use of stereo imaging which helped to pioneer "headphones-only" rock. Panning effects are used to create the illusion that guitar is swirling around the listener. The song's lyrics imply that Hendrix is an alien from outer space—a possible double metaphor for a drug experience, or simply referring to Hendrix's otherworldly guitar skills.

**Go to Chapter 6 playlist example "EXP" Jimi Hendrix, 1967**

The Experience's third and final release was a 1968 double album called *Electric Ladyland*. This is considered by many to be Hendrix's crowning achievement and was by far the band's most commercially successful effort. Sessions for the album, which were marked by Hendrix's intense perfectionism, caused friction between the guitarist and producer Chas Chandler. Hendrix also invited several guest artists into the studio as well as many friends and guests resulting in a chaotic atmosphere during the process. This all proved too frustrating for Chandler and ended in his quitting in midstream. Production duties were thus assumed by Hendrix himself. He also played many of the bass parts as Redding had become involved in his own solo project. The best-selling single from the album, and in fact the band's best-selling single ever, was a reworking of Bob Dylan's "All Along the Watchtower" with which Dylan himself was thoroughly impressed; so much so that he adopted elements of Hendrix's version into his own performance of the song from then on.

**Go to Chapter 6 playlist example "All Along the Watchtower" Bob Dylan arr. Jimi Hendrix, 1968**

Growing tensions between Hendrix and Redding on the road and in the studio led to the breakup of The Experience in 1969. Their last performance took place at the Denver Pop Festival at Mile High Stadium on June 29. The festival was marred by police tear gassings and the band's narrow escape in the back of a rental truck.

In August, Hendrix made a headlining appearance at the Woodstock Festival with drummer Mitch Mitchell, Billy Cox on bass, rhythm guitarist Larry Lee, and percussionists Juma Sultan and Jerry Valez, a group which Hendrix dubbed just prior to the performance, a Band of Gypsys. There he performed his now mythical rendition of "The Star-Spangled Banner." Hendrix's version of the American national anthem with a screaming electric guitar has been cited by many as *the* defining moment of the counterculture and the entire late 1960s era; a strong statement against the war in Vietnam as well as a celebration of liberty and personal expression.

**Go to Chapter 6 playlist example "The Star-Spangled Banner" F.S. Key (arr. Jimi Hendrix), 1969**

The visionary live album, *Band of Gypsys*, was recorded over two consecutive nights January 1 and 2, 1970, at the Fillmore East in New York City. It would be the only live recording Hendrix would release in his lifetime. Following the Woodstock performance, Hendrix began working on demo recordings of new material with bassist Cox and drummer Buddy Miles. The album would be a prime influence of the development of funk and jazz–rock fusion as well as heavy metal of the 1970s as it explored odd time signatures, proto-funk rhythms and textures, stratospheric improvisations, and punishing guitar riffs. The band was extremely short lived and gave their final performance on January 28 at Madison Square Garden.

**Go to Chapter 6 playlist example "Who Knows" Jimi Hendrix, 1970**

**Go to Chapter 6 playlist example "Machine Gun" Jimi Hendrix, 1970**

By 1970, Hendrix had developed a reputation as a hard drinker and drug user. In 1969, he was arrested in Toronto for possession of what was believed to be hashish and heroin but was later acquitted on the grounds that the drugs had allegedly been planted in Hendrix's bag without his knowledge. On September 18, 1970, Hendrix was pronounced dead at St Mary Abbot's Hospital in London of what a coroner later determined to be death by asphyxia brought on by barbiturates. Monika Dannemann, a young lady with whom Hendrix had spent the previous evening, later revealed that he had taken a handful of her prescription sleeping medication.

Jimi Hendrix's guitar playing was more than just virtuosic; it was a quantum leap forward for rock guitar. Hendrix was a sonic sculptor who, in realizing his own original vision, created a new musical vocabulary for the electric guitar, brought a level of unprecedented musicianship to rock, and inspired legions of young musicians to reach for more. Hendrix single-handedly speeded the development of hard rock, funk, heavy metal, and hip-hop, and has impacted nearly every pop rock genre in some way. Dozens, if not hundreds of the most important musicians that came in Hendrix's wake have commented on the significance of his music in their own careers. His awards and distinctions are numerous and include being named number one on *Rolling Stone* magazine's list of the "100 Greatest Guitarists" and a posthumous Grammy Lifetime Achievement Award (1992). Hendrix's enduring popularity is evident in his current annual album sales which, more than forty-five years after his death, exceed the levels reached in his own lifetime.

## Music Festivals

When The Beatles performed at Shea Stadium in 1965, they opened the floodgates for large-scale rock concerts. By 1967 the open-air rock festival had become a reality. On two consecutive week-ends in June, both the Fantasy Fair Magic Mountain Music Festival held on San Francisco's Mount Tamalpais, and the Monterey Pop Festival in Monterey, California, took place. The success of these festivals encouraged enterprising concert promoters, and by 1969 dozens of multiday festivals with extensive rosters of performers were happening all over the world. Many bands of the era gained a commercial foothold by performing at these festivals. There were the inevitable instances of criminal activity or violence that occasionally occurred, but by and large festivals were pleasurable and successful gatherings. These festivals were an important aspect of the counterculture as well. It was not uncommon to have public speakers in between musical acts presenting a wide variety of political and social views.

The most legendary festival of the decade, and perhaps of all time, took place between August 15 and 18, 1969 on a dairy farm in Bethel, New York. The concert was originally planned to be held in the town of **Woodstock** but there were many legal and logistical issues that could not be resolved. In the end, the concert was held on Max Yasgur's farm, and due to the completely overwhelming and unanticipated number of attendees—more than four hundred thousand—there were not enough resources to build adequate fencing to keep unpaid fans away. Woodstock ended up being a free concert as well as a defining moment in counterculture history.

Image 6.5: The crowd at Woodstock pours in, 1969

## The San Francisco Scene

If there was a geographical hub for the hippie counterculture of the late 1960s, it was San Francisco. Campbell and Brody state:

> Throughout the sixties, the San Francisco Bay Area was a center for radical thought and action. The free speech movement led by Mario Savio got started at the Berkeley campus of the University of California in 1964; it led to confrontations between student protestors and university administrators over student rights and academic freedom. In 1966, in Oakland—next to Berkeley and across the bay from San Francisco—Huey Newton, Bobby Seale and Richard Aoki formed the Black Panthers, a radical black organization dedicated to revolutionary social reform by any means necessary, including violence. Hippies generally followed a less confrontational path.
>
> For hippies, mecca was San Francisco; their counterpart to the Sacred Mosque was Haight and Ashbury, an intersection in a heretofore ordinary neighborhood in San Francisco, near Golden Gate Park, the largest public park in the city. The area became a destination for those who wanted to "make love, not war" and travel the fast route to higher consciousness by tripping on psychedelic drugs. Migration to San Francisco peaked during the 1967 "summer of love." When an estimated 75,000 young people flocked to the city. (p. 229)

Central to the confluence of hippies in the Bay Area was rock music and the bands that thrived amid these hordes of young idealists. Artists like the Grateful Dead and Jefferson Airplane lived communally among, and played in, the burgeoning local music scene, which included clubs like the Fillmore (west) and the Avalon Ballroom, parties, festivals, and the so-called "be-ins," loosely organized gatherings meant to emphasize personal empowerment, heightened consciousness, and environmental awareness, among other counterculture modes of thought. The Bay Area in the late 1960s was home to a staggeringly diverse and significant pod of bands and musicians. In addition to the folk rock–based jam band, the Grateful Dead, and the more pop rock–oriented Jefferson Airplane, there was the gritty powerhouse blues of Janis Joplin and her band Big Brother and the Holding Company, the tight, radio-friendly rock of Creedence Clearwater Revival, the Latin-based rock of guitar master Carlos Santana, and the pioneering funk music of Sly and the Family Stone.

## The Grateful Dead

There may be no greater embodiment of hippie culture in music than the **Grateful Dead**. "The Dead," as they are familiarly known, single-handedly pioneered the **jam band** genre. Formed in 1965 by guitarist and singer **Jerry Garcia** (1942–1995), guitarist **Bob Weir** (b. 1947), keyboardist **Ron "Pigpen" McKernan** (1945–1973), bassist **Phil Lesh** (b. 1940), and drummer **Bill Kreutzmann** (b. 1946), their music was a unique blend of folk, bluegrass, country, jazz-like improvisation, rock, and psychedelia; and because of its highly improvisational nature, it was particularly well suited to live performance. Their rise to fame can best be described as "organic." They were at ground zero of the San Francisco scene in the late 1960s and not only performed there regularly but participated in "acid tests" (gatherings with music, poetry, and copious amounts of LSD), lived among their fans, played free and charity concerts, and espoused the hippie lifestyle in every way. As the band took to the road, they built one of the most devoted breeds of rock fan ever known: the "Deadhead." Joseph G. Schloss, Larry Starr, and Christopher Waterman have this to say:

> If The Grateful Dead were a unique musical institution, their devoted fans—"Deadheads"— were a social phenomenon unparalleled in the history of American popular music. Traveling incessantly in psychedelically decorated buses and vans, setting up camp in every town along the tour, and generally pursuing a peaceful mode of coexistence with local authorities, hardcore Deadheads literally lived for their band. And the band recip- rocated: In retrospect, one of The Grateful Dead's lasting legacies was the creation of a business model that accommodated itself to the needs of their fans, rather than forcing the fans to accommodate them. (156)

The Dead, throughout their long career, had little help from radio or other mainstream commercial sources of music. Their lasting appeal had much to do with their genuine devotion to touring, perform- ing, and pleasing their fans. The Dead have performed more than twenty-three hundred concerts.

The Grateful Dead's lifestyle and appetites were costly: there were various drug arrests; "Pigpen" McKernan would die in 1972 from complications related to alcohol abuse. He was twenty- seven. During the 1970s and 1980s the band turned to using heroin and freebase cocaine; in 1985 Garcia went into a diabetic coma for five days and nearly died; latecomer keyboardist Brent Mydland died of a narcotics overdose in 1990; and in 1995 Jerry Garcia died of heart failure due to his diabetic condition that had been exacerbated by decades of heroin and cocaine abuse, as well as a cigarette habit. The band has continued in several incarnations without Garcia but it has never been quite the same without him.

The song "Casey Jones" from the band's fifth album, *Workingman's Dead*, was one of the few Dead tunes to become a staple on classic rock radio. The song was a regular part of their live show from 1969 to 1974. The interested student is encouraged to explore the extensive catalog of both studio and live recordings by the Grateful Dead.

**Go to Chapter 6 playlist example "Casey Jones" Jerry Garcia/Robert Hunter, 1970**

## Janis Joplin and Grace Slick

The feminine presence in the San Francisco rock scene was represented by two commanding figures: **Janis Joplin**, a powerhouse, full-tilt blues singer and **Grace Slick**, a psychedelic rock diva with a pop flair.

Janis Joplin (1943–1970), a troubled outcast from Texas, moved to San Francisco in 1966 and joined a band that had been working in the Bay Area called **Big Brother and the Holding Company**. Performing in the local scene with the likes of The Dead and other area musicians, the band came to the fore after their appearance at the Monterey Pop Festival in 1967. Joplin's unrelenting performance style and deeply expressive voice were reminiscent of the great female blues singers of old; Big Mama Thornton, Ma Rainey, and Bessie Smith. In 1968, the band's album *Cheap Thrills* rose to number one on the pop charts and made Joplin an international star. The trappings of fame proved too much for the young singer and she soon turned to heroin. Joplin's sound and persona presented a strange contradiction—that of a sensitive and artistic human being hiding behind a gruff exterior of hard rock and hard drugs.

In 1969, Joplin embarked on a solo career which involved two different projects: the **Kozmic Blues Band** and the **Full Tilt Boogie Band**. By this time her heroin use had reached epic proportions. She would round out the decade with acclaimed performances at Woodstock and Madison Square Garden despite her drug- and alcohol-addled condition. On October 4, 1970, when Joplin failed to show up at a recording session, her producer Paul Rothchild went to her hotel where he found her dead on the floor beside her bed. The official cause of death was a heroin overdose likely compounded by alcohol. She was twenty-seven.

One of Joplin's most famous recordings during her brief but brilliant career was "Summertime," a remake of a George and Ira Gershwin classic from the 1935 American opera *Porgy and Bess*. It was recorded by Joplin with Big Brother in 1968.

**Go to Chapter 6 playlist example "Summertime" George and Ira Gershwin arr. Janis Joplin, 1968**

Image 6.6: Janis Joplin several months before her death

The 1967 album, *Surrealistic Pillow*, was the second studio album by the band **Jefferson Airplane** and their first to feature newly hired vocalist **Grace Slick** (b. 1949). The album reached number three on the *Billboard* charts and launched **Jefferson Airplane** on a multi-decade career as **Jefferson Starship** and later just **Starship**. The band was actually the first to draw national attention to the San Francisco scene and the 1967 release, *Surrealistic Pillow*, is now considered a quintessential counterculture psychedelic rock album. The two hit singles from the album "Somebody to Love" and "White Rabbit" were both composed by Slick.

"White Rabbit" is a clearly a drug song and is based on images from Lewis Carroll's *Alice in Wonderland*. The song is, in effect, one long crescendo which peaks on the line "feed your head," a clear and obvious reference to LSD and other psychedelics.

**Go to Chapter 6 playlist example "White Rabbit" Grace Slick, 1967**

## Creedence Clearwater Revival

**Creedence Clearwater Revival** or "CCR" represents yet another facet of the late 1960s scene in San Francisco. Their music has been called roots rock, swamp rock, bayou rock, and southern rock. In any case, the band and its leader and main creative force, **John Fogerty** (b. 1945), were extremely skilled at writing tight, well-made singles. They enjoyed a great deal of commercial success from 1967 to 1972 and have enjoyed an enduring presence on classic rock radio. Their 1969 hit "Fortunate Son" is a counterculture anthem that attacks the privilege of the elite ruling class: The "millionaire's son" is not called to fight in the war. The song is a straightforward verse/chorus, riff-heavy rock tune with all of the core elements in plain view. The second chorus:

*It ain't me, it ain't me, I ain't no millionaire's son, no, no*

*It ain't me, it ain't me, I ain't no fortunate one, no*

**Go to Chapter 6 playlist example "Fortunate Son" John Fogerty, 1969**

## Santana

The Santana Blues Band was formed in 1967 by Mexican-born guitarist **Carlos Santana** (b. 1947) and was later shortened to just **Santana**. The music of Santana represents a fully integrated stylistic fusion of Afro-Cuban elements and rock elements that came to be known as **Latin rock**. Rock 'n' roll musicians of the 1950s like Fats Domino and Bo Diddley incorporated Latin elements into their music but more as an overlay into a fundamentally R&B-based context. With Santana, we hear the first true fusion of Latin music and rock music into an entirely new genre. The Latin elements exist primarily in the rhythms and percussion (timbales, congas, and various metallic instruments) while the rock elements are clearly in the guitar, bass, drum set, and keyboards.

Santana released their self-titled debut album in 1969 with Carlos on guitar, Gregg Rolie on keyboards and vocals, David Brown on bass, Michael Shrieve on drums, and Michael Carabello and Jose Areas both handling percussion. The album was released on the heels of the band's appearance at the Woodstock Festival, their first major festival performance. They made a lasting impression on the audience, particularly with their performance of the instrumental "Soul Sacrifice," as it provided a contrast to the other bands at the festival. *Santana* peaked at number four on the album charts and established the band as a global force in Latin rock. Over half the music on the album is instrumental.

The song "Soul Sacrifice" highlights the best of everything that Santana has to offer: There is an intricate interplay of rock licks between Santana and Rolie, a heavy battery of percussion, and various solo passages, including a drum solo.

**Go to Chapter 6 playlist example "Soul Sacrifice" Santana, 1969**

## Sly and The Family Stone

**Sly and The Family Stone** were another important genre defining band to emerge from the late 1960s San Francisco scene. The first major American rock act to feature a lineup that was fully integrated in both race and gender, the group was also central in the development of **funk** and **funk rock**. The band had some difficulty breaking into the mainstream, but did so with their fourth studio album, *Stand!*, released in 1969 just ahead of their appearance at Woodstock. The album produced several hit singles including "Sing a Simple Song," "I Want to Take You Higher," "Stand," and "Everyday People."

The band is comprised of horns, keyboards, guitars, bass, drums, and harmonica and explores richly complex layers of riffs and rhythm based on the **sixteenth note** layer. The result is an unprecedented danceable energy. Nearly every instrument is treated percussively. Their lyrics connected deeply with counterculture ideals of tolerance, equality, peace, love, and drug use.

**Go to Chapter 6 playlist example "Sing a Simple Song" Sly Stone, 1969**

### The End of the Beginning

In nearly every aspect of life, the 1960s were arguably the most transformative years in American history, and while the decade was marked by remarkable social and technological progress, it was also marred by unutterable violence, intolerance, and intense conflict. The assassinations of Martin Luther King, Jr. and Robert Kennedy, just a month apart in 1968, horrified the world and reminded Americans that true freedom was still much more of a concept than a reality. In virtually the same moment that humans walked on the moon, they were slaughtering each other in the jungles of Southeast Asia.

As the 1960s drew to a close, a postmodernist cultural revolution in the United States had come to pass; rock music and its attendant values and attitudes had taken over the mainstream and there would be no going back. The diversity of rock reflected its diverse fan base; at its best, rock spoke to their deepest concerns, expressed their deepest longings for individual freedom and touched the very core of what it meant to be a pluralistic society.

## Suggested Chapter Related Activities

- Explore post-2000 **folk rock**. Can you find modern examples of activist folk rock? What similarities and differences can you hear in the musical backgrounds, in the subject matter?

- Compare modern music festivals like Coachella to the festivals of the late '60s (i.e. Woodstock, Monterey Pop). What traditions have survived? How are modern festivals informed by those of the past?

- Can you locate post-2000 examples of what might be called "psychedelic" or "acid rock?" Are the reasons it is perceived as such musical, lyrical, cultural or a combination of some or all of these? How does this modern acid rock connect to the music of the late '60s? How does it differ?

## Suggested Discussion Topics

- Life in the pre-modern era (the Middle Ages) has been characterized as a "*dance* around a central point" while life in the modern era has been called a "*race* toward a goal or object." Postmodernism was, in many ways, a reaction to the "race;" the notion that science and technology had become a means of increasing human suffering rather than alleviating it. Modern warfare was/is perhaps the most glaring example of this failure. Besides the obvious anti-war songs, discuss how the counterculture and its music connected to these postmodern ideals.

- Do you feel that another counterculture movement is necessary or possible? Is a counterculture akin to that of the 1960s developing today and, if so, does music play any role?

- When considering the state of modern culture and world affairs, what efforts of the counterculture do you view as successful and which have failed?

## Image Credits

Image 6.1: John Paul Filo, https://en.wikipedia.org/wiki/File:Kent_State_massacre.jpg. Copyright © 1970 by Valley News-Dispatch.

# CHAPTER 7
# Mainstream Rock in the Seventies

*The great thing about rock and roll is that someone like me can be a star.*

-Elton John

## Cultural Context

As America moved into a new decade and the rock counterculture symbols of the late 1960s—long hair, wild clothes, peace signs and the like—had merged with the mainstream, many people might have taken it as an indication that some of the hurdles of the previous decade had been cleared; some were: The gradual termination of US involvement in Vietnam and the end of the draft in 1973 were clear victories as were new attitudes toward integration and equality. However, the widespread acceptance (and subsequent commercialization) of rock and rock counterculture, while it was ultimately very good for rock, did not spell a complete transformation for society as a whole. The 1970s were filled with new issues regarding social progress: The questions of segregation in the 1960s had morphed into the questions of diversity in the 1970s. By the early 1970s, the highly visible social upheaval of the previous decade may have subsided, but ever-emerging problems would develop to keep society in a relative state of instability. To be sure, America had moved forward in the struggle for equality—but still, ideological divergence on major issues remained prevalent on many fronts; many of the gains of the previous decade, though not eradicated, had been stalled. The 1970s were marked by a shift back toward conservative policies, unprecedented political scandals, global economic upheaval, and major trends that often seemed to be at cross-purposes with one another.

On April 22, 1970, the first Earth Day was observed as a day to honor the planet and to embrace the concept of peace, yet the war in Vietnam would not officially end until 1975. While the decade witnessed the birth of the Women's Liberation Movement in the United States and feminism grew around the globe, many of the efforts of the African American Civil Rights Movement began to crumble as frustration increased—tangible change had become slow to nonexistent, and many blacks felt obliged to choose isolation over negotiation. The Nixon administration opened US relations with China and signed the Anti-Ballistic Missile Treaty with the Soviet Union in 1972, yet in 1974 Richard "Tricky Dick" Nixon resigned from the office of president in disgrace; he faced impeachment proceedings spurred by the Watergate scandal (Nixon was pardoned of any criminal wrongdoing by incoming president Gerald Ford, much to the chagrin of most Americans). As the 1970s unfolded, much of the bristling energy of the counterculture was gradually pushed aside by growing cynicism, fatigue, and dispiritedness. Joseph G. Schloss, Larry Starr, and Christopher Waterman state:

> One of the most pervasive stereotypes about the 1970s—famously captured in novelist Tom Wolfe's epithet, the "Me decade"—has to do with a shift in the values of young adults, away from communitarian, politically engaged ideals of the 1960s counterculture, toward more materialistic and conservative attitudes. While this generalization should be taken with a large grain of salt, it is undeniable that the early 1970s did see a kind of turning inward in American culture. The majority of Americans had grown weary of the military conflict in Vietnam, which drew to a close with the U.S. withdrawal from Saigon in 1975. Around the same time, popular attention was focused on domestic problems, including the oil and energy crises (1973 and 1979) and economic inflation, which threatened the financial security of millions of Americans. If the assassination of President Kennedy in 1963 had robbed many Americans of a certain political idealism, the Watergate hearings—viewed by millions on television—and the subsequent resignation of President Nixon (1974) occasioned a growing cynicism about politics.[1] (pp. 179–180)

Even as these general changes in society were occurring, the aftereffects of the counterculture movement were manifesting in new ways and filtering into the mass media: As rock music became more commercialized and self-indulgent, television stepped in to carry the torch of seriously tackling contemporary social issues; most commonly in the unlikely form of weekly thirty-minute sitcoms (the comedic backdrop served as a psychological buffer). From 1970 to 1977, *The Mary Tyler Moore Show* aired on CBS. The show was the first to depict a never-married, independent career woman in the leading role. It dealt with subjects such as income inequality among women, divorce, premarital sex, adoption, and infertility. In 1971 the ground-breaking series *All in the Family* debuted on CBS where it ran for nine years. The show centered on a working-class, bigoted WWII veteran

---

1   Joseph G. Schloss, Larry Starr, and Christopher Waterman, Rock: Music, Culture, and Business, pp. 179-180, 183-184. Copyright © 2012 by Oxford University Press. Reprinted with permission.

named Archie Bunker and explored such serious topics as racism, homosexuality, religion, gender inequality, poverty, labor relations, rape, abortion, birth control, and menopause. Television shows about minority families and the problems they faced also appeared in the 1970s. *Sanford and Son*, *Good Times*, and *Chico and The Man* were noteworthy examples of this emerging phenomenon. In music television, Don Cornelius' *Soul Train* premiered in 1971 as the black counterpart to Dick Clark's *American Bandstand* and provided a mass media forum for black musical styles including funk, soul, R&B, disco, and even some of the earliest commercial rap. These shows helped pioneer the world of television and expanded the social role of the small screen through the 1970s and beyond.

**Consumer-level electronics** in the 1970s provided a new kind of media for people, especially teens, in several revolutionary forms. Video arcades replete with games like *Space Invaders*, *Asteroids*, and *Pac-Man* were enormously popular places to converge, and in 1977, both Atari and Apple brought video games and computing into the home; the former with its Atari 2600 video game console and the latter with the Apple II, the first mass-produced home computer. New technologies made music portable and customizable in the 1970s as well, first with the 8-track cartridge and later with the standard audio cassette (including recordable blanks). Portable players for car installation became fairly affordable and commonplace by mid-decade; those designed for personal use would surge late in the 1970s and into the 1980s.

## Mainstream Rock

By 1970, rock was not only developing out in all directions and into various subgenres; it had now been around long enough that it was forming a sense of its own history. Rock had become a multigenerational affair, and what sounded good to the older fans of rock now likely sounded out of date to younger audiences. In the 1950s, *rock 'n' roll* meant music for teens; in the 1970s the market for popular rock opened up to focus on two broad age groups: teens to young adults looking for music that spoke to their youthful energy, and adults aged twenty-five to forty whose tastes had become more mature and possibly a shade or two more conservative. This marketing model, while it may seem blatantly capitalistic, allowed for one of the most richly diverse decades in rock music history: there was something for *everyone* and a viable market for *all* of it. We now turn to some of the fundamentally new developments in the way that music was packaged, marketed, and sold.

The long-play LP rock album emerged and began to flourish in rock after *Sgt. Pepper's*, and by the 1970s it had become the standard format for rock recordings. Many rock musicians had justifiably come to consider themselves artists and their albums as unified artistic statements, rather than just a collection of singles. This brought significant changes to the way albums were recorded and in many cases, the length and complexity of individual songs. It also gave rock fans something more substantial by way of a product. Albums often contained lyrics, photos, and liner notes as well as engaging cover art that nourished a highly enthusiastic fan base.

Radio, particularly FM radio, stepped in to support these changes. The so-called "album-oriented rock" station (**AOR**) came into existence in the early 1970s. These stations promoted rock albums by playing several "focus tracks" (and taking caller requests) rather than promoting singles. An insightful article at www.wow.com/wiki/Album-oriented_rock describes AOR thusly:

> Most radio formats are based on a select, tight rotation of hit singles. The best example Is Top 40, though other formats, like country, smooth jazz and urban all utilize the same basic principles, with the most popular songs repeating every two to six hours, depending on their rank in the rotation. Generally there is a strict order or list to be followed and the DJ does not make decisions about what selections are played. AOR, while still based on the rotation concept, focused on the album as a whole (rather than singles). In the early 1970s many DJs had the freedom to choose which track(s) to play off a given album—as well as latitude to decide what order to play the records in. Later in the 1970s AOR formats became tighter and song selection shifted to the program director or music director, rather than the DJ. Still, when an AOR station added an album to rotation they would often focus on numerous tracks at once, rather than playing the singles as they were individually released.

Massive concert tours in arena and stadium settings became an integral part of the rock landscape in the 1970s. After the success of The Beatles at Shea and with the growth of the open-air festival in the late 1960s, the technology and techniques that supported live sound reinforcement increased rapidly, as did special effects like massive light shows, pyrotechnics, and elaborate stage props. It is important to realize that concert tours in the predigital age were not about generating profits in and of themselves, but rather about promoting record sales. It was fairly simple: If a band was touring, they had a new album out. Concerts were frequent occurrences in every major city and many minor ones. Many tours turned a profit, but as long as a tour did not *lose* money, the objective was met. Because of this fundamental difference with the postdigital market, where musicians are forced to rely on concert revenue as a *primary* source of income, tickets were far less expensive, even in relative financial terms.

As a result of the high level of artistry that went into many recordings, the mass media presence and marketing, and larger-than-life arena shows, the 1970s was when the romantic concept of the "rock star" really took shape. These gifted individuals, isolated by fame, awash in hedonistic behavior, and flush with the monetary rewards they had earned in return for the musical gems they bestowed upon society, became the heroes of a generation and created the soundtrack to the lives of millions. As Schloss, Starr, and Waterman note:

Though it is now such a part of our cultural landscape that we may take it for granted, the concept of the rock star was deeply tied to the specific character of rock in the seventies. At its foundation, the concept was based on the newly emergent idea that you could actually get rich as a rock musician. Beyond that, there was a growing feeling that wealth and fame could *contribute* to the quality of one's art, rather than detract from it, a position that would have been viewed with suspicion even five years earlier. There are several reasons for the change in attitude. First, there was the sense that wealth was the best path to the artistic independence that artists had been seeking since the 1960s. Simply stated, rich rock stars could do what they wanted. Even if what they wanted was no longer political revolution but just "sex, drugs and rock 'n' roll," that could still represent a kind of cultural revolution. And if rock was supposed to be about the liberating potential of self-indulgence, then who better to perform it than a rich outlaw? At the same time, part of what made this kind of indulgence acceptable was the belief that artists had earned it through their cultural output. In other words, the persona had an aspirational quality that the average person could relate to, much like winning the lottery. Rock stars, almost by definition, were working-class or middle-class kids with an almost religious commitment to the ideals of rock 'n' roll, who had struggled, paid dues and finally seen their dreams come true. From this point of view, the rock stars enjoyed wealth and debauchery almost on behalf of their fans. (pp. 183–184)

Mainstream popular rock in the 1970s included multiple subgenres, many of which occasionally overlap. The era was characterized by extreme diversity and an embarrassment of musical riches. In this chapter we will discuss some of the more prominent acts in the basic categories of pop rock, including singer-songwriter, soft rock, country rock, funk, and soul. This categorization is generally based on the artist's primary style and is by no means comprehensive. We begin with "solo" artists.

## Elton John

In the 1970s, no musician came to embody the self-indulgent, megasuccessful artist/rock star better than British musician **Elton John** (b. 1947). On recordings his musical skill is formidable and in performance his flamboyant style and fantastical stage costumes placed him in the top echelon of arena rockers of the 1970s. John's breakthrough came with his second album, a self-titled 1970 release, produced by Gus Dudgeon, that featured his first major hit "Your Song," a mid-tempo rock ballad, as well as the bluesy rock piece "Take Me to the Pilot," and the gospel-influenced "Border Song." His music throughout the decade ranged from soft ballads like "Daniel" to harder-edged rockers like "Saturday Night's Alright for Fighting." He recorded covers of The Who's "Pinball Wizard" and The Beatles' "Lucy in the Sky with Diamonds," on which John Lennon made a guest appearance. Elton John had seven consecutive number one albums in the 1970s as well as dozens of hit singles.

Unlike most of the singer-songwriters of the rock era, Elton John never wrote his own song lyrics. For most of his career, he collaborated with lyricist **Bernie Taupin** (b. 1950) with whom he has completed more than thirty albums and later with Tim Rice on soundtracks for the animated films *The Lion King* and *The Road to El Dorado*. John has also produced Broadway musical theater works with both lyricists. The list of musicians with whom he has performed and recorded is extensive and extremely diverse and includes everyone from Stevie Wonder and Paul McCartney to Lady Gaga and Eminem.

John's extraordinary songwriting skill has propelled a five-decade career and earned him nearly every major industry award clearly establishing his standing among rock's greatest. His particular type of song craft was well suited to the trends and tides of 1970s AOR radio in that he was a master of verse/chorus form, but he could handle more expansive nonstandard forms with equal proficiency. Two examples below illustrate:

Go to Chapter 7 playlist example "Goodbye Yellow Brick Road" Elton John/Bernie Taupin, 1973

Go to Chapter 7 playlist example "Tiny Dancer" Elton John/Bernie Taupin, 1971

Image 7.1: Elton John in performance, 1975

Elton John's personal struggles with drugs, his own sexuality (he came out as bisexual in 1976 and has been openly gay since 1988), and the deaths of his friends Ryan White and Queen singer Freddie Mercury from AIDS (discussed later in this chapter) have resulted in enormous charitable efforts and awareness-raising activities on John's part. Since the early 1990s, he has helped to raise hundreds of millions of dollars for AIDS research through concerts, recordings, and other events, and has been a champion for LGBT and same-sex marriage movements.

## Billy Joel

If Elton John had an American counterpart in the 1970s, it was **Billy Joel** (b. 1949). Although Joel's career wouldn't skyrocket until his 1977 album, *The Stranger*, he had some modest success early in the decade with the songs "Piano Man" (which would become his signature song), "The Entertainer," and "Say Goodbye to Hollywood." With *The Stranger* Joel soared to international fame and emerged as one of the great American songwriters; a role he has substantiated for over four decades. *The Stranger*, produced by Phil Ramone, highlights Joel's versatility at writing everything from sensitive pop ballads like "Just the Way You Are" to large-scale compositions like "Scenes from an Italian Restaurant."

**Go to Chapter 7 playlist example "Just the Way You Are" Billy Joel, 1977**

**Go to Chapter 7 playlist example "Scenes from an Italian Restaurant" Billy Joel, 1977**

While Joel was often considered a soft rock artist, he was quite adept at producing songs with a harder edge. These efforts were rendered more authentic by Joel's tough New York "street kid" image. The following track from 1978's chart-topping album *52nd Street* illustrates:

**Go to Chapter 7 playlist example "Big Shot" Billy Joel, 1978**

Billy Joel was one of the first of a small number of American musicians to play in the Soviet Union in the late 1980s during what would be the final years of the Cold War. Since 1994, he has been half of the famous series of "Face to Face" tours with Elton John during which he and John performed their own music, each other's music, and duets.

## Stevie Wonder

A child prodigy, **Stevie Wonder** (b. 1950) began his professional career as "Little" Stevie Wonder at the age of eleven in 1962. A skilled multi-instrumentalist and a gifted songwriter, he was left blind as an infant due to complications from a premature birth. Wonder's most classic work dates from his young adulthood in the 1970s. He was, in fact, the most influential and successful black artist of the decade. His self-produced fifteenth studio album, *Talking Book* from 1972, is considered by many to represent the beginning of his most important artistic period. The album earned Wonder his first Grammy and produced two number one hits, the ballad "You Are the Sunshine of My Life" and the infectiously funky

"Superstition," which features British rocker Jeff Beck on guitar. Wonder was a pioneer in his extensive use of electronic keyboards, special effects, and emerging synthesizer technology.

**Go to Chapter 7 playlist example "Superstition" Stevie Wonder, 1972**

Wonder's next album, *Innervisions*, released in 1973, marks his shift toward lyrics with a social and political message, perhaps drawing on a combination of lingering counterculture energy and Marvin Gaye's groundbreaking 1971 album *What's Going On* (discussed later in this chapter). The song "Higher Ground" expresses Wonder's feelings about reincarnation and higher consciousness, while "Living for the City" deals with systematic racism. Wonder plays every instrument on both tracks and employs a heavy dose of keyboard effects and early synthesizer technology.

**Go to Chapter 7 playlist example "Higher Ground" Stevie Wonder, 1973**

**Go to Chapter 7 playlist example "Living for the City" Stevie Wonder, 1973**

Just days after the release of *Innervisions*, Wonder was involved in a serious automobile accident which left him in a coma for several days. Fortunately, he would eventually make a full recovery and begin performing again in March of 1974. Stevie Wonder reached his commercial peak in the 1980s and participated in numerous large-scale charity efforts as well as major collaborations with other artists. He was also instrumental in the campaign to establish Martin Luther King Day as a national holiday.

Image 7.2: Stevie Wonder recording in 1973

## Carole King

**Carole King** (b. 1942) began her career as a songwriter with her lyricist partner and husband Gerry Goffin in New York's Brill Building. Together, the team wrote a string of now classic hits throughout the 1960s, many of which were recorded by Motown stars and other artists like Aretha Franklin and The Righteous Brothers. The King/Goffin song, "Chains," originally recorded by Little Eva was later covered by The Beatles. After divorcing Goffin in 1968, King moved to Los Angeles' Laurel Canyon where she befriended fellow songwriters James Taylor and Joni Mitchell. Taylor and King would collaborate often and with great success. In 1970, King embarked on her own solo recording career with the album *Writer*, which proved only modestly successful, peaking at number eighty-four. Undaunted, she released her now landmark follow-up, *Tapestry*, in 1971 with producer Lou Adler. The album was enormously successful, garnering four Grammys including Album of the Year and Best Pop Vocal Performance. She was also the first female artist to win Song of the Year for "You've Got a Friend," a song which would later be covered by James Taylor. Taylor and Mitchell also appear on *Tapestry*, both providing backing vocals with Taylor handling acoustic guitar duties as well.

King's songwriting is firmly grounded in gospel, folk, and pop traditions. She delivers with consummate musical skill on both vocal and piano.

### Go to Chapter 7 playlist example "It's Too Late" Carole King/Toni Stern, 1971

Although *Tapestry* was her most successful album (it is ranked thirty-six on *Rolling Stone*'s 500 Greatest Albums of All Time) and considered by many to be her defining work, the rest of the 1970s were very good to Carole King. She would continue to write hits for other artists and would release nine more solo albums by the end of the decade, all of which were well received. The track "Jazzman" from the 1974 album *Wrap Around Joy* shows another side of King's style.

### Go to Chapter 7 playlist example "Jazzman" Carole King, 1974

King's emergence in the pop world was timely. Her image as a strong, independent woman would resonate with the various feminist movements of the period; many of her songs were played at feminist gatherings and events. In 1977, King became involved in causes related to environmental issues, most notably in her work toward the passage of the Northern Rockies Ecosystem Protection Act.

## James Taylor

Following an early solo career that was stalled by drug addiction and a motorcycle accident, **James Taylor** (b. 1948) would find success in 1970 with his second studio album, *Sweet Baby James*. Hailed by critics as a folk rock masterpiece, the album, produced by Peter Asher, established Taylor as a mainstream artist and launched a career that has spanned nearly fifty years. The breakthrough hit from the album was "Fire and Rain," a confessional tale inspired by Taylor's battle with drugs and the loss of a childhood friend to suicide. The song showcases the conversational approach to music and storytelling that will come to define Taylor as an artist. It also highlights his deceptively simple guitar style as well as his exceptional attention to detail in songwriting.

The song is an alternating verse/chorus structure (there is no interlude), though each time the chorus repeats there are subtle differences in either the orchestration, the contour of the vocal line, or both, lending a sense that the chorus doesn't just repeat but that it evolves.

**Go to Chapter 7 playlist example "Fire and Rain" James Taylor, 1970**

As was mentioned earlier, Taylor and Carole King were friends and frequent collaborators (she played the piano part for "Fire and Rain"). Taylor's next album *Mud Slide Slim and the Blue Horizon*, also produced by Asher, contained his first number one hit, his cover of Carole King's "You've got a Friend." Moreover, the song itself was inspired by the line "I've seen lonely times when I could not find a friend" from Taylor's "Fire and Rain."

**Go to Chapter 7 playlist example "You've Got a Friend" Carole King arr. James Taylor, 1970**

Taylor would continue to produce albums and hits through the rest of the decade and well beyond (his 2015 album *Before This World* knocked Taylor Swift from the number one spot). The 1970s saw a concept album from Taylor (*One Man Dog*, 1972) as well as an extensive list of collaborations with many of the era's biggest stars, including Paul McCartney, Stevie Wonder, David Crosby, Bonnie Raitt, and Linda Ronstadt. In 1972, Taylor married fellow songwriter Carly Simon, with whom he would also collaborate.

James Taylor has become a familiar part of American culture. In addition to music, he has been involved in various social causes for decades, has done cameo appearances in movies and television, and has even been good-naturedly caricatured in the animated series *The Simpsons*.

## Lennon and McCartney after The Beatles

After The Beatles disbanded in 1970, all four members went on to successful solo careers, though Lennon and McCartney's were by far the most substantial. Lennon would collaborate with his wife, Yoko Ono, and McCartney with his, Linda McCartney (née Eastman).

Taking up residence in New York City, Lennon became involved in highly publicized war protests throughout the early 1970s. He became such a powerful political voice against Richard Nixon that the Nixon administration embarked on a serious effort to have Lennon deported. These efforts dragged on for four years and were ultimately unsuccessful. In 1971 John Lennon released two of his most powerful anthems, the first, "Power to the People," with the Plastic Ono Band and the second "Imagine," as a solo work, both in 1971. Both songs were produced with Phil Spector.

**Go to Chapter 7 playlist example "Power to the People" Plastic Ono Band, 1971**

**Go to Chapter 7 playlist example "Imagine" John Lennon, 1971**

Lennon remained active until 1975, collaborating with Ringo Starr, Elton John, and cowriting David Bowie's first US number one hit "Fame" before retiring in 1975 to be a stay-at-home dad to his son Sean. He resurfaced from his self-imposed retirement in October 1980 with the release of the single "Starting Over" followed by the album *Double Fantasy* in November, just one month before he was slain in New York City.

Paul McCartney would take another direction, forming the band Wings in 1970 following his first post-Beatles solo album, *McCartney*, earlier that same year. Paul McCartney and Wings would go on to become one of the most successful bands of the decade releasing seven studio albums between 1971 and 1979. All of the band's albums made the top 10 and produced twenty-three top 40 singles. In 1972, McCartney reunited with producer George Martin to record the hit "Live and Let Die" as the title track to the 1973 James Bond film. It features Martin's dramatic orchestrations.

**Go to Chapter 7 playlist example "Live and Let Die" Paul McCartney and Wings, 1973**

McCartney's penchant for writing love songs often showed through with Wings, as evidenced in the song "My Love" from the 1973 album *Red Rose Speedway*. It was also the first US number one single for the band.

**Go to Chapter 7 playlist example "My Love" Paul and Linda McCartney, 1973**

McCartney's activism has taken many forms over the decades and includes work with PETA, the Humane Society, the Make Poverty History campaign, the Save the Arctic campaign, Band Aid, Live Aid, and many others (Band Aid and Live Aid are discussed in Chapter 10).

## Marvin Gaye

On May 21, 1971, one of the most important albums of the decade, *What's Going On*, was released by **Marvin Gaye** (1939–1984). While Gaye's music clearly represents the soulful side of rock it draws on late 1960s psychedelia, rock, and blues. Moreover, his lyrics connect deeply to counter-cultural ideals and the social issues that spilled over into the 1970s, particularly those of income inequality, police brutality, the environment, and the Vietnam War. Critics have called it an inner city response to *Sgt. Peppers*. The album is ranked number six on *Rolling Stone*'s 500 Greatest Albums of All Time.

*What's Going On* is a concept album that links all nine tracks musically and topically. The final track "Inner City Blues" sums up many of the album's themes and is a good representation of Gaye's approach to his inventive sonic universe.

**Go to Chapter 7 playlist example "Inner City Blues" Marvin Gaye/James Nyx, Jr., 1971**

Marvin Gaye would remain in high demand through most of the 1970s but by the end of the decade he was struggling with cocaine addiction, a divorce, and problems with the IRS. In a self-imposed exile, he relocated to London in 1980. By 1982 he had gotten himself back into shape both financially and physically and was enjoying his ascent back to commercial prominence with a successful album and several hit singles. In 1983, while on tour, Gaye relapsed into cocaine use and as the tour ended he retreated to his parents' house where tensions were high between him and his father, Marvin, Sr. In an altercation between the two, which erupted on April 1, 1984, and during which Gaye reportedly beat his father badly, Marvin Sr., in retaliation, shot Gaye to death. An autopsy later showed both cocaine and PCP in Gaye's system. With this evidence and the photographs of Marvin Sr.'s injuries from the fight, Marvin, Sr. was only sentenced to probation.

## Paul Simon

**Paul Simon's** (b. 1941) career began in the mid19'60s as half of the folk rock duo Simon & Garfunkel; though his most influential work would occur in the early 1970s as he embarked on a solo career. Simon is credited as a fundamental force in the popularization of the so-called world music and world beat genres: he seamlessly connected musical elements of reggae, Latin, mbaqanga, zydeco, and other world styles with that of American rock, folk, pop, and R&B in his own hip, urban fashion. His 1972 album *Paul Simon* produced the hit "Me and Julio Down by the Schoolyard" which uses a Brazilian percussion instrument called a cuíca which is often used in samba music (it sounds like a laughing monkey), as well as the reggae-based hit "Mother and Child Reunion," which is said to be one of the first instances of reggae music recorded by a white musician.

**Go to Chapter 7 playlist example "Me and Julio Down by the Schoolyard" Paul Simon, 1972**

**Go to Chapter 7 playlist example "Mother and Child Reunion" Paul Simon, 1972**

Simon's released two more albums by 1975 when he won Grammys for Album of the Year and Best Male Pop Vocal for *Still Crazy After All These Years*, coproduced by Simon and Phil Ramone. This album marked a bit of a departure from his previous two in that it was a bit more somber in character, likely due to Simon's recent divorce. The album produced several hits, notably the cynical "50 Ways to Leave Your Lover," which is centered around what has become one of the decade's most famous drum riffs (played here by drumming legend Steve Gadd).

**Go to Chapter 7 playlist example "50 Ways to Leave Your Lover" Paul Simon, 1975**

The remainder of the 1970s saw Simon's album output dip as he dabbled in several other projects including scoring a film; though he released a greatest hits album in 1977. He would return in 1980 with *One-Trick Pony* and his groundbreaking album *Graceland* in 1986, the two albums most commonly attributed with stimulating massive interest in world music.

Simon's charitable work has been considerable. He has been raising money for music in primary education since 1970 through benefit concerts and other activities, and since 2003 he has supported Little Kids Rock, an organization that provides free musical instruments and lessons to children in public schools. He is also involved in a number of charities that promote health and medical care to children in underserved areas.

## Bruce Springsteen

*Born to Run*, released in 1975, was the third studio album released by **Bruce Springsteen** (b. 1949) and his breakthrough effort into the world of mainstream 1970s rock. Springsteen, the son of working-class parents, fell in love with rock after hearing Elvis and, upon seeing The Beatles on *Ed Sullivan*, he began to pursue music in earnest. As luck would have it, he failed the military medical exam after being drafted to go to Vietnam at age eighteen. He formed his first bands and began playing clubs in and around the Jersey Shore area where he would pepper sets of covers with his own original music. By the early 1970s, he was a veteran of the Jersey Shore scene and signed his first record deal with Columbia in 1972. His first two albums won the hearts of critics but not the general public, and sales were low. In 1975, that all changed with the release of *Born to Run*. The album reached number three and the songs "Born to Run," "Thunder Road," "Tenth Avenue Freeze-Out," and "Jungleland" were all enormous hits on AOR. Springsteen toiled meticulously with every detail in recording the album, taking more than fourteen months in the studio, and the payoff produced some of the most classic hits in Springsteen's enormous catalog. Springsteen's music is "big" and extremely well made—although in a wholly unpretentious way. He connects to powerful American images with an incomparable authenticity; we can clearly sense that he has been there.

**Go to Chapter 7 playlist example "Born to Run" Bruce Springsteen, 1975**

Springsteen is a master songwriter who can shift effortlessly from an epic rock piece like "Born to Run" to a thoughtful ballad or a pop tune; he can equally and effectively deliver a scathing social commentary or a song about the innocence of childhood. Springsteen would release his most successful album, *Born in the U.S.A.*, in 1984, which will be discussed in greater detail in Chapter 10.

## Carly Simon

**Carly Simon's** (b. 1945) solo career began in 1970 with the release of her self-titled album and the top 10 hit "That's the Way I've Always Heard It Should Be." Her second album, *Anticipation*, also released in 1970, produced the hit single of the same name. Her first number one song, "You're So Vain," would come in 1972 from her third album, *No Secrets*. The song became a kind of running pop culture riddle as to the identity of its subject. Simon's various professional dealings and relationships with people like Mick Jagger, actor Warren Beatty, and mogul David Geffen all fueled public speculation. Simon remained reticent on the subject, although she occasionally dropped hints in interviews and on talk shows. In 2003, Simon auctioned off the subject's identity in a charity event with the provision the winner not reveal the information. In 2015 she revealed that the song is actually about three men and that the second verse only is about Warren Beatty. She has yet to reveal the other two.

**Go to Chapter 7 playlist example "You're So Vain" Carly Simon, 1972**

Simon married James Taylor in 1972 and the two frequently appeared on each other's recordings. Simon saw a dip in her popularity around mid-decade but came roaring back with the hit "Nobody Does It Better," which served as the title theme for the 1977 James Bond film *The Spy Who Loved Me*. It was her second best–selling single. She followed up in 1978 with the smooth and jazzy "You Belong to Me."

**Go to Chapter 7 playlist example "Nobody Does It Better" Carly Simon, 1977**

**Go to Chapter 7 playlist example "You Belong to Me" Carly Simon, 1978**

Simon's music has been covered by a diverse group of musicians ranging from Marilyn Manson and the Foo Fighters to Jennifer Lopez and Liza Minelli. Many contemporary pop stars, including Carly Rae Jepsen, Taylor Swift, and Tori Amos cite Simon as a primary influence.

## Linda Ronstadt

One of the most popular and versatile female artists of the 1970s, **Linda Ronstadt** (b. 1946) has been called "The First Lady of Rock," "The Queen of Rock," and the first "arena-class rock diva." Her musical ventures helped to pioneer country rock and solidify the role of women in rock. By the end of the 1970s she was the highest-paid female rock musician and had produced numerous multimillion-selling albums; her tours were filling arenas and stadiums around the world. Ronstadt was criticized by some for the fact that most of her hit songs were covers, but praised by others for her interpretive skills and musicality. The Eagles (discussed below) were formed by members of her early 1970s backup band and she has collaborated with many artists including Frank Zappa, Johnny Cash, Warren Zevon, and Dolly Parton. She has released more than thirty studio albums and has made guest appearances on more than 120 records. She has earned the highest honors in pop, rock, country, and even a Latin Grammy Award.

Ronstadt's version of Hank Ballard's R&B song "You're No Good" was a number one hit for her in 1974. The track appeared on her album *Heart Like a Wheel*, produced by Peter Asher.

**Go to Chapter 7 playlist example "You're No Good" Hank Ballard arr. Linda Ronstadt, 1974**

Her 1977 album, *Simple Dreams*, also with Asher, included a song written by the up and coming Warren Zevon called "Poor Poor Pitiful Me," which became one of Ronstadt's signature hits.

**Go to Chapter 7 playlist example "Poor Poor Pitiful Me" Warren Zevon arr. Linda Ronstadt, 1977**

## Rod Stewart

With an early history in the British scene in the 1960s, most notably fronting the Jeff Beck Group from 1967 to 1969, **Rod Stewart** (b. 1945) had his solo breakthrough in the United States in 1971 with the hit "Maggie May" from the self-produced album *Every Picture Tells a Story*. Alternately recording as a solo artist and with the band Faces until 1975, Stewart was by then a household name. For the rest of the 1970s and well beyond, he produced a string of diverse albums with hits ranging from folk-flavored songs to ballads to blues-infused rockers.

**Go to Chapter 7 playlist example "Maggie May" Rod Stewart/Martin Quittenton, 1971**

**Go to Chapter 7 playlist example "You're in My Heart" Rod Stewart, 1977**

**Go to Chapter 7 playlist example "Hot Legs" Rod Stewart, 1977**

Rod Stewart has enjoyed several resurgences in his popularity since the 1980s. One of the best-selling artists of all time, he has been honored with a Grammy, a Brit Award, a Legend Award, and induction into several halls of fame.

We now survey of a small sampling of some of the era's most influential and successful groups, which, like the solo artists, represent the heterogeneous nature of 1970s mainstream pop music.

## Fleetwood Mac

Originally formed as a blues band in 1967 by guitarist **Peter Green** (b. 1946), drummer **Mick Fleetwood** (b. 1947), and bassist/singer **John McVie** (b. 1945), by 1975 **Fleetwood Mac** would evolve into its most familiar lineup and adopt a more pop-oriented style. The 1975 lineup saw the departure of Green and included John McVie's wife, keyboardist/singer **Christine McVie** (b. 1943), singer **Stevie Nicks** (b. 1948), and guitarist **Lindsey Buckingham** (b. 1949) (Nicks and Buckingham were in a romantic relationship at the time and came as a "package deal"). The newly assembled quintet released their self-titled album that year (it was actually the second to be called *Fleetwood Mac*; the first was released in 1968) and it rapidly climbed to the number one position on the *Billboard* chart. The album produced several hits including the Nicks composition "Rhiannon."

**Go to Chapter 7 playlist example "Rhiannon" Stevie Nicks, 1975**

Fleetwood Mac's interpersonal dynamic provided ample inspiration for their next album, the wildly successful *Rumours*, released in 1977. Christine and John McVie divorced in 1976; Buckingham and Nicks had ended their relationship; and Mick Fleetwood was in divorce proceedings with his wife. Success, wealth, and rock stardom had brought with it heavy cocaine and alcohol use within the band, and coupled with the other tensions, it is nothing short of miraculous that they were able to keep working. They did, however; and the resulting music is among the finest of its kind. The album exposes the emotional upheaval through which the band were going in a most artful and sincere fashion. *Rumours* would produce numerous hits, win a Grammy for Album of the Year, and come to represent Fleetwood Mac's best-known work. With more than 40 million copies sold it is one of the best-selling albums of all time.

"The Chain" is the only track on the album that was written as a full-band collaboration. It is a near-textbook verse/chorus form, though it supplants a return to a third chorus with an extended outro. Stylistically the song is a combination of folk, rock, psychedelia, and highly polished pop.

**Go to Chapter 7 playlist example "The Chain" Fleetwood Mac, 1977**

"Gold Dust Woman" is a song about infidelity.

**Go to Chapter 7 playlist example "Gold Dust Woman" Stevie Nicks, 1977**

Not all of the music on *Rumours* was reflective of the soured relationships within the band. The optimistic "Don't Stop" written by Christine McVie offered a message of hope in the midst of despair. The song is based on the long-short shuffle pattern and its brisk tempo adds to the uplifting character.

**Go to Chapter 7 playlist example "Don't Stop" Christine McVie, 1977**

Fleetwood Mac continued to produce hit albums until the early 1980s when they decided to take a hiatus. Nicks, Buckingham, and Christine McVie all embarked on successful solo careers during that time. The *Rumours* lineup of the band would make one more album in 1987 before officially disbanding. They have reunited with various personnel for tours and recordings since 1990.

## Queen

Formed in 1970 by guitarist **Brian May** (b. 1947), drummer **Roger Taylor** (b. 1949), bassist **John Deacon** (b. 1951), and singer/pianist **Freddie Mercury** (1946–1991), the British rock band **Queen** began down a path toward progressive/art rock with their first two albums, *Queen* and *Queen II*. Though the band would never lose its connection to their progressive and diverse beginnings, or their penchant for complex multilayered textures, from their third album on they would adopt a more commercially oriented approach. *Sheer Heart Attack*, released in 1974 and produced by Roy Thomas Baker, brought Queen to the international stage. The album successfully combines the elements of several diverse styles such as hard rock, vaudeville, ragtime, camp, and Caribbean. Two of the album's notable songs were "Killer Queen," which was its biggest hit, and "Stone Cold Crazy," which, with its aggressive riffs and brisk tempo, was a significant precursor to the "thrash" metal of the 1980s.

**Go to Chapter 7 playlist example "Killer Queen" Freddie Mercury, 1974**

**Go to Chapter 7 playlist example "Stone Cold Crazy" Queen, 1974**

While each member of Queen deserves recognition for their own fundamental contributions, the towering presence of Freddie Mercury, in all aspects—creativity, musical ability, charisma, and live performance skills—made Queen a band of enduring influence and historical and musical significance. Mercury's boundless creative energy and virtually limitless vocal ability made him one of the true giants of the twentieth century. He and Queen have been cited as a primary influence for a diverse body of many of the greatest bands and musicians of the last quarter of the twentieth century and well into the twenty-first. Even Mercury's death in 1991, discussed below, had a profound impact on the lives of millions.

Queen's fourth album, *A Night at the Opera*, would produce one of the most significant songs in rock history, a Mercury composition called "Bohemian Rhapsody." The song is a true rock epic, unfolding in several sharply contrasting sections of widely disparate styles. The introduction and subsequent piano/guitar ballad sections are followed by an operatic/symphonic rock section with elaborately arranged vocal harmonies. The vocals in this section alone required over three weeks to record and employed 180 vocal overdubs. The "hard rock" section follows, building to a climactic ascending guitar/piano run. This leads back to the introspective outro through the use of a musical device called a *ritardando* (gradual slowing of the tempo). The outro serves as a point of resolution, both musically and lyrically.

"Bohemian Rhapsody" has become a legacy unto itself. Simultaneously, it represents the fairly specialized genre of 1970s progressive rock coming to what would be its peak popularity, but also the 1970s *mainstream* listener's willingness to embrace music of a more daring nature. Although the song has clearly demonstrated a multigenerational appeal, it is interesting to speculate about how it would be received if it were released in today's relatively homogenized and unchallenging pop music market. The accompanying promotional video for the song also had a remarkable impact on the future of music video. Bands had been making the occasional promotional video clip and videos for some time by 1975; even The Beatles had made "videos." The success of "Bohemian Rhapsody" and the accompanying video made it a common practice and popularized the music video as a medium in and of itself. This is a considerable distinction; it set in motion an entire era, an era in which the music video would be *the* dominant factor in commercial music.

**Go to Chapter 7 playlist example "Bohemian Rhapsody" Freddie Mercury, 1975**

The 1970s would see three more hugely successful and influential albums: *A Day at the Races* (1976), *News of the World* (1977), and *Jazz* (1978). After parting ways with producer Roy Thomas Baker in 1976 to self-produce, the band would reunite with him to coproduce *Jazz*. A musical sample from each album follows:

**Go to Chapter 7 playlist example "Good Old-Fashioned Lover Boy" Freddie Mercury, 1976**

**Go to Chapter 7 playlist example "We Are the Champions" Queen, 1977**

**Go to Chapter 7 playlist example "Fat-Bottomed Girls" Brian May, 1978**

Queen's success endured through the 1980s and their work included collaborations, charity events, many singles with videos, and some of the most legendary concert performances in history. Mercury released two solo albums with one venturing into the realm of opera and musical theater.

The title track to his album *Barcelona* became the official anthem for the 1992 Summer Olympics held in that city.

Upon completion of their 1986 tour, Queen continued to record but seldom made public appearances. Following an appearance by Mercury at the 1990 Brit Awards, at which he looked very emaciated, reports began to circulate that the legendary musician was suffering from AIDS, a disease which was very little understood at the time. Mercury maintained that he was simply suffering from exhaustion. On November 23, 1991, Mercury issued an official press release that he had indeed contracted from the disease. He died a little more than twenty-four hours later. In spite of the rumors swirling around at the time, his death stunned the world.

Image 7.4: Freddie Mercury bringing it to the New Haven Coliseum in 1977

Mercury was the first major music star to die from AIDS. His death prompted a huge growth in public awareness and resulted in the generation of hundreds of millions of dollars for research, including money and proceeds willed by Mercury himself. In 1992, the Freddie Mercury Tribute Concert, the largest rock benefit ever staged, was held at Wembley Stadium in London. In addition to the seventy-two thousand spectators present, the concert was viewed by 1.2 *billion* viewers worldwide. It helped to generate tens of millions of dollars for AIDS charities. Many rock stars and other media personalities have created endowments and charitable funds in Mercury's name. In death, as in life, Freddie Mercury's impact was profound.

## The Eagles

As mentioned earlier, the Eagles were formed by members of one of Linda Ronstadt's early backup groups. Drummer/singer **Don Henley** (b. 1947), guitarist/singer **Glenn Frey** (1948–2016), bassist/singer **Randy Meisner** (b. 1946), and guitarist/singer **Bernie Leadon** (b. 1947), came together (with Ronstadt's assistance) in 1971 as the original lineup. Veteran producer Glyn Johns (The Who, The Beatles' Abbey Road sessions) worked with the band on their self-titled 1972 release and is credited for helping to cultivate the country rock sound that characterized the band's first several recordings. He sought to capitalize on the band's rich harmony singing and country backgrounds. The Eagles had their first hit with the song "Take It Easy" which features Frey on lead vocals and the rest of the band singing the sumptuous harmonies that would help generate their mass appeal. The successful fusion of country and rock elements is evident in the recording: An acoustic guitar riff accompanied by a clean, twangy electric guitar and just a hint of a bass line opens the song; a gentle rock beat comes in just before the vocal. The lyrics paint a picture consistent with stereotypical country music imagery: trucks, women, rambling, and the quest for a simple good time.

**Go to Chapter 7 playlist example "Take It Easy" Glenn Frey/Jackson Browne, 1971**

The Eagles' second album, 1973's *Desperado*, was a "theme" album that compared the lives of old west outlaws to that of rock stars, but did not sell well. By the time they began work on their third album, the Eagles were interested in moving their sound closer to hard rock and after sessions began, clashes with Glyn Johns led to his dismissal. Bill Szymczyk was hired to produce. Szymczyk recruited **Don Felder** (b. 1947) as an additional guitarist in an effort to bring more of a rock edge to their sound. The album produced some edgier music but still had country leanings.

The band broke through the international market in June 1975 with their fourth studio album, *One of These Nights*, which continued to lean more toward rock than country. The album earned the band their first Grammy and was the first of four consecutive number one albums.

**Go to Chapter 7 playlist example "One of These Nights" Don Henley/Glenn Frey**

Leadon left the band late in 1975, displeased with the direction they were taking and was replaced by singer/guitarist Joe Walsh. With Walsh, the band's sound would grow even edgier and they would produce some of their best known music. Taking nearly a year and a half to complete, *Hotel California* was released in late 1976. It would become one of the best-selling albums of all time and earned the band two Grammy Awards. The classic title track illustrates the band's sound in full flower as well as their fully developed songwriting style.

**Go to Chapter 7 playlist example "Hotel California" Don Felder/Don Henley/Glenn Frey, 1976**

The Eagles would release one more album, *The Long Run*, before the end of the decade, however, without Meisner. He left the band in 1977 and was replaced by **Timothy B. Schmit** (b. 1947). The Eagles broke up in 1980 amid serious personal tension and rancor. During the 1980s all five band members had substantial solo careers, with Henley's generally considered to be the most successful. Several "reunion" albums and concert tours occurred, beginning in 1994, and were extremely successful.

## America

The success and popularity of the band America through the 1970s was indicative of the enduring popularity of folk rock in the mainstream. The group's creative core consisted of American-born multi-instrumentalists/vocalists **Dewey Bunnell** (b. 1952), **Gerry Beckley** (b. 1952), and **Dan Peek** (1950–2011) who met in Britain as sons of US military personnel stationed there. Playing clubs in London in 1970 drew the attention of Warner Bros. Records who signed the band in 1971. The young musicians had envisioned their music moving toward a more psychedelic sound but their producer, Ian Samwell, convinced them to develop the folk rock style with which they began. Their self-titled debut that same year rose to number one in the United States and spawned two hit singles, "A Horse with No Name" and "I Need You."

**Go to Chapter 7 playlist example "A Horse with No Name" Dewey Bunnell, 1971**

Several very successful albums, a string of hits, and a Grammy followed. In 1975 the group began a series of recordings with ex-Beatles production team, George Martin and Geoff Emerick, though a big-name producer is no guarantee of commercial success. Their popularity went through a succession of peaks and valleys throughout the late 1970s. In 1977, Peek left the band to pursue his faith and record Christian music. Beckley and Bunnell forged on through the 1980s with sporadic results similar to the latter part of the 1970s. America has endured into the new millennium, although they never enjoyed the same success of the early 1970s. Their music from that era was highly influential and remains popular on classic rock radio.

**Go to Chapter 7 playlist example "Ventura Highway" Dewey Bunnell, 1972**

**Go to Chapter 7 playlist example "Sister Golden Hair" Gerry Beckley, 1975**

## Parliament/Funkadelic/P-Funk

Masterminded by visionary musician **George Clinton** (b. 1941), the band Parliament, alternately known as Funkadelic and P-Funk is a collective of more than fifteen musicians who pioneered the genres of funk, funk rock, and psychedelic funk in the early 1970s. Through several phases and various incarnations of each group, the musicians combined elements of psychedelic rock, soul, progressive, glam, and R&B with concepts of science fiction/fantasy and political activism.

All incarnations of Clinton's bands were praised for their high-level musicianship and dazzling stage shows, and are credited for speeding up the development of disco, hip-hop, electronica, and new wave. Offshoot bands from the collective include Bootsy's Rubber Band and The Brides of Funkenstein, as well as many solo projects by various members. Notable among the group is **Bootsy Collins** (b. 1951) who pioneered a highly influential style of percussive bass playing known as "slap bass." With a discography that includes dozens of albums, Clinton and his collective touched the future of music in innumerable ways. Clinton remains active as a performer, recording artist, and producer. Most recently, he made a guest appearance on Kendrick Lamar's 2015 album, *To Pimp a Butterfly*.

The following track is from the 1975 Parliament album *Mothership Connection*:

**Go to Chapter 7 playlist example "P-Funk (Wants to Get Funked Up)" Clinton/Collins/ Worell, 1975**

## Bob Marley and Reggae

Reggae originated in Jamaica in the late 1960s as a type of dance music. It is essentially a fusion of native calypso music, and American R&B and jazz styles. It is characterized by heavily syncopated rhythms emphasizing backbeats (2 and 4), upbeats (the "ands" between the beat), simple chord progressions, and heavy bass lines. Reggae bands are often a core rock ensemble with various Latin and Afro-Cuban percussion, horns, and vocals. Lyrically, reggae is rife with political and social criticisms which reflect the social climate in Jamaica, particularly in the 1960s and 1970s, but there are numerous songs of a personal, nonpolitical nature as well.

Image 7.5: Bob Marley live in concert in Zurich, Switzerland, 1980

Reggae music exerted a significant influence on American and British popular styles beginning in the late 1970s and grew even stronger through the 1980s.

**Bob Marley** (1945–1981) is credited with bringing reggae to the world stage in the mid-1970s and is, generally speaking, the musician most commonly associated with the style. He and his group the Wailers rose to world fame with their 1975 hit "No Woman, No Cry." Their rise was aided by Eric Clapton's cover of Marley's "I Shot the Sheriff" in 1974. Bob Marley died an untimely death in 1981 at the age of thirty-six as a result of cancer. Throughout the late 1970s, his music spread around the world, along with his image as a man of peace.

**Go to Chapter 7 playlist example "I Shot the Sheriff" Bob Marley, 1973**

**Note**: The artists and song samples listed in this chapter, while they represent a reasonable cross-section, only amount to small fraction of the popular music and musicians of the 1970s. The takeaway for the student should be these several principal realities:

1. The world of popular rock and rock related styles was *extremely* diverse.

2. Much of the popular music of the period presented an intellectual challenge to the listener in that songs had grown typically longer, more complex, and—in general—required a commitment from the serious listener.

3. While tuneful melodies were ubiquitous in the mainstream, *simple tunes* were not; nor was there any lack of rhythmic development and innovation in the percussive treatment of non-percussion instruments.

## Other Developments in Pop Music

A booming 1950s rock 'n' roll–based nostalgia market emerged around mid-decade in several forms: a rockabilly revival, which would continue into the 1980s; the 1974 network television premiere of the sitcom series *Happy Days*, about a typical middle-class 1950s family and their ducktail, leather jacket–donning neighbor, The Fonz; and the popularity of the Hollywood production of the rock 'n' roll Broadway musical *Grease* in 1978.

The world mourned as Elvis Presley died of a drug overdose at his Graceland mansion in Memphis on August 16, 1977. He was forty-two.

**Disco** and disco dancing peaked in popularity between roughly 1974 and 1978. The culture of disco music and dancing—though widely criticized for its lack of musical depth—for a time seemed poised to topple rock as the dominant style. There was a divisive sentiment between many rock fans and their disco counterparts. Phrases like "rock is dead" and "disco sucks" could be seen on T-shirts and bumper stickers. By the end of the decade, however, it was often difficult to tell the two apart as crossover hits and the inevitable hybridization of rock and disco elements began to occur.

Disco style was also ground zero for the first "electronic dance music" and played a major role in the development of 1980s popular styles, including early rap and electronica. An exemplar of disco is the Donna Summer/Giorgio Moroder electronic disco hit "I Feel Love." Note the sixteenth note base and the hypnotic, repetitive character:

**Go to chapter 7 playlist example "I Feel Love" Summer/Moroder, 1977**

We now turn to the harder, heavier side of rock in the 1970s.

## Suggested Chapter Related Activities

- As always, listen for and count along with the underlying rhythmic structures in each song. What do you discover?

- Analyze and compare the forms of Elton John's "Goodbye Yellow Brick Road" and "Tiny Dancer." How do the forms serve the lyrics?

- Compare and contrast the music of The Beatles with that of Lennon and McCartney's solo music.

- Locate several post-2000 singer/songwriters and compare them to their 1970s counterparts. Which elements have remained and which have evolved? How do lyrics, form and rhythms compare?

- See if you can locate a post-2000 example of a song with multiple stylistic juxtapositions such as those found in Queen's "Bohemian Rhapsody."

## Suggested Discussion Topics

- Compare your ideas of the modern rock or pop star with the concept discussed in this chapter. How do the roles differ? What part does the media play in our perception of the rock star?

- Discuss the level of diversity in mainstream '70s rock music (i.e. the idea that a singer like Bob Dylan can exist comfortably alongside a singer like Freddie Mercury). Do we encounter this level of diversity in modern mainstream music? Does it exist at all anymore?

## Image Credits

## CHAPTER 8

# Hard Rock, Punk, and Heavy Metal in the Seventies

*I used to have a drug problem. Now I make enough money.*

-David Lee Roth of Van Halen

### Another Word Regarding Labeling Music

As we learned in Chapter 1, and as we have seen at points thus far, the various problems that arise when labeling music are manifold. Case in point: in the last chapter we outlined a number of "mainstream" artists of the 1970s. In fact, many of the bands we will detail in this chapter, particularly those we will call "hard rock," were *also* mainstream. They were wildly popular, launched successful concert tours, received massive airplay, and sold millions of albums. Additionally, there are a lot of musical characteristics that overlap between all rock bands. It should therefore be clarified that the artists we call "hard rock," "heavy metal," and "punk" in this chapter *generally* exhibit some or all of the following distinguishing musical traits with considerable regularity:

- a blues-like approach to soloing, harmonic progression, vocal inflection
- riff-based textures
- heavy and more "distilled" beat keeping
- heavy guitar distortion
- gritty, rough-edged vocals
- fast tempos
- a strong connection to each other

Moreover, many of the hard rock bands we will discuss below became popular with the help of AOR radio and not primarily through their "hit" singles on Top 40 radio and other formats, as the majority of the bands in the previous chapter had; the bands referred to as "mainstream." Furthermore, most punk and metal bands received little or no airplay. These styles were thus referred to as "underground."

## Led Zeppelin

Recall that The New Yardbirds, formed by Jimmy Page, officially became Led Zeppelin in 1968. Their potent blend of psychedelic blues, heavy grooves, folk and Celtic elements, ultra-catchy guitar riffs and vocal lines, and even elements of country, jazz, and reggae, brought them to the forefront of 1970s hard rock. The band's prodigious creativity, their sheer diversity, their staggering impact on the music business, and their enduring presence and influence rival that of The Beatles. The overall cultural impact, which extends far beyond their music, is also comparable to that of The Beatles.

In terms of live performance, Led Zeppelin defined the arena hard rock experience in the 1970s and beyond. Their tours consistently set new attendance and earnings records as well as new standards for the rock concert as a sheer spectacle. Unlike many of their predecessors, Led Zeppelin frequently turned down offers to perform on major television shows, stating that their fans preferred to see them live in concert. As their arena status grew, so did their reputation for debauched, alcohol- and drug-fueled off-stage behavior.

> **Note**: Although Led Zeppelin would release their first two albums in 1969, their music is quintessentially '70s and will be considered as belonging more to that decade than the 1960s. We now sample each album from their 1969 debut, *Led Zeppelin*, through the 1979 release, *In Through the Out Door*, all of which were produced by Jimmy Page.

Financed by Jimmy Page and the band's manager, Peter Grant, the recording of *Led Zeppelin* was completed in a relatively short time. The band had not yet signed with a label and did not have the luxury of spending excessive amounts of time in experimental recording sessions. That Page envisioned the album to emulate a live performance—without excessive overdubs—and that the material was worked out well before sessions began allowed for a highly successful result; the master tapes enabled Led Zeppelin to negotiate a contract with Atlantic Records which was conducive to Page's desire for artistic freedom and autonomous control of the band's commercial affairs. Although the initial release of the album met with a largely unfavorable critical reception (many of those same critics which panned the album have since come to praise it), it was commercially quite successful, reaching the number ten spot on the US album chart and number six in the United Kingdom. Three of the album's nine tracks were covers, two of bluesman Willie Dixon, and a Robert Plant arrangement of an Anne Bredon folk song, reflecting the band's deep roots in both traditions.

The opening track "Good Times Bad Times" gives a clear indication of the band's intended "live" sound on the record, which is distinctively heavy; the song showcased drummer John Bonham and his rapid-fire bass drum figures.

**Go to Chapter 8 playlist example "Good Times Bad Times" Led Zeppelin, 1969**

The second album, simply titled *Led Zeppelin II*, was a commercial success and was better received by critics than their debut. It reached number one in both the United States and the United Kingdom. *Zeppelin II* is arguably the band's heaviest album. Regardless, it set a new standard for songs centered on the guitar riff, as opposed to songs whose hook is provided by a vocal part in the verse or chorus. In that way particularly, the album has also been called a "blueprint" for heavy metal.

"Whole Lotta Love" epitomizes this guitar-centered, blues-derived approach that will form the foundations of heavy metal, as well as a heavily distorted sound. There is also a prominent psychedelic section in the song which employs a variety of guitar and vocal effects and a theremin solo played by Page. Some of the material in the song is an adaptation of Willie Dixon's "You Need Love." Dixon is listed in the writing credits.

**Go to Chapter 8 playlist example "Whole Lotta Love" Led Zeppelin/Willie Dixon, 1969**

Released in the summer of 1970, *Led Zeppelin III* was written primarily by Page and Plant while they took a break from the hectic tour schedule to which they had been subject through the previous year. The two retreated to a rural cottage in Wales with no electricity and no running water to work out new material. The bucolic surroundings and lack of electric power inspired them to reconnect with their acoustic folk roots, which became a partial focus for the album. The album put forth the band's most diverse collection of songs to date. As is often the case when a band departs from popular and critical expectations, the album met with a fairly unkind critical reaction, although it sold and charted well. Most critics have since softened their stance as time has allowed for a fuller understanding of the album's breadth.

"That's the Way" is an acoustic track that is considered to be one the most tender and thoughtful pieces in the Zeppelin catalog:

**Go to Chapter 8 playlist example "That's the Way" Page/Plant, 1970**

Led Zeppelin's fourth studio effort was left untitled, in part, as a response to the harsh criticism they had received following *Led Zeppelin III*. It was unofficially dubbed by fans "Led Zeppelin IV." The album cover featured no band name or print whatsoever, just a puzzling image of a rustic oil painting portraying a man with a bundle of sticks on his back. Additional cover art presents an image called "The Hermit" which originated from a deck of tarot cards, along with the four famous "symbols" (often called "runes") meant to represent each band member. The band's intention was to create a sense of anonymity which would baffle the press. The net effect, although unintended, went much farther: they conjured a powerful mystique that would envelope the band and add another essential dimension to the image of the "rock star."

Image 8.1: The enigmatic "Led Zeppelin IV" front cover

Image 8.2: The fully opened inner album cover art (left) and the liner jacket with runes (right)

On a purely musical level, the album was astonishing. It was also successful commercially and won the highest praise from critics; it has been called everything from a "genre masterpiece" to a "monolithic cornerstone." The album features some of Zeppelin's most classic music, including the strangely groovy "Black Dog," the bluesy "When the Levee Breaks" and perhaps the most classic Zeppelin song, if not the most classic *rock* song of all time, "Stairway to Heaven." Moreover, "Zeppelin IV" confirmed the band's 1970s megastar status and reinforced their standing as one of the greatest rock bands in history. The album has sold nearly 40 million copies and is ranked among the most popular recordings in history.

"Stairway to Heaven" is a true rock epic, clocking in at just over eight minutes. It is frequently hailed as one of the greatest rock songs of all time. There are four distinct sections in the song: an acoustic introduction with finger-picked guitar part and four recorders (a wind instrument whose tone resembles a flute) giving it a distinctively Renaissance flavor; the "main" slow rock section, which emerges subtly from the introduction and builds in intensity, particularly as the drums enter around the midpoint of the song; a long unfolding guitar solo section follows; and a final hard rock section that ends by "hanging" an unresolved chord over an *a cappella* epilogue.

**Go to Chapter 8 playlist example "Stairway to Heaven" Page/Plant, 1971**

The band's fifth studio effort, *Houses of the Holy*, marked a deeper immersion into advanced studio techniques and overdubbing; a shift away from heavy blues derivation; stylistic explorations of reggae, funk, and progressive rock; and a healthy dose of atmospheric keyboard and synthesizer effects. Released in March 1973, the album was an immediate commercial success but still met with some mixed criticism, mainly due to its stylistic diversity. "The Crunge," a funk-based song with that features the shifting time signatures common to progressive rock left critics particularly baffled.

**Go to Chapter 8 playlist example "The Crunge" Page/Plant, 1973**

In 1975, Led Zeppelin released their sixth studio album, *Physical Graffiti*, a double-length collection of eight new originals and seven previously recorded but unused tracks. As the new music exceeded the length of a single album format, the band decided to include older material to make it a double album. Additionally, it was Zeppelin's first release on their own newly formed record label, Swan Song. The album was an instant success with both critics and fans. It was the first album ever to reach sales of one million in advance orders alone. It also reignited interest in older Zeppelin material as well; all previous Zeppelin albums reentered the top 200 charts following the release of *Physical Graffiti*. Critics at the time described it as "Led Zeppelin's *Sgt. Pepper's*," "towering," and a "tour de force of musical styles."

A particular highlight is the song "Kashmir." The song can be best described as Eastern-influenced orchestral rock and is at once cosmic, exotic, progressive, and driving. The drums are processed through a phase shifter lending a psychedelic effect to Bonham's powerhouse style. "Kashmir" was reportedly a band favorite as well and was performed at virtually every concert following its release.

**Go to Chapter 8 playlist example "Kashmir" Page/Plant/Bonham, 1975**

By 1975, Zeppelin was the biggest hard rock band on the planet. Their stage shows and tours had grown to an unprecedented scale and they were selling out arenas worldwide, although their fortunes were about to take a downward turn. Robert Plant and his wife were involved in an automobile accident in Greece in August 1975. His injuries resulted in the cancellation of an upcoming autumn tour. During his recuperation, the band wrote new material. In the spring of 1976, they released *Presence*, which sold well but received a mixed reaction on all fronts. Compared to the artistic path the band had been on, *Presence* was seen as a disappointment to many. The album was intended to mark a return to the band's straightforward rock roots; it had no keyboards and little in the way of acoustic guitar or intricate arrangements. As such, many fans and critics suspected that the band's excesses had finally overwhelmed them. Although some criticism has softened over the years and it does contain some great music, the album is still generally considered as an artistic low point for the band.

**Go to Chapter 8 playlist example "Nobody's Fault but Mine" Page/Plant, 1976**

Led Zeppelin returned to the road again in 1977 in promotion of *Presence* and their 1976 debut film, *The Song Remains the Same*. The film was compiled from concert footage taken in 1973 and mixed with documentary and several short "fantasy" sequences. The tour was financially successful but was plagued by a series of riots, arrests, and injuries. The tour was ultimately cut short in July when Plant received news that his young son, Karac, had died of a stomach virus.

It wasn't until August 1979 that Zeppelin would release *In Through the Out Door* which—unbeknownst to them at the time—would be their last full album of original material. The band did not tour heavily in 1979, but were playing sporadic concerts in Europe in the early summer of 1980 in preparation for a major world tour in the fall. That June, drummer John Bonham collapsed during a preview performance in Germany and was hospitalized. Rumors spread in the press that it had been the result of drugs and alcohol, although this was firmly denied by the band. On September 24, 1980, Bonham had begun to consume large quantities of alcohol early in the morning and continued throughout the day as the band rehearsed. As the band finished for the day they ended up at Page's house in Windsor. Bonham apparently passed out and was placed in bed. The next day he was found dead. An autopsy revealed his death to be asphyxiation from vomit and it was ruled an accident. He was thirty-two years old.

The song "Fool in the Rain" from *In Through the Out Door* highlights Bonham's musical skill in its subtly powerful "halftime" shuffle beat. The pattern Bonham played in the song is based on a blues shuffle but is distinguished by its slow, heavy rock groove which emphasizes the third beat of every measure. A distinct middle section in the song is based on a Latin samba rhythm and features multiple Latin percussion instruments such as maracas, timbales, agogo bells, claves, a marimba, and a whistle.

**Go to Chapter 8 playlist example "Fool in the Rain" Page/Plant/Jones, 1979**

Following Bonham's death the upcoming tour was cancelled and in spite of various rumors, no replacement was sought. The band issued a statement in December 1980 announcing that Led Zeppelin could not continue without John Bonham. An album of previously unreleased material called *Coda* was released in 1982 and there have been various box sets, films, and "reunion" performances with other drummers, including John Bonham's son, Jason, and even as their popularity has endured to this day, Led Zeppelin the band essentially ended in 1980. No other band defined hard rock in the 1970s and far beyond as Led Zeppelin did. Musicians too numerous to count cite Zeppelin as a primary influence.

## Deep Purple

Originally formed in 1968 as a progressive rock group, England's Deep Purple settled into its most commercially successful and musically influential lineup between 1969 and 1973 (and again from 1984–1988). This lineup consisted of vocalist **Ian Gillan** (b. 1945), guitarist **Ritchie Blackmore** (b. 1945), bassist **Roger Glover** (b. 1945), organist **Jon Lord** (1941–2012), and drummer **Ian Paice** (b. 1948). As early progenitors of hard rock and heavy metal, the band ranks among the most significant of the era.

Deep Purple are credited with merging the instrumental virtuosity found in baroque and classical music with the world of hard rock and heavy metal. These efforts would come to full flower in the band's 1971 release, and arguably their defining record, *Machine Head*. The album features several of the band's best-known songs, including "Smoke on the Water," "Space Truckin'," and "Highway Star," and became one of the most influential recordings of the decade.

It is revealing to compare some of the keyboard music of **J.S. Bach** (1685–1750) with the work of Jon Lord, who was himself a classically trained pianist. Lord, Blackmore, and Gillan, in fact, all substantiated the influence of Bach and other Great Masters of baroque and classical in the music of Deep Purple. This is perhaps nowhere more overt than in the keyboard solo of "Highway Star" (beginning around 2:10) which clearly owes to the toccata section of Bach's Toccata and Fugue in D minor.

**Go to Chapter 8 playlist example "Toccata and Fugue in D minor" J.S Bach circa 1704**

**Go to Chapter 8 playlist example "Highway Star" Deep Purple, 1971**

The fusion of classical music and hard rock was essential to the development of the heavy metal genre of rock, particularly as it pertains to many of the bands of the British Heavy Metal Invasion of the 1980s and—to some extent—in bands from the United States and elsewhere. Deep Purple's pioneering work in this area has influenced bands such as Iron Maiden, Judas Priest, Def Leppard, Metallica, Rush, and Van Halen. Moreover, the concept and application of musical virtuosity, as it comes from the classical traditions into rock music, is central to the evolution of the musical language of other several other types of rock, namely progressive rock and art rock. In that sense, Deep Purple's influence cannot be overstated. Deep Purple's reemergence in the 1980s will be discussed in Chapter 11.

## Aerosmith

Aerosmith came together in 1970 in Boston, Massachusetts with singer **Steven Tyler** (b. 1948), guitarist **Joe Perry** (b. 1950), bassist **Tom Hamilton** (b. 1951), drummer **Joey Kramer** (b. 1950), and guitarist Ray Tabano. Tabano was replaced in 1971 by guitarist **Brad Whitford** (b. 1952) to solidify the lineup of the band as it would exist for most of the rest its lifespan.

As Aerosmith began to write music and build a following in local clubs, they were noticed by Columbia Records who signed the band in mid-1972. Their debut album followed in January 1973 and produced their first significant hit song, "Dream On." While the band did not create a huge sensation with their debut, nor with their follow up, *Get Your Wings*, they had laid the foundations of a distinctly American sound of blues rock which they would perfect by their third album, *Toys in the Attic*.

Released in 1975, *Toys in the Attic* launched Aerosmith into the hard rock mainstream and marked an important development in the rhythmic evolution of rock and pop music as a whole. The now classic hard rock staple "Walk This Way" represents a shift toward a more aggressive sixteenth note rhythmic basis for hard rock music. This rhythmic conception had been developing in the funk music of Sly Stone, George Clinton, and some of the music of Stevie Wonder; however, Aerosmith were among the first blues rock bands to build on this fundamental shift. An aural survey of "Walk This Way" reveals the how rock began to get "funky" by tapping into the sixteenth note layer in the mid-1970s.

**Go to Chapter 8 playlist example "Walk This Way" Steven Tyler and Joe Perry, 1975**

## Lynyrd Skynyrd and Southern Rock

Another uniquely American flavor of rock to emerge in the 1970s was **southern rock** or **southern-fried rock**, a style that merges rock 'n' roll, blues, boogie-woogie, country, and honky-tonk. Vocal stylings typically lean toward a southern drawl and much of the culture was associated with the working class, rowdy good times, hard partying, and dancing. Early 1970s southern rock bands like The Allman Brothers Band, Blackfoot, and Molly Hatchet helped to bring the style to a larger audience, although no group had more impact and influence in the genre than **Lynyrd Skynyrd**.

Formed in Jacksonville, Florida, around 1970, the creative core of the band would morph into several incarnations bearing several different names before coming to the lineup of 1972 which featured vocalist **Ronnie Van Zant** (1948–1977), guitarist **Gary Rossington** (b. 1951), guitarist **Allen Collins** (1952–1990), bassist **Leon Wilkeson** (1952–2001), drummer **Bob Burns** (1950–2015), and pianist **Billy Powell** (1952–2009). By this time the band had gained momentum as a popular regional act in the South. They were noticed in Atlanta by producer Al Kooper who signed them to his label Sounds of the South, a subsidiary of MCA. With Kooper in the producer's chair, the band would record their debut album, *(pronounced 'Lĕh-'nérd 'Skin-'nérd)* in 1973. During the recording of the album they hired guitarist/bassist **Ed King** (b. 1949) to handle some of the session work. King was kept on as a third guitarist following the album's release. The album fared quite well with both fans and critics. It contains some of the band's best-known music including the classic rock anthem "Free Bird" and the surprisingly tender "Tuesday's Gone."

**Go to Chapter 8 playlist example "Free Bird" Collins/Van Zant, 1973**

**Go to Chapter 8 playlist example "Tuesday's Gone" Collins/Van Zant, 1973**

1974's *Second Helping* would prove to be a very successful follow-up and would spawn several more classic Skynyrd songs, such as "Sweet Home Alabama," "The Needle and the Spoon," and the J.J. Cale number "Call Me the Breeze." It would also be the last album to feature Bob Burns on drums, who was replaced by **Artimus Pyle** (b. 1948) in 1975. That same year Skynyrd released *Nuthin' Fancy*, which did not meet with the same success as their previous albums. King would leave the band during the supporting tour citing exhaustion. The group also decided to part ways with producer Kooper.

For their fourth album, *Gimme Back My Bullets*, Skynyrd hired producer Tom Dowd and also employed a trio of backup singers called The Honkettes which consisted of **Cassie Gaines** (1948–1977), **Leslie Hawkins** (b. 1951), and **JoJo Billingsley** (1952–2010). Although they recorded and toured with the band, they were never officially added as members of Lynyrd Skynyrd. Still seeking a replacement guitarist for Ed King, the band were introduced to Cassie Gaines' younger brother, **Steve Gaines** (1949–1977). He was brought in as a permanent member in 1976 and featured on the band's next release, a live double album called *One More from the Road*. The recording was well received and put Skynyrd back at the top of the southern rock world. Then tragedy struck.

On October 20, 1977, the band was touring in support of their newly released album, *Street Survivors*, when the plane they were traveling in crashed in Mississippi. Ronnie Van Zant, Steve Gaines, and Cassie Gaines were all killed, as were the pilot and several members of the band's road crew. The rest of the group—Powell, Rossington, Collins, Wilkeson, Pyle, and Hawkins—were all seriously injured. JoJo Billingsley had refused to board the plane, claiming that she had had a dream several nights prior that the plane would go down.

The crash occurred just three days after the release of *Street Survivors*. The staggering tragedy at the height of the band's popularity cemented Lynyrd Skynyrd's standing in the annals of rock history. The surviving members disbanded until 1980 and then reformed in various incarnations as the Rossington Collins Band and again as Lynyrd Skynyrd with Ronnie Van Zant's younger brother, Johnny, on vocals. As legendary as the band had become, they never again reached their precrash level of success.

The song "You Got That Right" from *Street Survivors* was one of several written by the team of Van Zant and Steve Gaines:

**Go to Chapter 8 playlist example "You Got That Right" Van Zant/Gaines, 1977**

## ZZ Top

The power trio of singer/guitarist **Billy Gibbons** (b. 1949), bassist **Dusty Hill** (b. 1949), and drummer **Frank Beard** (b. 1949) came together as **ZZ Top** in 1969 in Texas, connected by their love of blues, rock, boogie, and American roots music. The group has endured in its original lineup for well over four decades. They broke into the mainstream of hard rock in 1973 with their third album *Tres Hombres*. The album established ZZ Top as a hard-edged, blues rock power trio with musical abilities comparable to Cream and The Jimi Hendrix Experience. Propelled by Gibbons' distinctive guitar style and Beard's "finesse with power" drumming, *Tres Hombres* melded polished perfection with the expressive power of the blues.

**Go to Chapter 8 playlist example "La Grange" ZZ Top, 1973**

A half-live, half-studio album, *Fandango*, followed in 1975 featuring music recorded on their recent, highly successful tour in support of *Tres Hombres*. Live tracks included music by John Lee Hooker and Willie Dixon and demonstrated the band's musical prowess on stage as well as in the studio. *Fandango!* (1975) reached the top 10 in the album charts and featured the AOR hit, "Tush."

**Go to Chapter 8 playlist example "Tush" ZZ Top, 1975**

ZZ Top would finish out the 1970s with platinum, major-label success. Their signature look (chest-length beards, dark glasses, and fur-covered guitars) served them well as the MTV era dawned. Although they would go through a period of experimentation with the heavy use of synthesizers and sixteenth note layer rhythms, their blues roots always remained clear. The compelling groove of "Cheap Sunglasses" from their 1979 album, *Degüello*, showcases the band at the peak of their '70s power.

**Go to Chapter 8 playlist example "Cheap Sunglasses" ZZ Top, 1979**

## Heart

Fronted by sisters **Ann Wilson** (b. 1950) and **Nancy Wilson** (b. 1954), vocals and guitar, respectively, Heart found success in 1976 with their debut album *Dreamboat Annie*. The rest of the creative core of the band consisted of guitarist **Roger Fisher** (b. 1950), guitarist/keyboardist **Howard Leese** (b. 1951), bassist **Steve Fossen** (b. 1949), and drummer **Michael DeRosier** (b. 1951). The group developed a highly effective mix of hard rock and folk which would propel them to mainstream stardom, place the Wilson sisters in the top echelon of female rock musicians, earn Heart widespread praise as one of the most diverse bands of the 1970s, and produce many hit albums and singles. The hits "Magic Man" and "Crazy on You" appeared on *Dreamboat Annie*. Both are demonstrative of the stylistic blend for which the band became famous.

**Go to Chapter 8 playlist example "Magic Man" Ann and Nancy Wilson, 1976**

**Go to Chapter 8 playlist example "Crazy on You" Ann and Nancy Wilson, 1976**

A legal battle ensued in 1977 when Heart opted to leave their early label, Mushroom Records, and signed with Portrait Records, a satellite of CBS. This resulted in the nearly simultaneous releases of *Magazine* on Mushroom (comprised of partly finished, previously recorded tracks and not authorized for release by the band) and *Little Queen* on CBS. *Magazine* was eventually recalled so that it could be properly mixed and edited, and was re-released in 1978. Both albums, as well as both issues of *Magazine* were well received and produced AOR singles. The song "Barracuda," featured on *Little Queen*, became a signature song for Heart as well as a pioneering effort in the development of percussive heavy metal guitar.

**Go to Chapter 8 playlist example "Barracuda" Wilson/Wilson/Fisher/DeRosier, 1977**

Image 8.4: Nancy Wilson and Roger Fisher performing in 1978

Heart's final album of the decade was 1978's multimillion-selling *Dog & Butterfly*, an album conception resembling Bob Dylan's half-acoustic half-electric *Bringing It All Back Home*: the "Dog" side of the album features hard rockers while the "Butterfly" side features ballads (with a single exception: the album's closing track "Mistral Wind"). "Straight On" and "Dog & Butterfly" represent each side.

**Go to Chapter 8 playlist example "Straight On" Wilson/Wilson/Sue Ennis, 1978**

**Go to Chapter 8 playlist example "Dog and Butterfly" Wilson/Wilson/Sue Ennis, 1978**

Heart continues to record and perform. They experienced a decline in popularity in the early 1980s but came back with a more pop-oriented approach around mid-decade. There have been numerous lineup changes but the Wilson sisters have remained at the band's core. Heart has been honored with numerous awards and they stand as one of the most respected bands of the 1970s.

# AC/DC

Formed in Australia in 1973 by guitar-playing brothers **Angus Young** (b. 1955) and **Malcolm Young** (b. 1953), the hard-rocking "thunder from down under," **AC/DC**, rose to international fame in 1976. By that time the lineup had solidified to include vocalist **Bon Scott** (1946–1980), drummer **Phil Rudd** (b. 1954), and bassist **Mark Evans** (b. 1956), although Evans would be replaced by **Cliff Williams** (b. 1949) in 1977. The band had risen to national prominence in Australia during their early years and released their first two studio albums in 1975: *High Voltage* and *T.N.T.* In 1976 the band was signed by Atlantic Records who repackaged and reissued *High Voltage*. The international release included selected tracks from the band's *T.N.T.* album. One in particular became a well-known hit and the unofficial anthem of singer Bon Scott: "It's a Long Way to the Top." The song is unique in rock in that it features a bagpipe (which was played by Scott).

**Go to Chapter 8 playlist example "It's a Long Way to the Top" Young/Young/Scott, 1975**

AC/DC's third studio album, *Dirty Deeds Done Dirt Cheap*, released in 1976, would ultimately become the third best–selling record for the band, establishing them internationally. It features the classic double-entendre track "Big Balls."

**Go to Chapter 8 playlist example "Big Balls" Young/Young/Scott, 1976**

Their next album, *Let There Be Rock* (1977), would include Evans in the studio, although he would depart before the supporting tour. Cliff Williams replaced him and remains a member to this day. 1978 saw the release of *Powerage*. The album did not meet with an overwhelming critical response although it enjoyed robust sales. There was a conscious approach by the Young brothers to create heavier riffs and a more aggressive sound overall. Many consider this to be AC/DC's most under-rated work.

The real breakthrough to international superstardom came in 1979 with the album *Highway to Hell*. Working with producer Robert "Mutt" Lange, the band moved much closer to what would become their mature sound. Lyrics shifted away from their earlier facetious style to reflect themes more fundamental to rock. The title track as well as the hit "Beating Around the Bush," reflect the band's change in lyric direction, while the instrumental writing and production show a band that has truly discovered itself and is fully in touch with its blues roots.

**Go to Chapter 8 playlist example "Highway to Hell"** Young/Young/Scott, 1979

**Go to Chapter 8 playlist example "Beating Around the Bush"** Young/Young/Scott, 1979

Sadly, Bon Scott would not enjoy the fruits of the band's labor for long. On February 19, 1980, following a session of heavy drinking, Scott passed out in the back seat of a friend's car. Unable to waken him, the friend left him there to sleep it off. The next morning Scott was still in the car and unresponsive. He was rushed to a hospital where he was pronounced dead of asphyxiation from vomit. The official cause of death cited "acute alcohol poisoning." He was thirty-three.

The other members of AC/DC had considered disbanding but were encouraged by Scott's parents to carry on in his absence. Strengthened by this, the band began considering his replacement. The Young brothers had a recollection of a singer named **Brian Johnson** (b. 1947) about whom Scott had raved some time earlier. Johnson was in an English band called Geordie that performed regularly in Australia and was not difficult to locate. He was auditioned and hired within several days.

AC/DC had been working on the material for *Back in Black* when Scott died. They recorded the album with Johnson in April and May of 1980, again with Lange as producer, and released it in June. Its all-black cover was meant as a tribute to Scott. There was some apprehension on the part of the band that their loyal followers would not accept Scott's replacement. They could not have been more wrong. Not only was *Back in Black* an overnight critical and commercial success, it became one of the most popular albums ever recorded. It has sold more than 50 million copies and stands as the second best–selling album of all time, second only to Michael Jackson's *Thriller*.

Image 8.5: The iconic cover of *Back in Black*

*Back in Black* set the tone for much of what was to come in 1980s hard rock. It became one of the yardsticks by which all subsequent hard rock albums were measured. The title track and the song "Hells Bells" amply display AC/DC's mastery of their riff-driven, blues-soaked style.

**Go to Chapter 8 playlist example "Back in Black" Young/Young/Johnson, 1980**

**Go to Chapter 8 playlist example "Hells Bells" Young/Young/Johnson, 1980**

AC/DC found a winning formula with *Back in Black* and continued on with virtually no stylistic deviation or experimentation for more than three decades. In recent years, health issues have curtailed the band's concert appearances, and at the time of this writing, a recent report regarding Brian Johnson's failing aural health may spell the end for AC/DC.

## Journey

The first incarnation of **Journey** was formed in 1974 in San Francisco by veterans of Santana, guitarist **Neil Schon** (b. 1954) and keyboardist/singer **Gregg Rolie** (b. 1947). They were joined by bassist **Ross Vallory** (b. 1949), guitarist **George Tickner** (b. 1946), and drummer **Aynsley Dunbar** (b. 1946). Dunbar had built a reputation working with Frank Zappa and with John Lennon as a session drummer. The band recorded three albums between 1975 and 1977 in the jazz–rock fusion genre (discussed in Chapter 9), but were not finding much success. Tickner had parted with the band following their first album. At the behest of their label, Columbia, they added a devoted frontman, Robert Fleischman, and shifted their musical approach to a more radio-friendly rock style. Fleischman left the band after less than a year and was replaced by **Steve Perry** (b. 1949), the singer with whom they would soon rise to international fame.

Working with producer Roy Thomas Baker, Journey released their breakthrough album, *Infinity* in 1978. The album spawned several AOR hits including the single "Wheel in the Sky" and "Feeling That Way/Anytime," which are listed as two separate tracks but were, and are, often paired. The song pairing highlights the dual-lead vocals of Perry and Rolie. With *Infinity*, Journey combined high-level musicianship, straightforward pop rock song structures with a bluesy delivery, richly layered vocal harmonies, distorted guitars, big drum sounds, and infectiously catchy hooks.

**Go to Chapter 8 playlist example "Wheel in the Sky" Schon/Fleischman/Diane Valory, 1978**

**Go to Chapter 8 playlist example "Feeling That Way/Anytime" Journey/Fleischman, 1978**

For their 1979 release, *Evolution*, Journey would continue their partnership with Baker; however, Dunbar was replaced by drummer **Steve Smith** (b. 1954). The album increased the band's renown and spawned two successful singles: the blues-based, slow-shuffling "Lovin', Touchin', Squeezin'" and another dual-lead vocal piece called "Just the Same Way."

**Go to Chapter 8 playlist example "Lovin', Touchin', Squeezin'" Steve Perry, 1979**

**Go to Chapter 8 playlist example "Just the Same Way" Rolie/Schon/Valory, 1979**

Working with producers Geoff Workman and Kevin Elson on their 1980 album *Departure*, Journey sped the development of a phenomenon that would, by the end of the 1980s, become almost a genre unto itself: the **power ballad**. These were songs that showed the softer side of hard rockers and had an enormous commercial appeal. Power ballads will be discussed in detail in Chapter 11. The song "Stay Awhile" is an early prototype.

**Go to Chapter 8 playlist example "Stay Awhile" Perry/Schon, 1980**

Throughout most of the 1980s, Journey would continue to produce highly polished rock hits and had particular success with their power ballads. Songs like "Open Arms" and "Faithfully" became massive hits as did some of their harder-edged songs like "Stone in Love" from 1981. Lineup changes and various solo projects produced some hills and valleys in their career and singer Steve Perry would eventually be forced to retire from the band due to health issues. Their music has become well integrated into the popular culture through numerous placements in film, television, video games, and even the Broadway stage.

## Van Halen and the Guitar Solo Heard 'Round the World

Dutch-born, American-raised brothers **Eddie Van Halen** (b. 1955) and **Alex Van Halen** (b. 1953) formed the band that bears their name in 1974 in Pasadena, California. Completed by vocalist **David Lee Roth** (b. 1953) and bassist **Michael Anthony** (b. 1954), Van Halen brought rock music to new heights of virtuosity and showmanship. The musical centerpiece of Van Halen is unquestionably Eddie's revolutionary guitar playing, though as an *instrumental* power trio (not a trio in a technical sense) Van Halen also relies on the solidifying presence of its rhythm section. This it has in abundance: the musicianship of Alex Van Halen and Michael Anthony is superb. That they were somewhat overshadowed by Eddie's guitar playing and Roth's flamboyant stage antics cannot diminish their importance to the success of Van Halen. It was, however, Eddie's guitar skills that catapulted the band, almost immediately, to legendary status.

By dazzling audiences in the vibrant Los Angeles club scene with their brilliant musicianship and Roth's over-the-top stage persona and acrobatics, Van Halen had built a substantial regional reputation for themselves by the mid-1970s. The band caught the attention of producer Ted Templeman of Warner Bros. Records in the summer of 1977 and negotiated a recording contract. They entered the studio with Templeton in September and emerged within a month with their first full-length album, *Van Halen*. The album was recorded without excessive overdubs in order to recreate the band's live sound; there were even slight imperfections purposely left on the recording. The album was released in February 1978 and reached the top 20 in the album charts.

While *Van Halen* was commercially and critically successful, its true significance lies in Eddie's wildly innovative guitar playing; it marked the beginning of a new age of guitar virtuosity and inspired an entire era of "guitar gods." This is arguably the most singularly defining recording in the history of rock guitar. To be sure, the album displayed an abundance of all of the elements that scream rock, right down to the attitude (the first line of the opening track is "I live my life like there's no tomorrow"), but Eddie's technique was such that the world had never seen. In the second track on the album, a one-minute-forty-second guitar solo called "Eruption," he opened up a heretofore unknown sonic universe of blazing speed, unorthodox sound production and surgical precision. Michael Campbell and James Brody describe it nicely:

> Eddie Van Halen expanded the sound possibilities and raised the level of virtuosity on his instrument more than any performer in any genre—classical, jazz, rock or country—since the diabolical nineteenth-century violinist Nicolo Paganini or his pianist counterpart Franz Liszt.[1] (p. 435)

Joseph G. Schloss, Larry Starr, and Christopher Waterman have this to say:

> Eddie Van Halen's approach is characterized first and foremost by its emphasis on technical virtuosity. Up to that point, heavy metal guitar—and, in most cases, rock guitar in general—was associated with ragged-but-right soulfulness. Even widely praised guitarists like Eric Clapton and Jimi Hendrix were mainly appreciated for the way their technical skills facilitated emotional expression more that for the technical skills themselves. Eddie Van Halen, by contrast, ushered in an era in which a guitarist's notes-per-second rate was viewed as a good guide to the person's value as a musician. But although Van Halen was one of the fastest guitarists in rock history up to that point, his skills went far beyond simple speed. His solos showed a great deal of melodic and harmonic sophistication, and he also pioneered specific playing techniques that extended these skills even further. He was particularly noted for his use of "tapping," a technique whereby a guitarist quickly "taps" a note with the index finger of his or her right hand while still playing normally with the left hand. By alternating notes played the conventional way with tapped notes, a guitarist can play twice as fast as would otherwise be possible, while also making huge melodic leaps between notes. Tapping, then, allowed Eddie Van Halen to construct guitar solos that were almost inhumanly fast and melodically complex, a style of guitar playing that would later come to be known as "shredding."[2] (p. 283)

**Go to Chapter 8 playlist example "Eruption" Eddie Van Halen, 1978**

---

1   Michael Campbell and James Brody, Rock and Roll: An Introduction, pp. 435. Copyright © 2008 by Cengage Learning, Inc. Reprinted with permission.
2   Joseph G. Schloss, Larry Starr, and Christopher Waterman, Rock: Music, Culture, and Business, pp. 283. Copyright © 2012 by Oxford University Press. Reprinted with permission.

While many saw Van Halen as a "heavy metal" band, and they did in fact help to build a bridge between the heavy music of the early 1970s and the ascendance of metal that will occur in the 1980s, it was clear that their music encompassed elements that were more stylistically diverse. Their early studio efforts were by no means experimental, nor did they explore significant stylistic fusions; however, Van Halen demonstrated a facility for the popular rock genre with the song "Jamie's Cryin'" from their debut and with their first major hit single "Dance the Night Away" from their 1979 follow-up, *Van Halen II*. There is also a short acoustic guitar piece on *Van Halen II* called "Spanish Fly" which features hints of flamenco style, peppered with Eddie's signature techniques as well as the hard-rocking "Outta Love Again."

**Go to Chapter 8 playlist example "Dance the Night Away" Van Halen, 1979**

**Go to Chapter 8 playlist example "Spanish Fly" Eddie Van Halen, 1979**

**Go to Chapter 8 playlist example "Outta Love Again" Van Halen, 1979**

By the early 1980s, Van Halen had grown to a stadium-sized hard rock attraction. Roth's grand gestures (martial arts–style spinning back kicks, standing back flips and high-flying leaps) and motormouth patter gave the band an enormous stage presence, as did the overwhelming musicianship of Eddie, Alex, and Michael Anthony. Tension began to grow between Roth and Eddie Van Halen by the time they entered the studio for their fourth album, *Fair Warning* as is often the case when well-defined personalities have conflicting goals: Eddie was interested in writing more musically complex material while Roth had more pop-oriented aspirations. Additionally, Eddie, also a trained classical pianist, had begun to dabble in synthesizers and was interested in incorporating these into the band's sound. The use of synthesizers and keyboards would come to play a more prominent role in the band's later music, although we can hear the inklings of this on *Fair Warning* with the track "Sunday Afternoon in the Park" which segues into the more hard-rocking "One Foot Out the Door."

**Go to Chapter 8 playlist example "Sunday Afternoon/One Foot Out the Door" Van Halen, 1981**

Van Halen's strong visual element made them a perfect fit for MTV. We will discuss the band's endeavors and their continued success in the 1980s in Chapter 11.

## Kiss

By their own admission, **Kiss** consider themselves "entertainers" as opposed to "musicians." Their music, by extension, was far less significant to the development of rock than their presence as entertainers, their live shows, their "glam" image, and their massive merchandising endeavors. They developed an impressive live show, replete with heavy special effects and theatrics such as elaborate stage lighting, fog, pyrotechnics, fire breathing, blood spitting, and their signature gimmick: the dramatic costumes and makeup that would come to be iconic in pop culture.

Formed in 1973 by guitarist **Paul Stanley** (b. 1952), bassist **Gene Simmons** (b. 1949), drummer **Peter Criss** (b. 1945), and guitarist **Ace Frehley** (b. 1951), Kiss exploded into the public consciousness in 1975 with the release of *Alive!*, a live double album. Although the band had been touring and gaining mass media exposure, their studio albums were not selling well and their label, Casablanca, was on the verge of bankruptcy. *Alive!* changed their fortunes. The album sold very well and produced their anthemic hit "Rock and Roll All Nite." Kiss followed up with a string of hugely successful albums, including solo albums from each member in 1978. Their commercial success, if not their music, was staggering. The band represented the "marketing" of rock at its extreme. Besides recorded music, the band released a movie in which they possessed "super powers," and licensed an unprecedented range of products including comic books, lunchboxes, dolls, trading cards, Kiss makeup kits, Halloween masks, toy guitars, and even a pinball machine. This mass marketing of rock did not go unnoticed—or unchallenged…

Image 8.6: Kiss in character, 1976

## Punk Rock

By the mid-1970s, mainstream rock music had unquestionably taken on a decidedly commercial cast. Punk rock sprung from a position of rejecting the excess that was apparently eroding the soul of rock and the music industry. (This perceived excess included art rock and progressive rock; these are discussed in Chapter 9.) As a style, and eventually a globally relevant culture, punk was meaningful; as a reawakening of the original rebelliousness of rock, it was perhaps inevitable and necessary. The extremes of punk informed subsequent generations, not by invention but by *reinvention* and *intensification*. Punk bands were the garage bands of a new era, plain and simple; they played louder and faster and with more abandon, but they were *not* original nor did they advance the *state-of-the-art* of rock music. In point of fact, punk rock bombed rock music, songwriting, and the recording arts back into the Stone Age. As an expression of rock's *original values*, though, punk played a major role in *inspiring* the advances of the next decade.

There is a wealth of thought-provoking irony in the rock music scene in the late 1970s.

Rock, the quintessential "underdog" had risen from the obscure position of "rebel" music and fought tooth and nail to take over the kingdom. Kiss, more than just about any other rock band at the time, resembled nothing so much as Napoleon declaring himself Emperor. Herein lies just one of the ironies: Kiss' "kid-friendly" products and their powerful image inspired countless young children and teens to aspire to rock stardom, which had a major impact on the future of rock; numerous rock stars of the 1980s and 1990s cite Kiss as a primary influence. Yet, at the same time, Kiss' (and others) massive commercialization of rock would help to fuel the punk movement, its cultural antithesis. Paradoxically, punk rock would also exert an immense influence on many of those *same* young children and teens. In other words, both had a profound—if conflicting—effect on what rock (and metal) would become.

The irony of punk is like peeling away an onion: It is at once powerful yet ridiculous; expressive yet unmusical; profound yet superficial; brutal yet sublime; the *attitude* punk purported had an infinitely more far-reaching impact than the *music itself*. In terms of raw musical materials and ability punk rock music and musicians worked with extremely limited resources: Some of them could just barely play their instruments, and very few of them could really sing. Though in doing what they did, in the way they did it, the punk rockers reaffirmed so much of what rock was about in the first place: inclusion. That Johnny Ramone and Eddie Van Halen, or Johnny Rotten and Freddie Mercury could have coexisted as "rock stars" in the same universe speaks volumes about the inclusionary nature of rock.

Perhaps the richest irony of all is this: Punk was rock music rebelling against *itself*.

The epicenters for punk were primarily New York City and London; it happened in a handful of small "dive" bars in those cities. Although the earliest rumblings of the movement can be traced back to the late 1960s with the MC5 album *Kick Out the Jams* and what is now commonly referred to as "protopunk," it only began to gain serious traction in the early to mid-1970s. The Stooges, The New York Dolls, The Pink Fairies, and The Deviants were some of the more noteworthy acts involved in the articulation of the underground punk movement, however, no two bands embody the spirit, sound, look and attitude of punk rock more distinctly than New York's Ramones or London's Sex Pistols. We discuss each in turn.

## The Ramones

1974 saw four young (unrelated) musicians from Queens, New York, come together to form the Ramones. Taking on the pseudonym, inspired by Paul McCartney's erstwhile Silver Beetles alias, Paul Ramon, bassist **Dee Dee Ramone** (1951–2002), guitarist **Johnny Ramone** (1948–2004), singer **Joey Ramone** (1951–2001) and drummer **Tommy Ramone** (1949–2014) played their first gig at the downtown Manhattan club **CBGB** in August 1974. An underground music scene had been building at the now landmark venue, and to a lesser extent at Max's Kansas City, also in the downtown Manhattan area. The performance was described by one critic as a "wall of noise." They were loud and fast, their songs were all short and direct (their entire set spanned less than twenty minutes), and they had a distinctive appearance, donning blue jeans, leather jackets, and long hair. Their debut performance secured them a regular spot at the club and by the end of the year the Ramones had performed more than seventy shows at CBGB, drawing a considerable amount of attention.

Image 8.7: Joey Ramone performing circa 1980

By late 1975, the Ramones were leading of the New York underground punk scene. They were offered a contact with Sire Records and released their debut album, *Ramones*, in April 1976. The album contained fourteen songs yet it clocked in at just over twenty-nine minutes. It cost around

$6,000 to record (a relatively low price tag) and was finished in one week. Commercially, the album was a dismal failure and critical reviews were mixed, although it is now recognized as a genre-defining work of enormous influence which resonated far into the future. The track "Now I Wanna Sniff Some Glue" sums up the band's sound and attitude.

**Go to Chapter 8 playlist example "Now I Wanna Sniff Some Glue" Dee Dee Ramone, 1976**

The Ramones' legacy and their standing as cultural icons is incongruent with their lack of commercial success. The band toured almost constantly for more than twenty years, racking up well over two thousand performances. They are widely recognized by many mainstream publications, Halls of Fame, and other media for their broad and enduring influence.

## The Sex Pistols

In 1975, after spending a brief time New York where he had had various small-time dealings in the burgeoning punk scene there, a visual artist–turned-businessman named **Malcolm McLaren** (1946–2010) returned to his native London to resume his affairs. He ran a clothing and apparel shop there with his business partner Vivienne Westwood that catered to the various trendy rock tastes of hip, young Londoners. The shop had recently been rethemed toward marketing sadomas-ochist-inspired apparel and was renamed simply SEX. McLaren's business sense, his interest in the punk scene, and his flair for the outrageous motivated him to become involved with several young musicians who frequented his shop. Among these were guitarist **Steve Jones** (b. 1955), bassist **Glen Matlock** (b. 1956), and drummer **Paul Cook** (b. 1956), who played in a band called The Strand. McLaren introduced the musicians to a young customer who had caught his eye named **John Lydon** (b. 1956), proposing that he be their new singer. Lydon himself had given no thought to the idea. He gave a very impromptu audition and was brought into the group. With Lydon, who would soon change his name to **Johnny Rotten**, the band settled on the name the **Sex Pistols**.

The Sex Pistols began working on material and playing small gigs while McLaren went to work promoting the band, developing their look (mostly with clothing from his shop) and booking gigs. The band soon became known for hard-partying, anarchist-themed songs and the occasional bar fight. Steve Cook stated in an early interview, "we're not into music, we're into chaos." Increasingly outrageous performances and tabloid-style press contributed to the band's renown. In October 1976 they signed with EMI and entered the recording studio to make their first album. Though the Ramones by this time were understood to be the main influence on punk, Rotten claims that he had little interest in them or what they had to say. Instead, his lyrics were more political and caustic, as their first single "Anarchy in the U.K." indicates. The opening lines reveal the song's acerbic nature:

> I am an anti-Christ
>
> I am an anarchist

**Go to Chapter 8 playlist example "Anarchy in the U.K." Sex Pistols, 1976**

In 1977, a man by the name of John Simon Ritchie (1957–1979), aka **Sid Vicious**, would replace Matlock on bass. Disputes had begun between Rotten and Matlock over the lyrics of a song Rotten penned called "God Save the Queen." Sid Vicious did not even play bass when he joined the band but had been a friend of Rotten's and a fan of the Sex Pistols. He had a look and a reputation and he worked hard to learn the instrument in rehearsals. "God Save the Queen" was released as a single in 1977 and caused a massive public outcry in England for its sneering, antiroyal lyrics. It also soared into the number two position on the British charts.

**Go to Chapter 8 playlist example "God Save the Queen" Sex Pistols, 1977**

Image 8.8: The Sex Pistols (Sid Vicious left, Steve Jones center, and Johnny Rotten right) performing in Trondheim in 1977

The Sex Pistols basically self-destructed in 1978 due to internal conflict, McLaren's exploitation of the band, and Sid Vicious' increasingly problematic behavior, exacerbated by his heroin addiction.

Vicious died of a heroin overdose in 1979. He and his girlfriend, Nancy Spungen, were staying at the Hotel Chelsea and shooting heroin on October 11, 1978. Spungen was found dead the next morning with a stab wound to her stomach. Vicious was charged with the murder but managed to get released on bail. While out, he was involved in an altercation after which he was arrested and held at Riker's Island for nearly two months. Forced to detox while incarcerated, upon his release on February 1, 1979, Vicious partied with some friends and was found dead the next morning of an apparent overdose. He was twenty-one.

The Sex Pistols embodied life on the edge and burnt out as quickly as they rose. Their brief but influential presence figures prominently in the history of rock music. As the vanguard of the British punk movement and punk's true revolutionaries, they were a primary influence on the music and careers of some of the most significant artists of 1980s and 1990s.

**New wave**, as it was called, also emerged alongside of punk. Like punk, it sought a return to the musical simplicity that characterized early rock 'n' roll but with a modern approach that did not reflect the smooth, bluesy sound of earlier rock. New wave, however, had ties to popular music as well; pop song structures and devices were common; the incorporation of synthesizers and other electronic sounds as well as a great amount of diversity set new wave apart from punk. Bands like **Talking Heads** and **Blondie** helped to build a bridge between new wave and early 1980s pop rock. New wave will be discussed in greater detail in Chapter 10.

### Heavy Metal in the 1970s

The line between hard rock and heavy metal is fairly thin. Both genres share many of the same musical characteristics. Both feature heavily distorted guitars, bluesy or flashy guitar solos, thundering bass and drum sounds, intense rhythmic drive and energy, and hard-edged vocals. The primary distinction between hard rock and metal is the consistent and stylized use of **power chords** and **modal progressions** (your instructor can play examples)—metal bands base all or very nearly all of their harmonic and melodic language on these; whereas hard rock bands certainly make use of power chords, it only provides a portion of their harmonic language. These commonalities were behind the erroneous labeling of bands like Zeppelin, Van Halen, and Deep Purple as heavy metal bands.

Aside from this primary difference, there are other distinguishing traits that metal generally exhibits on a stylistically consistent level. Song structures tend to be more elaborate and frequently include extended guitar and other instrumental solos. Typically, the proportion of instrumental to vocal sections is much greater and, as the style developed, an absolute premium was placed on instrumental virtuosity. By the 1980s, the number of technically proficient musicians playing metal far exceeds those in other genres of rock. To the serious metal musician, advanced technical skills including speed, power, and precision were held up as a badge of honor. These traits are often linked with classical music; heavy metal bands adapted classical models as a basis for musicianship, structure, feel, and texture.

Lyric themes tended to focus on darker or more serious subject matter as well. Drug use, particularly its ill effects, is a common subject; as are themes regarding depression and mental illness, suicide, war, nuclear proliferation, the occult and, of course, sex. Concept albums are common as well. Many heavy metal lyricists have had to publicly defend their lyrics, sometimes even in courts of law. Specific instances of this will be discussed in subsequent chapters.

In the 1970s and early 1980s, heavy metal musicians and, by and large, their fan base, were mostly disenfranchised young people; commonly, but by no means exclusively, white males. These were the children of subsistence-level, working-class people who did not grow up in a world of privilege or advantage, as their middle- and upper-class counterparts had. Metal served as an outlet for musicians and a community for the fans. That heavy metal was perhaps the most misunderstood, underappreciated, and vilified style of all rock genres only served to solidify the feeling of unity within the metal community. An "us versus them"—"them" being anyone who did not understand or who criticized the music and its culture—prevailed.

Heavy metal received little to no help from the mainstream media in the 1970s and into the early 1980s. It was disseminated through recordings and in live performance, and also spread through underground media like independent magazines (fanzines), fans trading and sharing music, and simple word of mouth. Metal came to thrive because of a strong work ethic on the part of the musicians, perhaps shaped by the blue-collar culture from which many of them originated. Bands would tour constantly and for extended periods of time to promote their music; lesser known bands often strung tours together in clubs and small theaters. Their persistence would eventually pay off.

## Black Sabbath

Ask any aficionado of heavy metal (these people are commonly referred to as "metalheads" or "headbangers") who the first true heavy metal band was and chances are you will get the answer "Black Sabbath" (most likely accompanied by the same look you might get if you just emerged from an alien spacecraft). Guitarist **Tony Iommi** (b. 1948), bassist **Geezer Butler** (b. 1949), drummer **Bill Ward** (b. 1948), and singer **Ozzy Osbourne** (b. 1948) formed a band in 1968 in their hometown, the industrial city of Birmingham, England. Originally called Earth, the band changed its name to **Black Sabbath** after discovering that there was another Earth performing in the area. This incarnation of the band was stable for over a decade; a series of lineup changes began in 1979 when Osbourne was fired from the band (his solo career will be discussed in Chapter 12). For our purposes, we will discuss Sabbath as they existed in their original form in the 1970s.

In 1969, while still calling themselves Earth, there happened to be a horror movie showing near the band's rehearsal space called *Black Sabbath*. The title of the film inspired them to write a song of the same name. It was with the song "Black Sabbath" that the group found their ominous signature sound. They liked what they had done so much that they decided to move distinctly in the same direction with their subsequent music. It was shortly after this when they discovered the other local band called Earth and changed their name. The band, now called Black Sabbath, was discovered by and signed to Philips Records in late 1969 and recorded some early demo singles. They had also recently gained national exposure in England by performing several songs, "Black Sabbath" among them, on a rare live radio broadcast.

Sabbath used their newfound sound and name as a basis for building the themes and images for which they would become legendary. Images of the occult, crosses, references to heaven and hell in their music, and their dark personae helped to cultivate a mystique that would become synonymous with heavy metal. In some ways it was a "shock" tactic, and in others it seemed quite in keeping with the musical sounds they were creating. That the whole notion of "Black Sabbath" was inspired by a horror movie and written by young men living in a bleak, dirty, industrial environment says quite a bit in itself.

They recorded their self-titled debut album in a single twelve-hour session in October 1969 and released it on Friday the 13th of February 1970. The album reached number eight on the UK album chart but was torn apart by many mainstream critics. It has since been almost universally recognized as the birth of heavy metal. The title track amply demonstrates the distinctly dark and heavy sound and a band that has transcended blues rock.

**Go to Chapter 8 playlist example "Black Sabbath" Black Sabbath, 1970**

The follow-up, *Paranoid*, came quickly in September 1970. It rose to number four on the UK album chart, though the critics still were brutally unkind. The US release was held up until January 1971 as *Black Sabbath* was still making a strong showing in the album charts there. When *Paranoid* was released in the United States, the album reached number twelve, with almost no airplay whatsoever. The song "War Pigs/Luke's Wall" demonstrates the band's facility for writing longer forms, while the lyrics launch a scathing attack on the people who make war. While this was timely with the Vietnam protest movement and in keeping with the counterculture's condemnation of those who were perpetuating the war, there are differences in the expression of contempt in "War Pigs." This is not a plea to end the war, nor is it a simple political statement, as was common with many antiwar songs. This song portrays the makers of war as loathsome, detestable creatures who must, in the end, burn in hell for their sins against humanity. This kind of severe expression of antiestablishment concepts will inform metal for generations. In other words, the gloves were off and the verbal fists were flying. An excerpt from the final verse:

> *Day of judgement God is calling,*
> *On their knees the war pig's crawling.*
> *Begging mercy for their sins,*
> *Satan laughing spreads his wings, oh lord yeah!*

**Go to Chapter 8 playlist example "War Pigs/Luke's Wall" Geezer Butler, 1970**

Black Sabbath followed with *Master of Reality* in 1971, which contained the infamous "Sweet Leaf," the band's first ode to marijuana, as well as the heavily modal and rare acoustic forays "Solitude" and "Orchid." "Children of the Grave," another antiwar epic reflected lyricist Geezer Butler's growing pacifist ideals as well as his strong belief in civil disobedience, a widespread counterculture protest tactic.

The period from around 1971 saw the band engaging in increasingly self-destructive drug use, which would eventually lead to Osbourne's dismissal. Success meant access, and the band members indulged. They entered the studio to record *Masters of Reality* with what Bill Ward characterized as "more studio time and a briefcase full of cash to buy drugs." Nevertheless, they were able to produce genre-defining classics and music that would shape two generations of heavy metal—and then some.

Image 8.9: A well-worn Black Sabbath performing in 2014

Black Sabbath would release several more highly successful and influential albums with Osbourne before the end of the decade: *Vol. 4* (1972), *Sabbath Bloody Sabbath* (1973), *Sabotage* (1975), *Technical Ecstasy* (1976), and *Never Say Die!* (1978). Their commercial success experienced several peaks and valleys, although the band toured almost constantly, staging large arena shows all around the globe. Although Black Sabbath are now recognized as one of the most important bands in all of rock, critical reception throughout the 1970s and into the 1980s remained frigid at best and scathing at its worst. Their drug and alcohol use, especially Osbourne's, reached almost mythical proportions until it finally brought the band to a low point by 1978. Their opening act support for the *Never Say Die!* tour was an up-and-coming, youthful, and highly energetic Van Halen whose performance, by contrast, made Black Sabbath look like strung-out old men.

Black Sabbath would go through numerous lineup changes with the only constant being Tony Iommi. The band would feature important and influential vocalists like Ronnie James Dio, Ian Gillan, Glenn Hughes, and Tony Martin. The band eventually reunited in their original lineup for two separate periods, 1997–2006 and 2010–2014. Their future still holds potential for touring and recording.

In spite of the critical bashing and almost complete lack of airplay in the 1970s, Black Sabbath changed everything. Their originality and persistence were crucial to metal, which would rise in the 1980s to become the dominant style of rock. Nearly every major metal musician, as well as the minor ones, over the next three decades praised Sabbath in interviews, through tribute shows and recordings and through obvious emulation of what Sabbath did—not just musically, but in inspiring metal themes, culture, performance, and image.

Several other important and influential metal bands emerged from Great Britain, the United States and elsewhere in the last years of the 1970s. The so-called New Wave of British Heavy Metal (NWOBHM) produced bands like Judas Priest, Motörhead, Iron Maiden, and Def Leppard in those years; and in America, Ratt, Quiet Riot, and others were causing a stir on the West Coast. As the bulk of the important work of these bands will happen after 1980, they—and others—will be discussed in detail in Chapter 12.

We now examine another richly diverse and highly influential subgenre of rock, art/progressive rock, as it came of age in the 1970s.

### Suggested Chapter Related Activities

- Many important bands like Boston, Foreigner, Bad Company, Nazareth, Blue Öyster Cult, Free, Montrose, The Runaways, Thin Lizzy and others are not discussed in this chapter for reasons of space. Student research papers/presentations on these bands or others present an opportunity to explore their contributions.

- Compare the distinguishing features of punk to '70s hard rock trends.

- Compare and contrast the musical forms of several Led Zeppelin songs in the chapter. Which can you connect to the past and which can be distinguished as more innovative and original?
- Through careful listening and analysis, make a list of stylistic common ground between Journey, AC/DC and Heart. Do the same thing with ZZ Top and Lynyrd Skynyrd.

## Suggested Discussion Topics

- Discuss the idea of punk rock as a "reformation" movement.
- Discuss the cultural similarities between punk and heavy metal. Consider the necessity of each.
- Consider and discuss the many levels of irony in the punk movement and in the massive commercialization of rock in the 1970s.
- Does punk rock still serve a purpose?

## Image Credits

# CHAPTER 9

# Art Rock, Progressive Rock, and Fusion in the Seventies

*Hey you, don't help them to bury the light Don't give in without a fight*
-David Gilmour of Pink Floyd (from "Hey You")

## Art Rock or Progressive Rock?

If there's a thin line between heavy metal and hard rock, the terms *art rock* and *progressive rock* (alternatively referred to as "prog rock" or simply "prog") are virtually interchangeable. Both terms have historically been used to designate music that aspires to an elevated artistic status, to serve as an artistic statement as opposed to simply providing entertainment, and to present itself as music whose sole purpose is to exist in, of, and for itself. The ideal goal of art rock and prog is to create a listening experience that inspires contemplation and reflection. Both art rock and prog place demands on the musician and the listener; both demand a breadth of musical sensibility to create; and both require an intellectually and emotionally committed listener in order to be fully appreciated. Many of the criticisms of art and progressive rock have likewise been the same or very similar; both have been called out as self-important and overdone, pretentious and inaccessible, haughty and abstruse. And both have been derided for forsaking rock's original spirit by putting on airs.

Musical characteristics common to both art rock and prog may include: expanded structural forms that may begin with but move well beyond verse/chorus, or the introduction of novel structures (either usually results in songs that tend to be relatively long); a greater sense of rhythmic freedom is commonly favored over standard dance rhythms (more complex rhythmic structures, for example, those that move in groups of 5 or 7 or 11, as opposed to 4 are not infrequent, nor are tempo changes); nonstandard rock, instrumentation, synthesizers, experimental sounds, or "found" sounds often working in conjunction with rock instruments; advanced harmonic progressions; unified musical themes; and the "borrowing" or fusion of standard techniques and instruments common to other styles like jazz, classical, and even medieval and renaissance music.

Lyrics and lyric themes tend toward deeper, more philosophical topics, or the intellectual and philosophical approach toward common or universal topics. The depth of thematic ideas tends to result very often in concept albums or at least thematically linked songs. Subject matter may be connected to or inspired by literary genres and often employs literary devices such as metaphor, allegory, advanced imagery, and irony; science fiction themes, including many dystopian or apocalyptic themes and those dealing with the dehumanizing effects of technology are not uncommon; lyrics may reflect an intellectual perspective on social and political issues. These issues are sometimes addressed satirically. Fantasy themes and mythology are also familiar art rock and prog lyric fodder. These are only a few examples. Whatever the theme or subject matter, art rock and prog generally exhibit a thoughtful, cerebral approach with an emphasis on conveying something meaningful in a way that is commensurate with the music. Moreover, there is an abundance of purely instrumental pieces—even entire albums.

Album cover art was conceptually representative as well. Art and prog rock centered on the "full album experience" and bands often worked with well-known visual artists or specialty companies to create powerful images. Many album covers became iconic in their own right, spawning images that still pervade rock and popular culture. Surrealist or representational imagery was common in the heyday of art/prog as were images related to science fiction, fantasy, and technology. Lyrics were typically printed somewhere inside the album while photographs of the musicians were often not, or if they were they were downplayed in deference to the artwork. One of the great losses in the modern era of mp3 downloads and streaming music is the relative lack of concrete visual art connected to recordings.

Image 9.1: The cover of *The Dark Side of the Moon*

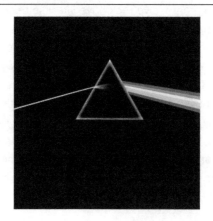

The iconic album cover image for *The Dark Side of the Moon* was designed by the George Hardy at the graphics company Hipgnosis. The company would come to be famous for many album cover designs in the 1970s. Roger Waters of Pink Floyd has said that the image represents three ideas: the light show of their live concerts, the album's lyric content, and their desire for a striking, clean design. Other interpretations have been offered. A widely regarded one states that the white light represents unified consciousness and as it moves through the prism (which represents the human state of existence) it becomes split apart into seemingly separate beams of light, representing the absence of original unity.

To many rock music scholars and commentators, the most discernible distinction between art rock and prog is that prog more often involves advanced instrumental techniques such as those commonly demonstrated by classical music virtuosi. This is problematic because it implies that art rock musicians avoid or are incapable of executing such techniques. This is simply not the case. There are also those who will distinguish art rock by its use of unconventional sounds and the use of "controlled noise" or other sounds that are not necessarily associated with musical instruments or standard instrumental technique. Art rock may be regarded as more "challenging," associated with the so-called *avant garde* or experimental music genres and involve novel sonic constructs. These blanket statements tend to be misleading and inaccurate as well.

We have seen some early examples of these two highly related styles evolving in the 1960s. Brian Wilson and The Beach Boys' work on *Pet Sounds* as well as their single "Good Vibrations," a good deal of The Beatles' late 1960s material, the music of Frank Zappa and The Who's invention of rock opera were among the earliest examples of rock aspiring to an elevated artistic status, as was the late 1960s work of bands such as Procol Harum, Jethro Tull, The Moody Blues, King Crimson, and The Nice. By about 1970, there was a clearly articulated set of practices surrounding art/prog that had grown into a relevant and well-received subgenre of rock. The early to mid-1970s were the peak years for the style. As mentioned in the previous chapter, the punk rock movement was partially inspired by the perceived pretensions of art rock and prog. The growth of punk and its repercussions effectively ended the golden age of art/prog. Although the genre(s) have persisted and evolved to this day (some artists have even fused art/prog with elements of punk), they have never experienced the same popularity as in the 1970s.

As the commonly held distinctions between art rock and prog are far fewer than the similarities, we will approach a categorization thusly:

Category 1) art rock bands with progressive leanings

Category 2) progressive bands with art rock leanings

These are loose categorizations and are by no means absolute. We start with Category 1:

## Pink Floyd

The earliest incarnation of British band **Pink Floyd** dates from 1965 when guitarist **Syd Barrett** (1946–2006), bassist **Roger Waters** (b. 1943), drummer **Nick Mason** (b. 1944), and keyboardist **Rick Wright** (1943–2015) formed in London under the creative leadership of Barrett. This lineup produced the successful debut album, *The Piper at the Gates of Dawn*, in 1967.

Syd Barrett had begun experimenting with LSD as early as 1965 and by 1967 his use of the drug had reportedly become heavy and frequent, often resulting in severe dysfunction. It reached a point where the band could not rely on Barrett. There were performances during which he would wander offstage or stop playing or just not show up at all. His increasingly erratic and unpredictable behavior, both on and off the stage, prompted the other band members to hire Barrett's longtime friend, guitarist **David Gilmour** (b. 1946). The idea was that Gilmour could be there as assurance if Barrett were to exhibit his ever more frequent problematic behavior. By early 1968, Gilmour and the rest of the band were excluding Barrett from shows and recording sessions and by April he was officially removed from Pink Floyd.

Barrett's image and legacy is that of the shadowy, troubled genius. His life and career went down a somewhat rocky path following his split with Pink Floyd. He released some solo music but he ultimately retreated from the music industry to pursue other endeavors. That he would be forever associated with Pink Floyd in many ways, including in the band's musical tributes to him, transformed him into a living legend, as well as one of rock's most enigmatic and intriguing figures. He is the subject of the song "Shine On You Crazy Diamond" from *Wish You Were Here* (1975) as well as partial inspiration for the album's title; the main character of the 1979 concept album *The Wall* is largely based on aspects of Barrett's personality.

Following Barrett's departure, Pink Floyd continued to develop along the shared creative visions of Waters, Wright, Gilmour, and Mason with Waters serving as the band's primary lyricist. Six studio albums came between 1969 and 1972 during which time the band became well known in the London underground scene for their expansive sound palette, which relied little on catchy hooks or predictable chord progressions, as well as their innovative live performances. It was in 1973 with the release of *The Dark Side of the Moon* that Pink Floyd would become a global force in art/prog rock.

The album is a conceptually based whole that explores themes of greed, violence, mental illness, the passage of time, the pressures of travel, and mortality. It paints an unsettling picture of the modern world. In addition to standard rock instrumentation and saxophone, Pink Floyd makes ample use of synthesizers. Perhaps the most notable extramusical effects are the "found" sounds and spoken dialogue (collectively known as *musique concréte*) which appear in the form of a cash register, clinking coins, ticking clocks, a helicopter (rendered by a synthesizer), a simulated beating heart sound, various spoken phrases, and the disturbing, maniacal laugh featured prominently in the song "Brain Damage."

Although there are no classical instruments on *The Dark Side of the Moon*, there is nevertheless a significant nod to the classical tradition: In an exceedingly common classical form known as sonata form, a composer introduces the musical material, or themes, which are subsequently developed into the full-blown composition, during an opening section called the *exposition*. Another way to think of it is that all of the musical "DNA" of the piece is contained in the exposition and, like a living thing, the piece "grows" from this "DNA." In the opening track of *The Dark Side of the Moon*, "Speak to Me," we are introduced to all of the album's thematic "DNA." The modern twist on this is that all of the themes in Pink Floyd's "exposition" are *musique concréte*). Nonetheless, this compositional technique links Pink Floyd firmly to the traditions of the Great Masters of classical music, and in a very subtle and clever way.

Image 9.2: Pink Floyd performing *The Dark Side of the Moon*, 1973

In this short introductory track, we hear the clock (time), the cash register and coins (greed), the spoken dialogue referring to madness and the bizarre laughter (mental illness), the helicopter (pressures of travel), and a nightmarish scream (violence)—all tied together with the beating heart effect (mortality). This is effectively a thematic exposition.

**Go to Chapter 9 playlist example "Speak to Me/Breathe" credited to Nick Mason, 1973**

An instant critical and commercial success, *The Dark Side of the Moon* brought Pink Floyd great wealth. It is one of the best-selling rock albums ever with around 45 million copies sold. With massive global success came possibilities for greater studio experimentation and expansion of their live show. The rest of the decade was extremely fruitful for the band although the interpersonal relationships were becoming increasingly fractured, mostly on the grounds of artistic differences. 1975 witnessed the release of *Wish You Were Here*, a concept album with a dual meaning: It reflects lyricist Waters' feelings regarding the deteriorating interpersonal dynamic of the band, including the effects of Barrett's departure and mental state; it also serves as a critique of the greed of the music industry and the power that money has to trump artistic integrity.

The track "Welcome to the Machine" is about the allure of wealth in the music industry.

**Go to Chapter 9 playlist example "Welcome to the Machine" Gilmour/Wright/Waters, 1975**

1977's *Animals* is based on the Orwellian concept of various classes in society being represented by different animals (and their characteristic behavior) from his novella *Animal Farm*. The album was very well received and the band set off on a world tour in support of it. During the tour, relationships between the band members became more and more distant. Waters was known to leave immediately following performances and to travel alone. At one point Wright threatened to quit, and Gilmour said that when the tour ended he felt he had reached a low point in his career, ironically because they had attained their goals of massive success and there was now nothing left to accomplish. Moreover, Waters was known to have a strong distaste for playing in large arenas and stadiums as he felt it created too much distance between the audience and himself as a performer. Waters' sense of isolation on the tour, both from his bandmates and audiences, would provide inspiration for the concept of the band's 1979 album, *The Wall*.

By the time Pink Floyd recorded *The Wall*, relationships within the band had all but broken down and Waters had assumed almost total creative control. Producer Bob Ezrin and engineer James Guthrie were hired to assist Waters and Gilmour. Ezrin helped to serve as a mediator between Waters and Gilmour, although by some accounts, his own strong personality often added to the tensions. The album itself is one of the most ambitious rock recordings ever made. It employs a small army of auxiliary musicians including a full orchestra and both adult and children's choirs. Recording took nearly a year and occurred in several studios from France to New York to Los Angeles. Much of the work was done with each band member in isolation. By the end, Rick Wright had officially left the band but would be hired as a live musician for *The Wall* tour. The sheer scope of the album, its utterly seamless production, and its standing in the annals of rock are a testament to the force of artistic will over personal challenges.

*The Wall* is a rock opera which tells the story of "Pink," a protagonist based partially on Syd Barrett and partially on Waters. Pink suffers a series of deeply traumatic experiences throughout his life beginning with the death of his father in World War II. He then endures a childhood dominated by an overbearing mother and abusive teachers lending to his disdain for authority and a twisted sense of himself. As an adult, Pink becomes a rock star whose life is mired in dysfunction and torment. He marries, but the relationship is tainted by infidelity—both his wife's and his own—while Pink is on the road. By then, he has turned to drugs to cope but it only makes matters worse. He suffers outbursts of violence and an epic hallucination in which he believes he is a fascist dictator ordering the persecution of audience members. As the story unfolds, we learn that "The Wall" is a metaphor for Pink's growing sense of alienation from the rest of the world; each of his negative experiences are the bricks of which it is built. In the end, he must face himself as the "Judge" and stand trial for showing feelings. Convicted, he is sentenced to "tear down the wall" thus baring himself to the world. The final fate of Pink is left in ambiguity.

The use of recurring musical themes figures prominently on *The Wall*. For example, the opening notes of the album on the track "In the Flesh?" return as the melody of the album's closing track "Outside the Wall," and the organ sequence which interrupts these opening notes is heard again in the "evolved" iteration of "In the Flesh" (without the question mark) that happens toward the end of the album. Additionally, the main melody of "In the Flesh?" begins with the first three notes of the major scale in the guitar (scale steps 1, 3, 2, 1). The major scale signifies the hopeful feeling of a yet untarnished life. The feeling of hopefulness is soon pushed aside by the more disparaging minor scale and its first three notes as the second track "The Thin Ice" unfolds (we hear "ooh, ooh, ooh, ooh babe" on minor scale steps 2, 1, 3, 2). The same three minor scale tones then begin to pervade the album, as in the main riff of "Another Brick in the Wall (Part 1)," for example (1, 2, 3, 2). Your instructor can demonstrate these themes with a piano or a guitar.

**Go to THE WALL playlist example** *The Wall* **(full album) Waters/Gilmour/Ezrin, 1979**

The live performances of *The Wall* (there were thirty-one shows in four cities in 1980–1981) were as grandiose as the recording. During each concert, a forty-foot wall (symbolizing alienation) was gradually constructed between the band and the audience. Animated visuals produced by cartoonist/visual artist Gerald Scarfe depicting disturbing renderings of characters and scenes from the album's storyline were projected onto sections of the wall, while giant inflatable versions of various characters were floated on tethers above the stage. The end of the concert culminated in the wall's collapse. The shows were limited to arenas as Waters refused to play in larger stadiums even though popular demand would have supported it.

There was a movie version of *The Wall* released in 1982 featuring actor/musician Bob Geldof in the lead role. Scarfe's animations were also used in some of the film's most famous sequences.

Pink Floyd would manage to record one more album, *The Final Cut* (1983), before breaking up. Many consider the album a Waters solo project as he wrote all of the music and the lyrics. Following the 1985 reincarnation of Pink Floyd sans Waters, years of legal battles over the rights to the name, mudslinging, and many other contentions between the band members, Waters, Gilmour, Mason, and Wright finally reunited in an epic farewell concert known as "Live 8 Reunion" in 2005 at London's Hyde Park.

## David Bowie

**David Bowie** (1947–2016) began his career variously involved in art, theater, dance, and music including folk, psychedelic, art/prog, and pop styles. His second studio album brought mild success with the 1969 single "Space Oddity," a song about a fictional astronaut named Major Tom (a character Bowie would revisit in other songs for over a decade). Following a period of experimentation, including a hard rock album from 1970 called *The Man Who Sold the World*, Bowie's love of acting and theatrics led to the development of his earliest and perhaps best-known stage persona, **Ziggy Stardust**.

By 1972, Bowie had earned a reputation as a flamboyant performer and personality, appearing on stage in wild costumes and giving interviews while dressed in drag. *The Rise and Fall of Ziggy Stardust and the Spiders from Mars* (1972) brought Bowie, or rather Ziggy, to the world stage. The album presents the story of a bisexual alien rock star (Ziggy) who has come to earth to deliver a message of peace and hope, though the earth is doomed. The Ziggy character lives the rock star dream; he is sexually promiscuous and indulges heavily in drugs. Ziggy is ultimately destroyed in the end by his own consumptions. Ziggy's character is described in the song "Ziggy Stardust."

**Go to Chapter 9 playlist example "Ziggy Stardust" David Bowie, 1972**

Image 9.3: An array of Bowie costumes as displayed in the Rock and Roll Hall of Fame

Bowie's performances as Ziggy were wildly theatrical and included moments of "shock" such as simulating oral sex with a guitar. Bowie appeared in character at interviews and other media events as well and had some trouble distancing himself from the character. In order to move past the Ziggy character, Bowie invented others such as Halloween Jack for the 1974 album *Diamond Dogs*, an Orwell-inspired concept album dealing with urban disorder and anarchism that presages similar themes in the punk movement.

In 1975, Bowie entered his self-styled "plastic soul" period, thus called because of Bowie's infusion of elements of black soul music—though he described his music of the period as "the squashed remains of ethnic music as it survives in the age of Muzak rock, written and sung by a white limey." The resulting album, *Young Americans*, saw Bowie's first number one single "Fame," which was cowritten with John Lennon and Carlos Alomar. Bowie and Alomar would continue to collaborate for the next three decades.

**Go to Chapter 9 playlist example "Fame" Bowie/Lennon/Alomar, 1975**

By 1976, Bowie had made his acting debut in the British sci-fi film, *The Man Who Fell to Earth* (a secondary career that would eventually include credits in more than twenty films). That same year he would develop a new stage persona called the "Thin White Duke" for the album *Station to Station*. By this time Bowie was living in Los Angeles and had become seriously addicted to cocaine. He appeared extremely thin and exhibited unusual behavior often making bizarre comments to the press. In an effort to regain himself, he moved to Switzerland and began painting, writing, studying classical music, and collecting art.

Bowie moved to Berlin at the end of 1976 where he continued his recovery from cocaine addiction in part by remaining very active. He was involved as a cowriter on two albums with Iggy Pop and in 1977 had begun releasing what would become an album trilogy of his own. Working with coproducer Tony Visconti and with contributions from ambient music pioneer Brian Eno, Bowie released *Low* (1977), an album which dealt with the pain of addiction, *"Heroes"* (1977), an album that explored Cold War themes (featuring guitarist Robert Fripp of King Crimson), and *Lodger* (1979), a dual-themed album, the first half portraying a homeless drifter through prototypical "world music," and the second half a critique of problems inherent in Western civilization.

**Go to Chapter 9 playlist example "African Night Flight" from *Lodger*, Bowie/Eno, 1979**

Over the next several decades, David Bowie would explore numerous musical styles and artistic endeavors. The 1980s brought enormous pop and MTV success and saw Bowie involved in a variety of collaborations with other mainstream artists like Queen, Pete Townshend, Mick Jagger, and Tina Turner, among others. His legacy as an experimental art/prog rock artist is matched by his contributions to "glam" rock and theatrics in rock. Bowie was an artist who continually reinvented himself and explored an expanse of artistic territory few others can claim.

We now explore several important acts who we will consider to be generally more progressive with art rock leanings (Category 2).

## Genesis

Formed in 1967 by keyboardist **Tony Banks** (b. 1950), bassist/guitarist **Mike Rutherford** (b. 1950), and singer/flutist **Peter Gabriel** (b. 1950), the British band **Genesis** would begin to find their stride when they were joined by drummer/singer **Phil Collins** (b. 1951) and guitarist **Steve Hackett** (b. 1950) in 1970. This lineup completed the album *Nursery Cryme* in 1971, which was not terribly successful in England but was very much so on the European continent. Genesis toured Europe for about nine months and built an enthusiastic following there, while gaining valuable performance experience.

*Foxtrot* was recorded in the summer of 1972 with producer Dave Hitchcock and boasts a twenty-three-minute epic suite called "Supper's Ready," as well as the melodramatic "Watcher of the Skies." Critics praised the album variously as a "milestone," a "creative peak," and a "pinnacle of art rock." The band toured for nearly a year in support of *Foxtrot* in both Europe and North America during which time Gabriel began developing elaborate stage costumes which included fluorescent face paint, bat wings, and capes. Audiences were quite receptive to Gabriel's theatrics as well as the band's complex music.

> **Go to Chapter 9 playlist example "Watcher of the Skies" Genesis, 1972**

*Selling England by the Pound* came in 1973 and kept the band touring. They had by now built a modest but devoted global following and the album sold fairly well, reaching number three in the United Kingdom. Critical praise was positive but cooler than it had been for *Foxtrot*. Most critics now consider *Selling England by the Pound* one of the most influential prog rock albums of all time.

> **Go to Chapter 9 playlist example "Dancing with the Moonlit Knight" Genesis, 1973**

Genesis' next project was a mammoth undertaking: a double-length concept album entitled *The Lamb Lies Down on Broadway* (1974). Coproduced by Genesis and John Burns, the album and subsequent tour would be Peter Gabriel's last with the band as creative and other differences would lead to his departure in 1975. The album is one of the most complex concept albums in rock, with a sophisticated and surrealist plot centered on a character name Rael. Rael finds himself on a dreamlike journey in search of his brother, though it has been suggested that Rael is a split personality and is really looking for himself. The album explores themes of mythology, heaven and hell, fantasy, sexuality, and consumerism.

Following Gabriel's departure, Collins assumed the role of lead vocalist. The quartet would release two more albums in 1976, *A Trick of the Tail* and *Wind & Wuthering* before Hackett left the band in 1977 to pursue a solo career. The trio of Collins, Rutherford, and Banks would continue with 1978's *... And Then There Were Three ...*, taking the band's sound in a more commercial direction with shorter songs and more conventional rock forms. The album was their most commercially successful up to that time. The hit single "Follow You Follow Me" is representative of the band's new direction.

**Go to Chapter 9 playlist example "Follow You Follow Me" Genesis, 1978**

Although the 1980s would be a decade of massive commercial success for Genesis—as well as for individual members as they embarked on solo careers (Phil Collins was particularly successful)—they never totally lost touch with their progressive beginnings. Though fans and critics who praised them in the 1970s are often critical of their 1980s shift to a more commercial approach (and vice versa), they remain one of the most important and enduring prog bands of all time. The hit title track from 1981's *Abacab* is a good representation of the middle ground Genesis struck between prog and mainstream rock.

**Go to Chapter 9 playlist example "Abacab" Genesis, 1981**

## Emerson, Lake & Palmer

Guitarist/bassist/singer **Greg Lake** (b. 1947) and keyboardist **Keith Emerson** (1944–2016) met in 1969 while they were each in different bands, King Crimson and The Nice, respectively, who were performing a series of concerts together at the Fillmore in San Francisco. Each learned that the other was unhappy in their current situation and interested in forming a new band. A mutual friend guided them to drummer **Carl Palmer** (b. 1950) who was in a newly formed band called Atomic Rooster. The two convinced Palmer to join them in an impromptu jam session, upon which all three knew they had found the right musical chemistry.

**Emerson, Lake & Palmer**, familiarly **ELP**, began performing in the summer of 1970. They landed a spot on the Isle of Wight Festival in August and were noticed and immediately offered a contract by Ahmet Ertegün, president of Atlantic Records. Their self-titled debut followed in November and climbed to number four in the United Kingdom. The album contains three instrumental tracks, all of which were based on existing classical pieces, a drum solo, and the now classic AOR single "Lucky Man."

**Go to Chapter 9 playlist example "Lucky Man" Greg Lake, 1970**

The band's follow-up album, *Tarkus*, was recorded in January 1971. The whole of side one is a seven-part concept piece dealing with the futility of religion and war, framed around the fictional creature Tarkus, a being who is half-tank and half-armadillo. The album reached number one in the United Kingdom and number nine in the United States and established ELP as one of the premier prog bands in the world.

ELP's first live album was a recording of their prog rock adaptation of Russian composer Modest Mussorgsky's 1874 piano masterpiece, *Pictures at an Exhibition*. The band had intended to release their *Pictures at an Exhibition* before *Tarkus* (it was recorded at England's Newcastle City Hall in March 1971) but their label thought this a bad idea, citing that a recording of a classical suite was not likely to perform well. Following the success of the June 1971 release of *Tarkus*, *Pictures at an Exhibition* was released in November and reached number three in the United Kingdom and number ten in the US album charts; an almost unheard-of chart performance for an adaptation of a classical work.

Emerson, Lake & Palmer would release their third studio album, *Trilogy*, in July 1972, reaching their commercial peak at number two in the United Kingdom and number five in the United States. The music proved problematic to perform because of extensive studio overdubs. Their following album, *Brain Salad Surgery* (1973) was approached with live performance specifically in mind. The band purchased an abandoned cinema in which to write and rehearse the album, paying special attention to keep the music suited to a concert situation. The album is, according to many critics, their creative peak. As with ELP's previous efforts, the album contains a mix of original music and adaptations of existing classical works. "Still ... You Turn Me On" and "Karn Evil 9: 1st Impression, Part 2" are both examples of the former:

**Go to Chapter 9 playlist example "Still ... You Turn Me On" Lake, 1973**

**Go to Chapter 9 playlist example "Karn Evil 9: 1st Impression, Part 2" Emerson/Lake, 1973**

A global promotional tour for the album followed. It would prove to be ELP's largest and most ambitious tour and was replete with a rotating drum riser and revolving keyboards. The show required nearly forty tons of equipment to produce. *Welcome Back My Friends, to the Show That Never Ends ... Ladies and Gentlemen*, a triple live album of concert performances from the tour was released in 1974. It reached the top 5 in both the UK and US album charts.

Following an extended break from 1974 to 1977, ELP returned with *Works, Volume 1* and *Works, Volume 2* in succession. Neither album was well received nor was 1978's *Love Beach*. It seemed that Emerson, Lake & Palmer had taken their music a bit too far for all but the most ardent prog fans. One critic stated: that an "overbearing sense of self-importance turned ELP from one of the 1970s' most exciting new groups into the definition of masturbatory excess and self-aggrandizement in only a few short years" and that "in their fall from grace, [ELP] represented everything wrong with progressive rock." Nevertheless, the early work of ELP stands as groundbreaking and influential prog rock. Highly significant artists such as metal greats Iron Maiden and modern prog metal band Dream Theater cite ELP as a primary influence.

Emerson, Lake & Palmer reunited in the 1990s and 2000s for various studio and live projects including live performance DVDs. Sadly, in March 2016, Keith Emerson took his own life.

## Yes

With twenty studio albums and fourteen live albums between 1969 and 2015, **Yes** is one of the most prolific bands of the rock era, and with a lineup that has included nineteen different members, they have boasted some of the greatest names in art/prog rock as part of their roster. Originally formed by bassist **Chris Squire** (1948–2015) and singer **Jon Anderson** (b. 1944) in London in 1968, the band at the beginning of what is widely considered their most significant period (1971–1977) included Anderson, Squire, guitarist **Steve Howe** (b. 1947), keyboardist **Tony Kaye** (b. 1946), and drummer **Bill Bruford** (b. 1949). Additionally, most of their music during this period was recorded with producer Eddy Offord.

After two critically acclaimed but commercially unsuccessful albums in 1969 and 1970, the band was in danger of being dropped by their label. Howe, who joined Yes for their third album, brought with him eclectic tastes and inclinations that his predecessor, Peter Banks, did not possess. Sessions with Howe produced the 1971 recording *The Yes Album* and brought the band the commercial success they and their label were seeking. The album reached number four in the United Kingdom and eventually sold more than a million copies. The AOR hit "Yours Is No Disgrace" is representative of the band's maturing sense of musical identity. Tony Kaye would depart following Yes's 1971 European tour due to artistic differences. He was replaced by classically trained keyboardist and studio musician **Rick Wakeman** (b. 1949).

**Go to Chapter 9 playlist example "Yours Is No Disgrace" Yes, 1971**

The next album, *Fragile*, also released in 1971, represented a new conception for the band. It contains nine tracks, four group-conceived pieces and five pieces based on ideas from each individual member. The entire album marked an increase in the band's use of the more sprawling formal structures associated with classical music. The album contains one of Yes' best-known songs and their first US chart single, "Roundabout." *Fragile* reached number four in the United States and number seven in the United Kingdom.

"Roundabout" is a complex, multi-sectioned song. Following a brief acoustic guitar introduction there are two verses followed by a bridge (with the lyric "In and around the lake..."). The bridge leads to a third verse and a repeat of the bridge. We then have a third major section characterized by a repeated riff overlaid with complex vocal lines. This eventually arrives back at the acoustic opening, only now the guitar is accompanied by an atmospheric keyboard part and segues to a mellow vocal section. Lengthy instrumental solos follow and lead back to a verse section much like the beginning. As one last twist in the form, a richly arranged vocal "scat" section brings the song to a quiet close on a descending acoustic guitar riff.

**Go to Chapter 9 playlist example "Roundabout" Anderson/Howe, 1971**

In 1972, Yes released *Close to the Edge*. The album contained three compositions and the band's longest single piece to date, occupying the whole of side 1 and clocking in at around nineteen minutes. Critics praised the band as being "light years ahead of their emulators." The album reached number three in the United States and number four in the United Kingdom. Drummer Bill Bruford left the band before the album tour citing his displeasure with the band's direction. He was replaced by **Alan White** (b. 1949) who had become known for his session work with both John Lennon and George Harrison.

Several highly successful albums and tours followed, as did lineup changes. *Tales from Topographic Oceans*, a concept album based on Hindu scripture came in late 1973. Keyboardist Rick Wakeman would depart following the album's tour to pursue a solo career. Swiss keyboardist Patrick Moraz was hired as Wakeman's replacement, though the subsequent album *Relayer* (1974) would prove to be Moraz's only recording with Yes. *Relayer* featured a twenty-two-minute composition called "The Gates of Delirium" based on Leo Tolstoy's novel *War and Peace*.

Solo albums from each of the band members were released between 1975 and 1976 and in 1977 Rick Wakeman returned to Yes to record *Going for the One*. The album featured mostly shorter tracks and contained no overarching themes as the band felt it was time to lighten things up a bit and adopt a more celebratory tone. Two singles were released including the title track and "Wonderous Stories." The album has been called the most overlooked album in the Yes catalog. The album's closing track, "Awaken," is the only large-scale composition, clocking in at nearly sixteen minutes.

**Go to Chapter 9 playlist example "Awaken" Anderson/Howe, 1977**

*Tormato* from 1978 would be the last Yes album of the decade. Even though there are no songs exceeding seven minutes, critics were fairly harsh, claiming the album represented the bloated excesses of early 1970s prog. That the album was released in the height of the punk movement may account for some of the scathing reviews.

Yes disbanded in 1981 only to return in 1983 with a new lineup and a major comeback album, *90125*. A much more media-friendly commercial approach to form marked the band's eighties sound, although they always maintained the highest standards of musicianship and continued to work with the advanced musical materials of their most progressive music, as we hear in the track "Leave It." Yes remains one of the most respected and influential bands of the rock era.

**Go to Chapter 9 playlist example "Leave It" Squire/Rabin/Horn, 1983**

## Rush

The original lineup of the Canadian band **Rush** from 1971 consisted of bassist/singer/keyboardist **Geddy Lee** (b. 1953), guitarist **Alex Lifeson** (b. 1953), and drummer **John Rutsey** (1952–2008). Their 1974 self-titled debut album would be the only recording to feature Rutsey. He departed Rush following its release due to health issues. His replacement, drummer/percussionist **Neil Peart** (b. 1952) would join shortly after and subsequently assume duties as the band's primary lyricist. Peart will play a dominant role in shaping the band's identity. Not only did he bring his literary-minded and highly intelligent lyric style to Rush, his skill as a drummer places him squarely among the greatest musicians of all time—in any style. Often recognized as one of the hardest-working bands in rock, Rush has released twenty studio albums, eleven live albums and various box sets, compilations, and anthologies to date. Their lineup has remained the same for more than four decades.

Their second album, *Fly by Night* (1975), the first recorded with Peart, will also see the addition of producer Terry Brown who, between 1975 and 1982, would go on to coproduce seven albums with Rush. *Fly By Night* and to a greater extent the following album, *Caress of Steel*, also released in 1975, are often considered transitional or developmental for the band as they increasingly embraced progressive elements not present on their first album. Although *Caress of Steel* was a commercial failure at the time of its release, it has nonetheless come to be highly regarded by both fans and critics. Their fourth studio effort, *2112*, would firmly establish Rush as progressive rock icons and pave the way for their continued commercial and critical success.

Although their label at the time, Mercury Records, warned Rush that another progressive-flavored album with concept pieces, such as they had recorded on *Caress of Steel*, just would not do, Rush stayed true to their artistic vision and created what has now come to be known as one of the greatest prog albums of all time as well as a signature recording for the band. It would also prove to be the band's commercial breakthrough. *2112*, released in 1976, is half concept album (side 1) and half unrelated songs (side 2). For our purposes, we will discuss the concept portion of the record, the seven-part suite for which the album is titled.

> **Note**: While Peart acknowledges the "genius of Ayn Rand" in the liner notes as inspiration for the story and lyrics of "2112" (it bears similarities to the Objectivist Rand's novella *Anthem*) he has stated that he did this so as not to encounter any legal repercussions from Rand or her publisher. Nevertheless, the band faced negative backlash for the association with Rand and her right-wing extremism. Peart, while contending the individual is paramount in matters of justice and liberty, specifically dissociated himself from a strictly Objectivist (Randist) line.

"2112" is part science-fiction, part cautionary tale. The story is told in part through the lyrics and in part through the accompanying album liner notes. Here is a summary:

In the year 2062, following an interplanetary war, a union of planets is formed under the rule of the Red Star of the Solar Federation. All activities of society, including work, media, literature, and entertainment are controlled by the Priests of the Temples of Syrinx ("We've taken care of everything, the words you read, the songs you sing, the pictures that give pleasure to your eye …"). The protagonist of the story, who lives happily (he thinks) among this highly controlled society, stumbles upon a guitar in a cave one day. Fascinated with the "strange device," he begins toying around with it and eventually teaches himself to play it. Unable to contain his joy at the prospect of what the guitar can mean to society ("I can't wait to share this new wonder, the people will all see its light. Let them all make their own music, the Priests praise my name on this night …"), he takes his find to the Temples of Syrinx. Upon presenting the guitar to the Priests, they simply dismiss it saying "Yes we know it's nothing new, it's just a waste of time"/"Another toy that helped destroy the elder race of man, forget about your silly whim, it doesn't fit the plan…" They smash the guitar at his feet. Distraught, our hero runs away to the cave and falls into a restive sleep. He dreams of an oracle telling him of the return of the elder race to free humankind from its bonds. Awakening to find that it was only a dream, he takes his own life. As he dies, the piece ends ambiguously with an ominous voice repeating "Attention all planets of the Solar Federation, we have assumed control," suggesting that the dream was actually a vision of the future of Earth.

**Go to Chapter 9 playlist example "2112" Rush, 1976**

Rush would finish out the 1970s with two more albums, *A Farewell to Kings* in 1977 and *Hemispheres* in 1978. Both albums contain richly progressive music and heady lyrics such as the song series "Cygnus X-1" which explores the dichotomy of human logic and emotion through an allegorical lens of sci-fi and Greek mythology. With *Hemispheres*, Rush also begins to create more conventional, AOR-friendly tracks like their now-classic metaphorical song, "The Trees." In it, the oaks and the maples represent two distinct classes of society, presumably the wealthy and the poor. The first verse:

*The trouble with the maples*
*(And they're quite convinced they're right)*
*They say the oaks are just too lofty*
*And they grab up all the light*

**Go to Chapter 9 playlist example "The Trees" Rush, 1978**

Image 9.5: Neil Peart in concert with Rush circa 2004

1980's *Permanent Waves* marked a new era of synthesizer experimentation, shorter compositions, and commercial success for Rush, though their music continually retained its progressive qualities. Uncompromising artistry and nearly nonstop touring have defined Rush for more than forty years. Among their most classic work is 1981's *Moving Pictures* and the AOR staple "Tom Sawyer."

**Go to Chapter 9 playlist example "Tom Sawyer" Rush, 1981**

## Supertramp and Progressive Pop

Formed in London in 1970 by multi-instrumentalists/vocalists **Rick Davies** (b. 1944) and **Roger Hodgson** (b. 1950) and following only modest success with their first two albums, **Supertramp** began their ascent to the popular mainstream in 1974 with their album *Crime of the Century*. The lineup of the band by this time came to include bassist **Dougie Thomson** (b. 1951), drummer **Bob Siebenberg** (b. 1949), and woodwind player **John Anthony Helliwell** (b. 1945). The album was a successful blend of art and prog musical elements with pop sensibility and radio-friendly formats. It spawned two major hits, "Dreamer" and "Bloody Well Right" and reached the top 10 in the UK album charts.

**Go to Chapter 9 playlist example "Dreamer" Davies/Hodgson 1974**

**Go to Chapter 9 playlist example "Bloody Well Right" Davies/Hodgson, 1974**

Two more mildly successful albums would follow in 1975 and 1977—*Crisis? What Crisis?* and *Even in the Quietest Moments...*, respectively. It was 1979's release, *Breakfast in America*, which would launch Supertramp to international superstardom and help give progressive pop an enduring presence on rock radio. The album topped charts all around the world and produced four hit singles, "Breakfast in America," "The Logical Song," "Take the Long Way Home," and "Goodbye Stranger." It is widely regarded as one of the greatest albums of the era and has been lauded as "faultless" and "extraordinarily melodic." Conversely, one critic called it a "perfect demonstration of why punk had to happen."

**Go to Chapter 9 playlist example "Take the Long Way Home" Davies/Hodgson, 1979**

## Kansas and American Prog

Although most influential art/prog rock bands were British, there were some noteworthy American bands as well (most American prog has a distinctly hard rock edge). Boston and Styx are among a memorable few, the latter being best known for hits like "Come Sail Away," "Fooling Yourself," and "Blue Collar Man" (Styx will be discussed in Chapter 11). Arguably, the most significant American art/prog band in the 1970s was **Kansas**.

Kansas was formed from a collective of musicians working in Topeka in the early 1970s: the original incarnation of Kansas and a group called White Clover who basically merged, split, and reformed. The resulting second incarnation of Kansas was made up of keyboardist/ vocalist/percussionist **Steve Walsh** (b. 1951), guitarist/keyboardist/vocalist **Kerry Livgren** (b. 1949), violinist/vocalist **Robby Steinhardt** (b. 1950), guitarist **Rich Williams** (b. 1950), bassist **Dave Hope** (b. 1949), and drummer **Phil Ehart** (b. 1951). Their self-titled debut album came in 1974 and got the band off to a fairly slow start. It received mixed reviews and charted rather poorly, but Kansas had begun to build a small cult following through persistent performance and promotion.

Their second album, *Song for America*, came the following year and was praised for its intensity, yet only met with mild commercial success. The title track, a ten-minute symphonically structured piece, was also edited down to a three-minute single. Neither version had a significant impact at the time but the longer version has come to be known as one of Kansas' masterpieces from their obscure early period and appears on several greatest hits collections and anthologies released in later years.

Go to Chapter 9 playlist example "Song for America" Kerry Livgren, 1975

Kansas's breakthrough would come in 1976 with their fourth album, *Leftoverture*. It would reach number five on the album chart and produce one of the band's best-known songs, "Carry On Wayward Son." This marked the beginning of Kansas' peak commercial period that included their next album, *Point of Know Return* (1977). Both the title track and the deeply philosophical ballad "Dust in the Wind" would become hit singles as well as enduring classics of rock radio.

Go to Chapter 9 playlist example "Carry On Wayward Son" Livgren, 1976

Go to Chapter 9 playlist example "Point of Know Return" Ehart/Steinhardt/Walsh, 1977

Go to Chapter 9 playlist example "Dust in the Wind" Livgren, 1977

Beginning in 1981, Kansas would go through several lineup changes and commercial peaks and valleys. Although they never enjoyed the commercial success of 1976–1977, their music has become engrained in popular culture through movies, television, and video games. They have continued to record and tour and have earned the rare station as one of America's classic art/ prog bands.

## Brand X and Fusion

Jazz–rock fusion, or **fusion**, is a subgenre of art/prog that developed from the influences of jazz, psychedelia, progressive music, and the visceral power of rock, and evolved along its own lines in the 1970s. Fusion artists had little concern for generating mass commercial appeal, but instead favored artistically ambitious and complex music. Fusion shares many characteristics with art/prog but often takes those characteristics to even greater extremes: Purely instrumental pieces were the rule, not the exception; improvisatory solo passages, difficult time signatures, and intricate time signature changes; dense textures; highly advanced and unconventional harmonic progressions; and extreme virtuosity all pervade the genre. In other words, fusion is the most intensely "artistic" of the art rock genre.

There were a number of significant bands and artists in this specialty genre whose influence can be followed into later generations and whose art was deeply respected, if not commercially successful, in its own time, particularly by other musicians. Weather Report, The Mahavishnu Orchestra, Nucleus, Traffic, The Eleventh House, and The Pat Metheny Group are among the most notable. Additionally, many well-established artists, most of them coming from jazz, were involved in experimental fusion projects. Among the jazz notables who experimented with fusion are Miles Davis, Chick Corea, Herbie Hancock, Jean-Luc Ponty, Maynard Ferguson, and Buddy Rich.

**Brand X** is representative of the genre. The band was formed in 1975 by guitarist **John Goodsall** (b. 1953), bassist **Percy Jones** (b. 1947), and would ultimately include eighteen other musicians between 1975 and, 1980 and 1992 and 1999. **Phil Collins** of **Genesis** played drums and sang on three of the four albums the band would release in the late 1970s. He was forced to depart the band sporadically due to obligations arising with Genesis. He left the band permanently in 1979. Their 1976 debut album, *Unorthodox Behaviour*, also included keyboardist/vocalist **Robin Lumley**. The following tracks, "Nuclear Burn" and "Smacks of Euphoric Hysteria" are great examples of the extreme musicianship and musical complexity that distinguished the genre:

**Go to Chapter 9 playlist example "Nuclear Burn" Brand X, 1976**

**Go to Chapter 9 playlist example "Smacks of Euphoric Hysteria" John Goodsall, 1976**

Jazz–rock fusion evolved in several different directions in 1980s and 1990s. For example, so-called "smooth jazz" became a highly commercialized fusion-based style in the 1980s. Artists like George Benson, David Sanborn, and Chuck Mangione and jazz rock bands like Chicago and Steely Dan fused jazz, rock, and pop elements into a lightweight, radio-friendly style. Many "purists" denounced smooth jazz and jazz rock for their comparative lack of depth and complexity. The technically challenging nature of fusion has influenced the so-called "math rock" and progressive metal bands of the 1980s, 1990s and beyond. Bands like Dream Theater, Meshuggah, Planet X, The Mars Volta, and Porcupine Tree have helped to carry the spirit of complex fusion into the twenty-first century.

## The Legacy of 1970s Rock

The commercialization of rock in the 1970s was ironic in the extreme. On one hand, it seemed to undermine rock's core values as an expression of rebellion and dissent. On the other hand, the benefits of financial success for artists afforded them access to the tools and technologies to expand their art to heretofore unimaginable proportions and to bring the spectacle of the live rock show to millions of people. Commercialization spurred a reactionary rebirth of the rebellious spirit, as we have seen with the punk movement, but it was also significant in facilitating the staggering amount of musical diversity in the 1970s; the permeation of rock into mainstream popular culture ultimately advanced its inclusionary nature. Joseph G. Schloss, Larry Starr, and Chris Waterman conclude:

> In the seventies, rock became solidly established as both a cultural force and as a business enterprise. The profits generated by recordings, mass media and live performances were brought into a self-perpetuating relationship that would last for decades. The "rock star" ideology flourished; stadium concerts, platinum albums, and mega-tours became commonplace; and a cultural infrastructure developed to support (and to critique) the genre. At the same time, the massive expansion of rock and its audience opened the door for the music's fragmentation into specialized subgenres, a trend that would continue with even greater intensity in the decades to follow.[1] (p. 213)

## Suggested Chapter Related Activities

- Locate several examples of post-2000 art/prog songs or albums. What similarities does modern art/prog share with that of the '70s? How has it evolved?
- Watch the movie *The Wall*. Try to draw your own sense of meaning in its metaphorical content.
- Locate several examples of post-2000 concept albums. Are there recurring themes in modern concept albums? Do these themes draw inspiration from art rock of the '70s?
- See if you can find modern songs that employ metaphor similar to Rush's "The Trees."
- As a particularly challenging exercise, map out the form of a song like "Tom Sawyer" or "Carry On Wayward Son."
- Locate post-2000 examples of jazz-rock fusion or other new types of creative fusion styles.

---

1    Joseph G. Schloss, Larry Starr, and Christopher Waterman, Rock: Music, Culture, and Business, pp. 213. Copyright © 2012 by Oxford University Press. Reprinted with permission.

## Suggested Discussion Topics

- Do you find art/prog rock to be overblown and pretentious or do you feel that it represents important artistic pioneering in rock?

- Do you think that art/prog rock represents musical elitism? Does it undermine the spirit of the "garage band" or does it inspire garage bands to become more accomplished musicians?

- Why do you think most modern listeners are alienated by challenging music? Does it have to with shorter attention spans (i.e. "multitasking") or does it reflect something deeper like the lack of emphasis on early music education, apathy, etc.? Does it say something about our society?

## Image Credits

# UNIT THREE
# THE EIGHTIES AND NINETIES

Image 10.1: Fictional rock star Nigel Tufnel's Marshall amp that "goes to eleven"

# CHAPTER 10

# Mainstream Rock in the Eighties

*There is no political solution*
*To our troubled evolution*

-Sting (from "Spirits in the Material World")

## Cultural Context

The 1980s have been called the "Age of Excess." The decade saw a rebirth of the so-called "conspicuous consumption" that characterized middle-class America the 1950s, although it did not begin on an economic or political high note. In fact, by the end of the 1970s many people around the world had lost faith in their leadership. In the United States, the Watergate scandal of the mid-1970s, the deepening economic recession and high unemployment, the ongoing Cold War, various conflicts in the Middle East, and the Iran hostage crisis under the Carter Administration had most Americans feeling that there was very little about which to feel optimistic.

In the 1980 US presidential race, Ronald Reagan, a Hollywood actor-turned-politician, defeated incumbent Jimmy Carter on the platforms of lower taxes, smaller government, states' rights, and a massive defense budget plan. Reagan's "supply-side" economic policies, later dubbed "Reaganomics," achieved the desired effect—at least in the short term—of stimulating economic growth and creating millions of new jobs. Reagan implemented policies that included cutting government spending on social and domestic programs and increasing spending on defense and defense-related technologies (resulting in a record increase for peacetime defense spending). There was also government deregulation of many industries under Reagan, including the financial sector, the energy industry, and the further deregulation of the communications industry, which began in the 1970s. In 1981, the resulting markets for cable television gave us MTV (discussed below) and by 1983, the economy had taken a substantial upturn.

**Note:** Critics of Reagan's policies and his political legacy note that his deregulation of the financial sector was a fundamental cause of the financial crisis of 2008 and that the easing of regulations on energy and other industrial sectors has led to environmental catastrophes and the outsourcing of millions of US jobs to foreign countries where cheap labor equates to more profits. Reagan's policies and their outgrowths have also been blamed for global corporatization and the massive wealth gap.

The American economy grew dramatically during the 1980s, and renewed economic prosperity brought with it a focus on wealth, power, status, and materialism. Mass media in particular idealized wealth, youth, and beauty. The term "yuppie" (young urban professional) was attached to a new generation of college-educated young people who had high-paying jobs and lived and worked in or near large cities. The yuppie lifestyle was replete with the luxuries of sophisticated urban culture, such as fine automobiles, designer clothing, well-appointed homes or condos, certain types of recreation and fitness, and a generally expected, typically pretentious social poise. Many yuppies worked in technology, law, finance, and consulting professions. The 1987 film *Wall Street* encapsulates the culture of greed and self-interest espoused by the stereotypical yuppie: The main character of the film, an unscrupulous stock market shark Gordon Gekko, became a symbol for unrestrained self-indulgence.

The current age of digital technology is rooted in many of the significant developments of the 1980s. As John Covach and Andrew Flory note:

> The American economy grew in many ways during the 1980s, but no sector advanced as impressively and publicly as high tech. The space program had provided many spin-off benefits and technologies, and the development of ever-smarter, more powerful computers made it possible for home computers to be useful and affordable to most Americans. The earliest Apple computers from the mid-1970s were made from kits. By the early 1980s, however, Steve Jobs and Steve Wozniak were marketing a more refined home unit, while Microsoft founders Bill Gates and Paul Allen were offering the MS-DOS operating system for the IBM PC. In 1984, a now famous commercial during the Super Bowl announced the arrival of the Macintosh computer, and by 1985, the first version of Windows was available for the PC. These years also marked the beginning of Internet use by the general public; CompuServe offered home email in 1979 and real-time chat in 1980, and the number of users increased throughout the decade, though the real Internet explosion would not occur until the 1990s.[1] (pp. 410-11)

Gates, Allen, Jobs, and Wozniak, along with several other tech pioneers were to become the twentieth- and twenty-first-century analogue to the first billionaire industrialists, the so-called

---

1    John Covach and Andrew Flory, What's That Sound?: An Introduction to Rock and Its History, pp. 410-411, 421. Copyright © 2012 by W. W. Norton & Company, Inc. Reprinted with permission

"robber barons" of old, like Carnegie, Vanderbilt, Rockefeller, Morgan, and others. A new age of digital technology had arrived and there was fierce competition to cash in on its expansion.

Other developments in technology greatly affected the way music was consumed and recorded. Early in the decade, portable cassette players in the form of "boomboxes" and the Sony Walkman, a personal cassette listening device, were fairly ubiquitous. By late in the decade, the compact disc became widely available and began to take over as the medium of choice; digital recording became widely accessible—although still very expensive—by around 1987. Digital recording would eventually have a profound impact on the way music was and is captured and edited in the studio. One of the many criticisms of modern popular music is its "cut and paste" quality, made possible through digital editing technology (that is, using a digital copy of the chorus of a song each time it is heard). Also criticized are digital technologies like "auto-tune" which allows a singer to "cheat" in the studio to compensate for lackluster vocal intonation, as well as "the grid" which is an ultra-precise tool used to temporally align musical events in a song: Digitally manufactured perfection of rhythm and timing are blamed for music feeling too "mechanical." There are growing factions within the modern recording industry that are reverting to analog technology, citing its warmth, depth of sonic dimension, and "humanness" as something that recorded music in the digital age has lost.

## From "Me" to "We"

In the music world of the 1980s, there were aspects of culture much more akin to the activist spirit of the 1960s. For example, in 1984, musician and actor Bob Geldof, after seeing a BBC broadcast on famine-stricken Ethiopia, rallied several of his famous musician friends together to record the song "Do They Know It's Christmas?" which he had cowritten with Midge Ure. Among those who appeared on the recording were Paul McCartney, Sting, Bono, Phil Collins, and Boy George. The song was released just before Christmas and all of the proceeds were donated to famine relief efforts under the **Band Aid Trust**. Shortly thereafter, inspired by Geldof's work, Michael Jackson—along with one of the most impressive rosters of rock, pop, country, and soul musicians ever assembled—recorded "We Are the World." The song and accompanying video, under the project name **USA for Africa**, would raise more than $50 million for famine relief. Several subsequent large-scale events organized by Geldof, John Mellencamp, and others followed, as well as the high-profile individual activism and charity efforts of a host of major rock and pop music celebrities. Michael Campbell and James Brody say:

> These events and others like them (such as Farm Aid) put the "we" back in rock. In the six-ties, rock had defined itself as a "we" music: first in the bands themselves (names like the Beatles, the Beach Boys, the Who, the Rolling Stones gave bands a collective identity) then in the bond between music and audience. The "we" in rock was a generation who didn't trust anyone over 30. The seventies, by contrast, have been dubbed the "me" decade: in

music, self-involvement (what about me?) and the pursuit of success seemed to negate the sense of community created in the sixties. There was no Woodstock in the seventies.

The massive fund-raising events of the eighties signaled the return of rock's conscience, but with a huge difference. In the sixties, rock gave voice to a generational revolution. It provided the soundtrack for an assault on the establishment, and by overthrowing the pop music establishment, it led by example. In the eighties, rock *was* the establishment, the dominant segment of the music industry. As a result, it could leverage the celebrity of its artists in projects that served a greater good. In the eighties, "we" in rock not only included the musicians, the music industry and the audience, but also those whom it sought to help. The success of their efforts was a strong signal of the enormous cultural presence of rock-era music in the latter part of the twentieth century.[2] (p. 423)

## AIDS/HIV

The AIDS epidemic that began in the early 1980s would become a central topic of cultural discourse and social activism as the decade progressed. In 1985, Rock Hudson, a Hollywood movie star from the 1950s through the 1980s, was the first major public figure to die from complications of the disease Hudson's homosexuality was apparently well known in Hollywood circles, although he never officially outed himself and was, in fact, in a heterosexual marriage at one point in the 1950s. Upon his death, his sexuality was made public. AIDS was very little understood in 1985. It was not understood exactly how the disease was transmitted or who was most at risk. It was known that many intravenous drug users and homosexuals were contracting AIDS. That Hudson was homosexual fueled the early common misconception that AIDS was a "gay" disease, although his death would actually help raise research money and general public awareness. His friendly, wholesome on-screen image ultimately went a long way in changing people's attitude about the disease. As mentioned in Chapter 7, when Queen frontman Freddie Mercury died from complications of AIDS in 1991, fund-raising events and awareness-raising efforts were kicked into high gear, particularly in the music industry.

### Television in the 1980s

Many mainstream network television programs reflected the changing values in American society. Americans' obsession with wealth and power was evident in the popularity of shows like *Dallas* and *Dynasty*, both of which dramatically portrayed the sagas of enormously wealthy families. Fabulous mansions, private jets, yachts, and limousines were part and parcel to the characters' lifestyles,

---

2   Michael Campbell and James Brody, Rock and Roll: An Introduction, pp. 423, 430-431, 404. Copyright © 2008 by Cengage Learning, Inc. Reprinted with permission.

as were greed, revenge, deception, and treachery. Americans fell into a love/hate relationship with despicable characters like J.R. Ewing and Blake Carrington—power-driven, often ruthless men bent on preserving their legacies through vast family fortunes using whatever means were necessary.

Sitcoms also addressed a changing society. The popular Michael J. Fox series, *Family Ties*, featured Fox as Alex Keaton, in a reversal of traditional generation gap roles: Alex was a teenage conservative Republican and budding yuppie. His liberal, former hippie parents comically fought to come to grips with their son's materialistic values and world view and to teach him that compassion and humanity were more important than monetary success and power. *The Cosby Show*, one of the most popular sitcoms of the decade, reflected changing attitudes and situations in the black community as well as the visibility of an expanding black middle class in America. Bill Cosby's character, Cliff Huxtable, and his wife Clair (played by Phylicia Rashad) were both professionals (he was a doctor and she a lawyer) living in an upper middle–class neighborhood in Brooklyn. The comic trials they faced in raising their children had little or nothing to do with problems of race or equality, but rather the more commonplace issues faced by middle America.

Television itself experienced massive growth and diversification in the 1980s. For many years, there were very few choices in TV programming: ABC, CBS, and NBC were the "Big 3" in broadcasting, and alongside a few local stations and PBS (Public Broadcasting) constituted all that TV had to offer. Cable networks expanded rapidly in the mid–late 1970s and began offering premium movie channels through a cable subscription fee. This allowed for the fragmentation of the market by providing revenues from sources other than advertising and paved the way for MTV in 1981 and its sister station, VH1, in 1985.

## MTV and VH1

That the first video to air on MTV on August 1, 1981 was "Video Killed the Radio Star" by the Buggles was perhaps a little prophetic. Videos wouldn't kill the radio star but would utterly transform what it meant to be a pop star. Music videos were nothing new in 1981. In fact, bands and artists had been making promotional videos for nearly two decades; The Beatles were using videos to promote their music as early as 1964 and Queen's promo video for "Bohemian Rhapsody" had taken video production to a more artistic level in 1975. What *was* new was the idea of a television station that aired videos twenty-four hours a day.

Originally conceived as a television analogue to AOR FM radio, MTV was formatted to play rock music videos. Early on, videos followed the approach of the traditional promo video which The Beatles and others had used during the 1960s: They were not artistic ends in and of themselves, but rather marketing tools used by record labels to promote album sales. Furthermore, MTV was not available everywhere at first. This proved advantageous in that it created a demonstrable impact in areas where MTV was aired: Within a short time, record stores in areas within MTV's reach began selling music that was not being played on local radio, but only on MTV.

MTV effectively incited the so-called Second British Invasion in the early 1980s. Groups in the United Kingdom had been involved in producing videos to a greater extent than many American bands. British rock videos gained importance in New Zealand and Australia as well before they were of any major cultural or market significance in the United States. As MTV faced the challenge of filling a twenty-four-rotation cycle of rock videos, they programmed videos by these British acts. The Buggles were a British new wave rock band, as were early MTV feature bands and artists like Adam Ant, Eurythmics, Culture Club, Duran Duran, The Human League, A Flock of Seagulls, Billy Idol, Simple Minds, and others. Established British artists like Bowie, The Who, Rod Stewart, and Phil Collins also had a significant presence on MTV.

In that MTV was meant to emulate an AOR station, and that most of the bands playing the specific kind of music MTV was airing were white, the network faced allegations of racism in its early years. Executives at MTV claimed that, as it was only one station as opposed to the diverse radio market, the allegations were unfair and unreasonable. However, in 1983 the argument would become irrelevant. Michael Jackson's *Thriller* album, released in late 1982, and the subsequent video for the single "Billie Jean," along with Prince's "Little Red Corvette," broke the color barrier on MTV. The change was not immediate or absolute, but by 1984, black artists like Lionel Richie, Stevie Wonder, Aretha Franklin, Donna Summer, and many others were enjoying regular heavy rotation on MTV. Programming would soon diversify to include multiple genres of rock, rap, pop, and dance music.

The cultural impact of MTV in the 1980s is inestimable. Beyond the music itself, videos and artists influenced everything from fashion to dance to popular lingo to body language. By mid-decade popular relevance for musicians was measured in terms of their MTV presence. Or, conversely, as in the case of Metallica, intentionally *not* having a video on MTV became an equally powerful "antiestablishment" statement. The development of the video-as-art-form will take on dramatic new dimensions beginning with Michael Jackson's "Thriller" video and continuing on through the 1980s and early 1990s. Throughout the MTV era, we will encounter both the positive and negative repercussions of the increasing centrality of artist's visual "image" in rock and pop music.

VH1 was launched in 1985 as a response to the enormous popularity of MTV, but was designed to target a slightly older audience. The station featured soft rock by artists like Elton John, Billy Joel, and Carly Simon as well as Top 40, smooth jazz, R&B, and urban contemporary artists like Marvin Gaye, Chicago, and Spyro Gyra.

## New Wave–Influenced Mainstream Rock in the 1980s

The punk movement of the late 1970s and its cultural next of kin, new wave, helped to bring rock back to a state of simplicity, directness, and edginess that was seemingly lost in the elaborate expressions of art rock and the softening of much of the mainstream rock of the 1970s. New wave and punk shared a similar ethos and a common audience. The most conspicuous difference between pre-1970s rock and new wave was that new wave (and punk) lacked the rhythmic smoothness of the blues. A jittery, tense sense of rhythm prevails in new wave as do thinner textures. New wave, however, was far more diverse than punk and often exhibited traits of pop rock, such as form and a focus on polished production. There was also a heavy presence of synthesizers in new wave music. By the 1980s, both new wave and punk music from both sides of the Atlantic had exerted a significant influence on mainstream rock, as had disco, reggae, and funk.

## The Police

Formed in London in 1977, **The Police** were at the forefront of the new wave–inspired Second British Invasion of the early 1980s. Singer/bassist/keyboardist **Sting** (b. 1951), guitarist/keyboardist **Andy Summers** (b. 1942), and drummer **Stewart Copeland** (b. 1952) brought together the influences of rock, new wave, reggae, and punk to create one of the freshest and most popular sounds of the new decade. Their early period saw two albums which were successful in the United Kingdom and produced one of the band's signature songs, "Roxanne," as well as the heavily reggae-influenced "Can't Stand Losing You."

**Go to Chapter 10 playlist example "Can't Stand Losing You" Sting, 1978**

The title track from their second album, *Reggatta de Blanc*, earned The Police a 1980 Grammy for Best Rock Instrumental Performance. It is one of the only Police songs written as a full-band collaboration.

**Go to Chapter 10 playlist example "Regatta de Blanc" The Police, 1979**

The Police broke into the US singles chart in 1980 with releases from their third album, *Zenyatta Mondatta*. Both "Don't Stand So Close to Me" and "De Do Do Do, De Da Da Da" landed in the top 10, the former garnering a Grammy Award for Best Rock Vocal Performance. "Don't Stand So Close to Me" is about an inappropriate liaison between a high school teacher and one of his students. Sting's earlier work as a high school teacher is said to have inspired the tale. The subsequent video was also a hit on MTV in 1981. The Police, and Sting in particular, were handsome young blond men with a great deal of visual appeal. As such, they were a perfect fit for the new video station.

**Go to Chapter 10 playlist example "Don't Stand So Close to Me" Sting, 1980**

The 1981 album *Ghost in the Machine* produced three more hit singles and reached number one on the UK album chart and number two in the United States. By this time, The Police had become one of the biggest bands in the world. A world arena tour followed and the band seemed unstoppable. Their politically charged song "Spirits in the Material World" was one of the album's featured hits. It is an indictment of government and capitalism but ultimately offers a positive message regarding the transcendental nature of human consciousness. The song demonstrates the band's increasing use of synthesizers, which would be employed even more liberally on their next album.

**Go to chapter 10 playlist example "Spirits in the Material World" Sting, 1981**

By the time The Police released what would be their final album—*Synchronicity*, in 1983—they were MTV superstars and a stadium-sized draw. Feeling that the band had reached its climax, each member began pursuing solo projects. They reconvened for several charity concerts for Amnesty International in 1986 and entered the studio that year with the intention of recording another album; however, tensions caused the project to collapse and the band members went their separate ways. Each would find their own fruitful paths, Sting as a globally successful rock and pop solo star, Summers involved in several solo efforts as well as projects with other musicians and Copeland enjoying a career as a film composer and drummer in two progressive rock bands, Animal Logic and Oysterhead. The Police only reunited once in 2007 for a brief 30th anniversary tour. Still, after more than twenty years of absence as a group, the tour was the third highest–grossing of all time with a total gate of $358 million.

The Police played a significant role in bringing new wave– and reggae-infused rock into the mainstream. *Rolling Stone* magazine lists four of their five albums in their 500 Greatest Albums of All Time.

## Talking Heads

By 1980, **Talking Heads**, led by vocalist/guitarist **David Byrne** (b. 1952), had released four albums and were well established in the underground new wave scene in New York City. The group—which also included drummer **Chris Frantz** (b. 1951), bassist **Tina Weymouth** (b. 1950), and keyboardist **Jerry Harrison** (b. 1949)—formed in 1975 after they met as art school students in New York City. They had gained recognition with the modestly successful singles "Psycho Killer," "Life During Wartime," and a cover of Al Green's "Take Me to the River." Byrne's characteristic nervous-sounding voice was complemented by the band's punk/new wave–inspired minimalist approach.

Following a three year hiatus from 1980 to 1983, the band scored their mainstream commercial breakthrough with the hit single "Burning Down the House" from their fifth studio album, *Speaking in Tongues*. The video enjoyed heavy rotation on MTV, as did others that followed.

**Go to Chapter 10 playlist example "Burning Down the House" Talking Heads, 1983**

1985's *Little Creatures* spawned another hit single for Talking Heads, "And She Was." In 1986, Byrne cowrote, directed, and starred in a film called *True Stories*. Talking Heads supplied some of the music for the film and released an album by the same name that year. The hit "Wild Wild Life" comes from this album. The band's final album, *Naked*, came in 1988. It was not a commercial success but marked Byrne's growing interest in world music with its heavy component of African percussion and complex polyrhythms drawn from traditional African music. Byrne would continue down the world music path as he embarked on a solo career in 1989.

Go to Chapter 10 playlist example "And She Was" David Byrne, 1985

Go to Chapter 10 playlist example "Wild Wild Life" David Byrne, 1986

## Blondie

**Blondie**, another band with its origins in the New York new wave underground scene of the late 1970s, emerged as mainstream rock superstars early in the 1980s. Founded by singer **Deborah Harry** (b. 1945) and guitarist **Chris Stein** (b. 1950), Blondie had its first international hit single, "Heart of Glass," in 1979. More disco than rock, the song was actually a reworking of a reggae-influenced song that Stein and Harry had written earlier in the 1970s. The rise of disco influenced them to change the basic rhythmic feel of the song. In February 1980, the Richard Gere film *American Gigolo* premiered with the theme song "Call Me" by Blondie. Harry collaborated on the song with Italian composer, producer, and electronics wizard Giorgio Moroder. (Moroder had become well known for his work with disco queen Donna Summer in the late 1970s).

Go to Chapter 10 playlist example "Call Me" Harry/Moroder, 1980

*Autoamerican*, released in 1980 produced two more hit singles for Blondie and offers a good indication of the diverse direction the mainstream would take throughout the decade. "The Tide Is High," a cover version of a Jamaican reggae song by the group The Paragons, became a number one hit for Blondie, as did their rap-laced song "Rapture." Although it is not a rap song *per se*, it was the first number one hit in the United States to feature any kind of rapping. The song's lyrics also name two rap pioneers, Fab Five Freddy and Grandmaster Flash, who were soon to come into their own fame.

Go to Chapter 10 playlist example "The Tide is High" The Paragons arr. Harry/Stein, 1980

Go to Chapter 10 playlist example "Rapture" Harry/Stein, 1980

Blondie broke up in 1982 but would reform in 1997. They are still active and are widely recognized as an important force in bringing new wave elements to the mainstream in the early 1980s.

## Duran Duran

**Duran Duran** rose from the British new wave scene in the early 1980s. Their self-titled 1981 debut album would lead to global success and their massive exposure on MTV placed them at the vanguard of the Second British Invasion. Their music was catchy and wellcrafted and their small-screen video image was a carefully tailored blend of sexuality, theatrics, fashion, and glamour.

Singer **Simon Le Bon** (b. 1958), keyboardist **Nick Rhodes** (b. 1962), bassist **John Taylor** (b. 1960), drummer **Roger Taylor** (b. 1960) (not to be confused with Roger Taylor of Queen), and guitarist **Andy Taylor** (b. 1961) formed the most commercially successful lineup of Duran Duran from 1981 to 1986. Their first hit single was "Girls on Film" from their 1981 debut. The original video was intended by the band to be viewed in adult-age dance clubs and on premium pay–TV channels and was thus fairly R-rated. The film showed topless women engaged in pillow fights, mud wrestling, and other fetish-like scenes. The heavily edited MTV version was a hit nonetheless. For those modern listeners unfamiliar with the sound effect at the beginning of the song, it is the sound of a 35mm film camera's motor drive common to fashion model photo shoots in the days before digital photography.

**Go to Chapter 10 playlist example "Girls on Film" Duran Duran and Andy Bates, 1981**

Duran Duran's second album, *Rio*, from 1982, produced by Colin Thurston, spawned four chart singles and accompanying videos. The album was such a sensation that it earned Duran Duran the nickname "The Fab Five" (recall that the Beatles were often referred to as "The Fab Four"). The ballad "Save a Prayer" demonstrates the band's more pensive side as well as their versatility.

**Go to Chapter 10 playlist example "Save a Prayer" Duran Duran, 1982**

The last Duran Duran album featuring the original lineup (until a reunion in 2004) was 1984's *Seven and the Ragged Tiger*. The album contained the hit singles "Union of the Snake" and "New Moon on Monday." Its most successful song was the number one single "The Reflex." The version from the album underwent a substantial remix by producer Nile Rodgers (of the band Chic) before being released as a single. It subsequently became the most successful single of the band's career.

**Go to Chapter 10 playlist example "The Reflex" Duran Duran/Rodgers Remix, 1984**

1985 saw Duran Duran with a hit title track to the James Bond film *A View to a Kill* as well as an appearance at the mammoth US Live Aid festival in front of a JFK stadium crowd of more than ninety thousand and an estimated TV audience of 1.5 billion. That year would also see the departure of Andy Taylor and Roger Taylor due to solo career conflicts and exhaustion from touring. Le Bon, Rhodes and John Taylor would continue on as a trio, working with Nile Rodgers and other studio musicians to produce the album *Notorious* in 1986. The album met with fairly harsh reviews and marked a decline in popularity for the band over the rest of the decade. Duran Duran continues to record and tour, although they never matched their popularity of the first half of the 1980s. Their videos from that period are classics of the early MTV years.

## Culture Club

Formed in 1981 and fronted by the androgynous **Boy George** (b. 1961), the British band **Culture Club** also included guitarist/keyboardist **Roy Hay** (b. 1961), bassist **Mikey Craig** (b. 1960), and drummer **Jon Moss** (b. 1957). The band created a catchy blend of new wave, pop, reggae, and soul music to become one of the top acts of the early 1980s. Boy George built a certain aura around the band with his ambiguous sexuality. He never confirmed or denied any queries to determine his sexuality, but rather used what became his famous pat response to the question: "I prefer a nice cup of tea to sex."

Culture Club entered the US charts and heavy rotation on MTV in 1982 with the single "Do You Really Want to Hurt Me," a reggae- and gospel-influenced pop song from their debut album, *Kissing to be Clever*. The video is a disconnected series of scenes alternating between a courtroom (with a jury of blackface minstrel-style performers), a jazz club, a health spa, and a jail cell. Like many early MTV videos, the music and the videography had little or nothing to do with one another. The practice of creating videos connected to the actual storyline of the song varied greatly but often had nothing to do with whether a video succeeded or failed.

Two other singles from the album, "Time (Clock of the Heart)" and "I'll Tumble 4 Ya" charted in the top 10 distinguishing Culture Club as the first band since The Beatles to have three songs from a debut album reach the top 10.

**Go to Chapter 10 playlist example "Do You Really Want to Hurt Me" Culture Club, 1982**

**Go to Chapter 10 playlist example "I'll Tumble 4 Ya" Culture Club, 1982**

*Colour by Numbers*, the band's follow-up album, reached number one in the United Kingdom and number two in the United States following its 1983 release and produced Culture Club's best-selling single, "Karma Chameleon." The album was warmly received by critics and would go on to sell more than 16 million copies. The single "Karma Chameleon" would eventually reach number one in more than thirty countries.

**Go to Chapter 10 playlist example "Karma Chameleon" Culture Club/Phil Pickett, 1983**

By 1984, Boy George was becoming increasingly dependent on cocaine. His use of the drug escalated rapidly into a full-blown addiction and by 1986 he was also using heroin. Additionally, and unbeknownst to the public at the time, Boy George and drummer Jon Moss were romantically involved. Their relationship was often troubled and involved physical and verbal abuse. In spite of Boy George's involvement with Bob Geldof's Band-Aid project in 1985, Culture Club's popularity was waning. Their third and fourth albums were far less successful then the previous two. In July of 1986, Boy George was arrested for possession of heroin and Culture Club disbanded. They have reunited on several different occasions and are actively touring at the time of this writing.

## Eurythmics

Consisting of only two official members, **Annie Lennox** (b. 1954) and **Dave Stewart** (b. 1952), Eurythmics formed in London in 1980. Lennox and Stewart had met in the London underground punk scene in 1975 and played together in the punk bands The Catch and The Tourists. As Eurythmics, they decided to handle all of the creative aspects as a duo and hire studio and live musicians as needed. Eurythmics were signed to RCA records and worked with influential and innovative electronic music producer Conny Plank on their 1981 debut album, *In the Garden*. Unfortunately, commercial success proved elusive.

Following their first effort, the duo set up their own recording space and put together several singles which also failed to perform well. Stewart had begun experimenting heavily with electronic sounds and mixing them with live instruments. Their second album, *Sweet Dreams (Are Made of This)*, would provide the commercial success the duo were seeking. The title track topped US and UK charts and the accompanying video was a major hit on MTV. Almost overnight, Lennox became a pop rock idol, appearing on the cover of *Rolling Stone* magazine and many other popular publications. Her soul-tinged vocals and her visual appearance (her hair was cropped and she often wore men's suits) created a powerful feminine mystique and a strong MTV presence.

"Sweet Dreams" is built around a dark and heavy analog synthesizer bass line. Stewart programmed the drum part on a rare early drum machine called a Movement Systems Drum Computer and Lennox multitracked her rich harmony vocal lines. The song has been covered many times, most notably by Marilyn Manson, Tori Amos, and actress Mario Bello in her 2000 movie *Duets*.

**Go to Chapter 10 playlist example "Sweet Dreams (Are Made of This)" Eurythmics, 1983**

Eurythmics produced their third album quickly in order to maintain their momentum. *Touch* was released late in 1983 and rapidly rose to number one in the UK album chart and number seven in the US chart. It produced three hit singles and videos: "Who's That Girl?," "Right by Your Side," and "Here Comes the Rain Again." The success of their previous album afforded Lennox and Stewart the luxury of hiring the string section of the British Philharmonic and conductor Michael Kamen to work with them in the studio.

In addition to the heavy synthesizer sounds, the orchestral strings play prominently in "Here Comes the Rain Again."

**Go to Chapter 10 playlist example "Here Comes the Rain Again" Eurythmics, 1983**

1985's *Be Yourself Tonight* demonstrated a stylistic expansion for Lennox and Stewart. The music was much less synthesizer based; but rather, focused on traditional rock instruments and encompassed Motown, pop, and R&B elements. Guest appearances included Stevie Wonder and Elvis Costello as well as Aretha Franklin singing a duet with Lennox on the hit feminist anthem "Sisters Are Doin' It for Themselves." *Be Yourself Tonight* would become Eurythmics' best-selling studio album.

**Go to Chapter 10 playlist example "Sisters Are Doin' It for Themselves" Eurythmics, 1985**

Eurythmics continued down a path of chart success and maintained a strong MTV presence through the rest of the 1980s. Their output was a diverse mix of traditional rock and heavily synthesized elements. All of it was both commercially and critically successful. By 1990, the pressures of success and heavy touring had caused a rift between Lennox and Stewart. They parted ways and each embarked on solo careers. Eurythmics would reunite in 1999 and again in 2014 to perform in a massive tribute concert marking the 50th anniversary of The Beatles' first appearance on *The Ed Sullivan Show*.

> **Note:** Since the 1980s, Annie Lennox has been a major force as a political and social activist and has championed a variety of causes and charitable organizations, including the establishment of her own SING Campaign to raise funds and awareness for women and children living with AIDS. She has been involved with Greenpeace, Amnesty International, the Treatment Action Campaign, UNESCO, and others. Although she is heterosexual, her image and her strong ties to feminism have earned her a substantial following in the LGBT community.

## Billy Idol

British singer **Billy Idol** (b. 1955) represents the crossover of punk into the early 1980s mainstream. Idol began his career in the British punk band Generation X in the late 1970s and embarked on a solo career in 1980. He teamed up with whiz-kid metal guitarist **Steve Stevens** (b. 1959) in a songwriting partnership that would produce some of the biggest hits of the decade. Idol and Stevens both projected a charismatic glam/punk image that was well suited to video. Idol's 1981 debut album, *Billy Idol*, produced by disco pioneer Keith Forsey, did fairly well in the album charts and spawned the hit single "White Wedding." It would become one of Idol's most recognizable songs and the video became a staple of early MTV. Idol would, in fact, become a kind of poster boy for MTV, appearing in memorable promos with his trademark sneer, clenched fist and thick Cockney accent declaring "I want my MTV!"

**Go to Chapter 10 playlist example "White Wedding" Billy Idol, 1981**

The 1983 release, *Rebel Yell*, also produced by Forsey, would catapult Billy Idol to international stardom. MTV ran videos of the title track, "Eyes Without a Face," "Flesh for Fantasy," and "Catch

My Fall" in regular heavy rotation following the album's release. The music on *Rebel Yell* blends hard rock, punk, and new wave with a clear pop sensibility. Most of the songs follow standard verse/chorus form and employ a well-produced and effective blend of synthesizers and standard rock instrumentation.

**Go to Chapter 10 playlist example "Rebel Yell" Idol/Stevens, 1983**

**Go to Chapter 10 playlist example "Eyes Without a Face" Idol/Stevens, 1983**

Billy Idol would enjoy massive success on records and MTV for the rest of the decade. 1986 saw the release of the platinum selling *Whiplash Smile* and *Charmed Life* in early 1990. A serious motorcycle accident in 1990 nearly cost Idol his leg and put him out of regular action for a time. During his recovery he still managed to film videos (he was shot from the waist up). His career has been on-again, off-again since around 1993.

Image 10.4: Billy Idol

# U2

**U2** are unique among mainstream new wave/punk-inspired rock bands of the early 1980s in several ways: they originated in Ireland; they not only maintained a relevant position throughout the 1980s, they continued to evolve musically and actually grew in popularity throughout the 1990s and 2000s to become one of the most successful bands of all time; from their beginnings, their music, and lives—both as a band and as individuals—have been steeped in humanitarian and political causes and philanthropic endeavors. U2 have recorded thirteen studio albums, sold over 170 million records and hold the record for the highest-attended, highest-grossing concert tour of all time with their 2009–2011 promotional tour for their *No Line on the Horizon Album* (2009). Campbell and Brody have this to say about U2:

> From the start, U2—lead vocalist Bono (b. 1960), guitarist/keyboardist The Edge (b. 1961), bassist Adam Clayton (b. 1960) and drummer Larry Mullen (b. 1961)—have had a sense of their own destiny. In 1981, three years after the group came together, Bono told *Rolling Stone*, "Even at this stage, I do feel we are meant to be one of the great bands. There's a certain spark, a certain chemistry, that was special about The Stones, The Who and The Beatles, and I think it's also special about U2." They have fulfilled their destiny because they have stayed together and because they have never lost their passion for rock and what it can be. As recently as 2000, after more than two decades of touring, recording and sending their message out into the world, Bono told *USA Today* that "There is a transcendence that I want from rock. ... I'm still drunk on the idea that rock and roll can be a force for change. We haven't lost that idea." (pp. 430-31)

Following their formation in 1978, U2 began performing in their native Ireland where they caught the attention of Irish music press and eventually executives at Island Records, who signed the band in 1980. Working with producer Steve Lillywhite, their debut album *Boy* followed, as did their first hit single, "I Will Follow" and a world tour. Critics were taken with Bono's charismatic presence as well as the band's energy. Their 1981 follow-up, *October*, was not as well received and for a time, the band were in danger of losing their contract.

U2 released their third album, *War*, in 1983. The album was a great commercial success in spite of its far grittier and guitar-based sound amid the wave of synthesizer-based pop rock that had been dominating the mainstream. U2 established themselves as important social critics with *War* as well. The album opens with the protest song "Sunday Bloody Sunday," a song about the 1972 massacre in Ireland known as Bloody Sunday, and includes the tracks "New Year's Day" about the Polish Solidarity Movement and "Seconds," a song about nuclear proliferation. Both "Sunday Bloody Sunday" and "New Year's Day" were hit singles in the United States and United Kingdom and their videos were aired heavily on MTV.

**Go to Chapter 10 playlist example "Sunday Bloody Sunday" U2, 1983**

**Go to Chapter 10 playlist example "New Year's Day" U2, 1983**

Seeking a change of direction for their next studio project—in order not to become stagnant and pigeonholed—U2 sought out and convinced ambient music pioneer and producer Brian Eno and his engineer Daniel Lanois to work with them. The resulting album, *The Unforgettable Fire*, came in 1984. Thanks in large part to Eno's contributions, the record dramatically expanded U2's range and musical vocabulary. It contains material which is at times atmospheric and richly orchestrated, yet still retains the rhythmic drive and direct rock energy for which U2 had become known. Bono's lyrics also moved in a more poetic direction. He had been occupying his mind with various works of fiction, philosophy, and poetry, which had a major influence on his approach as a lyricist. The song "Pride (In the Name of Love)" was the album's biggest hit. It is about the life and death of Dr. Martin Luther King, Jr. A major arena tour followed, as did a highly acclaimed performance at the UK Live Aid festival at London's Wembley Stadium. Seventy-two thousand were in attendance with an estimated 2 billion TV viewers.

**Go to Chapter 10 playlist example "Pride (In the Name of Love)" U2, 1984**

The 1987 *Joshua Tree* album would be U2's most successful work of the decade. It fused American and Irish roots elements, U2's straightforward rock approach, and Eno's atmospheric style into hits like "I Still Haven't Found What I'm Looking For" and the utopian-themed "Where the Streets Have No Name." In the time between *The Unforgettable Fire* and *The Joshua Tree*, Bono and his bandmates had developed a great love of the cultural richness of the United States; Bono had immersed himself in the literature of radical American writers like Norman Mailer and Raymond Carver. The band had also been motivated by their recent experiences in meeting and performing with musicians like The Rolling Stones and Bob Dylan to dig deeper into the roots music of the United States as well as their own Irish musical heritage. The various inspirations that resulted in *The Joshua Tree* helped to established U2 as rock megastars of their generation. They were awarded Grammys in 1988 for Album of the Year and Best Rock Performance by a Duo or Group with Vocal.

**Go to Chapter 10 playlist example "Where the Streets Have No Name" U2, 1987**

U2's history is still being written. They have remained a potent and innovative force for more than three decades and continue to labor as high-profile activists for a number of causes and to provide much-needed social commentary from the world of popular rock music.

**Madonna, Michael Jackson, and Prince: Pop Rock's Holy Trinity**

There were no bigger pop rock superstars in the 1980s than Madonna, Michael Jackson, and Prince, and each brought something unique to the table. Madonna, a capable vocalist and song-writer (although most of her biggest hits were written by other people), was more known for her racy performances, risqué videos, and music business acumen. She capitalized on her sex appeal and rose to the top of her field as a trend-setting, take-no-prisoners pop queen. Michael Jackson, at least until a sexual abuse scandal rocked his career in 1993, presented a fascinating mix of childlike innocence and devastating talent as an entertainer. There is no question that Jackson's music and vocal abilities were great (although he also did not write all of his songs), but it was his dancing (and videos) that set the pop world ablaze. Prince was a musician and songwriter of the absolute highest order. His skill as a multi-instrumentalist alone was staggering. He performed all vocals and played more than twenty instruments on his first album, which he released at the age of nineteen. He was a virtuoso guitarist and a master keyboardist, drummer, and percussionist. His abilities as a songwriter were no less impressive. Not only did he write all of his own music (which itself is so stylistically diverse as to defy categorization), he composed dozens of hits for other artists. He was a highly adept producer and was quick to employ emerging electronic technology in his music. We discuss these three pop rock giants in turn.

## Madonna

Following her early beginnings in entertainment as a dancer and then a guitarist in a band called Breakfast Club, **Madonna** (b. 1958) began her solo career in 1981, signing with Sire Records. Her earliest singles became quite popular in the dance club scene and reached high positions on *Billboard's* Dance charts. Her debut album, *Madonna*, came in 1983. It was cowritten and copro-duced by Reggie Lucas and John Benitez. The singles from the album were important in bridging the gap between late disco, dance pop, and rock music in the early 1980s, but it was the videos that introduced Madonna the person as a vivacious, street-smart, independent woman with no interest in holding with the "girl-next-door" cliché. Her style and sound would become the model for the so-called "pop diva" of the 1980s and well beyond. Moreover, Madonna's videos contained many postmodern motifs relating to provocative subjects such as interracial and homosexual relation-ships, religious freedom, and nontraditional gender roles. She became an important catalyst for public discourse regarding these lingering taboos.

---

Her video for the song "Borderline" is an excellent early example of her representational style. It has been heavily analyzed by academics and social scientists. In it, Madonna portrays the girlfriend of a Latino man living in the barrio. She is wooed by a wealthy white fashion photographer and the promise of fame. This creates a rift between her and her boyfriend. Her taste of fame is tainted by the reaction she receives when she tries to express her own sense of creativity and she ultimately returns to the barrio, her roots, and her original lover. The video has been noted for its use of symbolism to express feminine power, independence, and racial inequality. The lyrics and the video bear little or no direct relationship to one another. Here the video transcends the meaning of the song to become an entity unto itself.

**Go to Chapter 10 playlist example "Borderline" Reggie Lucas, 1983**

Madonna continued to shock, surprise, and innovate throughout the 1980s. Her overwhelming media presence literally changed the landscape of pop music. Before Madonna, most pop stars were male; after her they were almost all female. She challenged mainstream thinking, used controversy as a tool, and served as a role model not only for women in music but women in business. Covach and Flory write:

> Madonna's albums and singles in the mid-1980s established her as one of the most important figures in pop music, and she remains among the most successful acts in the music business. She has continually challenged aspects of what she perceives to be society's most troubling issues and practices. Early on, her "boy toy" image cast her as a sex object, although this was done with great irony—Madonna put on the role of sex object in order to call it into question, and a link can be made to previous figures who adopted personae, such as Jim Morrison and David Bowie. In this way, Madonna has exploited the boundaries of sexual conduct, racial issues, women's roles and spirituality. Detractors have accused her of seeking publicity by titillating and shocking audiences, while her supporters have praised her methods of raising important social issues for debate. Whatever position you take on Madonna's place in popular culture, video images clearly played a central role in her music. Her videos are rich in symbolism and striking juxtapositions—a factor that has caused many academics to offer extended interpretations of their deeper meanings. (p. 421)

**Go to Chapter 10 playlist example "Like a Virgin" Billy Steinberg/Tom Kelly, 1984**

**Go to Chapter 10 playlist example "Material Girl" Peter Brown/Robert Rans, 1984**

## Michael Jackson

With a career that began at Motown Records as a child pop star in the 1970s performing with his older brothers as the lead singer of The Jackson 5, **Michael Jackson** (1958–2009) was no stranger to the song and dance world. Jackson left Motown and began his mature solo career, as well as an enormously fruitful relationship with producer Quincy Jones, in 1979 with the album *Off the Wall*. The recording was hailed by critics as a successful transition from his early Motown work. However, it was in 1982 with the release of his pop rock epic *Thriller* that Michael Jackson would ascend to almost divine status.

As mentioned earlier, the videos from *Thriller* helped to break down the racial barrier on MTV. Michael Jackson seemed tailor made for the burgeoning video station. He had the moves, the music, and the charisma, and his videos became the standard by which all other pop videos were measured. "Billie Jean," "Beat It," and the mini-film "Thriller," cited by many as the best music video ever, featured dancing and choreography the likes of which had not heretofore been seen in music video. After Jackson, it would become the norm: pop singers could no longer just stand in front of the microphone and deliver their song; there had to be at least *some* dancing, though even the most skilled usually fell short next to Jackson. Nobody could move like this guy.

The music on *Thriller* was not to be outdone by the videos. It is one of the most immaculately produced recordings of all time. Four of the nine tracks were written by Jackson with contributions by British songwriter Rod Temperton, James Ingram, Steve Porcaro of the band Toto, lyricist John Bettis, and producer Quincy Jones. There are no filler tracks. Moreover, the album boasts an impressive list of guest artists. Campbell and Brody write:

> Although only three of the tracks were shot as videos, all of the songs on *Thriller* have a distinct identity. There is considerable contrast from song to song, as the musical settings capture the tone and content of the lyric. For example, the hard-edged riffs that open "Wanna Be Startin' Somethin'" anticipate the lyric's schoolyard-style provocation. The punk-inspired beat and Eddie Van Halen's guitar underscore the message of "Beat It." The loping rhythm (a shuffle bat on top of a rock beat), the use of pre-rock pop harmony, and the soft synth sounds reinforce the friendly rivalry between Michael and Paul McCartney in "The Girl Is Mine." And a setting that mixes an open middle range—just a simple synthesizer riff—with the irritation of a persistent bass riff and percussion sound characterizes the emptiness of the groupie-style relationships in "Billie Jean." Both the songs and Quincy Jones' masterful settings give the album an expressive range that compensates for the one dimensional quality of Jackson's singing. (p. 404)

**Go to Chapter 10 playlist example "Billie Jean" Jackson, 1982**

**Go to Chapter 10 playlist example "Beat It" (featuring Eddie Van Halen) Jackson, 1982**

**Go to Chapter 10 playlist example "Thriller" (featuring Vincent Price) Temperton, 1982**

**Go to Chapter 10 playlist example "The Girl Is Mine" (featuring Paul McCartney) Jackson, 1982**

*Thriller* is the best-selling album of all time with estimated sales of more than 70 million copies.

Michael Jackson has been called the greatest entertainer of all time and his contributions to popular culture cannot be overstated. To be sure, his changing appearance due to plastic surgery and a condition called vitiligo, which caused his skin to lighten, were the topic of overmuch tabloid and other media coverage, as were the allegations of child sexual abuse which occurred in 1993 and again in 2003 (he was not found guilty of any wrongdoing in both cases), although most felt that Jackson was unjustly targeted. In addition to his contributions to music, he was a humanitarian and activist whose efforts changed the lives of millions. His untimely death at the age of fifty due to a prescription drug overdose shocked the world. Michael Jackson's music, dancing, and spirit of humanitarianism will unquestionably continue to be influential for many decades to come.

# Prince

**Prince** (1958–2016) began his recording career in 1978. He was richly creative throughout his entire career and, even early on, attained a level of mastery over a widely diverse range of styles. His output extends into pop, rock, funk, R&B, soul, disco, rap, jazz, electronica, and gospel; he often seamlessly merged multiple styles together in the same song. Where Madonna wove her sex appeal into performances and videos, Prince wove his into his music. Simply put, Prince's music is *sexy*. Where Michael Jackson dubbed himself the "King of Pop," Prince seemed only mildly concerned with pop success; his music was about itself in a way that spoke to artistic integrity over mainstream appeal. This is apparent in songs like "Sexy MF," "Gett Off," "Head," "Do Me, Baby" and "Jack U Off." The titles and lyrics of these songs—and others—clearly suggest that there was no concern for mass media or MTV exposure. To be sure, if Prince *wanted* to write a pop hit, it was well within his purview; although unlike nearly every other pop star, it was not always his goal.

> **Note:** At the time of this writing, Prince has only recently passed away and there is reliable speculation that he has at least one thousand unreleased songs. There is still much to be sorted out in terms of his estate, but the release of this treasure trove of material could expand his stylistic reach into uncharted territory.

By 1982, Prince had released five studio albums, including the wildly successful *1999*. The title track was simultaneously an indictment against nuclear proliferation and a declaration of the intent to enjoy life in spite of it. It would become one of his best-known songs. With his first videos on MTV and his Hollywood film debut of *Purple Rain* (and its soundtrack) in 1984, Prince became a household name. The soundtrack album *Purple Rain* has sold more than 20 million copies and is ranked among the best albums of the twentieth century. Its first two singles, "When Doves Cry" and "Let's Go Crazy," were the album's first global hits; all five singles released from *Purple Rain* would eventually become worldwide hits. The album also earned Prince two Grammy Awards.

One of *Purple Rain's* songs, "Darling Nikki," with its references to masturbation, would serve as an impetus for the formation of the Parents Music Resource Center (PMRC) by then-Senator Al Gore's wife, Tipper Gore, and several other Washington wives—and their eventual implementation of Parental Advisory warning labels on recordings with explicit sexual or violent lyrics/images. (This will be discussed in greater detail in Chapter 12.)

Prince was a dominant force in pop music all through the 1980s and well beyond, and continued to perform until just before his death in April 2016. In 2015, he released a song called "Baltimore" as a tribute to Freddie Gray, who died as a result of police brutality. Prince was one of the only major artists who was visible in relation to the 2015 Black Lives Matter movement, an organized effort started in response to a rash of murders of unarmed black citizens at the hands of police officers. Prince was universally respected as an artist, activist, and champion of racial and gender equality. There is no question that his life and music will continue to awe and inspire far into the future.

> **Note**: As Prince's music is unavailable on the site used for the chapter playlists, your instructor may choose to obtain Prince recordings for demonstration in class.

## American Roots Rock in the 1980s

There was a brand of rock which began to emerge in the late 1970s and would become most prominent in the early and mid-1980s that related to the lives and struggles of **blue-collar** America in the midst of the postindustrial decline. The music drew on folk elements as well as rock, while the lyrics (and powerful video images) were often concerned with issues such as the disintegration of the working class, the slow death of the labor union brought on by conservative politics and the Reagan Administration, social isolation, and the marginalization of a once vital segment of the American workforce. There were also many lyrics that spoke to the plight of those adversely affected by the ongoing social, physical, and emotional fallout of the Vietnam era. Sometimes referred to as "Heartland" rock, its major proponents in the 1980s supported the notion that rock music had a social and communal purpose. Much of the activity of Geldof and others mentioned earlier connect to this genre, although there were artists whose entire careers were built on the foundations of bringing rock music to a position of social and political relevance.

### Bruce Springsteen

In 1980s mainstream rock there was no greater champion for the working-class than "The Boss," Bruce Springsteen. Having made a serious mark on the mainstream in the 1970s with *Born to Run*, he had become a familiar figure in the American rock scene. Springsteen had also gotten involved in humanitarian causes as early as 1979 when he and his band joined Musicians United for Safe Energy (MUSE) and performed at a concert series known as the "No Nukes" concerts, which were captured on a live album as well as a documentary film.

In 1980 he continued his musical exploration of working-class life with his album *The River*, and in 1982 he released *Nebraska*, a collection of acoustic songs that deal with blue-collar strife, but also depart from that theme to explore social outcasts, criminals, and even mass murderers. There are no songs with anything resembling an optimistic message, save the final track, "Reason to Believe." The album did not enjoy the commercial success of his previous albums but was deeply praised by critics for its emotional challenge and dark sophistication. It has come to be one regarded as one of Springsteen's most influential recordings. The title track is an unsettling tale based on the true story of serial killer Charles Starkweather and his girlfriend, Caril Fugate, who embarked on a two-month killing spree in the late 1950s. Starkweather was put to death by electrocution. Springsteen delivers the disturbing narrative in the first person rendering it all the more chilling.

**Go to Chapter 10 playlist example "Nebraska" Bruce Springsteen, 1982**

Springsteen's most significant work, at least in the 1980s, came in 1984 with *Born in the U.S.A.* The album produced seven top 10 singles and has sold more than 30 million copies. More importantly, many of the songs addressed some of the most crucial working-class social developments of the era. The title track itself paints a picture of the utter isolation and disenfranchisement that a working-class man who had returned from conscripted service in Vietnam experiences. It also alludes to those who never returned. The accompanying video presents potent images of blue-collar, subsistence-level life following the Vietnam era interspersed with scenes from a deeply passionate live concert performance of the song, all of which lent potency to the song's message.

As *Born in the U.S.A.* was dominating the charts and receiving massive amounts of press coverage, the 1984 presidential campaign was in full swing. In a moment of classic buffoonery, campaigning incumbent Ronald Reagan attempted to benefit politically by associating himself with Springsteen at a campaign stop in New Jersey. Reagan's complete lack of understanding of Springsteen's lyrics and liberal political views resulted in media ridicule of Reagan. Springsteen himself, at a concert performance the following week, gently but effectively mocked the president for his ignorance.

**Go to Chapter 10 playlist example "Born in the U.S.A." Bruce Springsteen, 1984**

The first verse:

> *Born down in a dead man's town*

> *The first kick I took was when I hit the ground*

> *You end up like a dog that's been beat too much*

> *Till you spend half your life just covering up*

In contrast to the big, anthemic sound of "Born in the U.S.A." and the brooding acoustic folk flavors on *Nebraska*, the song "My Hometown" (from *Born in the U.S.A.*) further demonstrates Springsteen's musical versatility as well as his ability to deliver a narrative in an unaffected and tender fashion. The song is a medium-paced, synthesizer-based piece about the very real postindustrial phenomena of the economic death of the American small town.

**Go to Chapter 10 playlist example "My Hometown" Bruce Springsteen, 1984**

Bruce Springsteen's status as a working-class hero was augmented by his concert performances. He has become legendary for playing concerts in excess of four hours in length, almost as a rule. Not only does this demonstrate a passion for performing and his commitment to his fans, it speaks to the blue-collar work ethic on a subconscious level: to the working class the sense of self-worth comes not so much from the product of the work (that is, the coal that is mined or the automobile that is assembled), but from the intrinsic value of *work itself*. When Springsteen plays a four hour–plus concert, he connects to this value in a very real way.

The Boss is much more than a rock star. In terms of his socially conscious lyrics, he picked up the torch lit by Woody Guthrie that was later carried by "folkies" like Pete Seeger and early Bob Dylan. His decades-long involvement in charitable activities, humanitarian efforts, and social activism are considerable. In nearly every disaster-relief effort that the music world organizes, Springsteen rolls up his sleeves and digs in to help. High-level efforts in recent times include an appearance on the 2015 broadcast of *Shining a Light: A Concert for Progress on Race in America* as well as his ongoing activism for LGBT rights and his support for gay marriage. Bruce Springsteen is a national treasure and the epitome of postmodern philosophy in rock music. In a 2008 speech, Springsteen said "I spent most of my life as a musician measuring the distance between the American dream and American reality."

Image 10.6: Bruce Springsteen in 2008 with drummer Max Weinberg

# John (Cougar) Mellencamp

Following a series of failed attempts to break into the American mainstream rock world in the late 1970s and early 1980s, singer/guitarist **John Cougar** (b. 1951) found major success with his 1982 album *American Fool*. He had changed his surname to Cougar at the behest of his first manager (a decision he soon regretted). After achieving international fame as John Cougar, he would later transition through John Cougar Mellancamp to his given name John Mellencamp by 1991. *American Fool* rose to the top of the *Billboard* album chart in 1982 and earned Cougar a Grammy for Best Male Rock Vocal Performance. The hits "Hurts So Good" and "Jack & Diane" epitomize Cougar's so-called heartland style. The focus is clearly on traditional rock instrumentation (with the occasional fiddle, dulcimer, or accordion), standard verse/chorus forms, and a plain-spoken vocal style.

"Jack & Diane" is Cougar's most successful hit single to date. The video became an MTV standard as well. It featured grainy images of Cougar's childhood photographs and home movies set against those of him performing the song, presumably in the present. The images of Americana, hot rod cars, motorcycles, diners, and a budding romance set in Midwestern scenery created a simple but powerful backdrop for the song.

**Go to Chapter 10 playlist example "Jack & Diane" John Cougar, 1982**

In 1983, he released *Uh-huh*, the first album under the name John Cougar Mellencamp. The album spawned several more hit singles, affirming the magnetism of the singer's tell-it-like-it-is delivery and his earthy roots rock musical settings. One of those hits, "Pink Houses," is a song that addresses the myth of equality in America.

**Go to Chapter 10 playlist example "Pink Houses" John Cougar Mellencamp, 1983**

Mellencamp's 1985 release, *Scarecrow*, would lead to his central involvement in organizing the **Farm Aid** benefit concert series, along with Willie Nelson and Neil Young. The series was established to assist family farmers in their struggles against losing their farms to mortgage debt and corporate takeover of their land and livelihood, as well as to raise awareness to the importance of family farming. The song "Rain on the Scarecrow" speaks directly to this and became somewhat of an anthem for the first concert. The Farm Aid benefit concerts have been an annual event since 1985; they have included dozens of popular musicians and raised tens of millions of dollars for family farmers.

**Go to Chapter 10 playlist example "Rain on the Scarecrow" John Cougar Mellencamp, 1985**

**Note:** Mellencamp is also a highly skilled visual artist. His work has been the focus of numerous exhibitions. He also continues to write and record music that explores themes of problems in society and the quest for personal truth. His most recent album was 2014's *Plain Spoken*.

## Rock's Ongoing Diversification

Rock became increasingly fragmented into subgenres as the 1980s wore on: In contrast to the mainstream and MTV, so-called "alternative" styles emerged. Some called it "post-punk" or "indie" or "college" music, and a good deal of it would eventually move into the mainstream. Brand new fusions like funk rock and rap rock emerged as well. Many bands and artists from the 1960s and 1970s remained quite popular; progressive and art rock remained relevant, and blues-based rock was alive and well on AOR radio stations and the newly established "classic rock" stations. VH1, as mentioned earlier, provided a high-visibility home for the softer rock that generally appealed to an older audience; many 1970s soft rock superstars held firmly there alongside a new generation of soft rock artists. In 1980, the two preexisting and closely related styles of hard rock and heavy metal were undergoing a rebirth thanks in large part to the appearance and impact of Van Halen as well as the powerful influence of Zeppelin, Sabbath, Deep Purple, and the so-called New Wave of British Heavy Metal. By mid-decade both hard rock and heavy metal would be thriving, though heavy metal particularly would be well on its way to becoming the dominant genre of rock. Hard rock will build on its connection to the blues while heavy metal will draw together blues elements with punk, prog, and glam to forge its own path to the top of the rock heap. Both will play central roles in making the 1980s the "Age of Excess."

In the next chapter, we explore hard rock, including funk rock and rap rock, as they developed in the 1980s. Since "alternative" forms rock became more prominent in the 1990s, they will be discussed in Chapter 14.

## Suggested Chapter Related Activities

- Compare four or five Prince songs released between 1984 and 1990. Make notes on rhythmic structures, forms, instrumentation, connection between lyrics and music.

- Compare/contrast the pop of Madonna and Michael Jackson with several pop stars of today (i.e. Katy Perry, Lady Gaga, Miley Cyrus, etc.). What elements are universal? Does modern pop sound better to you or more sterile and predictable?

- Locate at least two examples of post-2010 musicians who relate to the working class. How do they do this? Are they rock musicians or some other style?

- Find some examples of modern British pop-rock and see if you can hear the influence of new wave sounds similar to those of the 1980s. If not, what are the fundamental influences?

- Compare the way Madonna used controversy to her advantage with the way modern pop divas like Miley Cyrus, Beyonce and others do.

## Suggested Discussion Topics

- How do you feel sites like YouTube compare to MTV? How does each platform positively and negatively affect music/musicians?

- Do you feel the enduring popularity of musicians like Springsteen, Madonna and The Stones changes the modern perception of what is culturally defined as "old?"

- Compare your perception of tolerance (sexual, religious, lifestyle) in the 1980s to what it is today. Have we progressed as a society or does it seem we are moving in the wrong direction? If we have regressed, what do you see as the root cause(s)?

- Digital music was a reality by the end of the 1980s. Have you ever listened to music recorded in analog on a record disc? What are your thoughts on the sound characteristics compared to digitally recorded music?

## Image Credits

# CHAPTER 11

# Hard Rock in the Eighties

*And when you're high you never, ever wanna come down...*

-Axl Rose of Guns N' Roses (from "Welcome to the Jungle")

## Hard Rock Around 1980

Hard rock was alive and well as the 1980s dawned. This was evident in the success of quintessential hard rockers Van Halen as it began with their debut in 1978 and grew through the early 1980s, as well as in the overwhelming popularity of 1980 releases like AC/DC's *Back in Black*, Pat Benatar's *Crimes of Passion*, and the 1979 hard rock hit single "Renegade" from the band Styx. That the second video to air on MTV in August of 1981 was Pat Benatar's hard-rocking cover of The Young Rascals' "You Better Run" and the fourth video was The Who's "You Better You Bet" is a testament to the continued relevance of hard rock as well.

Where punk revisited the original simplicity and rebelliousness of garage rock, late 1970s hard rockers like Van Halen, AC/DC and Pat Benatar reaffirmed the potent expressive influence of the blues in rock and repackaged it with greater levels of production, musicianship, and raw power. Hard rock would evolve in different ways throughout the decade—sometimes blending elements of art/prog rock, classical music, and pop rock—but always maintaining a distinctly hard edge.

### Van Halen in the 1980s

Van Halen would go through two distinct phases in the 1980s owing to a lineup change in 1985. The early 1980s, the David Lee Roth era, is fundamentally a continuation of the over-the-top, guitar-driven rock that brought the band international fame in the late 1970s. When Roth departed in 1985, Van Halen joined forces with vocalist Sammy Hagar for what came to be known as the "Van Hagar" era. As mentioned in Chapter 8, Van Halen began to sparsely incorporate synthesizers into their sound around 1981. However, their use of these would become more fundamental by 1984 and would accelerate after Hagar joined.

From 1980 to 1984, Van Halen released four albums with Roth (for a total of six, all produced by Ted Templeman). 1980's *Women and Children First* solidified the band's status as the premier hard rock act on the planet. It opens with the now classic rock radio staple "And the Cradle Will Rock...," an obvious play on the line from the classic nursery rhyme. The album was heavier than the previous two and featured a greater use of studio overdubbing. Van Halen's blues influences are clear, yet quite individually distinctive, on the tracks "Take Your Whiskey Home" and "Could This Be Magic?"

**Go to Chapter 11 playlist example "Take Your Whiskey Home" Van Halen, 1980**

**Go to Chapter 11 playlist example "Could This Be Magic?" Van Halen, 1980**

The album *Fair Warning* came in 1981. One critic called it some of the fiercest music Van Halen has ever made. Its opening track, "Mean Street," begins with a short but stunning guitar instrumental that segues into a highly syncopated main riff, which is quite heavy and unexpectedly funky. The rhythmic structure of the piece is built on the sixteenth note rhythm lending to the funky feel.

**Go to Chapter 11 playlist example "Mean Street" Van Halen, 1981**

"Sinner's Swing!" is an aggressive blues rocker with all the standard Van Halen signature elements:

**Go to Chapter 11 playlist example "Sinner's Swing!" Van Halen, 1981**

1982's *Diver Down* features twelve songs, five of which are covers and three of which are instrumentals. A remake of Roy Orbison's "(Oh) Pretty Woman" is one of the album's highlights. A video was made for the song but was banned by MTV—one of the first banned videos—for being too sexually suggestive. "Big Bad Bill (Is Sweet William Now)" is a cover of a 1924 jazz tune by Milton Ager and Jack Yellen. The Van Halen version features Jan Van Halen, Eddie and Alex's father, on clarinet.

**Go to Chapter 11 playlist example "(Oh) Pretty Woman" Orbison/Dees, arr. Van Halen, 1982**

**Go to Chapter 11 playlist example "Big Bad Bill" Ager/Yellen arr. Van Halen, 1982**

Stylized in Roman numerals as *MCMLXXXIV* on the album cover, *1984* came that same year and would prove to be the last album Van Halen would record with David Lee Roth until a reunion in 2012. *1984* became the band's best-selling album at more than 20 million copies, and it saw Van Halen's explosion onto the small screen with three enormously popular videos: "Jump," "Panama," and "Hot for Teacher." Eddie's ongoing desire to make greater use of synthesizers was realized on *1984*. The instrumental title track, which opens the album, is a full-on synthesizer piece, and the tracks "Jump" (Van Halen's only number one single) and "I'll Wait" are synthesizer-centered band pieces, although they each appropriately feature a guitar solo. In spite of the use of synthesizers, *1984* contains some of Van Halen's most aggressive and technically complex music. The contrast between high-tech synth and screaming guitars was praised by critics and well received by fans. The following examples from the album demonstrate each:

**Go to Chapter 11 playlist example "1984/Jump" Van Halen, 1984**

**Go to Chapter 11 playlist example "Hot for Teacher" Van Halen, 1984**

Various tensions between Roth and the other band members led to his departure following the tour for *1984*. Roth would enjoy his own successful solo career in the years that followed. When Eddie met Sammy Hagar and asked him to join Van Halen, Hagar was already an experienced rocker, first with the band Montrose and later as a solo artist. Hagar, also a skilled guitarist, would sometimes play the instrument with Van Halen on stage to enhance the band's sound.

*5150*, the first album with the new singer, came in 1986. In spite of the lineup change and an even heavier keyboard/synth element, the album rose to the number one spot on the *Billboard* charts with the lead single "Why Can't This Be Love" reaching number three. A massive tour followed with live footage being released in 1987. Although there were dramatic changes in Van Halen's sound during this period, they were not remiss in letting the world know that they were *still* Van Halen, as is evident in the song "Get Up," a hard-driving rock piece with all of the classic Van Halen elements.

**Go to Chapter 11 playlist example "Why Can't This Be Love" Van Halen, 1986**

**Go to Chapter 11 playlist example "Get Up" Van Halen, 1986**

The last Van Halen album of the 1980s would also reach number one in 1988. *OU812* (Oh, you ate one too) was a mix of heavy guitar-based jams and deceptively simple synthesizer-driven, pop rock–oriented songs, all of it of extremely high quality in production and execution. Part of the supporting tour was the now legendary Monsters of Rock series stadium tour of 1988. The show featured a little-known blues-based rock band called Kingdom Come, an up-and-coming metal act called Metallica, the quasi-glam band Dokken (featuring guitar ace George Lynch), the German metal masters Scorpions, and Van Halen headlining. The tour stopped in thirty cities between May 23 and July 30. The song "When It's Love" was the best-charting single from *OU812*, reaching number five on the *Billboard* singles chart.

**Go to Chapter 11 playlist example "When It's Love" Van Halen, 1988**

Van Halen's momentum carried them well into the 1990s when they would reach their peak popularity and win their first Grammy. By 1995, creative tensions were rising between the Van Halen brothers and Hagar. He would depart in 1996. Various incarnations and reunions of the band with both Roth and Hagar have occurred and have even included Eddie's son, Wolfgang, on bass guitar. Van Halen *defined* hard rock as it would exist in the early 1980s and they *refined* it throughout the decade. They have earned a position as one of the greatest bands of the twentieth century—as has Eddie, as one of the most brilliant and influential guitarists of all time.

## Pat Benatar

With a musical life that began as a classically trained singer, **Pat Benatar** (b. 1953) made the move to rock in her early 20s. She was noticed by Chrysalis Records executive Terry Ellis while performing in a night club in New York City in April 1978 and signed a contract shortly thereafter. She would release her debut rock album, *In the Heat of the Night* in 1979. By early 1980, *In the Heat of the Night* had reached number twelve on the album chart. Its second single release, "Heartbreaker," written by Geoff Gill and Cliff Wade, became a hit as well. The song helped to build a commercial presence for Benatar and to create the enthusiasm which would propel her second album, *Crimes of Passion*, to number two on the album chart following its release in August 1980.

**Go to Chapter 11 playlist example "Heartbreaker" Gill/Wade 1979**

Image 11.2: The hard-rocking Pat Benatar

*Crimes of Passion* would include Benatar's fully formed backup band, several of whom would make songwriting contributions. The band included guitarist Neil Giraldo (whom Benatar would marry in 1982), guitarist Scott Sheets, bassist Roger Capps, and drummer Myron Grombacher. The album produced the hit singles "Treat Me Right" and "Hit Me with Your Best Shot," which would become Benatar's signature song. It also contains the single "You Better Run" which, as mentioned earlier, was the second video to air on MTV. The album earned Benatar her first Grammy for Best Female Rock Vocal Performance and would go on to be the best-selling album of her career with more than 4 million copies sold in the United States alone.

**Go to Chapter 11 playlist example "Hit Me with Your Best Shot" Eddie Schwartz, 1980**

**Go to Chapter 11 playlist example "Treat Me Right" Pat Benatar/Doug Lubahn 1980**

*Precious Time*, Benatar's third studio album released in the summer of 1981, would reach number one on the album chart and secure her position as the top female hard rock singer in the world. Its lead single "Fire and Ice" earned Benatar a second Grammy for Best Female Rock Vocal. By the end of 1981, she was a regular on MTV. *Precious Time* would be the last Pat Benatar album to feature guitarist Scott Sheets.

**Go to Chapter 11 playlist example "Fire and Ice" Tom Kelly/Scott Sheets/Pat Benatar, 1981**

Benatar's 1982 album, *Get Nervous*, extended her critical and commercial success. It spawned another hit single and video for "Shadows of the Night," supported a sold-out world tour and garnered a third Grammy for the singer. The album also saw the addition of keyboardist Charlie Giordano to her band. The prominent keyboard element had begun to take the hard rock, guitar-driven edge off of Benatar's sound, and pressure to keep up with pop rock trends on MTV would lead to the video for the hit single from 1983's *Live from Earth*, "Love Is a Battlefield," which featured Benatar in a Jackson-esque choreographed dance sequence. Nevertheless, it too was a major hit and earned Benatar her fourth consecutive Grammy for Best Female Rock Vocal.

**Go to Chapter 11 playlist example "Shadows of the Night" D.L. Byron 1982**

**Go to Chapter 11 playlist example "Love is a Battlefield" Holly Knight/Mike Chapman 1983**

The rest of the 1980s saw Benatar and her band experimenting with synth-driven pop rockers and pop ballads (she even a made jump band blues record in 1991 called *True Love*). 1988's *Wide Awake in Dreamland* marked a brief return to the guitar-driven hard rock roots that brought Benatar into the limelight, though her hard rock of the early 1980s is her best-remembered music. She would become less active in the 1990s as she took periods of time to devote to her family. Pat Benatar's music has become engrained in many facets of popular culture through films, television, and video games.

# Billy Squier

Guitarist/singer/songwriter **Billy Squier** (b. 1950) enjoyed a meteoric rise to stardom in the early 1980s, beginning with his 1980 debut solo album, *The Tale of the Tape*, which Squier coproduced with Eddy Offord. Although none of its songs broke the singles charts, several were popular AOR hits and the album itself peaked at number seven. Not only did it get Squier's solo career off the ground, one of the songs from the album, "The Big Beat," would come to be sampled numerous times by major hip-hop artists including Run–D.M.C., Alicia Keys, and Jay Z, to name a few, enshrining Squier in modern music.

**Go to Chapter 11 playlist example "The Big Beat" Billy Squier, 1980**

Squier's follow-up effort, 1981's *Don't Say No*, saw him soar to international fame. The album peaked at number five and stayed in the charts for more than two years. Several hit singles and videos came and Squier became a fixture on MTV by late 1981. His videos were usually fairly straightforward, most featuring him in performance mode, either shot from live concert footage or simulated on a sound stage. "The Stroke" was the biggest hit from the *Don't Say No*.

**Go to Chapter 11 playlist example "The Stroke" Billy Squier, 1981**

In 1982, Billy Squier released *Emotions in Motion* with cover art by famous pop artist Andy Warhol. The album climbed to number five and produced another of Squier's best-known songs, "Everybody Wants You." The accompanying video was an enormous hit on MTV and ran in regular rotation for several months. The song demonstrates all of Squier's musical strengths as well as the best of his catchy, hard-rocking style of the early 1980s. Additionally, the album featured Queen's Freddie Mercury and Roger Taylor providing backing vocals on the title track. They were listed in the album credits as "Emotional Support."

**Go to Chapter 11 playlist example "Everybody Wants You" Billy Squier, 1982**

**Go to Chapter 11 playlist example "Emotions in Motion" Billy Squier (feat. Mercury and Taylor), 1982**

Squier toured extensively in support of *Emotions in Motion* including shared billing with Queen, Foreigner, and The Who. He is also credited with helping to introduce a young British heavy metal band, Def Leppard, to US audiences as they opened for Squier during part of the tour.

*Signs of Life* (1984), Squier's fourth studio album, would become his third consecutive multi-million-seller. Ironically, the album's biggest hit song (and Squier's highest-charting career single), "Rock Me Tonite," featured an accompanying video that would prove to be his undoing. In what has been frequently described as the worst video ever made, Squier is shown waking up in a satin sheet covered bed and then performing a kind of dance to the song that can only be described as terribly unskilled and awkward. The video met with massive ridicule and Squier's popularity declined rapidly. His next album would only sell around three hundred thousand copies. Squier himself blames the video for derailing his career. The video is a classic "What was I thinking?" moment for the singer. Sadly, Squier would never again enjoy the same popularity he had in the early 1980s, although the hits from that period are now classic rock radio staples, and the video incident is a strong testament to the *negative* potential of MTV.

## Styx

Formed in the early 1970s, the band **Styx** straddled the fence between progressive rock and hard rock through most of the decade. As such, they are quite difficult to classify. Unlike many prog bands of the 1970s, Styx had a strong tendency toward catchy rock hooks and the occasional pop-esque ballad. They recorded nine albums between 1972 and 1979 and had achieved moderate success on AOR by mid-decade. By 1976, the band would include vocalist/keyboardist **Dennis DeYoung** (b. 1947), bassist **Chuck Panozzo** (b. 1948), drummer **John Panozzo** (1948–1996), guitarist **James Young** (b. 1949), and their newest member, vocalist/guitarist **Tommy Shaw** (b. 1953). Through their most successful years, DeYoung and Shaw shared lead vocal duties.

Styx had their major commercial breakthrough in 1977 with their seventh album, *The Grand Illusion*. It spawned the hits "Come Sail Away" and "Fooling Yourself (The Angry Young Man)" which have become classic rock radio standards. The album contains many art/prog elements. It is not a concept album but it does contain overarching lyrical themes. There are also several tracks with expansive forms, prog-like harmonic progressions, and a heavy synthesizer/keyboard component, though these are interspersed with hard rock elements like distorted guitars, gritty vocals, and heavy drums and bass.

The 1978 album, *Pieces of Eight*, marked a move to a more distinctly hard rock sound largely due to Shaw's input. The singles "Blue Collar Man (Long Nights)" and "Renegade" are indicative of this. Although "Blue Collar Man" is a keyboard-centric piece, the tone and style are quite heavy and even a bit reminiscent of the hard rock keyboard stylings of early 1970s Deep Purple. Both hits were written by Shaw and feature him on lead vocals.

**Go to Chapter 11 playlist example "Blue Collar Man (Long Nights)" Shaw, 1978**

**Go to Chapter 11 playlist example "Renegade" Shaw, 1978**

Styx' next album, 1979's *Cornerstone*, would show the band's propensity for pop rock hits and ballads. It moved away from the hard rock sound of *Pieces of Eight*, though their 1981 release, *Paradise Theater* would swing back to a heavier direction with the songs "Too Much Time on My Hands" and the anti-cocaine-themed "Snowblind." Dennis DeYoung confirmed that *Paradise Theater* is a concept album which uses metaphor to describe the changes occurring in America during the late 1970s to the turn of the decade. *Paradise Theater* would become the band's most successful album and would also lead to their greatest controversy: Several religious and anti-rock activist groups claimed that Styx, using a studio technique known as backmasking, had hidden Satanic messages in the song "Snowblind." This helped to fuel a political lobby that would lead to the PMRC hearings of 1985 (more on this in Chapter 12). The accusation was flatly denied by the band. DeYoung made light of the matter and was quoted as saying "We had enough trouble to make the music sound right forward."

**Go to Chapter 11 playlist example "Too Much Time on My Hands" Shaw, 1980**

**Go to Chapter 11 playlist example "Snowblind" Young/DeYoung, 1980**

The backmasking controversy inspired Styx' next album, *Kilroy Was Here*, in 1983, although it would prove to be the band's last studio album of the 1980s. *Kilroy Was Here* is essentially a progressive pop album. This shift back toward progressive flavors eventually drove a wedge between DeYoung and Shaw. Creative conflicts and antagonism on DeYoung's part led Shaw to depart following the *Kilroy* tour to pursue a solo career; the band would dissolve shortly thereafter. Styx reformed in 1989 without Shaw and would later reunite with the classic lineup on several occasions to record and tour from 1995 to the present, though they would never regain the popularity they enjoyed in the early 1980s.

## Triumph

Formed in the mid-1970s, Canadian hard rock power trio **Triumph** made their commercial breakthrough in 1979 and grew in popularity in the early and mid-1980s through persistent touring, AOR radio, and videos. The band included singer/drummer **Gil Moore** (b. 1953), bassist/keyboardist **Mike Levine** (b. 1949), and singer/guitarist **Rik Emmett** (b. 1953) for nearly their entire recording career, with the exception of their final studio album, *Edge of Excess*, in 1993, for which Phil Xenidis, also known as Phil X, replaced Emmett.

Following a period of recording, touring and earning scattered radio exposure between 1975–1979, Triumph's third album, *Just a Game* (1979), would provide the struggling band the commercial success they were seeking. The songs "Hold On" and "Lay It on the Line" gained significant exposure for Triumph, the former breaking the top 40 and both becoming enormous AOR hits. These early hits showed the band's depth of songwriting skill, their propensity for dramatic musical contrasts, and the superb musicianship that would earn them great respect among their fans and peers.

**Go to Chapter 11 playlist example "Lay It on the Line" Emmett, 1979**

**Go to Chapter 11 playlist example "Hold On" Emmett, 1979**

1981's *Allied Forces* brought Triumph further into the spotlight with the songs "Magic Power" and "Fight the Good Fight." "Magic Power," a song praising the power of music, reached number eight on the mainstream rock chart and became something of a youth-culture anthem. *Allied Forces* eventually sold more than 1 million copies in the United States.

**Go to Chapter 11 playlist example "Magic Power" Emmett/Levine/Moore, 1981**

**Go to Chapter 11 playlist example "Fight the Good Fight" Emmett/Levine/Moore, 1981**

By 1984, Triumph's lyrics had become decidedly more political. Their seventh album, *Thunder Seven*, is a concept album that explores the state of humanity at the turn of the twenty-first century. It is considered by most fans and critics to be the band's creative peak.

**Go to Chapter 11 playlist example "Follow Your Heart" Emmett/Levine/Moore, 1984**

Triumph became known well for their stunning live performances as well. They were one of the earliest bands to heavily incorporate laser light shows. They were also among the first bands to release music on the emerging compact disc format in 1984. They are currently inactive as a band but have not ruled out the possibility of a reunion.

As a band and individually, Triumph are noted for their support of a number of charitable causes and philanthropic endeavors including United Way of Canada, Kids With Cancer, Barrett House AIDS Hospice and the Children's Wish Foundation, among others.

## Joan Jett & the Blackhearts

Singer/guitarist Joan Jett (b. 1958) began her career as a member of the female punk/hard rock group The Runaways in the mid-1970s. She began to pursue a solo career when the Runaways disbanded in 1979. Following a series of false starts, shoestring-budget tours, and attempts to form a permanent backup band, Joan Jett & the Blackhearts released their first album, *I Love Rock 'n' Roll*, in 1981. The album was a mix of covers (including a Runaways cover written by Jett) and originals. It sold more than 10 million copies. The title track, originally written and released by The Arrows, was among the covers. Jett had first heard the song years earlier and it had become a regular part of her live show. Her recording of it with The Blackhearts was a massive hit single, selling more than 2 million copies. The video, a basic black-and-white live performance style piece, was aired heavily on MTV. The follow-up album, entitled *Album*, came in 1983 and was also a mix of originals and covers. The success of the video for "I Love Rock 'n' Roll" had made Joan Jett an MTV superstar. As a result, the video for the lead single from *Album*, "Fake Friends," received heavy airplay on the station upon its release.

Jett followed with more albums, a string of hits, her own New Year's special on MTV, a series of sold-out tours, and a role in the Michael J. Fox Movie *Light of Day*. One of Jett's most enduring hits, "I Hate Myself for Loving You," came in 1988 from the album *Up Your Alley*. It features former Rolling Stones guitarist Mick Taylor performing the guitar solo. The hit "Little Liar" was also featured on *Up Your Alley*. There were two videos shot for "Little Liar," both of which enjoyed heavy rotation on MTV.

**Go to Chapter 11 playlist example "I Hate Myself for Loving You" Joan Jett/Desmond Child, 1988**

**Go to Chapter 11 playlist example "Little Liar" Joan Jett/Desmond Child, 1988**

Joan Jett is one of the most successful female hard rock musicians in history. She has maintained an active career in music, film, and television for four decades and her music has become engrained in popular culture through television, film, and other media.

# Deep Purple in the 1980s

Following their success with *Machine Head* in 1972, British hard rock band Deep Purple underwent a series of lineup changes, commercial ups and downs, solo careers, and their official disbandment in 1976. In 1984, the classic lineup of Gillan, Blackmore, Lord, Paice, and Glover reunited to record the album *Perfect Strangers*. The revival of the hard rock market in the 1980s and their timely return to it proved successful for pioneering band. *Perfect Strangers* climbed to top positions on several European charts and reached number five in the United Kingdom. It would peak at number sixteen in the United States but a massive 1985 US tour in support of the album would be the second-highest gate of the year, topped only by Bruce Springsteen's *Born in the U.S.A.* tour.

While the following three tracks contain the core elements that made Deep Purple so influential in the early 1970s, they validate the band's seamless adaptation to a new era of hard rock. In other words, they didn't sound like a 1970s band trying to fit in as a 1980s band.

> **Go to Chapter 11 playlist example "Knocking at Your Back Door" Blackmore/Gillan/Glover, 1984**

> **Go to Chapter 11 playlist example "Nobody's Home" Deep Purple, 1984**

> **Go to Chapter 11 playlist example "Perfect Strangers" Blackmore/Gillan/Glover, 1984**

Deep Purple continues to record and tour despite several subsequent lineup changes and the death of keyboardist Jon Lord in 2012.

## The "Power Ballad"

Beginning in the 1970s and increasing greatly in popularity throughout the 1980s, the **power ballad**, as it came to be known, became one of the most popular song forms in rock. Lyrically, the typical power ballad most commonly deals with love or romantic storytelling. In the 1980s, the lifestyle of the rock musician was often romanticized in power ballads. Musically, the songs are slow paced and usually begin with a mellow acoustic section centered on guitar or piano with vocal. The power ballad builds in intensity to include the full amplified band, though the tempo remains subdued. Occasionally there is a return to the mellow intro section toward the middle of the song, but this occurs more commonly at the end. Alternatively, the song builds to a big, full-band chorus section and employs a classic studio fade-out as a way of concluding.

Bands like Journey helped to popularize the form in the late 1970s, and by the mid-1980s mainstream hard rock and glam bands were almost *expected* to produce at least one power ballad per album. It was not unusual for a hard rock band to become famous not because of their hard rock music, but because of a successful power ballad. Although there were many fine power ballads which demonstrated outstanding musicianship and deep emotional expression, the form was so over-commercialized by the end of the decade that power ballads had become almost self-parodic. Here are several classic examples of the finer kind of power ballad:

**Go to Chapter 11 playlist example "Faithfully" Cain (Journey), 1983**

**Go to Chapter 11 playlist example "Save Your Love" Williams/Russell (Great White), 1987**

**Go to Chapter 11 playlist example "I Remember You" Bolan/Sabo (Skid Row), 1989**

## Bon Jovi

Hailing from New Jersey in the early 1980s, **Bon Jovi** would become a global force in hard rock by mid-decade and would continue to top charts until their first major hiatus in 1990. Founded by singer/guitarist **Jon Bon Jovi** (b. 1962), pianist **David Bryan** (b. 1962), and drummer **Tico Torres** (b. 1953), the three members enlisted bassist **Alec John Such** (b. 1951) and guitarist/singer **Richie Sambora** (b. 1959) to complete the group in 1983.

Playing in local clubs and showcase events, Bon Jovi caught the attention of scouts at Mercury Records and were offered a record deal. They released their self-titled debut in 1984 and scored a hit with the single "Runaway," though the song was actually an earlier demo that Jon Bon Jovi had recorded with other musicians and released before Bon Jovi was formed. Nevertheless, it reached the top 40 and helped to put Bon Jovi on the map. "Runaway," unlike the rest of the material from their early period, would continue to be a regular part of the band's live performances for years to come. Tours followed their debut album, including landing coveted opening spots for bands like Kiss and Scorpions.

**Go to Chapter 11 playlist example "Runaway" Jon Bon Jovi/George Karak, 1981**

The band broke from touring to record their follow-up album *7800° Fahrenheit* in 1985. Three singles from the album were released and, although sales were not as brisk as Bon Jovi and Mercury had hoped, headlining tours in Japan and Europe were hugely successful. In order to enhance their fortunes, Bon Jovi decided to recruit professional songwriter Desmond Child and up-and-coming producer Bruce Fairbairn for work on their next album. The results of these collaborations would launch Bon Jovi to global megastardom.

*Slippery When Wet* was released in August 1986 and was an overnight success. It reached number one on the *Billboard* album chart and would go on to sell more than 12 million copies. Bon Jovi's presence on MTV increased greatly with videos for the singles "You Give Love a Bad Name," "Livin' on a Prayer," and the power ballad "Wanted Dead or Alive," all three of which were *Billboard* chart hits as well. "Livin' on a Prayer" won the MTV Video Music Award for Best Stage Performance. Soon, Bon Jovi were headlining arenas and stadiums all over the world including England's Monsters of Rock Festival in 1987.

**Go to Chapter 11 playlist example "You Give Love a Bad Name" Bon Jovi/Sambora/Child, 1986**

**Go to Chapter 11 playlist example "Livin' on a Prayer" Bon Jovi/Sambora/Child, 1986**

**Go to Chapter 11 playlist example "Wanted Dead or Alive" Bon Jovi/Sambora, 1986**

**Note:** In 1989, Jon Bon Jovi and Richie Sambora gave a stunning acoustic performance of "Livin' on a Prayer" and "Wanted Dead or Alive" at the MTV Video Music Awards. These acoustic versions of their rock hits served as inspiration for a phenomenal new series soon launched on MTV called "MTV Unplugged," in which rock performers would play acoustic arrangements of their music. Countless stars from numerous genres, from Bob Dylan to Lil Wayne, have appeared on the series over the years.

Bon Jovi's fourth album, *New Jersey* (1988), would confirm their standing as one of the biggest hard rock bands on the planet. The band continued the collaboration with Child and Fairbairn that had proved so successful on their previous record. Reaching number one on album charts in multiple countries and establishing a record for the most number one singles from a hard rock album with five, *New Jersey* would sell 7 million copies in the United States alone. In the final days of the Cold War, it was also the first album by an American artist to be released and sold legally in the Soviet Union.

Image 11.4: Jon Bon Jovi in concert in 2014

The music on *New Jersey* exhibited a greater level of diversity and experimentation for the band than previous efforts. In addition to hard rockers and power ballads, there is the atmospheric intro section to "Lay Your Hands on Me," a harmonica and organ trade-off in "Homebound Train" and a flamenco-style guitar opening section in "Wild Is the Wind."

**Go to Chapter 11 playlist example "Lay Your Hands on Me" Bon Jovi/Sambora, 1988**

**Go to Chapter 11 playlist example "Homebound Train" Bon Jovi/Sambora, 1988**

**Go to Chapter 11 playlist example "Wild Is the Wind" Bon Jovi/Sambora/Child/Warren, 1988**

Bon Jovi toured extensively in the late 1980s in support of *Slippery When Wet* and *New Jersey*. This included hundreds of shows and sojourns to more than twenty countries. In 1989, they were part of the now legendary Moscow Music Peace Festival, a monumental hard rock/heavy metal concert held in the former Soviet Union toward the end of the Cold War (this will be discussed further in Chapter 12). By 1990 Bon Jovi were suffering from professional burnout; many months of nonstop touring had taken its toll on the band members. Following the *New Jersey* tour they took a much-needed break before reconvening in 1992. Their career would take several different turns in the decades to come but in the last half of the 1980s, Bon Jovi sat in the top echelon of the hard rock world.

## The Cult

Formed in 1983 in the British post-punk scene, **The Cult** was masterminded by singer **Ian Astbury** (b. 1962) and guitarist **Billy Duffy** (b. 1961). The pair comprise the creative core of the band and are its longest-standing members. The Cult found its earliest commercial success in 1985 with their second studio album, *Love*. It reached number four in the United Kingdom and built momentum for the band abroad. In 1987, working with producer Rick Rubin, The Cult released *Electric*, a highly polished hard rock offering which brought the band mainstream success in the United States and a world tour. The lead single from *Electric* was "Love Removal Machine." It demonstrates the band's maturing hard rock style.

**Go to Chapter 11 playlist example "Love Removal Machine" Astbury/Duffy, 1987**

The Cult's major commercial breakthrough was 1989's *Sonic Temple*. The album was recorded with then–up-and-coming producer Bob Rock. *Sonic Temple* reached its highest chart position in the United States at number ten and the videos for "Sweet Soul Sister" and "Edie (Ciao Baby)" enjoyed regular rotation on MTV. Promotional tours for the album included opening spots with Aerosmith and Metallica as well as their own headlining engagements.

**Go to Chapter 11 playlist example "Sweet Soul Sister" Astbury/Duffy, 1989**

**Go to Chapter 11 playlist example "Edie (Ciao Baby)" Astbury/Duffy, 1989**

**Go to Chapter 11 playlist example "Soul Asylum" Astbury/Duffy, 1989**

**Go to Chapter 11 playlist example "New York City" Astbury/Duffy, 1989**

As of this writing, The Cult are actively recording and touring. Although their period of major success was fairly limited, they penned some of the great bluesy rock of the late 1980s. They were also an important stepping stone for producer Bob Rock, who will later play a significant role in Metallica's success, as well as drummer Matt Sorum—who, after rising to fame as a touring drummer with The Cult, would join Guns N' Roses for most of the 1990s.

## Guns N' Roses

Singer **Axl Rose** (b. 1962), guitarists **Slash** (b. 1965) and **Izzy Stradlin** (b. 1962), drummer **Steven Adler** (b. 1965), and bassist **Duff McKagan** (b. 1964) formed **Guns N' Roses** in 1985 in Los Angeles. Their persistent presence in the bustling Sunset Strip and Hollywood club scene gained the attention of several record labels. They signed with Geffen Records in 1986 and released a live demo to maintain a market presence while they retreated to work on their debut studio album. *Appetite for Destruction* was released in 1987 and for a time, performed rather poorly. The video for the lead single "Welcome to the Jungle" was simply not receiving any airplay on MTV. When Geffen president David Geffen finally persuaded MTV to air the video, they initially placed it during their late-night rotation. Shortly after airing, requests for the video began pouring in to MTV. "Welcome to the Jungle" was soon among the most popular videos on MTV.

The song and the video feature a connected narrative describing the allure—and the danger—of the city (presumably Los Angeles) and the pursuit of stardom ("... You can taste the bright lights but you won't get them for free..."). In the video, a rube-ish Axl Rose gets off a bus at a city street corner amid the sound of sirens. He immediately encounters a drug dealer (played by Izzy Stradlin)—from whom he flees—and a prostitute. It then cuts to the band performing in a club interspersed with scenes of TV broadcasts of violence and police raids. An intervening scene then shows a shocked Axl strapped in a chair and being forced to watch numerous TV monitors with graphic images. In the end, the rube-ish Axl is transformed into a cynical city dweller who, now transformed, shakes his head in indifference to the images on the TV screens.

**Go to Chapter 11 playlist example "Welcome to the Jungle" Guns N' Roses, 1987**

Along with "Welcome to the Jungle," singles for "It's So Easy," "Sweet Child o' Mine," "Paradise City," and "Nightrain" were released. After Guns N' Roses took MTV by storm, album and singles sales skyrocketed. The band embarked on a massive world tour which kept them on the road for well over a year. They variously opened for Mötley Crüe, The Cult, Alice Cooper, Iron Maiden, and

Aerosmith and headlined many concerts as well. By late 1988, Guns N' Roses were one of the biggest hard rock bands on earth.

**Go to Chapter 11 playlist example "It's So Easy" Guns N' Roses, 1987**

**Go to Chapter 11 playlist example "Nightrain" Guns N' Roses, 1987**

*Appetite for Destruction* made Guns N' Roses one of the most successful bands in history. It holds the record for the best-selling debut album of all time with around 30 million copies sold worldwide. Musically and culturally, the album was the *Back in Black* of a new generation; a generation that was dealing with the specter of AIDS and the stifling conservatism of Reagan–Bush Era politics. *Appetite* revisited "sex, drugs and rock 'n' roll" with bluesy, rebellious music. It was pure hedonism repackaged for the MTV era.

In 1988, Guns N' Roses released an album called *G N' R Lies*, a recording consisting of four preexisting tracks released from the band's 1986 live demo and four newly recorded acoustic tracks. The hit single "Patience" was among the latter.

**Go to Chapter 11 playlist example "Patience" Guns N' Roses, 1988**

The album stirred up controversy for the band as accusations of racism swirled around the song "One in a Million." The song, written by Rose, contains the n-word, the use of which he attempted to defend by contextualizing it in his own song as well as by comparison to the 1972 John Lennon song "Woman is the [N-word] of the World." The song also contains lyrics that were considered to be homophobic. Rose claimed that his lyrics were based on negative experiences in his life and that he was expressing his anger relating to these experiences. Slash, whose mother is a Black American-born English artist, claimed that he did not particularly favor the song but did regret the way the press portrayed the band's personal feelings.

Much controversy grew around Guns N' Roses, and Axl in particular, in the late 1980s and early 1990s. Rose would come to be perceived by many as a tantrum-throwing, immature, drug-addled male diva.

In 1990, Guns N' Roses underwent personnel changes, drummer Matt Sorum replaced Steven Adler and keyboardist Dizzy Reed joined the group. In 1991 they released two albums, *Use Your Illusion I* and *Use Your Illusion II*, simultaneously. The recordings demonstrated remarkable musical prowess and diversity, as well as the skills of producer Mike Clink, and both immediately rose to the number one and two positions in the album charts. The accompanying videos, especially the one for "November Rain," were enormously successful. Guns N' Roses seemed to transform from a gritty, blues-based rock band into a group capable of writing epic compositions and spouting serious political discourse.

**Go to Chapter 11 playlist example "November Rain" Rose, 1991**

**Go to Chapter 11 playlist example "Civil War" Slash/McKagan/Rose, 1991**

The promotional tour for *Use Your Illusion I* and *II* lasted for more than two years and while it was a massive financial success, it also saw numerous instances of riots and major controversies, most involving Axl Rose. In one infamous incident in 1992 in Montreal, while Guns N' Roses were coheadlining a leg of the tour with metal giants Metallica, Metallica frontman James Hetfield was severely burned in a pyrotechnic malfunction during an opening performance and had to be rushed off stage for medical treatment. This caused a long delay in the concert during which the audience became restless. When Guns N' Roses finally took the stage, Axl performed just a few songs and, claiming that his throat hurt, abruptly walked off. This sent the already agitated crowd into a riotous state which resulted in massive property damage, injuries, and arrests. In later interviews, members of Metallica stated that they believed Axl could have salvaged the concert, but instead chose to take the low road which fueled the ensuing situation. This was just one of many incidents that occurred on the tour and lent to the generally negative perception of Axl Rose.

Tensions between Rose and Slash would ultimately lead to Slash's departure in 1996, and ever since, the singer and guitarist have hurled negative comments toward each other in the press. The legendary bad blood between the two had prevented a reunion for two decades, in spite of much popular demand. At the time of this writing, Slash and Axl have just recently reunited in Guns N' Roses for a headlining performance at the 2016 Coachella Festival and a major stadium tour (dubbed the "Not In This Lifetime…" Tour) to follow. While the future of Guns N' Roses is uncertain, their status as the hard rock kings of the late 1980s and early 1990s is indisputable.

## Hard Rock Supergroups of the 1980s

The concept of a supergroup was discussed in Chapter 8. To reiterate, a supergroup is made up either partially or entirely of well-established, famous musicians coming from their own successful solo careers or bands to record and tour together. Most often, these supergroups were short-lived side projects, perhaps resulting in an album or two and the ensuing promotional tours. Many resulted in infamous ego clashes. Supergroups were generally seen as "money in the bank" for record companies and concert promoters, and they usually had no trouble generating sales. In the 1970s and 1980s, there were supergroups in nearly every style of music, from country to progressive rock and even in one famous instance, opera (The Three Tenors). Noteworthy among 1980s rock-oriented supergroups were Asia, The Firm, The Power Station, and Bad English. In hard rock music, a particularly successful supergroup was the late 1980s/early 1990s band, Damn Yankees.

### Damn Yankees

Formed in 1989 and led by **Tommy Shaw** of Styx, **Damn Yankees** included guitarist **Ted Nugent** (Amboy Dukes and solo), bassist **Jack Blades** (Night Ranger), and then-unknown drummer **Michael Cartellone**. Damn Yankees' self-titled 1990 debut was quite successful, producing three hit singles,

"Coming of Age," "Damn Yankees," and the power ballad "High Enough," and selling more than 2 million copies. Damn Yankees also produced videos which were successful on MTV.

**Go to Chapter 11 playlist example "Coming of Age" Blades/Nugent/Shaw, 1990**

**Go to Chapter 11 playlist example "Damn Yankees" Blades/Nugent/Shaw, 1990**

**Go to Chapter 11 playlist example "High Enough" Blades/Nugent/Shaw, 1990**

Damn Yankees launched a massive world tour in support of their first album that lasted for well over a year. The 1992 follow-up, *Don't Tread*, was not as successful but nonetheless produced several hits and sold nearly 1 million copies. It would be the last album for Damn Yankees.

**Go to Chapter 11 playlist example "Don't Tread on Me" Blades/Nugent/Shaw, 1992**

**Go to Chapter 11 playlist example "Mister Please" Blades/Nugent/Shaw, 1992**

## Funk Rock/Rap Rock in the 1980s

Funk rock can be traced back to the late 1960s in some of the music of Jimi Hendrix and Aerosmith in the mid-1970s. Funk as a well-defined style had its origins in the music Sly Stone and George Clinton. Rap's origins can be traced to the urban neighborhoods of New York, Los Angeles, and even Jamaica, and began to emerge as a style unto itself in the late 1970s. In the 1980s, innovative bands began fusing these styles together into a hip, rock-based fusion, much of which was laden with rapping and rap-style vocals as well as **virtuosic bass guitar playing**. In the mid–late 1980s, no two bands embodied a greater expression of these collective elements than Red Hot Chili Peppers and Primus.

## Red Hot Chili Peppers

Formed in 1983 by vocalist **Anthony Kiedis** (b. 1962), virtuoso bassist **Michael "Flea" Balzary** (b. 1962), guitarist **Hillel Slovak** (1962–1988), and drummer **Jack Irons** (b. 1962), Red Hot Chili Peppers' early years were plagued by lineup instability, production staff difficulties, and heroin addiction, which would ultimately lead to Slovak's untimely death in 1988. Three albums came between 1985 and 1987 (the second of which, *Freaky Styley*, was produced by funk pioneer George Clinton) and—in spite of numerous personal and professional issues both in the studio and on the road— the band gradually built a modest but devoted international following. Upon returning home from the tour for their third album, Slovak retreated from the company of his bandmates as he struggled with severe heroin addiction. He was found dead in his apartment on June 27, 1988, at the age of twenty-six from an apparent overdose. A distraught Irons left the band soon after. Kiedis and Flea debated whether or not to continue, but ultimately concluded that they did not want to abandon what they and Slovak had accomplished.

Kiedis battled with his own heroin problem and several more members would come and go before the band reached its stable 1989 lineup and released their fourth album, *Mother's Milk*. Guitarist **John Frusciante** (b. 1970) and drummer **Chad Smith** (b. 1961) rounded out what would be the lineup until 1992. *Mother's Milk* produced three singles including a cover version of Stevie Wonder's "Higher Ground." The album, produced by Michael Beinhorn, helped the band reach closer to the mainstream.

**Go to Chapter 11 playlist example "Higher Ground" Stevie Wonder arr. RHCP, 1989**

Working with producer Rick Rubin—who would go on to produce the band's next five albums— the Chili Peppers recorded 1991's *Blood Sugar Sex Magik*, the album that would catapult them to international superstardom and define commercial funk rock for over two decades. Major hit singles "Give It Away," "Under the Bridge," and "Breaking the Girl" followed, as did enormous MTV exposure. During this period, the band refined and fortified a sound that combined funk, rap, acid rock, art rock, and blues and brought it to the mainstream. The Chili Peppers became one of the most successful and influential acts of their time.

**Go to Chapter 11 playlist example "Give It Away" Red Hot Chili Peppers, 1991**

**Go to Chapter 11 playlist example "Under the Bridge" Red Hot Chili Peppers, 1991**

**Go to Chapter 11 playlist example "Breaking the Girl" Red Hot Chili Peppers, 1991**

Red Hot Chili Peppers are among the most enduring bands from the late 1980s. They enjoyed multi-platinum success throughout the 1990s with the albums *One Hot Minute* (1995) and *Californication* (1999). Their music and image permeates popular culture through movies and television and their activism extends into politics, disaster relief efforts, and other world affairs. The Chili Peppers' continued relevance is evident in recent successful recordings and tours as well as a 2014 Super Bowl halftime show appearance with current pop funk sensation Bruno Mars.

## Primus

Another important funk rock band who would have a career beginning in the late 1980s and extending into the 1990s was **Primus**. Founded in 1984 by singer, songwriter, and bass guitar virtuoso **Les Claypool** (b. 1963), by the time the band would have commercial success in 1989 it included guitarist **Larry LaLonde** (b. 1968) and drummer **Tim "Herb" Alexander** (b. 1965). Primus' sound was heavier than the Chili Peppers' and is sometimes referred to as alternative metal or funk metal. In 1989 Primus released their first full-length album, *Suck on This*, a live album recorded in Berkeley, California. The album is credited with helping to propagate the burgeoning underground genre of funk rock/metal in the late 1980s. The song "Harold of the Rocks" amply demonstrates Claypool's funky but heavy bass playing as well as the band's propensity for Zappa-esque musical eccentricities. (A studio version of the song appears on the follow-up studio album, *Frizzle Fry*.)

**Go to Chapter 11 playlist example "Harold of the Rocks," Claypool/Huth, 1989**

Image 11.5: The inimitable Les Claypool

1990's *Frizzle Fry* brought well-deserved critical praise to the band for their superb musicianship and unique sound. A video was released for the single "John the Fisherman" that featured a cameo appearance by Metallica guitarist Kirk Hammett. The song "Mr. Knowitall" demonstrates all of the characteristics that endeared Primus to their modest but rabid fan base at the end of the decade.

**Go to Chapter 11 playlist example "John the Fisherman," Primus, 1990**

**Go to Chapter 11 playlist example "Mr. Knowitall" Claypool/Huth, 1990**

Primus would go on to build a cult following and enjoy varied success in the 1990s and 2000s. Claypool has come to be one of the most respected bass players in rock. In 2000 he played in the supergroup Oysterhead with former Police drummer Stewart Copeland and Phish guitarist Trey Anastasio. Additionally, drummer Herb Alexander performed with the highly acclaimed Blue Man Group in the early 2000s. Primus is currently actively recording and touring. They—or at least their distinctive sound—have become widely recognized in popular television culture as the writers/performers of the theme song for the hit animated series *South Park*. Many bands and artists, including Deftones, Korn, Limp Bizkit, Muse, and Incubus cite Primus as a fundamental influence.

## Hard Rock and Metal

As detailed in Chapter 8, 1970s hard rock and heavy metal shared many common characteristics. This was no less true the early 1980s (particularly between "glam" bands and hard rock bands), although as metal grew, it would diversify into several musically and culturally well-defined, though mutually interconnected, subgenres. The three main arms of the metal monster that would dominate rock music by mid-decade began with the New Wave of British Heavy Metal (NWOBHM) in the late 1970s, the Los Angeles glam bands around 1980, and underground "thrash" and "speed" metal bands, primarily out of San Francisco and New York, in the early and mid-1980s.

In the following chapter, we will discuss the Golden Age of heavy metal in the 1980s.

## Suggested Chapter Related Activities

- As your counting skills have no doubt improved over the course of the semester, see if you can make a chart of the rhythmic attacks (see chapter 1) of the main riff in Van Halen's "Mean Street" (hint: the riff unfolds over two measures at the sixteenth note level). This will help you to see and hear how the syncopated sixteenth notes create a "funkier" overall feel.

- See how many other songs in the chapter exploit sixteenth-note layer syncopation.

- Songwriter Desmond Child had a hand in the hits of both Joan Jett and Bon Jovi. Can you identify characteristics in each song that might point to Child's signature style? Can you find other examples of Child co-written songs with similar elements?

- It was mentioned that the music of Billy Squier has been heavily sampled by contemporary rap and hip hop artists. See if you can locate other examples of modern hip hop artists sampling '80s hard rock.

- Locate several examples of post-2000 power ballads and compare them to their '80s counterparts in terms of form, instrumentation and stylistic influences.

- Compare/contrast the music of The Chili Peppers and Primus.

## Suggested Discussion Topics

- Discuss the enduring relevance of hard rock bands like Gun N' Roses and AC/DC, both of whom have headlined Coachella in recent times, as well as The Chili Peppers who performed at the 2014 Super Bowl halftime show alongside Bruno Mars.

- Consider and discuss the role of women in hard rock.

## Image Credits

Image 11.1: Copyright © GHOSTRIDER2112 (CC BY-SA 2.0) at https://commons.wikimedia.org/wiki/File:VAN_HALEN_2008.jpg.

Image 11.2: Copyright © Heidy Escobar (CC BY-SA 2.0) at https://commons.wikimedia.org/wiki/File:PAT_BENATAR_2007-09-07.jpg.

Image 11.3: Doorstepsnail, https://commons.wikimedia.org/wiki/File:Jett_Rocks.jpg. Copyright in the Public Domain.

Image 11.4: Copyright © Lunchbox LP (CC by 2.0) at https://commons.wikimedia.org/wiki/File:Jonbj2013.jpg.

Image 11.5: Xylon, https://commons.wikimedia.org/wiki/File:LesClaypool.jpg. Copyright in the Public Domain.

# CHAPTER 12
# Heavy Metal in the Eighties

*... It will be so loud that if we move in next door to you, your lawn will die.*

-Lemmy Kilmister of Motörhead

## Cultural Context

Where punk rockers reacted against contemporary political and social ills; Springsteen spoke to the plight of a disenfranchised post-Vietnam working-class; Prince sang about partying in spite of the specter of total annihilation; and Bowie and Kiss explored theatrical escapism, heavy metal bands of the late 1970s and 1980s combined these expressions into a style that was inspired musically by the ominous riffs and power chord–laden sounds of Black Sabbath, the high energy of punk, the earthy grit of blues rock, and the virtuosity and precision ensemble playing of Deep Purple and Van Halen.

The culture surrounding heavy metal in the late 1970s consisted of mostly young (aged 17 to 21), white, lower-class males, although this would diversify considerably as the 1980s unfolded. This typical early metal fan (as well as the metal musician) was the archetypal "angry young man." The feelings of alienation accumulated through social and economic obstacles (being seen as coming from "the wrong side of the tracks"), resisting social conformity, and generally thinking apart from the mainstream line, nourished a strong sense of identity: The early metalheads were outsiders in every sense of the word. The metal community bonded around this, as much as the music, and developed an "us versus them" mentality. The fan loyalty this generated, the understanding that the bands existed almost solely to provide a voice for their fans, played an absolutely crucial role in metal's survival through the punk and disco years: With a few exceptions, heavy metal bands had little or no help from radio, and when major labels became obsessed with punk, disco, and other mainstream rock in the mid–late 1970s, the New

Wave of British Heavy Metal spread in England and Europe by musicians and fans taking matters into their own hands; concert attendance, word of mouth, "fanzines" (homemade publications), and sheer persistence on the part of the musicians helped the movement grow. Ian Christe writes:

> Though the "old wave" of British heavy metal had existed mostly in the imaginations of hard rock fans, there was something catchy about the "New Wave of British Heavy Metal" that allowed the clunky moniker to stick. Musically, the NWOBHM cut 1970s hard rock into punk-size pieces, producing a highly focused form of guitar energy. Inspired by the self-actualizing elements of punk, many of the early efforts by Iron Maiden and Diamond Head were self-released or issued by bedroom labels such as Neat and Heavy Metal Records. Fans were clustered across England and Europe, wearing black leather jackets with denim vests covered in patches and pins promoting their favorite acts. By 1980, the movement was fully realized, with hundreds of 45s in print and a handful of landmark long-players by Motörhead, Saxon, Iron Maiden and Judas Priest. Though they were still very much London acts on the rise, these bands would dominate heavy metal for the next decade on the strength of their serious live capabilities. (p. 41)

From the beginning in heavy metal culture, extreme antiauthoritarianism and rebellion ruled. Like rock, there was a heavy party atmosphere surrounding metal bands and fans. Drugs and alcohol were often celebrated (although there are also a great number of songs that provide a cautionary view of addiction). Likewise, furious touring, fast living, and sexual promiscuity are all associated with metal bands. As the 1980s unfolded, major metal festival-style concerts became increasingly common and often featured British, glam, and underground bands (more below) on the same bill. Although these concerts were party scenes, in some ways they verged on ritual in heavy metal culture. Crowds engaged in headbanging, moshing, crowd surfing, and stage diving as a physical reaction—or type of "dancing"—to the music. To the uninitiated observer, these reactions often appeared to have a malicious or violent intent. Those who knew better knew it was all in good fun, albeit rough and tumble. The thrash and speed metal bands had the most intense crowd response; the "mosh pit" was a given at these shows.

## Tipper Gore and the Parent's Music Resource Center (PMRC)

The PMRC was formed in 1985 by four women—Tipper Gore, Susan Baker, Pam Howar, and Sally Nevius. The women were the wives of powerful Washington, DC political and business figures, the most well known being Tipper Gore's husband, then-Senator Al Gore. The PMRC would eventually expand to include twenty-two members. Their mission was to increase controls regarding access to certain music by minors—music that they deemed to contain explicit lyrical content regarding violence, drugs, and sex. Their main proposal was that the Recording Industry Association of America voluntarily label albums with explicit content, much the way that the film industry rates films. They also proposed that record stores should be forced to remove displays of albums with explicit content, keeping them out of the sight of customers, and that radio stations and video channels should be not be permitted to air songs or videos deemed explicit. Following an article published in the *Washington Post* stating the PMRC's position, retailers like Wal-Mart and Sears removed rock music and magazine displays from their stores.

The PMRC also compiled a list known as the **Filthy Fifteen**, fifteen songs that exemplified their objections to lyric content in popular and rock music. Nine of the fifteen bands were heavy metal bands; the list also included music by Prince, Madonna, and Cyndi Lauper, among others.

In September, 1985, a Senate hearing was held in order to determine the plausibility of the PMRC's request that music should be labeled. Among the PMRC's witnesses were two academics, a music professor named Joe Stuessy and a child psychiatrist named Paul King. Stuessy argued that heavy metal music was different than other forms of popular music like jazz or rock 'n' roll in that hatred was one of its core elements, while King stated that many adolescents read deeply into song lyrics. Other various arguments were made that pointed to overt expressions of sex, violence, drug taking, and the occult.

Arguing on behalf of the music industry and in defense of free speech were composer Frank Zappa, folk musician John Denver, and heavy metal singer Dee Snider of the band Twisted Sister. All three musicians made strong points against the proposal, variously citing the dangers of censorship in a free society, the possibility of misinterpretation of lyrics, enforcement problems, and the general infringement of civil liberties that were potentially involved in the proposed system.

In the end, record companies agreed to the demands of the PMRC, although many arguments have been made since that the labeling of explicit recordings actually increased record sales due to the "forbidden fruit" effect (I mean, who wants to sneak into a G-Rated movie?). Ironically, Frank Zappa, who was no friend of the PMRC, released an album of purely instrumental music called *Jazz from Hell* in 1986 that was labeled with a "Parental Advisory" sticker, in spite of the fact that the album contained *no lyrics*. The hearings—as well the PMRC and its individual members—have elicited an array of responses from musicians over the years ranging from humorous to openly hostile. By way of example, rap and metal musician, and currently well-known TV actor Ice-T and punk rocker Jello Biafra co wrote a song in 1989 called "Freedom of Speech." It contains the lyrics:

*Yo Tip, what's the matter? You ain't gettin' no dick?*

*You're bitchin' about rock'n'roll, that's censorship, dumb bitch*

## Heavy Metal Vilified in Prime Time

In 1988, TV personality Geraldo Rivera hosted a two-hour prime time network special called "Devil Worship: Exposing Satan's Underground." In it, Rivera attempted to draw a link between teenage

Satan worship, sacrificial murder, and heavy metal music. By selectively documenting several grisly murders in which teenagers were involved in ritual worship and committed murder, Rivera also noted that the teens were fans of heavy metal music, and that the music, lyrics, and album art were somehow responsible for influencing the actions of these obviously disturbed individuals. The music and album art of bands like Mötley Crüe and Iron Maiden were woven into the program, and singer Ozzy Osbourne, one of the most persecuted musicians in rock at the time, deftly defended his music and viewpoints via satellite feed.

While Rivera did manage to terrify millions of uninformed parents, he was also criticized by analysts for sensationalizing the connection between heavy metal music and violence with unsupported and poorly researched facts, as well as the utter lack of a critical journalistic approach. In other words, he failed to mention that the vastly overwhelming majority of perpetrators of brutal murders committed in the United States are fans of *all* kinds of music and are from a diverse range of religious and social backgrounds. He was also criticized for sidestepping any discussion on actually improving the mental health of teenagers, effective parenting strategies, the concept of personal responsibility, or the right to free speech. Rivera's "tabloid TV" approach seemed calculated to generate ratings, which it did: At the time, it set record-breaking ratings for a two-hour TV documentary.

It is not surprising that heavy metal music and musicians were targeted for public persecution. Like rock 'n' roll in the 1950s and rock in the 1960s, heavy metal music and lyrics challenged the right-wing, conservative cultural narrative of its time. This postmodernist opposition to entrenched societal values has historically fostered paranoia as well as the misattribution of cause and motive in juvenile crime. This was no different.

## The Moscow Music Peace Festival

In August 1989, in the last dark days of the Cold War, a momentous occasion took place in Moscow's Central Lenin Stadium. A host of American and European heavy metal and hard rock bands, along with several Russian bands, took to the concert stage in the name of world peace and, somewhat ironically, drug abuse treatment and prevention. The first of its kind in the Soviet Union, the **Moscow Music Peace Festival** drew hundreds of thousands of young Russian rock fans together in what has been called that country's equivalent to Woodstock. The event was sponsored by the charity, Make a Difference Foundation, in an effort to assist in educating Soviet doctors in learning the newest methods for treating drug addiction. Additionally, the concert signified the pinnacle of success for Soviet leader Mikhail Gorbachev's *Glasnost* (openness) policies, which greatly helped to end the Cold War. Among the performers were Ozzy, Mötley Crüe, Bon Jovi, Skid Row, and Scorpions.

The festival was quite successful in its fundraising and diplomatic efforts, although it was not without its problems: There were reportedly issues between bands and their management regarding everything from allotted performance times to who opened for whom, to arguments over the use of lighting and special effects and so forth. In other words, there were epic ego clashes backstage. All in all, the concert was and is viewed as an event of historical and political significance.

## The Three-Headed Metal Monster of the 1980s

As mentioned in Chapter 11, heavy metal in the 1980s can be basically—and more or less chronologically—divided into three subgenres: the New Wave of British Heavy Metal (fairly diverse in itself), American "glam" metal, and underground "thrash" (sometimes called "speed") metal. More fragmentation will occur by the end of the 1980s with so-called "death" metal, "doom" metal, "black" metal, and "power" metal establishing a presence, though for our purposes we will be concerned with the three major subgenres named. To be sure, these three subgenres overlapped; they shared many common characteristics and often a common audience. Indeed, they reacted to *each other* as well. Moreover, as with all labeling of music, problems of classification occur due to stylistic commonalities and should be understood as such.

We begin with the New Wave of British Heavy Metal and its foremost progenitors, Judas Priest, Motörhead, Iron Maiden, and Def Leppard, and, although Black Sabbath founding member Ozzy Osbourne was not technically part of the NWOBHM, his important and influential solo career began in 1980 and will be discussed here as well.

## Judas Priest

During an early 1970s experimental period of mingling metal, progressive, and blues elements, but finding limited commercial success, **Judas Priest** had released two studio albums by 1976. In 1977, the band signed with the major CBS Records (a rare accomplishment for a metal-oriented band in 1977) and included most of what would be their first long-standing lineup. Vocalist **Rob Halford** (b. 1951), guitarists **K.K. Downing** (b. 1951) and **Glenn Tipton** (b. 1947), and bassist **Ian Hill** (b. 1951) worked with session drummer **Simon Phillips** (b. 1957) (who would move on to his own very successful career) and producer Roger Glover (also bassist for Deep Purple) for their third studio album, *Sin After Sin*. The album marked an important step in Priest's stylistic development as they became more focused on the aggressive metal sound that would define them as a band in the 1980s and beyond; they had moved away from the more progressive elements that dominated their first two albums. Drummer **Les Binks** (b. 1948) would join the band for the album's tour and stay with them until 1979. *Sin After Sin* enjoyed robust sales and marked the beginning of a long period of commercial success for Judas Priest.

The song "Dissident Aggressor" showcases two important contributions Judas Priest made to early heavy metal: the precision two-guitar attack of Tipton and Downing and the aggressive double bass drum figures played by Phillips in the studio.

**Go to Chapter 12 playlist example "Dissident Aggressor" Halford/Downing/Tipton, 1977**

*Stained Class* (1978), Priest's fourth studio album, sold well and was the first Priest album to enter the US chart, even though it just barely did so. The album was markedly heavier than *Sin After Sin* and contained darker themes. American audience reaction was fairly mixed as Priest's presence there had just barely been established through recent touring. The darker lyrics may have contributed to the lukewarm response as well. Many American rock fans, having become accustomed to bands like Zeppelin and Aerosmith, simply were not ready for this music. The album is considered a seminal recording in the NWOBHM.

Judas Priest's cover of the Spooky Tooth song "Better by You, Better Than Me" from *Stained Class* would bring significant controversy to the band in 1990, more than a decade after its release. The parents of a teenage boy would force a civil action against Judas Priest after their son and his friend shot themselves in 1985 in an alleged suicide pact. The friend succeeded in his suicide attempt while the son of the parents bringing suit would die from his injuries several years later. The 1990 court action alleged that Judas Priest had hidden a subliminal message saying "Do It" in the song. The band denied the allegations and the suit was eventually dismissed, but it kept alive the ongoing social discourse on the topic of free speech and artist accountability.

**Go to Chapter 12 playlist example "Better by You, Better Than Me" Gary Wright, 1977**

1978 witnessed the release of the fifth Judas Priest studio album, *Killing Machine*. The title for the US release of the album was changed to *Hell Bent for Leather* due to an uproar over the original title. Around this time, Priest adopted a distinctive "biker" look which featured a considerable amount of leather clothing enhanced with metal studs. As an accoutrement to this new image, vocalist Rob Halford began taking the stage on a Harley-Davidson motorcycle, a move that would become a Priest concert hallmark. They also began to craft a more commercial approach to their music with heavy leanings toward straightforward verse/chorus structures and a slightly bluesier flavor. Guitarist Glenn Tipton, inspired by the techniques pioneered by Eddie Van Halen, began to employ guitar finger-tapping in his solos. Priest's lyrics took on a stronger tone of realism as well, though there was still a characteristically heavy edge: songs dealt in themes of sadomasochism/bondage, partying, and self-aggrandizement. Drummer Les Binks, displeased with the more commercial direction the band was taking, departed following the album's tour. He was replaced by **Dave Holland** (b. 1948) who would remain with Judas Priest until 1989.

**Go to Chapter 12 playlist example "Hell Bent for Leather" Tipton, 1978**

In 1980, Judas Priest released the album *British Steel*, which would push the band through to the world of AOR with its catchy but heavy music. It also had a broad rock/metal crossover appeal to millions of American rock fans, helping to initiate them by degrees to the bustling world of British heavy metal. The album featured two AOR hit songs which have since become classic rock radio standards. "Breaking the Law" is a rebellious power anthem while "Living After Midnight" is a celebration of the party life:

**Go to Chapter 12 playlist example "Breaking the Law" Tipton/Halford/Downing, 1980**

**Go to Chapter 12 playlist example "Living After Midnight" Tipton/Halford/Downing, 1980**

Judas Priest would continue down the same path of releasing heavy but accessible music, touring extensively, enjoying AOR exposure, and, by 1982, a fair amount of MTV support. The rest of the 1980s would see a stable lineup and a steady stream of multiplatinum albums. Judas Priest was fundamental in introducing heavy metal to the world. Their more radio-friendly music served as a gateway to their own heavier material as well as that of other metal bands. As fans became more attuned to heavy sounds, Priest delivered. The song "Eat Me Alive" from 1984's *Defenders of the Faith* album showed the bands propensity for edgy, aggressive music. The song's suggestive lyrics also earned it a spot on the PMRC's Filthy Fifteen list.

**Go to Chapter 12 playlist example "Eat Me Alive" Tipton/Halford/Downing, 1984**

By 1985, Judas Priest had helped to push British heavy metal much further into the mainstream of rock styles. This was evident not only in their commercial presence, but also in their inclusion in the 1985 US Live Aid Festival (along with Black Sabbath in a brief reunion of the original members).

The 1990s would see a lineup change in the band followed by Halford's unexpected departure in 1992. The addition of virtuoso drummer Scott Travis (formerly of the L.A. progressive metal band Racer X) in 1990 for what would be Halford's last Priest album of the twentieth century, *Painkiller*, marked a shift toward a dramatically heavier sound. This shift was likely inspired by Metallica's success (discussed later). The album's tour featured—as opening acts—some of the heaviest bands in metal at the time including Megadeth, Pantera, and South American death metal pioneers Sepultura. The title track, as well as the track "Leather Rebel," demonstrate Travis' outstanding contribution to the heavier Judas Priest sound.

**Go to Chapter 12 playlist example "Painkiller" Tipton/Halford/Downing, 1990**

**Go to Chapter 12 playlist example "Leather Rebel" Tipton/Halford/Downing, 1990**

Judas Priest was fundamental in the rise of metal. They, along with Black Sabbath, are considered to be the front line of metal's aural assault on the world in its earliest days. Priest's ability to adapt a metal sound into a commercially acceptable context in the late 1970s was a key element in introducing heavy metal, particularly British heavy metal, to a much broader audience. As musicians, their skills and contributions to the style are formidable. Tipton and Downing are among metal's most respected and emulated guitarists, and Halford's vocals inspired dozens of the greatest metal singers of the 1980s. Moreover, their "hell bent for leather" look inspired countless imitators.

In a 1998 MTV interview, Rob Halford revealed that he was homosexual. He stated that hiding his sexuality contributed greatly to a sense of isolation and to his heavy drug and alcohol abuse in the 1980s. He became sober in 1986 after a near-fatal overdose. Halford's self-outing also helped to dispel the lingering stereotype of homophobia among metal fans and bands. Rob Halford was and is one of the most respected metal musicians of all time. The revelation of his sexuality had no effect on fan perception or his status. Rob Halford is so revered, in fact, that he is often referred to simply as "The Metal God." Halford and Priest reunited in 2003 and have been actively touring and recording ever since.

Image 12.1: Rob Halford ("The Metal God") in concert circa 2006

## Motörhead

No British metal band of the late 1970s straddled the fence between punk and metal more than **Motörhead**. Founder and only lifelong member of the band, bassist/singer **Lemmy Kilmister** (1945–2015) solidified the band's first substantial lineup with drummer **Phil "Philthy Animal" Taylor**

(1954–2015) and guitarist **"Fast" Eddie Clarke** (b. 1950) in 1976. Various ups and downs characterized the band's first few years together but they built a devoted regional following. They would find early success in 1979 with their second studio album, *Overkill*. The album unexpectedly reached number twenty-four on the UK album chart and the momentum resulted in their next album, *Bomber* (1979), peaking at number twelve. The music from this period established Motörhead as a raunchy, raucous, speed-freak metal band that relied far more on energy than polish. Many of the songs from these early recordings were performed regularly by the band over the next thirty-five years.

**Go to Chapter 12 playlist example "Overkill" Motörhead, 1979**

**Go to Chapter 12 playlist example "Bomber" Motörhead, 1979**

Motörhead's fourth studio album, 1980's *Ace of Spades*, would represent, to many, the band's defining moment. The title track became a kind of unofficial Motörhead anthem and perhaps their best-known song. *Ace of Spades* reached number four on the UK album chart and the single peaked at number fifteen. In 1980, the band was gaining attention all over the United Kingdom and Europe with their definitive brand of metal and would soon be headlining tours in North America.

**Go to Chapter 12 playlist example "Ace of Spades" Motörhead, 1980**

Image 12.2: Lemmy in one of Motörhead's final performances in 2015

Over the next thirty-five years, Motörhead would maintain a consistent presence on the concert stage and in the recording studio. Although they were never to become a household name, they enjoyed a storied career, and their music—characterized by raw energy, power, and attitude—was always true to its origins. Several lineup changes in the 1980s and early 1990s finally stabilized in 1996 with a roster that featured drummer **Mikkey Dee** (b. 1963) and guitarist **Philip Anthony Campbell** (b. 1961) This incarnation of Motörhead would continue to record and tour until Lemmy's death in 2015, when it was announced that the band would not carry on without him. Motörhead released 22 studio albums, 9 live albums, 4 EPs, and many singles and videos. Although they would pioneer no new musical frontiers from 1980, their influence is incalculable. A sample of Motörhead's music from their later period confirms the band's enduring commitment to their heavy roots.

**Go to Chapter 12 playlist example "Rock Out" Motörhead, 2008**

**Go to Chapter 12 playlist example "End of Time" Motörhead, 2013**

## Iron Maiden

Bassist/songwriter **Steve Harris** (b. 1956) founded **Iron Maiden** in 1975 and is its only original member. After several brief, unsuccessful formations of the band, the first solid lineup featured Harris, guitarist **Dave Murray** (b. 1956), drummer **Doug Sampson** (b. 1957), and singer **Paul Di'Anno** (b. 1958). The quartet began performing in earnest in 1978. A demo recorded on New Year's Eve 1978 would gain the band their first substantial recognition. They delivered the four-song tape to Neal Kay, the owner of a London club called Bandwagon Heavy Metal Soundhouse in hopes of landing work. Kay liked what he heard and began playing the tape regularly at his club. It proved to be quite popular with the club's crowd and secured Iron Maiden steady gigs there as well. As the band grew in stature through local press and performances, they decided to self-release the demo they had given to Kay. They duplicated five thousand copies and sold them all in a matter of weeks. The demo, known as *The Soundhouse Tapes*, brought the band to the attention of EMI Records, who signed the band in late 1979.

Before Maiden could begin recording, drummer **Clive Burr** (1957–2013) would be hired to replace Sampson, who left due to health issues, and the band would add second guitarist **Dennis Stratton** (b. 1952) to fill out their sound. Maiden's first appearance on an album was as part of an EMI promotional compilation of NWOBHM bands called *Metal for Muthas* in 1980. That same year, the band released their own self-titled full-length debut which soared to the number four spot on the UK album chart. The album's title track was captured as part of a live video performance and would be the first heavy metal video ever shown on MTV on the station's very first broadcast day in August 1981.

Even early on, Iron Maiden began to display their proclivity for the "metal epic"—songs that tended toward lengthy, complex, progressive structures but were decidedly heavier than 1970s progressive rock. To be sure, Iron Maiden also wrote many songs that lean *toward* more traditional rock structures, although they would never deal in the same kind of radio-ready material as Judas Priest. In other words, even the shorter Maiden songs were more intricately structured than simple verse/chorus songs, although a typical Iron Maiden album contained both shorter songs and epics. Additionally, a number of Iron Maiden albums feature an instrumental piece. As such, it would be inaccurate to characterize Iron Maiden strictly as a "progressive" metal band, although their music will serve as partial inspiration for developments in progressive metal in the late 1980s. An example of a metal epic from the *Iron Maiden* debut album is the track "Phantom of the Opera."

**Go to Chapter 12 playlist example "Phantom of the Opera" Steve Harris, 1980**

**Note**: Beginning with the cover art for their first single, Iron Maiden adopted a "mascot" who is known simply as **"Eddie."** The artistic creation of Eddie, originally by artist Derek Riggs, is basically a menacing skeleton-like figure who is adorned in various "theme" guises from album to album. For example, on the Egyptian-themed cover of *Powerslave*, Eddie appears as a pharaoh-like statue; on the futuristic *Somewhere in Time* cover, he is half-skeleton, half-cyborg. "Eddie the Head" was a papier-mâché prop used in Iron Maiden's earliest stage shows and the inspiration for Riggs' renderings. Large robotic models of Eddie have since become staples in Iron Maiden's live show.

Image 12.3: A robotic Eddie stage prop in 2008

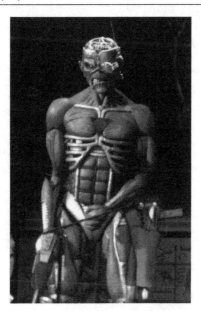

During the *Iron Maiden* album tour, which included supporting spots for Judas Priest and Kiss, as well as headlining shows, Dennis Stratton was fired over personal differences. His replacement, guitarist **Adrian Smith** (b. 1957), would be with Iron Maiden from 1980 until 1990, and from 1999 to the present.

The album *Killers*, released in 1981, was made up almost entirely of music written by Steve Harris before the recording of Maiden's debut album. The recording was the first to feature guitarist Adrian Smith, as well as the first of a string of albums produced by Martin Birch, who would work on every Iron Maiden record until 1992. Birch was a veteran rock producer and had worked with Fleetwood Mac, Deep Purple, and Black Sabbath before joining forces with Iron Maiden. The album was also Di'Anno's last. His excessive use of alcohol and cocaine had begun to interfere with his ability to perform resulting in his removal from the band immediately following the album tour. The song "Wrathchild" is a classic from this period and was one of the only songs from the album to remain a regular part of the band's live repertoire.

**Go to Chapter 12 playlist example "Wrathchild" Steve Harris, 1981**

The addition of vocalist Bruce Dickinson in late 1981 opened up a new world of possibilities for Iron Maiden. His operatic style and charismatic stage presence helped to thrust the band onto the world stage. The 1982 album *The Number of the Beast*, would bring significant success—and controversy—to Iron Maiden. The album rose to number one on the UK chart and made a good showing in the United States as well. Critics and fans praised *The Number of the Beast* and the album it has since become widely recognized as a genre-defining work. The album's cover art, as well as the title track, were fiercely attacked by religious conservatives, particularly in the United States. Demonstrations, album burnings, and boycotts plagued the tour. Steve Harris stated that the song was inspired by the 1978 horror film *Damien: Omen II*.

**Go to Chapter 12 playlist example "The Number of the Beast" Steve Harris, 1982**

"The Number of the Beast" and the epic "Hallowed Be Thy Name," are consistently held up as two of the greatest metal songs of all time. The latter is a fictional and philosophical first-person account about a convicted prisoner awaiting his execution.

As the protagonist of the song wrestles with the terror of facing his imminent demise, wonders if it's all a mad dream, and is marched to the gallows, in the final verse the condemned one ultimately comes to grips with his fate:

*I've gone beyond to seek the truth*

*When you know that your time is close at hand*

*Maybe then you'll begin to understand*

*Life down here is just a strange illusion*

**Go to Chapter 12 playlist example "Hallowed Be Thy Name" Steve Harris, 1981**

In December 1982, following *The Number of the Beast* tour, drummer Clive Burr was fired from Iron Maiden for reasons that were never clearly disclosed to the public. His replacement, **Nicko McBrain** (b. 1952) remains with the band to this day. The first album to feature McBrain, 1983's *Piece of Mind* would mark Iron Maiden's debut in the US album charts, and its singles "The Trooper" and "Flight of Icarus" began to receive minor airplay on American AOR stations. The album's lyrics reflect the band's interest in literature, drawing various inspiration from books like Frank Herbert's sci-fi classic *Dune* and Alfred Lord Tennyson's narrative poem *The Charge of the Light Brigade*. There are also references to Greek mythology as in the song "Flight of Icarus," and to cinema with "Where Eagles Dare" inspired by the 1968 Brian Hutton film of the same name.

**Go to Chapter 12 playlist example "The Trooper" Harris, 1983**

**Go to Chapter 12 playlist example "Flight of Icarus" Smith/Dickinson, 1983**

In answer to the 1982 protests staged by religious and other conservative groups along with accusations of being involved in Satan worship, Iron Maiden included a backwards "message" at the beginning of the track "Still Life." The clip itself is a recording of Nicko McBrain imitating another recording of British satirist John Bird mocking Ugandan dictator Idi Amin. Played backwards, it says: "What ho said the t'ing with the three 'bonce,' do not meddle with things you don't understand..." and then McBrain belches. Annoyed by being labeled as Satan worshippers, the band included the message as a tongue-in-cheek response to these allegations.

**Go to Chapter 12 playlist example "Still Life" Murray/Harris, 1983**

*Powerslave*, released in 1984, featured the aforementioned Egyptian-themed cover which related to the title track. The song, inspired by Egyptian mythology and symbolism, is about a pharaoh's journey to the underworld. The album also includes the popular "Aces High," a song about R.A.F. fighter pilots in the Battle of Britain; the blazing "Back in the Village," a song inspired by the 1960s British TV psycho-drama *The Prisoner*; and the fourteen-minute epic "Rime of the Ancient Mariner," based on Samuel Taylor Coleridge's poem of the same name.

**Go to Chapter 12 playlist example "Aces High" Harris, 1984**

**Go to Chapter 12 playlist example "Back in the Village" Smith/Dickinson, 1984**

**Go to Chapter 12 playlist example "Rime of the Ancient Mariner" Harris, 1984**

The remainder of the 1980s saw two more studio albums, a live album, and virtually nonstop touring from Iron Maiden. Adrian Smith departed in 1990, replaced by Janick Gers (b. 1957); and Bruce Dickinson would leave by 1993, having already begun a solo career in 1990 with his album

*Tattooed Millionaire*. As metal waned in popularity in the 1990s, Iron Maiden persisted. With the return of both Dickinson and Smith in 1999 (Janick Gers has remained in the band making them now a rare three-guitar act), the band have had a successful string of albums, tours, and massive festival performances up to the time of this writing. Their most recent album, *The Book of Souls* (2015), was supported by a thirty-five-country world tour.

Iron Maiden is arguably the most influential metal band in history having had a major impact on eighties bands like Metallica, Slayer, Megadeth, and Anthrax, as well as nearly every contemporary metal band. They are also credited as a fundamental influence in the development of progressive metal as its own style. Numerous bands have paid homage to Iron Maiden by mentioning them in their songs and in recorded cover song tributes. These tributes have not just come from metal artists but from acoustic bands, hip-hop acts, electronic artists, and even classical string quartets!

## The Remarkable Life of Bruce Dickinson

Heavy metal and rock music are full of interesting and colorful characters, but few have been as multifaceted as Iron Maiden vocalist Bruce Dickinson. In addition to traveling the globe with his band, he is a successful novelist and scriptwriter; he hosted his own radio show from 2002 to 2010 as well as a five-part Discovery Channel documentary series on aviation; he has been an internationally competitive fencing champion; an entrepreneur in fencing equipment, craft beer, and aircraft maintenance; and perhaps most interestingly, a commercial airline pilot. In fact, Dickinson himself pilots **Ed Force One**, Iron Maiden's commissioned Boeing 747 jumbo jet which they now use to tour. He has been recognized as an example of a *polymath* (a Greek term meaning "having learned much"), which places him in the company of people like Leonardo da Vinci and Galileo.

Image 12.4: The custom tail wing of Ed Force One

# Def Leppard

Of all the NWOBHM bands, **Def Leppard** were clearly the most commercially oriented and by far the most commercially successful with global album sales topping 100 million, but theirs is not an entirely happy story. At the start of their recording career Def Leppard consisted of vocalist **Joe Elliott** (b. 1959), bassist **Rick Savage** (b. 1960), guitarists **Pete Willis** (b. 1960) and **Steve Clark** (1960–1991), and drummer Frank Noon who was soon replaced by **Rick Allen** (b. 1963). Their 1979 three-song demo, called *The Def Leppard E.P.*, was self-produced on an extremely low budget. The band printed one thousand copies and either sold them or gave them away to anyone who would help spread the word. At a club performance at Sheffield University, Joe Elliott noticed prominent BBC DJ John Peel in the audience and leapt from the stage to hand him a copy of the demo. Peel, in turn, played the band's songs on his popular show, after which they began getting attention from the London music press.

Over the next year, Def Leppard's star began to rise. They developed a large following in London and were signed to Mercury Records and their newly hired manager, Peter Mensch, booked them as the opening act for an AC/DC UK tour. They released their full-length debut album, *On Through the Night*, in 1980 and followed with tours in the United States as the supporting act for Ted Nugent, Pat Travers, and again with AC/DC. Although the album charted fairly well at number fifteen in the United Kingdom and number fifty-one in the United States, the production was not commensurate with the commercial style the band were going for.

Enlisting producer Mutt Lange, who had recently come off of producing AC/DC's hard rock masterpiece *Back in Black*, Def Leppard found the studio chemistry they had been lacking. With Lange's skillful assistance, the resulting album, *High 'n' Dry* (1981) began to uncover Def Leppard's full potential as a world-class metal band. Though the album was only a mild commercial success initially, the video for the single "Bringin' On the Heartbreak" would make the band MTV regulars and introduce them to a huge American audience.

Def Leppard's lineup would include **Phil Collen** (b. 1957) on guitar after Willis was fired for showing up intoxicated to recording sessions for the band's third album, *Pyromania* (1983). Working once again with Lange, the album would launch Def Leppard to superstardom and go on to sell more than 10 million copies in the United States alone. The album features the hit "Rock of Ages," a hard-pounding yet highly commercialized metal anthem and the massive hit single "Photograph." The video for "Photograph" bumped Michael Jackson's "Beat It" video from the top spot as the most requested video on MTV. Def Leppard opened for Billy Squier for much of the *Pyromania* tour and headlined shows toward the tour's end.

**Go to Chapter 12 video example "Rock of Ages" Clark/Lange/Elliott, 1983**

**Go to Chapter 12 video example "Photograph" Clark/Willis/Savage/Lange/Elliott, 1983**

On New Year's Eve 1984, drummer Rick Allen was driving in his Corvette with his girlfriend in in the hills outside of Sheffield, England, when he lost control on a curve and hit a stone wall. His left arm was severed in the crash. Surgeons attempted to reattach the limb but were unsuccessful. At the age of twenty-one, with his band topping charts all over the world, the young drummer's future, as well as Def Leppard's, was in question. As he recovered, Allen's bandmates stood by him and encouraged him to continue. Bolstered by their support, Allen began formulating ideas about how to compensate for the missing limb. Working with engineers at electronic drum manufacturer, Simmons, and with friend and fellow drummer Jeff Rich, a drum kit was designed that allowed Allen to use foot pedals to trigger sounds he would normally play with his left hand. Allen worked diligently to develop his new technique. Rich was enlisted to provide drumming support as the band began to play live again. When he missed a show in Ireland and Allen was left to play alone, it became clear that the one-armed drummer was fine on his own. Allen made his official comeback performance at England's Monsters of Rock Festival in 1986 and was warmly welcomed with an enthusiastic ovation from the audience.

The following year, Def Leppard released their fourth album, *Hysteria*. The album took the number one spot in both the United Kingdom and the United States and produced seven hit singles. Three years in the making, Def Leppard's third effort with Lange would prove to be their most successful recording with more than 25 million copies sold worldwide. Though the music, in the context of mid-1980s metal, was as close to pop as it was to metal (Lange's stated intention was to create rock's answer to *Thriller*), the album is painstakingly produced down to the most infinitesimal detail. The album's videos were enormously popular as well.

**Go to Chapter 12 video example "Pour Some Sugar on Me" Clark/Collen/Elliot/Lange/Savage, 1987**

**Go to Chapter 12 video example "Women" Clark/Collen/Elliot/Lange/Savage, 1987**

*Hysteria* contained some notable power ballads as well. Among these, "Love Bites" became a number one hit single, clearly speaking to the popular appeal of the power ballad in the '80s.

**Go to Chapter 12 video example "Love Bites" Clark/Collen/Elliot/Lange/Savage, 1987**

Determined not to have another years-long gap between albums, Def Leppard took to the studio following a sixteen-month tour for *Hysteria*. The sessions, however, were plagued by Steve Clark's increasing dependence on alcohol. He entered rehab programs several times but to no avail. In late 1990, Clark took a leave of absence from Def Leppard ostensibly to seek treatment. He was found dead in his London home on January 8, 1991, from an apparent overdose of alcohol and prescription drugs. He was thirty years old.

The album *Adrenalize*, the project on which Def Leppard had been working at the time of Clark's death, was released in 1992 and was as instant success, as were its accompanying videos. In fact, its first video, "Let's Get Rocked," won MTV's Best Video of the Year award in 1992. As the rock music–buying public's taste changed dramatically and suddenly around 1992, *Adrenalize* would be knocked from the number one spot by grunge band Nirvana's *Nevermind* (more on Nirvana in Chapter 13).

**Go to Chapter 12 video example "Let's Get Rocked" Collen/Elliot/Lange/Savage, 1986**

Def Leppard carried on, hiring Whitesnake guitarist **Vivian Campbell** (b. 1962) in 1992. As metal declined in the 1990s, so too did Def Leppard's popularity. They have continued to record and tour and have been, along with many other metal acts of the 1980s, enjoying a resurgence in their popularity. Def Leppard, in spite of their later pop leanings, are often cited as an influence by many prominent metal artists such Metallica, Slayer, and Pantera. Drummer Rick Allen's dedication, as well as his bandmates' willingness to stick by him following his injury, served as inspiration to people from all walks of life.

## Ozzy Osbourne Goes Solo

Following Ozzy's firing from Black Sabbath in 1979, he set out to form a band of his own. He teamed up with bassist **Bob Daisley** (b. 1950), drummer **Lee Kerslake** (b. 1947), and guitarist **Randy Rhoads** (1956–1982). Ozzy recruited Rhoads from Quiet Riot, a Los Angeles metal band the young guitarist had formed in 1975. The newly formed band was to be called The Blizzard of Ozz, though after their debut album was recorded, Ozzy's record company decided to call the album *Blizzard of Ozz* (1980) and label it as an Ozzy Osbourne solo project. The album features "Crazy Train" which would become an Ozzy signature song. The world also stood up and took notice of the virtuosic playing of then-unknown Randy Rhoads.

**Go to Chapter 12 playlist example "Crazy Train" Osbourne/Rhoads/Daisley, 1980**

The album also featured a short, acoustic instrumental by Rhoads called "Dee." It was a tribute to his mother, Delores, who was a classical music teacher.

**Go to Chapter 12 playlist example "Dee" Rhoads, 1980**

The *Blizzard of Ozz* song "Suicide Solution" would bring significant controversy to Ozzy in 1984. In a situation similar to that of Judas Priest in 1990, CBS Records and Ozzy found themselves being sued by the parents of a teenager who took his own life. They sued for "encouraging self-destructive behavior" and claimed that Ozzy's song contributed to the death of their son. Ozzy contended that the song is about the slow death of alcoholism and was inspired by the death of AC/DC singer Bon Scott. In the opening verse he sings:

*Wine is fine but whiskey's quicker*

*Suicide is slow with liquor*

*Take a bottle and drown your sorrows*

*Then it floods away tomorrows*

Regardless that the plaintiffs were ignorant of the lyrics or simply misunderstood them, the case was dismissed on the grounds of Ozzy's First Amendment right to free speech.

**Go to Chapter 12 playlist example "Suicide Solution" Osbourne/Rhoads/Daisley, 1980**

In 1981, Ozzy released *Diary of a Madman*. Following the album's release, Ozzy's manager (and future wife) Sharon Arden, fired Daisley and Kerslake, replacing them with bassist **Rudy Sarzo** (b. 1950) and double bass drum pioneer, drummer **Tommy Aldridge** (b. 1950), and added keyboardist **Don Airey** (b. 1948) for the album tour. The album was well received by fans and critics and was especially noted for Rhoads' outstanding contributions. His clever infusion of classical elements into heavy metal guitar playing was termed "neoclassical" metal.

**Go to Chapter 12 playlist example "Flying High Again" Osbourne/Rhoads/Daisley/ Kerslake, 1981**

With two widely acclaimed albums to his credit Rhoads was garnering accolades from guitar industry magazines and had recently designed a signature model guitar with Jackson that was soon to go into production. It was clear that Randy Rhoads was rapidly rising to the status of "guitar god." Having grown up the son of a classical music teacher, and having studied classical guitar, Rhoads had an abiding interest in classical music that was becoming increasingly apparent in his work with Ozzy. He had even talked to Ozzy and his other bandmates of leaving rock for a few years to pursue a degree in classical guitar.

While on the *Diary of a Madman* tour, in Florida on March 19, 1982, the band had made a stop near an airfield where there were several small planes parked. With some of the band still asleep on the bus, tour bus driver Andrew Aycock, also a former commercial pilot, somehow started and took one of the planes, without permission, for a "joyride." Airey and tour manager Jake Duncan went up with Aycock on his first flight. He then took Randy Rhoads and makeup artist Rachel Youngblood up for a second flight. Apparently trying to buzz the tour bus, Aycock flew too close, clipped the bus with the wing of the plane causing it to crash and burst into flames. Rhoads, Youngblood, and Aycock were all killed instantly. Rhoads was twenty-five. Ozzy would release a tribute album of Randy Rhoads live concert recordings in 1987.

Deeply saddened but determined to carry on, Ozzy hired veteran guitarist **Jake E. Lee** (b. 1957) to record *Bark at the Moon* in 1983. Bob Daisley was rehired to write and record the bass parts and, although drummer Tommy Aldridge was part of Ozzy's touring band for several years in the early 1980s, *Bark at the Moon* is the only Ozzy studio album on which he appears. The album peaked at number nineteen on the US album chart, and would eventually sell more than 3 million copies in the United States. The title track, with Lee's stunning guitar work, has become an Ozzy classic.

**Go to Chapter 12 playlist example "Bark at the Moon" Osbourne/Lee/Daisley, 1983**

Ozzy"s next album would come in 1986. *The Ultimate Sin* was, at the time, Ozzy's highest-charting album. Bass player **Phil Soussan** (b. 1961) replaced Daisley, although Daisley still contributed material to the album, and drummer **Randy Castillo** (1950–2002) stepped in for Aldridge. 1988's *No Rest for the Wicked* would be Ozzy's final album of the decade and would introduce a young whiz kid guitarist named **Zakk Wylde** (b. 1967) to the world.

Go to Chapter 12 playlist example "The Ultimate Sin" Osbourne/Lee/Daisley, 1986

Go to Chapter 12 playlist example "Miracle Man" Osbourne/Wylde/Daisley, 1988

Image 12.5: Police provide security for Ozzy as he leaves a 2010 book signing event

Ozzy Osbourne is considered the "Godfather of Heavy Metal." He is also known by the tongue-in-cheek moniker, "The Prince of Darkness." Whatever one calls him, he is a household name and a fixture in modern culture. In music, his work as a solo artist and as a member of the reunited Black Sabbath has carried him to the present day. His life and career have been through a staggering series of ups and down involving drugs and alcohol, domestic issues, lawsuits, and other entanglements. He has been at the center of dozens of controversies over his music, his lifestyle, and his occasionally bizarre actions. There are few characters so engrained in modern popular culture and even fewer who have had the longevity and sustained popularity that Ozzy has.

## Glam Metal

Of the three subgenres of metal we discuss in this chapter, glam metal was by far the most popular through most of the 1980s. Its manifestation in the 1980s, as alluded to in previous chapters, was basically a combination of seventies glam (outfits, makeup, theatrics), punk (high energy), metal (heavy distortion, raw power), and pop rock (verse/chorus forms, commercial goals).

Of all the debauchery the rock and metal lifestyle, glam was arguably the *most* debauched. Part and parcel to glam metal was the "bad boy" (and in some cases "bad girl") image. Many bands used copious amounts of hard drugs and alcohol, were notoriously sexually promiscuous, and regularly engaged in behavior that would land most people behind bars or in the hospital. Occasionally glam rockers had run-ins with the law—sometimes serious ones—but most often they were granted special dispensation because of their unique position in society in the "age of excess."

Glam had two phases known as the first and second waves, lasting roughly from 1981–1985 and 1986–1991. The first wave was more developmental as the style became established and rose up to the fore of the rock mainstream. The second wave saw extended success for many first wave bands as well as an enormous influx of new acts, many of whom adopted a bluesier sound. Most glam bands were American and of those, most were from or relocated to Los Angeles. Christe states:

> There was a homegrown hard-rock scene in Los Angeles in the 1980s, struggling against disco in the name of Van Halen. Some bands took up outlandish stage antics in order to break the monotony—most just soaked up the rays, dyed their hair blond and tried to blend into a sea of club clones waiting for the big score. In New York nobody knew what to do with bands like Riot and Twisted Sister. Nonetheless, it mattered that these groups were competing with the English wave. For all intents and purposes Ozzy Osbourne's new band was an American entity. Along with Van Halen, Ozzy helped usher out Aerosmith, Heart, and the rest of the rock straphangers at the beginning of the 1980s. Soon, Mötley Crüe, Ratt and the *Metal Massacre* gang took heavy metal into a whole new direction. (p. 53)

In order to understand glam, we need look no further than to the band who were the utter embodiment of everything for which glam metal, and its excesses, stood—Mötley Crüe.

## Mötley Crüe

In 1981, bassist **Nikki Sixx** (b. 1958), drummer **Tommy Lee** (b. 1962), guitarist **Mick Mars** (b. 1955), and singer **Vince Neil** (b. 1961) came together to form **Mötley Crüe**, a band that would go on to sell more than 100 million records and help to define eighties glam metal through their music, their extravagant stage shows, their fashion and image, and their wildly hedonistic and self-destructive lifestyle; nobody lived harder than Mötley Crüe.

Gaining experience and a devoted following in the Hollywood Sunset Strip scene in the spring and summer of 1981, the band recorded and self-produced their first album, *Too Fast for Love*, and released it on their own independent label, Leathür Records, in November 1981. It initially sold twenty thousand copies before the band was signed to Elektra Records, when the album was remixed by producer Roy Thomas Baker and re-released in August 1982. It would go on to sell more than 1 million copies by 1986. The album was praised for its raw energy, as evinced in the lead single, "Live Wire."

**Go to Chapter 12 playlist example "Live Wire" Nikki Sixx, 1981**

Mötley Crüe's major breakthrough came in 1983 with the release of *Shout at the Devil*. It is considered by many critics and fans to be the band's heaviest album. Critics have called it "dark," "sleazy," "menacing" and "notorious, yet highly entertaining." The band's image at that time was inspired by the leather and studs look of Judas Priest but included the big hair and heavy makeup that would come to characterize eighties glam. The album's title and pentagram cover art drew fire from conservative and Christian groups, who associated it with Satan worship.

Image 12.6 The controversial *Shout at the Devil* album cover

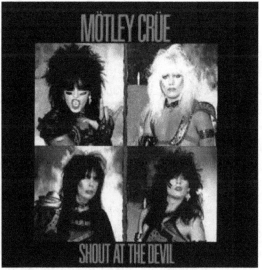

The album demonstrates a much greater level of studio polish than their debut, as well as the evolving sound of Mötley Crüe. The song "Looks That Kill" was a successful single and the accompanying video gained the band their first serious exposure on MTV. In 1985, the song "Bastard" made the PMRC's Filthy Fifteen list for violent lyric content.

**Go to Chapter 12 playlist example "Looks That Kill" Nikki Sixx, 1983**

**Go to Chapter 12 playlist example "Bastard" Nikki Sixx, 1983**

1984 was an eventful year for Mötley Crüe. Having captured the admiration of Ozzy Osbourne during their performance at the 1983 US Festival, the band was invited to open for Ozzy on his 1984 world tour. In December 1984, following the successful outing, the band was back home in Los Angeles when tragedy struck. Vince Neil and his friend, Hanoi Rocks drummer Nicholas "Razzle" Dingley, were traveling to Neil's home on a return trip from a liquor store in Neil's high-performance sports car. Neil, intoxicated and traveling too fast, lost control and hit another vehicle head-on. The occupants of the other vehicle were severely injured and Dingley was killed in the accident. Vince Neil was charged with DUI and vehicular manslaughter. He received a sentence of thirty days' jail time and a fine of $2,600,000. As community service, Neil also filmed a series of public service announcements warning of the dangers of driving while intoxicated.

The band's 1985 album, *Theatre of Pain*, was dedicated to Razzle Dingley. The album reached number six, sold more than 10 million copies, and pushed glam into the mainstream. It features the power ballad "Home Sweet Home," a song describing the life on the road and in the limelight. The song's video was aired heavily on MTV.

**Go to Chapter 12 playlist example "Home Sweet Home" Sixx/Neil/Lee, 1985**

*Girls, Girls, Girls* was released in 1987 as Mötley Crüe's notoriety was reaching epic proportions and glam metal was dominating the rock world. The title track (and its video) is an unabashed celebration of whiskey, drugs, strip clubs, and motorcycles. It names some of the world's most famous strip clubs and the band's exploits as patrons of these clubs. The song "Wild Side" represents a rarity for the party-oriented band: It approaches social consciousness by detailing the dark underbelly of urban life with themes of pimping, organized crime, and assault. Both were MTV and AOR hits. *Girls, Girls, Girls* was the band's highest-charting album at the time, reaching number two. It was held off of the number one spot by pop diva Whitney Houston's second album, *Whitney*.

**Go to Chapter 12 playlist example "Girls, Girls, Girls" Sixx/Lee/Mars, 1987**

Arena rock concerts in the glam era became almost a competition to see who could outdo whom with lighting, special effects, and pyrotechnics. Mötley Crüe's 1987 *Girls, Girls, Girls* tour arguably topped them all. As an added bonus to the already massive stage show, drummer Tommy Lee devised a drum kit that was periodically moved to front and center stage and then spun completely upside-down while Lee continued to play. This unique and stunning special effect was captured in the concert video for "Wild Side."

**Go to Chapter 12 playlist/video example "Wild Side" Sixx/Neil/Lee, 1987**

In December 1987, bassist Nikki Sixx was declared legally dead as he was transported to the hospital as the result of a heroin overdose. Paramedics revived him en route. Sixx would later author a book called *The Heroin Diaries: A Year in the Life of a Shattered Rock Star* (2007) chronicling his addiction and recovery. The incident led the band's management to cancel a European tour out of a genuine concern that some of the band would "come back in bodybags." They staged an intervention to convince the band members to enter rehab. Sixx's near-death experience also served as inspiration for the band's hit song "Kickstart My Heart" from the *Dr. Feelgood* album.

Released in 1989, *Dr. Feelgood* was a landmark recording for Mötley Crüe: It was their first album to reach number one on the album chart; it would be their best-selling album; and it was the first album the band recorded in a state of sobriety. Working with producer Bob Rock, the band recorded what is almost universally considered their finest album. Rock's production resulted in a meticulously detailed recording, adding an entirely new dimension to Mötley Crüe without sacrificing the band's inherently muscular sound. "Kickstart My Heart" and "Sticky Sweet" illustrate:

**Go to Chapter 12 playlist example "Kickstart My Heart" Sixx, 1989**

**Go to Chapter 12 playlist example "Sticky Sweet" Sixx/Mars, 1989**

Mötley Crüe retired in 2015 with a triumphant farewell tour. They experienced a series of peaks and valleys in the 1990s but rose again to prominence in the early 2000s. They were one of the great party bands of their generation. They never set out to be humanitarians or to change the world. Mötley Crüe just wanted to rock and celebrate excess—and in that, no one was more successful.

By the late 1980s there were dozens of highly successful glam bands dominating the record charts as well as MTV. Band like Mötley Crüe, Ratt, Twisted Sister, and others were enjoying regular, heavy airplay on MTV by 1984. In 1985, MTV began a monthly broadcast called *Heavy Metal Mania* which featured more obscure and heavier bands alongside the mainstream metal acts. In 1987, MTV launched a new repackaged version that aired weekly called *Headbangers Ball* which now included live-in-the-studio interviews with established as well as emerging bands. The show, one of the most popular in the network's history, ran for eight years and for a time was up to three hours long. MTV also added a show called *Hard 60*, a daily hour-long segment that was essentially a weekday afternoon version of *Headbangers Ball*.

Although the limited scope of this textbook does not allow for a more detailed history of the many glam bands that rose to fame in the 1980s, a partial list can provide the interested student some insight for further study. Other important glam bands of the 1980s include Ratt, Quiet Riot, Twisted Sister, W.A.S.P., Whitesnake, Cinderella, Warrant, Kix, Poison, Europe, Winger, Skid Row,

Dangerous Toys, Vixen, Lita Ford, Slaughter, L.A. Guns, Faster Pussycat, Dokken, Great White, and Black 'n Blue.

## Underground Thrash Metal

The heavy metal underground in the 1980s was a fairly complex world. The idea of being underground, in the simplest sense, meant not getting airplay or MTV exposure. It would be an oversimplification to say that that was all there was to the underground scene. Underground was as much about an attitude as it was about the lack of airplay or the music itself. Many underground metal bands, like purist punk bands of the 1970s, were wholeheartedly antiestablishment. Like punk, "thrash" and "speed" metal bands often expressed nihilistic perspectives, were seen as antisocial, and drew fire from mainstream critics for lacking musical skill. Unlike punk bands, and contrary to the views of most critics, many underground bands were in fact highly skilled musicians with deep a commitment to artistic principles over (or at least before) commercial success.

Musically, thrash and speed metal were an intensification all that metal had become by the early 1980s. It was faster, louder, more distorted, more technically demanding, and in general, more abrasive. It was also much less about melody and much more about rhythm.

In underground metal culture, the idea of "selling out"—altering one's musical style and principles for the sake of attaining commercial success—was akin to blasphemy. Given that, it was not surprising that when Metallica began to experience an increasing commercial presence in the late 1980s, many of their early fans felt that the band had abandoned them. As we will see, nothing could be farther from the truth. The fact is that most underground bands *wanted* to be successful but they wanted success on their own terms. They did not want to be shaped into a mold or to tone down their music to get airplay. As such, they were often forced to find alternative means to get their music heard. A host of independent record labels sprang up in Los Angeles and New York. Labels like Combat, Megaforce, Metal Blade, and Roadrunner became important mechanisms in the distribution of thrash and speed metal. There were also thriving club scenes that supported thrash and speed metal, most notably in San Francisco, but as the 1980s wore on, an increasing infrastructure of support grew in other major cities.

For the purposes of our discussion we will examine two genre-defining bands with similar origins but whose music and careers will develop along somewhat different paths: Metallica and Slayer.

### Metallica

Drummer **Lars Ulrich** (b. 1963) and guitarist/singer **James Hetfield** (b. 1963) met in late 1981 when Ulrich placed an ad in the Los Angeles newspaper, *The Recycler*, seeking metal musicians. Ulrich, an avid metal fan and ambitious young man, had already established a network of friends and connections in the early underground metal scene. Without yet having formed a band, he convinced Brian

Slagel, founder of the brand new Metal Blade Records, to reserve a spot for him on an upcoming metal promo compilation album called *Metal Massacre*. When Hetfield learned of the opportunity Ulrich had established, the two went to work finding other members. They advertised in *The Recycler* again and were answered by a guitarist named **Dave Mustaine** (b. 1961) who soon joined the band. The song "Hit the Lights" was recorded for the *Metal Massacre* compilation in early 1982 with Hetfield handling the rhythm guitar and bass parts. Shortly after finishing the recording, Metallica hired bass player **Ron McGovney** (b. 1962) and played their first gig in March 1982. The quartet recorded a self-funded four-song demo in April while awaiting the release of *Metal Massacre*, which occurred in June.

Later that year Hetfield and Ulrich attended a show at the Whisky where they saw a band called Trauma. The band's bass player, **Cliff Burton** (1962–1986) made an enormous impression on the pair and they asked him if he would join Metallica, feeling he would be a much better fit than McGovney. After initially declining, Burton later told Metallica that he would join them if they relocated to the San Francisco Bay Area where Burton was based. They agreed, fired McGovney, and moved to the Bay. The band began performing with their new bass player in March 1983 and recorded another self-funded demo.

In May 1983, the band traveled to New York to record their debut album after signing with the newly formed independent label Megaforce. The label was owned by concert promoter Johnny Zazula who offered the band a deal after hearing one of their earlier demos. Up to this point, Hetfield, Ulrich, and Burton had been having problems getting along with Mustaine as he apparently became abusive when he drank. Just before the band began recording they fired Mustaine. Guitarist **Kirk Hammett** (b. 1962), who was in another Bay Area thrash band called Exodus, was contacted and asked to join **Metallica**. He agreed and promptly came to New York. They rehearsed the songs with Hammett and began recording within a month. Hetfield, Ulrich, Burton, and Hammett would form the band's steady lineup for their next three albums, until 1986. Mustaine would go on to form his own successful band, **Megadeth**.

*Kill 'Em All*, Metallica's debut album was released in July 1983. The original title the band had wanted, *Metal Up Your Ass*, was rejected by Zazula. The album had very limited sales following its release but helped to build Metallica's following in the underground scene. *Kill 'Em All* is now universally recognized as one of the most important albums in metal history. It became the template for thrash metal. Its music and lyrics were decidedly set apart from the mainstream, yet it would inspire countless imitations. Several sample tracks illustrate just how different this music was from everything else in 1983.

**Go to Chapter 12 playlist example "Motorbreath" Hetfield, 1983**

**Go to Chapter 12 playlist example "The Four Horsemen" Hetfield/Ulrich/Mustaine, 1983**

**Go to Chapter 12 playlist example "Metal Militia" Hetfield/Ulrich/Mustaine, 1983**

Following several US and European club tours in support of *Kill 'Em All* which proved successful overall, the band traveled to Denmark in the summer of 1984 to record their second album with producer Flemming Rasmussen. The resulting work, *Ride the Lightning*, saw Metallica expand their boundaries to include more complex forms and sophisticated harmonies without forsaking their aggressiveness. This was due in part to the greater amount of input from Burton, who was versed in music theory. He lent his depth of musical knowledge to the band and they grew as a unit. Hetfield's lyrics became more socially oriented and philosophical around this period as well. He would come to be widely recognized as one of the greatest lyricists in metal. The album was initially released on Megaforce in July 1984, though Zazula did very little to promote it. Displeased, Metallica severed ties with him. A short time after, they were noticed at a performance in New York in late August by executives from Elektra Records. Impressed by what they heard, they offered Metallica a contract. *Ride the Lightning* was reissued on Elektra in November 1984. With *no radio or MTV exposure* it sold more than five hundred thousand copies by 1987. Samples from the album illustrate its appeal: "Fight Fire with Fire" is a song about the specter of mutually assured nuclear destruction. "Escape" is about shedding the figurative chains of social oppression.

**Go to Chapter 12 playlist example "Fight Fire with Fire" Hetfield/Ulrich/Burton, 1984**

**Go to Chapter 12 playlist example "Escape" Hetfield/Ulrich/Hammett, 1984**

*Ride the Lightning*, like its predecessor, is credited with changing the course of metal.

Metallica toured extensively in support of *Ride the Lightning* and soon established a global presence. In the summer of 1985, they were invited to play the Monsters of Rock festival in Donington Park, England. They opened for Ratt and Bon Jovi to a crowd of seventy thousand. Two weeks later they performed at the Day on the Green festival in Oakland, California, to a crowd of sixty thousand.

In the fall of 1985, Metallica headed back to Denmark to record their third studio album, and second with producer Flemming Rasmussen. *Master of Puppets*, released in March 1986, became thrash metal's first platinum album. It marked a turning point in metal history: It simultaneously opposed *and* redefined the mainstream. The band perfected what they had started with *Kill 'Em All* and expanded with *Ride the Lightning* with music that demonstrates absolute control of composition, texture, structure, energy, and pacing. Rasmussen and Metallica paid meticulous attention to every detail, creating an album with a clear sense of musical atmosphere and lyrical character. Critics of all stripes praised the album as a masterpiece; it has been consistently hailed as one of the greatest recordings of all time. In 2016, *Master of Puppets* was added to the National Recording Registry in the Library of Congress making it one of only 450 recordings, and the only heavy metal album, to do so. A sampling of the album gives a glimpse into the sheer musical and lyrical might Metallica were wielding:

The title track is a song that tackles cocaine addiction; the drug is the "master" while the user is the "puppet." "Disposable Heroes" is about how the military brainwashes young soldiers to do their dirty work with utter disregard for their humanity. "Damage, Inc." is a gloriously ferocious song that figuratively describes the power and aggression that Metallica poured into their music and "Orion" is a vividly detailed instrumental work.

**Go to Chapter 12 playlist example "Master of Puppets" Hetfield/Ulrich/Burton/Hammett, 1986**

**Go to Chapter 12 playlist example "Disposable Heroes" Hetfield/Ulrich/Hammett, 1986**

**Go to Chapter 12 playlist example "Damage, Inc." Hetfield/Ulrich/Burton/Hammett, 1986**

**Go to Chapter 12 playlist example "Orion" Hetfield/Ulrich/Burton, 1986**

Metallica took to the road as the opening act for Ozzy in support of *Master of Puppets* in March 1986. After completing the US leg of the tour in August, Metallica headed to Europe for a series of headline shows. Traveling in Sweden during the night on September 27, 1986, while the band members were sleeping, their driver lost control of the bus causing it to skid sideways and overturn several times. As the bus was flipping, bassist Cliff Burton was thrown from the window of his bunk compartment and was crushed beneath the bus as it landed. He was pronounced dead at the scene. Burton was twenty-four.

The rest of Metallica debated whether to carry on in Burton's absence. Concluding that their friend would have wanted them to forge on, and receiving support from Burton's family, Hetfield, Ulrich, and Hammett set out to find a replacement, taking little time to grieve. After holding several dozen auditions, Metallica hired bassist **Jason Newsted** (b. 1963), formerly of the thrash band Flotsam and Jetsam (and soon after dubbed him "Jason Newkid").

Upon completion of their tour, Metallica recorded an EP of covers by obscure NWOBHM bands called *The $5.98 EP: Garage Days Re-Revisited*. The recording was both an attempt to get a feel for their new bass player in the studio and to destress following the ordeal they had just been through. The EP also gave fans something to tide them over while Metallica recorded a new album. That album, *... And Justice for All*, came in August 1988. The album captured a surgically precise and progressive-oriented Metallica dealing in intensely thrashing riffs and richly complex structures light years away from verse/chorus pop rock. Lyric themes dealt with political injustice, social inequities, war, and censorship in a poetic and intelligent manner. Many critics found the album's audio production somewhat sterile, particularly when compared to *Master of Puppets*. This was attributed to the fact that, although Rasmussen was once again producing, he was unable to be present during the final mixing sessions due to previous commitments. Nevertheless, the album earned Metallica their first Grammy in 1990, sold 8 million copies in the United States, and entered the top 10 in charts all over the world. *... And Justice for All* confirmed the presence of thrash metal in the mainstream.

**Go to Chapter 12 playlist example "Blackened" Hetfield/Ulrich/Newsted, 1988**

**Go to Chapter 12 playlist example "Shortest Straw" Hetfield/Ulrich, 1988**

The album also saw Metallica release its first video, something the band had built a reputation for saying they would never do. This drew fire from some of their longtime fans, declaring that Metallica had "sold out." Regardless, the video for "One" rose to the number one–ranked spot on MTV following its debut.

**Go to Chapter 12 playlist/video example "One" Hetfield/Ulrich, 1988**

*... And Justice for All* would be Metallica's final album of the 1980s; however, with the release of *Metallica* (also known as "The Black Album") in 1991, Metallica would become a household name and held up by many as the "Led Zeppelin of their generation." Working with producer Bob Rock, *Metallica* was nearly nine months in the making. The album debuted at number one in ten countries, sold more than 16 million copies in the United States alone, and stands as a monument in heavy metal history. Metallica's approach was toward a slower but heavy sound with an emphasis on an expressive range that once again redefined metal. Although the album was a huge commercial success, it didn't have anything to do with pop structures nor does it lack a seriously heavy edge. As when Metallica released their first video, there were the naysayers who claimed Metallica had sold out, but in actuality, *Metallica* is arguably rock's final and most significant triumph. Critics praised the album as "disarmingly genuine," "versatile," and "twice as heavy as anything they've ever done before." A 1991 guitar industry publication featured James Hetfield and Kirk Hammett on the cover with the caption: "Metallica: They Didn't Reach Number One, It Came to Them."

**Go to Chapter 12 playlist example "Through the Never" Hetfield/Ulrich/Hammett, 1991**

**Go to Chapter 12 playlist example "Wherever I May Roam" Hetfield/Ulrich, 1991**

**Go to Chapter 12 playlist example "Of Wolf and Man" Hetfield/Ulrich/Hammett, 1991**

Metallica pounded through the 1990s and into the twenty-first century with no signs of relenting. They continue to record, tour, and are involved in a number of philanthropic endeavors. Their influence extends far beyond metal and has inspired countless tributes in a wide variety of genres from classical to bluegrass. Interested students are encouraged to explore their later music as well as their video albums and documentaries. With a legacy that is still unfolding Metallica is one of the most culturally significant and universally respected bands in rock history.

## Slayer

Guitarists **Kerry King** (b. 1964) and **Jeff Hanneman** (1964–2013), drummer **Dave Lombardo** (b. 1965), and singer **Tom Araya** (b. 1961) formed **Slayer** in 1981 in southern California and were soon playing a mix of metal covers and originals at parties and small clubs. Drawing on "spikey" punk fashion, the "leather" look of Judas Priest, and the occultist vibe of Black Sabbath, Slayer cultivated an image that both visually and lyrically alluded to Satanism, though the band has repeatedly denied being Satanists and have stated that it was only part of their "shock" value. Their stage sets would feature pentagrams and inverted crosses while the band donned black leather and homemade spiked armbands.

While performing in Anaheim in 1982, they were approached by Brian Slagel of Metal Blade Records, who by then was preparing the track listing for his upcoming *Metal Massacre III* compilation and wanted Slayer to be a part of it (recall that Metallica appeared on the *Metal Massacre* debut). Slayer agreed and recorded the song "Aggressive Perfector" for inclusion on the album. Following the release of the compilation, the song, along the band's live performances were causing such a buzz in the underground scene that Slagel offered Slayer a contract with Metal Blade Records.

*Show No Mercy*, Slayer's debut album, was released in 1983. Relentless touring helped to generate buzz about the album. The early Slayer tours were very low budget, self-managed, and almost entirely self-funded. These were far from the high-level arena tours of mainstream rock bands but served to unite the band members in their cause: getting their music out to the world by whatever means were available. The outings made an impact, and with thirty-five thousand copies of the album sold worldwide, it marked a sales milestone for the fledgling Metal Blade label. Critics were sharply divided over *Show No Mercy*. Some critics have praised the album, stating that it was "as seminal as *Kill 'Em All*" and that it "expanded the limits of metal;" others called it "pure unadulterated junk" and "amateurish." It has since come to be universally recognized as an extremely significant juncture in the development of metal.

**Go to Chapter 12 playlist example "The Antichrist (live)" Hanneman/King, 1983**

**Go to Chapter 12 playlist example "Die by the Sword" Hanneman, 1983**

*Show No Mercy* put Slayer on a path toward the perfection of thrash and speed metal. Successful club tours, an EP called *Haunting the Chapel*, and the release of a live concert video helped to boost Slayer's presence as well as their album sales. Their second full-length album, *Hell Awaits*, was released in 1985. Aside from being decadently heavy, the lyric themes became more focused around hell and Satan. The album showed a band that was not only maturing musically, but technically as well. Slayer was named "best live band" in a several magazine fan polls and Dave Lombardo was named best drummer by a major British metal magazine.

Slayer's magnum opus came in 1986 with *Reign in Blood*. Having gained a significant amount of attention in the underground scene, the band was approached by executives at the newly formed Def Jam Recordings, which had been having remarkable early success in the world of hip-hop. The band accepted the deal. Armed with a major label budget and assigned to a seasoned producer, Rick Rubin, Slayer would create one of the most devastating records in the history of metal. Slayer and Rubin kept things relatively simple in terms of song structure and length; the *entire album* (ten songs) clocks in at just under thirty minutes. In other words, there are no lengthy epics here. Instead, the band cranked up the tempo and delivered an ensemble performance that was honed to a razor-sharp edge. Rubin's approach to production brought every blindingly fast moment into clear focus. In terms of sheer metal brutality, speed, and precision, this record was light years ahead of anything else at the time. *Reign in Blood* has been credited—almost solely—with inspiring several entire subgenres of heavy metal, including so-called death metal, black metal, and crossover thrash. The album almost did not see the light of day. Def Jam's distributor, Columbia, refused to handle it due to its darkly provocative lyrics and cover art. After much negotiation, Geffen Records eventually agreed to distribute it. With no airplay whatsoever, *Reign in Blood* peaked at number ninety-four on the US album chart and number forty-seven in the United Kingdom.

Image 12.8: The controversial cover of Slayer's *Reign in Blood*

**Go to Chapter 12 playlist example "Angel of Death" Hanneman, 1986**

**Go to Chapter 12 playlist example "Necrophobic" King/Hanneman, 1986**

**Go to Chapter 12 playlist example "Reborn" King/Hanneman, 1986**

**Go to Chapter 12 playlist example "Epidemic" King/Hanneman, 1986**

On several occasions beginning in 1992, Lombardo would leave Slayer to be replaced by Paul Bostaph, return, and leave again, with Bostaph replacing him. At the time of this writing Paul Bostaph is currently drumming for Slayer. Sadly, guitarist Jeff Hanneman died of liver failure in 2013. His replacement, Gary Holt, was a longtime member of the 1980s Bay Area thrash band, Exodus.

Slayer remains active and has more or less continued in the same vein of extreme heavy metal, with some occasional experimentation. They would never enjoy the same level of commercial success as Metallica, although they are a member of what is known as "The Big 4," a quartet of the most influential and successful hardcore metal bands that includes Metallica, Megadeth, and Anthrax. Slayer's concerts are some of the most intense live music environments that have ever been staged. Slayer mosh pits are legendary. To date, Slayer has released twelve studio albums, performed thousands of concerts, and shows no signs of slowing.

Again, due to the scope of this book, it is impossible to discuss all of the important thrash bands of the 1980s and beyond. Having glimpsed those who were the most significant and influential, the student may wish to examine some or all of the following thrash/speed metal bands: Megadeth, Anthrax, Exodus, Testament, Metal Church, Overkill, Pantera, Sanctuary, Nuclear Assault, Flotsam and Jetsam, S.O.D., Forbidden, Heathen, Lääz Rockit, and Sacred Reich. This is by no means a comprehensive list but may serve as a starting point.

### Suggested Chapter Related Activities

- Students may prepare research papers/presentations on bands listed at the end of the sections on glam and thrash metal.

- To get a better sense of the range of heavy metal, compare and contrast "Aces High" by Iron Maiden, "Girls, Girls, Girls" by Mötley Crüe and "Master of Puppets" by Metallica. Your comparison should include tempo, level of distortion (guitar and bass) ratio of instrumental to vocal sections, vocal style (including harmonies), form and rhythmic texture.

### Suggested Discussion Topics

- Consider and discuss your views on the vilification of heavy metal in the '80s. Do you feel that the court rulings in the cases of Ozzy and Judas Priest were just? Should artists be held accountable on some level for their lyrics? If so, what does this mean in the context of free speech? Who gets to decide where lines are drawn? How does personal responsibility of the listener figure into the equation, or in the case of minors, parental responsibility?

- Do you feel that the PMRC was justified in its attempt to label music?

- Do the mass media and "authority figures" still connect popular music with harmful or destructive behavior? If so, what style(s) of music are most targeted? If not, do they assign blame for specific societal problems to other forms of entertainment/arts?

## Image Credits

# CHAPTER 13

# Grunge and Alternative Metal in the Nineties

*Into the flood again. Same old trip it was back then...*

-Layne Staley of Alice in Chains (from "Would?")

## Cultural Context

The 1990s were a time of significant change in global politics, technology, and media. A peaceful revolution in the Soviet Union, fueled by Soviet leader Gorbachev's policy reforms in the late 1980s led to the 1989 fall of the Berlin Wall and the eventual dissolution of the Soviet Union. The decades-long Cold War was over and America had emerged as the world's only remaining superpower. 1991 began with the first Gulf War and an American-led coalition pushing back Iraqi forces in order to protect American corporate and oil interests in the Middle East. The war was broadcast live from the front lines by CNN and other corporate news channels. Americans could tune in 24/7 and see images of high-tech "smart" bombs destroying their targets and humiliated Iraqi soldiers, dressed in rags, surrendering to coalition forces. President George H.W. Bush's approval rating soared.

Not everyone was so supportive of Bush and the Gulf War. Independent critical media outlets like Deep Dish TV produced programs that exposed media complicity in the promotion of the war, the interlocking interests of military and energy industries, and citizen reactions to the war that were not shown on the mainstream news. Many small local media outlets offered coverage of demonstrations, academic antiwar lectures, antiwar art exhibits, and protests against media bias in war coverage. Numerous critics of the elder Bush trace a direct line of responsibility to his administration for escalating American involvement in the ongoing turmoil in the Middle East, and the resulting decade-long wars in Iraq and Afghanistan in the 2000s.

Even though George H.W. Bush's approval ratings rose in the months that followed, broken campaign promises, an economic recession, and high unemployment would lead Americans to elect a youthful Democrat named Bill Clinton in 1992. The Clinton presidency was fairly successful overall. By the end of his first term in 1996, the economy was moving forward; by the end of his second term in 2000 the economy was robust (though this was largely due to the tech boom), and the federal budget was in the black by some $200 billion. Nonetheless, his legacy was tarnished when he was embroiled in a sex scandal involving White House intern Monica Lewinsky. To make matters worse, he lied to Congress about the affair. He was impeached for perjury and obstructing justice but was eventually acquitted. Still, the entire situation left most of the country feeling that their president was a philanderer and a liar, even if the actual fact of the affair had little to do with Clinton performing his duties as a public servant. This contributed to the general sentiment that had been commonplace—and growing steadily since Nixon—that the government, for many reasons, was not to be trusted. A feeling of powerlessness prevailed in the minds of the young and would come to the surface in many ways, including musical expression.

## Television in the 1990s

Television sitcoms were widely popular in the 1990s and, but for a few, were fairly unconcerned with making any kind of social statement. Notable exceptions were *Ellen*, whose main character, played by Ellen DeGeneres, was openly gay, and *The Fresh Prince of Bel-Air*, starring Will Smith, which shone a comic light on the ultra-privileged compared to the underprivileged. The ongoing fascination with wealth, beauty, and power was reflected in dramatic series like *Beverly Hills, 90210* and *Baywatch*. Arguably, the most poignant social satire came in the form of an animated sitcom called *The Simpsons*. The show's writers were merciless in their humorous interpretation of social stereotypes: They were completely unprejudiced in that they poked fun at *everyone*. The trend of modern "reality" TV also began in the 1990s with shows like *Cops* and MTV's *The Real World*. (As the decade wore on, MTV would become substantially *less* about music videos and far more involved in other types of programming.)

MTV *was* heavily involved in the 1992 presidential race with its "Choose or Lose" and "Rock the Vote" campaigns, their coverage of the party primaries, and their hosting of a town hall forum with Bill Clinton during which young people had an opportunity to question the candidate on his views. Although there is no accurate way to calculate MTV's impact, the voter turnout of 18–24-year-olds was higher in 1992 than it had been since 1972, the year that the voting age was lowered to eighteen.

CNN and other 24-hour news cable channels emerged in the early 1980s with the expansion of cable TV. By the end of the 1980s, 24-hour news had become the norm. Up to that point most Americans were content to read the newspaper and/or catch the six o'clock or eleven o'clock news broadcast. Many modern social scientists and psychologists link the nonstop barrage of graphic images associated with news broadcasts—including those from the first Gulf War—to a surge in acts of violence, including school, workplace, and other public shootings. Case in point: In 1999, the country stood horrified when two students at a high school in Columbine, Colorado, murdered twelve classmates and a teacher before killing themselves. Sadly, in recent times these types of tragic events have become almost commonplace. It is interesting to note that depression among youth rose sharply in the 1990s as well.

Television helped to confirm that racism and police brutality were alive and well in America when a bystander who happened to have a portable video camera inadvertently filmed a 1991 traffic stop involving four white Los Angeles police officers and a black motorist named Rodney King. King was stopped for speeding, but the officers proceeded to pull him from his car and brutally beat him with their fists, feet, and nightsticks. While this was likely nothing new for the LAPD, it was the first time this kind of unnecessary use of force was captured on camera. Americans were outraged, and when the four officers were acquitted, Los Angeles erupted in riots. It was all heavily covered on 24-hour TV news.

The line between violence and entertainment was noticeably blurred in the highly televised courtroom trial of football-star-turned-actor, O.J. Simpson. Simpson was accused of murdering his ex-wife Nicole Simpson and her friend Ron Goldman. The unprecedented media coverage began with the 1994 low-speed car chase leading up to Simpson's arrest and continued through every detail of the 1995 trial and verdict. Simpson's acquittal divided public opinion but more importantly, the cable news channels, as they had in the first Gulf War, shamelessly turned tragedy into entertainment.

## The Internet

The American economy underwent a vast expansion in the 1990s during Bill Clinton's eight-year presidency, though this was largely due to the unforeseen growth of the Internet and its benefits to related technologies and commerce. The Internet had existed for quite some time; however, the invention of the World Wide Web by Tim Berners-Lee in 1990, which created the basic language for commercial internet use, followed by the removal of the last remnants of Internet access restrictions by 1995, caused a rapid expansion in web commerce, communication, and the distribution of information. Personal computer sales skyrocketed as did large-scale corporate investment in the Internet. Countless industries rushed to cash in on the boom and restructure their businesses to fit the new model. Few could have foreseen how profoundly the Internet would reshape the modern world.

At first, the Internet seemed as if it would be a boon for independent musicians. There was now a viable avenue for bands to market their music to the world, independent of radio and other mass media. However, a sea change was coming and the music industry—including both signed and independent musicians—would be turned upside down. John Covach and Andrew Flory write:

> One of the most contentious segments of the Internet economy was in the music industry. In 1999, twenty-year-old Shawn Fanning created Napster, a file-sharing service that allowed users to exchange music, free of charge, over the Internet. Napster made music available to all, and cut record labels and artists out of the process. The Record Industry Association of America (RIAA), which represents five major record labels and a host of smaller labels, didn't like the effect of the Napster revolution on their profits and they sued. Napster was forced to shut down (though it was eventually reborn as a legal music company). As Napster proved, many Internet users felt that anything on the Web should be free—including artistic material. The music industry continues to struggle with issues of ownership to this day.[1] (p. 488-89)

Not only was Napster involved in the sharing of existing music, they were also responsible for the premature leaking of yet-unreleased music. Both Metallica and Madonna, among others, had singles leaked on Napster before their official release dates, costing the artists an undeterminable amount of money. Both Lars Ulrich of Metallica and rapper Dr. Dre sued Napster in separate and highly publicized cases. Napster settled on both suits.

Although Napster tried to make a case that it was helping unsigned and underground bands reach a broader audience, most *musicians*, independent or otherwise, felt that Fanning and his partner Sean Parker were detestable slackers whose sense of entitlement drove them to build a website that stole and distributed the intellectual property of others. The "culture of theft" started by Napster has orientated the millennial generation's mindset and created an enormous vacuum in the music industry damaging the livelihood of countless musicians. In order to fill this void, concert ticket prices have skyrocketed and many independent artists have been forced to sustain their music careers by selling T-shirts and other merchandise not at all related to their art form.

## Generation X

By the the mid–late 1980s, rock music had become fragmented into numerous subgenres; although by then, heavy metal and metal genres had the largest piece of the rock pie. Around the same time, a relatively new underground movement dubbed "alternative" rock was gaining a substantial fan base. The term alternative was a reference to music outside of the mainstream more than any specific *musical* style. Like early metal and thrash, the so-called alternative bands built their

---

1   John Covach and Andrew Flory, What's That Sound?: An Introduction to Rock and Its History, pp. 488-489. Copyright © 2012 by W. W. Norton & Company, Inc. Reprinted with permission.

followings through heavy touring, low-budget independent label recordings, and fan involvement, although many alternative bands had the added benefit of airplay on college radio as well as an occasional mainstream rock hit.

In 1991, Perry Farrell of the alternative rock band Jane's Addiction, along with the band's management, organized the first **Lollapalooza** festival—a touring, multistage, outdoor concert that hearkened back to Woodstock. In fact, inspired by the 1960s phrase "Woodstock Nation," Farrell dubbed the Lollapalooza audiences "Alternative Nation." The festival featured alternative artists from various genres as well as assorted nonmusical performers, art and technology displays, and tables and booths set up by groups promoting political ideas and various humanitarian causes (more on Lollapalooza in Chapter 14).

The mass media soon attached the name "Generation X" to this newly visible youth demographic, a term that was itself inspired by Douglas Coupland's 1991 novel called *Generation X: Tales for an Accelerated Culture*. In his novel Coupland describes a youth with few economic prospects, who are forced to work at "McJobs," low-paying, no-future positions in the service industry. The truth of the Gen X culture is that while they shared many traits with the counterculture, a liberal worldview, and support for equal rights for minorities, women, and other historically oppressed groups, they lacked the authenticity and much of the motivation of the 1960s counterculture: They were not inventing their *own* culture; but rather, they were in a sense, recycling their cultural vibe based on an decades-old model. More importantly they lacked a common cause. Deena Weinstein writes:

> Members of Gen X were deeply dissatisfied, but without an enemy in sight. They felt impotent, unable to act because there was no action that made any sense. Philosophers would understand their state of mind as existential despair. Political theorists would classify their situation as a crisis of legitimacy, where all social institutions—political, economic, religious, educational and the familial—are viewed with suspicion and disap- pointment. Their misgivings about commercial culture and the celebrity hype machine included rock itself. After all, Gen Xers didn't just emerge in 1991. They were already there in the mid-1980s, active in indie DIY rock scenes or just fans of its resultant music. (p. 248)

Where the hippie counterculture called out the establishment through protest and activism, Gen Xers were generally seen as apathetic and self-pitying. The most *visible* Gen Xers were children of privilege who embraced the outsider lifestyle because it was romantic and because they could, not because they had no choice. In 1993, Ben Kim, a correspondent for a Chicago alternative paper called *NewCity* wrote of the Gen X culture:

> Downward mobility is after all a central metaphor of bohemia, but even at our self-willed stoopidest [sic], we punk descendants realize how much of it is play, purchased from inherited privilege (and that includes our smarts). It's sexy and ridiculous to feel totally

fucked and useless, because we know we aren't really, we sons and daughters of the middle class. We can be as slack as we wanna [sic] be, because we can afford the joke. (p. 13)

The band Nirvana would come to be one of the representational symbols of Generation X. Their music, aptly labeled **grunge**, has a thick, sludgy sound that was heavily distorted like metal, but without the focus on precision or virtuosity. Lyrically, grunge was filled with angst, apathy, and alienation. Grunge acts were noted for their particular "fashion" as well: torn jeans, flannel shirts, and a basic "thrift store" look. The epicenter of grunge was Seattle and the rain-soaked environs of the Pacific Northwest.

## Nirvana

Singer/guitarist **Kurt Cobain** (1967–1994) and bassist **Krist Novoselic** (b. 1965) formed **Nirvana** in 1987 in Aberdeen, Washington. A series of drummers would eventually end with **Dave Grohl** (b. 1969) joining the band in 1990. Nirvana became well established in the little-known Seattle grunge scene in the late 1980s and had released their first album, *Bleach*, in 1989 on the independent label Sub Pop. *Bleach* did not sell well but was praised by critics as an album that defined the 1990s and showed Cobain's considerable songcraft. (*Bleach* is the only Nirvana album to feature drummer Chad Channing.)

**Go to Chapter 13 playlist example "Blew" Cobain, 1989**

**Go to Chapter 13 playlist example "Negative Creep" Cobain, 1989**

Unhappy with Sub Pop, Nirvana began pursuing major label interest. They secured a deal with DGC Records in 1990 and began work on their next studio album with producer Butch Vig. *Nevermind* was recorded between May and June of 1991 and released in August. As the band were behind schedule and the mixes not yet complete, Andy Wallace, who had recently mixed for Slayer, was brought in to finish the project; a decision that resulted in Nirvana's dissatisfaction with the final product: They claimed it sounded "too polished." DGC had only modest hopes for the record; however, exposure of the song "Smells Like Teen Spirit" on college radio in September created a spike in sales, shortly after the video debuted on MTV it began to create a buzz. By year's end, both the single and the album were global hits.

Nirvana's late 1991 European tour was sold out and heavily covered by the media. In January 1992 *Nevermind* bumped Michael Jackson's *Dangerous* album from the number one spot in the US chart and was topping charts in countries around the globe. Nirvana opted not to tour the United States citing exhaustion. They certainly didn't need to. *Nevermind* sold more than 30 million copies worldwide. The band performed at the 1992 MTV Video Music Awards where they also won Best Alternative Video and Best New Artist. The hits "Smells Like Teen Spirit" and "Come as You Are" epitomize the band's pop radio appeal and served to erode the meaning of the label "alternative" as they placed Nirvana squarely in the mainstream.

**Go to Chapter 13 playlist example "Smells Like Teen Spirit" Cobain/Grohl/Novoselic, 1991**

**Go to Chapter 13 playlist example "Come as You Are" Cobain, 1991**

Nirvana hired producer Steve Albini for work on their next album and entered the studio in February 1993. Albini had earned a reputation in the American alternative scene as a producer who understood the style and was not likely to over-apply studio polish. As it turned out, the album was finished in two weeks, although Cobain was again unhappy with the Albini's product. The deficiencies perceived by Cobain were corrected by producer Scott Litt and *In Utero* was released in September 1993. It quickly rose to number one on the Billboard album chart. The album is much less polished-sounding than *Nevermind* and reflects the bands grungier roots. Most critics praised the album as a triumph.

**Go to Chapter 13 playlist example "Heart-Shaped Box" Cobain, 1993**

**Go to Chapter 13 playlist example "Rape Me" Cobain, 1993**

While on tour in Europe in March 1994, Cobain suffered an overdose of prescription medication and alcohol in Rome and had to be hospitalized. The rest of the tour was cancelled and the band returned to Seattle. Cobain had also, by this time, become addicted to heroin. An intervention convinced him to enter rehab. Less than a week passed before Cobain snuck out of the facility and returned to his home. On April 8, 1994, Cobain was found dead in his home of a self-inflicted gunshot wound to the head.

Nirvana's short career and limited output did not limit their influence. Nirvana brought grunge, as well as nineties alternative rock to the mainstream and are considered to be one of the most important bands of the 1990s. Kurt Cobain has been called the "last real rock star." There are those who disagree with this, however, and say that—far from being the last real rock star—he is the first real *antirock star*. Compared to rock stars of previous generations—the Lennons and McCartneys, the Freddie Mercurys, the Bruce Springsteens, the James Hetfields—Kurt Cobain seems to be of another variety; that variety who deal in apathy rather than ambition, self-pity rather than self-growth, and believe that it really *is* "sexy and ridiculous to feel totally fucked and useless."

## Pearl Jam

Guitarists **Stone Gossard** (b. 1966) and **Mike McCready** (b. 1966), bassist **Jeff Ament** (b. 1963), vocalist **Eddie Vedder** (b. 1964), and drummer **Dave Krusen** (b. 1966) first formed as **Mookie Blaylock** in 1990 and began performing original material in the Seattle scene. After gaining the attention of Epic Records and signing a contract, they changed their name to **Pearl Jam**. The band entered the recording studio with producer Rick Parashar in March 1991 to record their first album,

*Ten*. The band's original name, Mookie Blaylock, is the name of a basketball player; his jersey number—10—was the inspiration for the album title. Krusen would leave the band before the album's release to seek treatment for drug addiction. He was briefly replaced by Matt Chamberlain and then by **Dave Abbruzzese** (b. 1968), who would complete the *Ten* album tour and remain with the band until 1994.

*Ten* was released in August 1991 and did not sell well at first. In the middle of 1992—in the wake of Nirvana—the album entered the top 10 and would remain in the Billboard charts for nearly five years. Critics called *Ten* a masterpiece and cited Vedder's vocal work as being from the gut and hypnotic. The music is intricate and, at times, dense and raucous, drawing as much from classic rock bands like Zeppelin as it did from its contemporaries. Vedder's lyrics deal with depression, suicide, alienation, and social concerns. The album's singles, "Alive," "Even Flow," and "Jeremy" all reached mainstream charts and their accompanying videos were awarded heavily at the 1993 MTV Video Music Awards. *Ten* would eventually sell more than 13 million copies in the United States alone. It remains Pearl Jam's best-selling album.

The song "Alive" is about a boy who finds out his father is really his stepfather and then is coerced into an incestuous relationship with his mother, by his mother. Her attraction to her son is sparked by a combination of her grief over the revelation and the boy's strong resemblance to his biological father.

**Go to Chapter 13 playlist example "Alive" Vedder/Gossard, 1991**

"Even Flow" is a song that offers a compassionate perspective on homelessness. An excerpt from the second verse:

> *Oh, feelin', understands the weather of the winters on its way*
>
> *Oh, ceilings, few and far between all the legal halls of shame, yeah*

**Go to Chapter 13 playlist example "Even Flow" Vedder/Gossard, 1991**

"Jeremy" is based on a true story of a high school boy who shot himself in front of his classmates. The video, though quite disturbing, was an enormous hit. It won four MTV awards in 1993.

**Go to Chapter 13 playlist example "Jeremy" Vedder/Ament, 1991**

Pearl Jam toured furiously in support of *Ten* and in 1992 had an appearance on *Saturday Night Live*, their own MTV *Unplugged* special and were part of the 1992 Lollapalooza tour.

Pearl Jam's second album, *Vs.*, was recorded in the spring of 1993 and released that October. The band hired producer Brendan O'Brien and aimed for a more aggressive sound. Most of the music was written from studio jam sessions in an attempt to capture the live band feel. The result is a looser, less polished product than *Ten* with more of the focus on power. The album features two acoustic ballads as well. One of these, "Daughter," a song dealing with child abuse, was a successful single. "W.M.A." deals with police racism and "Glorified G" is an attack on gun enthusiasts. *Vs.* sold nearly 1 million copies in the first week following its release.

**Go to Chapter 13 playlist example "Daughter" Vedder/Gossard, 1993**

**Go to Chapter 13 playlist example "W.M.A." Vedder/Abbruzzese/Ament, 1993**

**Go to Chapter 13 playlist example "Glorified G" Vedder/Gossard/McCready, 1993**

By this time, the trappings of fame had become troublesome for the band. As a result, they decided not to make any videos for the album and to cut back on commercial efforts—such as interviews, TV appearances, and press conferences—to promote it. Instead, the band focused its efforts on touring and connecting with fans. During the album tour, they imposed a cap on ticket prices to show appreciation for their concert-going fans.

During the tour, Pearl Jam discovered that corporate ticket giant Ticketmaster was adding service fees to the price of Pearl Jam tickets. After the tour, the band sued Ticketmaster for monopolizing the ticket industry. They also concurrently attempted to stage their own tours without Ticketmaster's involvement. These efforts failed and became part of their argument that the ticket giant had a stranglehold on the industry. The US Justice Department investigated Ticketmaster which resulted in Gossard and Ament being called to testify before Congress. The Justice Department eventually dropped its case but the band continued its boycott of Ticketmaster controlled venues on the tour for their following album. Pearl Jam's suit against Ticketmaster remained in litigation.

*Vitalogy* was released on vinyl in November 1994 and on CD the following month. Recording sessions were tense as the pressures of fame and the stress of the Ticketmaster suit had begun to take their toll. McCready entered rehab for cocaine and alcohol addiction during the album's postproduction. In many ways, Pearl Jam was imploding. Nonetheless, *Vitalogy* was praised by critics as "original" and "uncompromising." The album is perhaps the most stripped down of all of the early 1990s Pearl Jam recordings. In that way, it's much closer to a punk record. Still, there are moments of smoothness and musicality that have little to do with punk sensibility.

**Go to Chapter 13 playlist example "Spin the Black Circle" Vedder/Gossard, 1994**

**Go to Chapter 13 playlist example "Not for You" Vedder, 1994**

**Go to Chapter 13 playlist example "Immortality" Vedder, 1994**

Drummer Dave Abbruzzese was fired for personal reasons before the *Vitalogy* tour and was replaced by Jack Irons. The band toured successfully in Asia and Europe, although back in the United States, their continued boycott of Ticketmaster created many problems. Very few other bands showed any solidarity in joining them. Additionally, Vedder was experiencing health issues which caused the band to cancel a number of shows.

Pearl Jam experienced varying amounts of success through the rest of the decade. Their lawsuit against Ticketmaster would keep them more or less off of the road in the United States until 1998 when, having lost their case and returned to playing Ticketmaster-controlled venues, they finally were able to return to full-scale touring. Pearl Jam are considered one of the most influential bands of their generation. They have earned praise for their ideals and their personal and professional integrity as much as their music. They continue to record and tour and are involved in numerous social, humanitarian, and political causes both as a band and individually.

## Soundgarden

**Soundgarden** was formed in 1984 in Seattle by singer/guitarist **Chris Cornell** (b. 1964), guitarist **Kim Thayil** (b. 1960), and bassist **Hiro Yamamoto** (b. 1961). Drummer **Matt Cameron** (b. 1962) would join the band in 1986 and Yamamoto would be permanently replaced by **Ben Shepherd** (b. 1968) in 1990. Credited with helping to form the early grunge scene in Seattle along with Nirvana, Pearl Jam, and Alice in Chains (discussed below), Soundgarden would record two albums before finding major success in the wake of the Seattle grunge explosion of 1991 with their third studio album, *Badmotorfinger*.

Although many commentators consider *Badmotorfinger* to be a metal record, its sludgy, down-tuned sound, broad tempos, and odd time signatures make it difficult to classify. If time and place are factors, then it clearly belongs to the grunge genre. The lyric content hovers between metal and grunge as well. The singles "Jesus Christ Pose," "Rusty Cage," and "Outshined" enjoyed consider-able airplay on alternative radio stations while the videos for the latter two songs were heavily aired on MTV. The video for "Jesus Christ Pose" was removed from MTV in 1991 amid controversy over its images and lyrics being perceived as anti-Christian. Cornell stated that the lyrics to "Jesus Christ Pose" are a reference to celebrities who hold themselves up as being persecuted and martyred. The first verse:

> And you stare at me in your Jesus Christ pose
>
> Arms held out like you've been carrying a load
>
> And you swear to me you don't want to be my slave

**Go to Chapter 13 playlist example "Jesus Christ Pose" Cornell/Cameron/Shepherd/Thayil, 1991**

**Go to Chapter 13 playlist example "Rusty Cage" Cornell, 1991**

**Go to Chapter 13 playlist example "Outshined" Cornell, 1991**

To add to the confusion of exactly what Soundgarden was all about and where they really fit in musically, while promoting *Badmotorfinger*, they toured with hard rockers Guns 'N Roses and glam rock band Skid Row in North America before setting out on a headlining theater tour of Europe. They were also nominated for a Grammy in 1992 for Best Metal Performance.

By 1994, the sounds of grunge had become entrenched in the mainstream. When Soundgarden released their fourth album, *Superunknown*, it went straight to number one on the album chart. The album deals with themes of suicide, depression, and drug abuse. There is a considerable amount of musical experimentation on the album. Producer Michael Beinhorn encouraged the band to employ multiple layers of sound and he sought to expand their appreciation of other music. He made band members listen to a variety of other styles of music during the recording process. The result is a grungy, complex, punk-pop-psychedelic record that stands as a monument of the era. *Superunknown* has sold more than 9 million copies worldwide.

**Go to Chapter 13 playlist example "Black Hole Sun" Cornell, 1994**

**Go to Chapter 13 playlist example "Spoonman" Cornell, 1994**

**Go to Chapter 13 playlist example "My Wave" Cornell/Thayil, 1994**

Soundgarden released one more album in 1996 before breaking up. The album *Down on the Upside* was even more experimental than *Superunknown* and abandoned many of the heavy elements for which the band came to be known. Critics praised the album as a Zeppelin-esque exploration of crisp acoustic sounds; however, the album sold poorly. Touring with Metallica in 1996 as part of Lollapalooza, Soundgarden reached a boiling point internally and decided to disband following the tour. Matt Cameron would later say that they were "eaten up by the business." Soundgarden reunited in 2010 and has been active since. They are considered one of the originators of grunge in the 1990s and have been universally praised for their technical prowess, originality, and heartfelt music.

## Alice in Chains

Like Soundgarden, Seattle band **Alice in Chains** hovered around the gray area between metal and grunge in the early 1990s. Formed in 1987 by guitarist **Jerry Cantrell** (b. 1966) and singer **Layne Staley** (1967–2002), the early lineup included drummer **Sean Kinney** (b. 1966) and bassist **Mike Starr** (1966–2011). After hearing a demo tape of the band in 1989, executives at Columbia Records offered them a contract. A promotional EP was recorded in 1990 and the band's first single, "We Die Young" became a hit on metal radio stations.

**Go to Chapter 13 playlist example "We Die Young" Cantrell, 1990**

Columbia assigned producer Dave Jerden to work with Alice in Chains on their debut album. Jerden had worked as a mixing engineer with bands like The Rolling Stones, Frank Zappa, and Talking Heads in the 1980s. The album, *Facelift*, was released in the summer of 1990. It was not an immediate success but was hailed by critics as establishing a taste for grunge among heavy metal fans. When MTV began airing the video for "Man in the Box" in regular daytime rotation in 1991 amid the grunge craze, the album took off. "Man in the Box" is about censorship in the media and begins with a very catchy, wordless vocal melody that is doubled by a heavily-effected guitar.

**Go to Chapter 13 playlist example "Man in the Box" Staley/Cantrell, 1990**

Touring as opening support for the Clash of the Titans metal tour, which included Slayer, Anthrax, and Megadeth, Alice in Chains were rather poorly received. Apparently, many of the hardcore metal fans were not impressed by the slow, grungy stylings the band was offering. In spite of their lukewarm reception on the tour an EP called *Sap*, which was recorded between the tour and the follow-up album would sell over half a million copies, confirming the band's viability.

In 1992, Alice in Chains recorded and released their second studio album, *Dirt*. The recording is much darker than *Facelift* with almost half of its songs dealing with addiction, a subject with which the band were becoming intimately familiar. Critics raved over *Dirt*. It would go on to sell more than 4 million copies in the United States alone. The song "Would?" was written in response to the overdose death of Andrew Wood of the band Mother Love Bone and with whom Cantrell had been friends. The hit "Rooster" was written by Cantrell as a tribute to his father, who served in Vietnam. "Angry Chair," written by Layne Staley, is a philosophical reflection on the trappings of fame and the pain of addiction.

**Go to Chapter 13 playlist example "Would?" Cantrell, 1992**

**Go to Chapter 13 playlist example "Rooster" Cantrell, 1992**

**Go to Chapter 13 playlist example "Angry Chair" Staley, 1992**

A lengthy world tour followed the album with Alice in Chains opening for Ozzy on the North American leg and headlining in Europe. Bassist Mike Starr left the band part way through the tour to deal with substance issues and was replaced by **Mike Inez** (b. 1966). The band would also be featured as part of Lollapalooza in 1993. The tour would prove to be their last major outing with Layne Staley.

A highly successful EP called *Jar of Flies* followed in 1994. The recording is a low-key, mostly acoustic work which was written and recorded in one week. Following its release, Staley entered rehab to deal with his worsening heroin addiction. Upon his return, the band booked tour dates for 1994 with Metallica, as well as an appearance at Woodstock '94, but during rehearsals Staley relapsed and the band felt it best to cancel their tour dates. The song "I Stay Away" is representative of *Jar of Flies*.

**Go to Chapter 13 playlist example "I Stay Away" Cantrell/Inez, 1994**

The band's next album, *Alice in Chains*, came in late 1995 amid much press coverage of Staley's addiction. That the band did not tour for the album added fuel to the fires of speculation about his condition. Nevertheless, the recording showed a band in full possession of its expressive powers.

It would be told later just how painful the sessions were for Staley's bandmates; they watched helplessly as he was consumed by heroin. Cantrell sang lead vocals on three of the four album singles. Most of the album's themes deal with isolation, depression, and death.

**Go to Chapter 13 playlist example "Heaven Beside You" Cantrell/Inez, 1995**

**Go to Chapter 13 playlist example "Again" Cantrell/Staley, 1995**

In April, 1996, Alice in Chains appeared on MTV *Unplugged* and a live album of the concert was released. The band agreed to tour with Kiss for that band's 1996/1997 reunion outing but after only four shows, Staley was found unresponsive after overdosing on heroin. He was revived but the band were forced to back out of the tour and went on an extended hiatus. After a failed attempt to restart the band in 1998, Staley retreated from the company of his bandmates and family. He was found dead in his Seattle home on April 19, 2002, of an apparent heroin and cocaine overdose at the age of thirty-four.

Alice in Chains is considered to be a major influence on modern heavy metal. Their difficult-to-define but heavy sound has played a fundamental role in shaping artists like Opeth, Godsmack, Three Days Grace, Mudvayne, and Breaking Benjamin, among many others. Alice in Chains reformed in 2005 with vocalist William DuVall and continues to tour and record. Former bassist Mike Starr was found dead of a drug overdose in 2011 at his home in Utah.

Image 13.1: Layne Staley circa 1992

## Alternative Metal

With the rise of metal in the 1980s and Metallica's dominance in the early 1990s, the influence of metal was formidable as the decade progressed. Moreover, with alternative rock and grunge moving into the mainstream, and many grunge bands blurring the lines between grunge and metal, the idea of alternative music became increasingly ambiguous. This inevitably led to greater and greater sub-classifications of metal that was infused with "alternative" elements or vice versa. Critics, fans, and musicians were creating new terms like "stoner" metal, "industrial" metal, "gothic" metal, "noise" metal, "sludge" metal, and so on. To be sure, many of the distinctions were incremental at best and at times, had more to do with characterizing the audience or the culture rather than the music itself. There *were* very clearly identifiable stylistic fusions, like funk metal and rap metal as well.

For our purposes, we will place the following bands under the blanket distinction of "alternative" metal, maintaining two common characteristics as basic criteria: a strong connection to traditional metal and punk elements, and an approach toward experimentation. It should be noted that some of the bands we discuss here had their origins in the 1980s but came to prominence in the 1990s.

## Living Colour

Guitarist **Vernon Reid** (b. 1958) formed **Living Colour** in 1984. The band grew out of a New York music collective called the Black Rock Coalition, an organization Reid cofounded to attract black musicians interested in playing rock music. By 1988, the band consisted of Reid, Berklee-trained drummer **Will Calhoun** (b. 1964), vocalist **Corey Glover** (b. 1964). and bassist **Muzz Skillings** (b. 1965). Regular performances in and around New York City attracted the attention of Epic Records, who signed the band and put them in the studio with Ed Stasium and Mick Jagger coproducing. Their debut album, *Vivid*, was off to a slow start until MTV began airing the video for the single "Cult of Personality" in late 1988. By the end of the year the album had reached number six on the *Billboard* chart and sold more than 1 million copies. *Vivid* employs elements of funk, punk, and metal in fairly equal measure. It also features guest appearances by Mick Jagger, and Chuck D and Flavor Flav of the hardcore rap group, Public Enemy.

The song "Cult of Personality" is a critique of twentieth-century world politics and its domination of the masses through media and propaganda. The second verse:

*I sell the things you need to be*

*I'm the smiling face on your TV...*

*I exploit you, still you love me*

*I tell you one and one makes three*

**Go to Chapter 13 playlist example "Cult of Personality" Living Colour, 1988**

Living Colour's 1990 follow-up, *Time's Up*, was far more experimental, incorporating elements of jazz, blues, hip-hop, thrash metal, and art rock. The album featured an impressive lineup of guest appearances including Jagger, Little Richard, Queen Latifah, master saxophonist Maceo Parker, and voice-over by James Earl Jones. The album reached number thirteen and won a Grammy Award for Best Hard Rock Album. The songs "New Jack Theme," "Elvis Is Dead," and "Love Rears Its Ugly Head" illustrate the complex and experimental nature of the album.

**Go to Chapter 13 playlist example "New Jack Theme" Reid, 1990**

**Go to Chapter 13 playlist example "Elvis Is Dead" Reid, 1990**

**Go to Chapter 13 playlist example "Love Rears Its Ugly Head" Reid, 1990**

In 1993, Living Colour released *Stain*, a fairly aggressive and obscure album that was not as well received as their previous two. Internal issues with the band would lead to their dissolution in 1995 though they reunited in 2000 and continue to record and tour. The band had a brief but influential presence in the early 1990s and confirmed the popularity of experimental metal fusion. Vernon Reid is considered one of the primary forces in the development of funk-infused alternative metal.

## Faith No More

Following two independent label releases in 1985 and 1987 which met with limited success **Faith No More** found their stride after joining forces with vocalist **Mike Patton** (b. 1968) in 1989. By that time, the band included founding members, bassist **Billy Gould** (b. 1963), keyboardist **Roddy Bottum** (b. 1963), and drummer **Mike Bordin** (b. 1962), as well as guitarist **James Martin** (b. 1961).

Faith No More's third studio album, *The Real Thing*, was released in 1989 on the independent label Slash Records. Once again, MTV exposure proved a key ingredient to success. The video for the single "Epic" was aired heavily on the video channel and sent the song up the charts. Performances on the 1990 MTV Video Music Awards as well as *Saturday Night Live* bolstered the band's popularity, and combined with extensive touring, brought album sales in excess of 4 million copies.

"Epic" is a fusion of metal, funk, and rap elements with a nod to classical in the piano outro.

**Go to Chapter 13 playlist example "Epic" Gould/Bottum/Martin/Bordin, 1989**

Following their success in 1990, Faith No More followed up with *Angel Dust* in 1992. A complex, experimental recording which employs heavy sampling of a diverse array of existing pieces (everything from Simon and Garfunkel's "Cecelia" to Shostakovich's string quartet no. 8) alongside instrumental performances, the album had critics raving. It has been called a "startlingly original concoction" and "the most uncommercial follow-up to a hit record ever." In terms of popular reception, the album sold much better overseas than it did in the United States. Still, the album produced the US hit single "Midlife Crisis" and the prog-esque "Smaller and Smaller."

**Go to Chapter 13 playlist example "Midlife Crisis" Bottum/Bordin/Gould/Patton, 1992**

**Go to Chapter 13 playlist example "Smaller and Smaller" Patton/Gould/Bottum/Bordin, 1989**

Faith No More's subsequent albums became much less metal oriented and their popularity waned in the United States. The band broke up in 1998 only to reform in 2009. Faith No More served as inspiration for a diverse body of artists including Guns 'N Roses, Nirvana, Metallica, Limp Bizkit, and Korn. Many credit the band with inventing alternative rap rock/metal, though Red Hot Chili Peppers' singer Anthony Kiedis has accused Mike Patton of blatantly imitating his performance style and mannerisms.

## Ice-T and Body Count

That underground metal and rap shared many cultural similarities—both aggressively attacked the establishment, both spoke to social inequities, both derided economic oppression, both denounced political abuse of power including police brutality, and both were similarly attacked by critics—was not lost on emerging rap artists like **Ice-T** (b. 1958). Along with guitarist **Ernie C** (b. 1959), bassist **Lloyd "Mooseman" Roberts** (1973–2001), drummer **Victor "Beatmaster V" Wilson** (1959–1996), and guitarist **D-Roc the Executioner** (1959–2004), Ice-T formed the heavy metal band **Body Count** in 1990.

Ice-T debuted the new band during the 1991 Lollapalooza tour. Half of his set was devoted to Ice-T solo music and the other half to Body Count. Some of the rapper's less open-minded fans accused him of "selling out" for incorporating rock elements into his music. Ice-T responded to these accusations by including an interview excerpt in the introduction to the song "Body Count," which was included on Ice-T's 1991 album, *O.G. Original Gangster*. This was the first recording to feature Body Count as a band.

**Go to Chapter 13 playlist example "Body Count" Ice-T/Ernie C, 1991**

Body Count's self-titled debut was released in 1992 and quickly established Ice-T as an important crossover artist, though the album would soon create one of the most heated controversies in the history of rock, rap, and metal. The song "Cop Killer," included on the original release, was intended as an indictment of those police officers who abused their power by committing illegal acts of violence against civilians. Many took it as an attack on all police officers. Protests by police and other organizations rapidly spread across the country. Campaigns were launched against Body Count's record label, Warner Bros., to pull the album from record store shelves. Politicians and public figures spoke out against the record, including George H.W. Bush, who denounced Warner Bros., and actor/political conservative Charlton Heston, a stockholder in Warner, who demanded the company take action. There were as many angry citizens defending Body Count's right to free speech and understood that police brutality was and remains a serious issue, particularly in light of the Rodney King beating. Even the National Black Police Association supported Body Count saying that police brutality was the cause of an entrenched antipolice attitude, and recommended the formation of independent civilian review boards "to scrutinize the actions of our law enforcement officers."

In the end, Ice-T pulled the song from the album, not wanting to be seen as trying to cash in on the publicity, and desirous to refocus on the real issue of police brutality. Other issues addressed in the album included drug abuse, racism, and censorship. Unfortunately, the song "Cop Killer" is no longer available. Instead, we examine the song "There Goes the Neighborhood," which deals with racism and social stereotypes in rock and rap music.

**Go to Chapter 13 playlist example "There Goes the Neighborhood" Ice-T/Ernie C, 1992**

Ice-T and Body Count continued to stir things up and provide important social and political commentary throughout the 1990s. In spite of the deaths of several original members over the years, Ice-T and Ernie C have kept the band actively recording and touring to the present day, although no controversy like that which surrounded "Cop Killer" has since embroiled the band.

Image 13.2: Ice-T performs with Body Count in 2006

## Helmet

Finding success in 1990 with their debut album, *Strap It On*, New York alternative metal band Helmet stood out among their contemporaries. Their music possessed an eerie, hypnotic quality due to its repetitive, unrelenting rhythms and dense, drop-tuned textures. Moreover, Helmet spurned the long hair and wild clothing of metal bands of the era, opting for a "jeans and sneakers" look that was closer to what one might see at a college frat party than a rock concert. Founded by its only lifelong member and primary songwriter, guitarist/singer **Page Hamilton** (b. 1960), the band has gone through numerous lineup changes over the course of its career, which to date has produced seven studio albums, four of which were released in the 1990s. Helmet are widely recognized as a major influence on metal of the late 1990s and beyond 2000. A sample of their work from each album produced in the 1990s, *Strap It On* (1990), *Meantime* (1992), *Betty* (1994), and *Aftertaste* (1997) illustrates their approach:

> **Go to Chapter 13 playlist example "Repetition" Hamilton, 1990**

> **Go to Chapter 13 playlist example "In The Meantime" Hamilton, 1992**

> **Go to Chapter 13 playlist example "Milquetoast" Hamilton, 1994**

> **Go to Chapter 13 playlist example "Exactly What You Wanted" Hamilton, 1997**

## Rage Against the Machine

Guitarist **Tom Morello** (b. 1964), drummer **Brad Wilk** (b. 1968), vocalist **Zack de la Rocha** (b. 1970), and bassist **Tim Commerford** (b. 1968) formed **Rage Against the Machine** in Los Angeles in 1991 and have comprised the band's lineup since. Rage combines elements of metal, rap, funk, and thrash with caustic political and social commentary. They address serious issues such as corporatism, imperialism, government oppression, warmongering, institutional racism, and police brutality in nearly all of their music. They recorded their self-titled debut album in 1992 and produced two more albums, *Evil Empire* (1996) and *The Battle of Los Angeles* (1999) before decade's end. Samples of music and lyrics from each of their 1990s albums clearly demonstrate their volatile mix of music and politics:

"Killing in the Name:"

> *Those who died are justified, for wearing the badge, they're the chosen whites*

> *You justify those that died by wearing the badge, they're the chosen whites*

> **Go to Chapter 13 playlist example "Killing in the Name" Rage Against the Machine, 1992**

"Bulls on Parade:"

> *Weapons not food, not homes, not shoes*

*Not need, just feed the war cannibal animal*

**Go to Chapter 13 playlist example "Bulls on Parade" Rage Against the Machine, 1996**

"Testify:"

*Mister anchor assure me*

*That Baghdad is burning*

**Go to Chapter 13 playlist example "Testify" Rage Against the Machine, 1999**

## Korn

**Korn** was formed in Bakersfield, California in 1993 by guitarist **James "Munky" Shaffer** (b. 1970), bassist **Reginald "Fieldy" Arvizu** (b. 1969), drummer **David Silveria** (b. 1972), vocalist Jonathan Davis (b. 1971), and guitarist **Brian "Head" Welch** (b. 1970). The lineup would remain stable throughout the 1990s and produce four albums, all of which would be certified multiplatinum. Korn are considered the pioneers of so-called "nu" metal. Their music brings together heavy grooves, influences of 1970s hard rock, rap, 1990s alternative, funk, and avant garde–inspired dissonance. Their lyrics are deeply personal and tackle subjects such as bullying, child abuse, exploitation, depression, sexuality, and drug abuse. Korn has sold more than 35 million records, produced thirty-nine music videos, and won two Grammy Awards and two MTV Video Music Awards. A sample from each of their four albums released in the 1990s, *Korn* (1994), *Life Is Peachy* (1996), *Follow the Leader* (1998), and *Issues* (1999) show their early development:

**Go to Chapter 13 playlist example "Need To" Korn, 1994**

**Go to Chapter 13 playlist example "No Place to Hide" Korn, 1996**

**Go to Chapter 13 playlist example "Freak on a Leash" Korn, 1998**

**Go to Chapter 13 playlist example "Falling Away from Me" Korn, 1999**

## Sevendust

As a band that effectively represented the flavor of metal in the late 1990s, Atlanta, Georgia's **Sevendust** has been noted for their soulful vocals, quasi-progressive forms, raw melodies, innovative drumming, and powerful riffs. Formed in 1994 by drummer **Morgan Rose** (b. 1968), guitarist **John Connolly** (b. 1968), bassist **Vince Hornsby** (b. 1966), and later joined by vocalist **Lajon Witherspoon** (b. 1972), and guitarist **Clint Lowery** (b. 1971), the band released their self-titled debut album in 1997. Singles from the album included "Black," a song that deals with racism, and "Bitch," which deals with a relationship gone bad.

> **Go to Chapter 13 playlist example "Black" Sevendust, 1997**

> **Go to Chapter 13 playlist example "Bitch" Sevendust, 1997**

1999's *Home* confirmed the band's legitimacy as a world-class metal act for the new millennium. The singles "Denial," a song about drug abuse and "Waffle," a song about expressing one's individuality, clearly represent the state of alternative metal at the end of the twentieth century.

> **Go to Chapter 13 playlist example "Denial" Lowery/Rose, 1999**

> **Go to Chapter 13 playlist example "Waffle" Lowery/Rose/Witherspoon, 1999**

We now explore the diverse world of alternative rock in the 1990s.

## Suggested Chapter Related Activities

- Compare/contrast the music of Nirvana and Pearl Jam. Examine form, tempo, distortion, vocal style, rhythmic structure, lyric content, etc. Do a similar comparison of Soundgarden and Alice In Chains.

- What are the similarities between metal of the '80s and metal of the '90s? What are the differences?

- Find two post-2000 subgenres of "alternative" rock of your choosing, or by searching the internet. Pick several songs that exemplify each subgenre. Analyze the songs from subgenre each using the tools you've acquired in class. After comparing each, what similarities/differences do you find? Does the subgenre classification seem to have more to do with the actual music or the culture surrounding it?

## Suggested Discussion Topics

- Do you think "authenticity" in music/art can coexist with commercial success?

- What are your thoughts regarding the irony of the alternative movement of the '90s? How do you feel about the notion that Cobain was the first "anti-rock star?"

- What are your thoughts about "free" music on the Internet? Of all the music you "own," how much of it did you actually purchase?

## Image Credits

# CHAPTER 14
# Alternative Rock in the Nineties

*This isn't meant to last. This is for right now.*

-Trent Reznor

## An Alternative View on Alternative as Mainstream

As we have learned, the ethos of punk in the late 1970s was based in large part on the rejection of the mainstream pop rock values of the time. These mainstream values were rooted in commercialism, the grandiosity of arena rock, and the concept of the "rock star" as a wealthy, self-indulgent sort whose last vestiges of rebellion lay *in* self-indulgence. The perceived *musical* pomposity of art/prog rock was also seen an example of rock's self-indulgence. That punk rock would become commercially successful may not have occurred to many early punk musicians, although when it did, few turned their backs on that success. On the contrary, many embraced it as a possibility to make music for a *living* or simply as a means to spread their message. We have already noted the irony in punk's ascension.

Whereas punk rockers viewed reacting against the mainstream as pure *rebellion*, alternative musicians of the late 1980s and early 1990s based their form of rebellion on the philosophy that *commercial success* was somehow at odds with *artistic integrity*. Hence a different kind of existential dilemma arose when commercial success came. This raised serious questions of "authenticity" within the culture that weren't a part of the popularization of punk. The hypocrisy of the alternative movement also became apparent through musicians who indeed courted commercial success by signing major label contracts and making videos; yet in word eschewed commercialization. The awareness of this hypocrisy occasionally turned to internal antipathy: Kurt Cobain once called Eddie Vedder a "corporate sell-out."

Perhaps one way to understand this is that it reflected a certain ironic Gen X romanticism of feeling "totally fucked and useless." Another way of looking at it is that a *successful* rebellion of any sort is simply unsustainable. Once a rebellious movement takes over, it *becomes* the establishment (such as Napoleon declaring himself Emperor). As punk ignored the lessons of history, so too did the alternative movement.

As the decade wore on, alternative rock continued to blur with mainstream pop rock. By the late 1990s, even the purest elements of the music and culture of alternative rock had become fully sterilized and marketed by the major labels and their subsidiary labels. In fact, the marketing of alternative music on "independent" labels had really become an illusion by mid-decade. Most of the nonmajor labels were actually owned by the majors. Some had been bought up, others created outright by marketing experts in order to appeal to buyers who were attracted to "indie" bands. In regard to this questionable business practice, Joseph G. Schloss, Larry Starr, and Christopher Waterman write:

> The notion of a huge entertainment corporation cooking up a fake independent record label to satisfy an audience hungry for musical expressions of authenticity and rebellion may seem a bizarre contradiction at first glance. From an historical perspective, however, we can see this institutional development as the culmination of a decades-old trend within the music business. In the days before rock 'n' roll, genres such as blues, rhythm & blues, country music and ethnic music were predominantly the bailiwick of small independently owned and operated record labels. By the nineties, however, the major record companies had fully internalized the hard lesson of rock 'n' roll and had come to view independent labels as the functional equivalent of baseball farm teams: small, specialized, close-to-the-ground operations perfectly suited to sniff out the next big thing. In an era when most so-called independent labels were distributed, promoted and even owned outright by huge entertainment corporations, it became difficult to sustain a purely economic definition of alternative music as music that doesn't make money. To put it another way, the fact that a band's music, song lyrics, appearance, and ideological stance are anti-commercial doesn't mean they can't sell millions of records and thereby help to generate huge corporate profits.[1] (pp. 312–313)

So even though the term "alternative," as it applies to the music and musicians in this chapter, would go from being fairly ambiguous to being rendered totally meaningless, we have a look at some of the important and influential artists whose music was *understood* as alternative rock in the 1990s:

---

1   Joseph G. Schloss, Larry Starr, and Christopher Waterman, Rock: Music, Culture, and Business, pp. 312-313. Copyright © 2012 by Oxford University Press. Reprinted with permission.

## Jane's Addiction

**Jane's Addiction** officially formed in 1985 with singer/keyboardist **Perry Farrell** (b. 1959), bassist **Eric Avery** (b. 1965), and drummer **Stephen Perkins** (b. 1967), and would include guitarist **Dave Navarro** (b. 1967) by 1986 to form the most significant early lineup of the band. By late 1986, Jane's Addiction had become one of the hottest bands in the Los Angeles club scene and were courting offers from several different record labels. Opting for Warner Bros., the band recorded and released a self-titled live album as its major-label debut in January 1987. The idea of a live album was based on the band's desire to capture the raw energy of their live show without excessive studio garnish, though many of the tracks would be re-recorded later on studio albums. The band staged several club tours in Europe and the United States in support of the record and began building a worldwide cult following.

**Go to Chapter 14 playlist example "Trip Away" Jane's Addiction, 1987**

In 1988, Jane's Addiction released their first studio album, *Nothing's Shocking*. The album's first single, "Mountain Song," received almost no airplay and the video was banned from MTV for containing a scene with frontal nudity which Farrell refused to omit. As a result, sales were modest in the first year following its release. The single "Jane Says" reached number six on the Alternative chart but as no video was released, exposure was limited. Even as the band was recording *Nothing's Shocking*, internal pressures were causing serious friction. Navarro and Avery were becoming increasingly dependent on alcohol and heroin. There were also arguments over royalty percentages which had to be mediated by label executives to prevent a breakup. Nevertheless, the band toured successfully in support of the album, sharing stages with Iggy Pop and the Ramones and continued to grow their following.

**Go to Chapter 14 playlist example "Mountain Song" Jane's Addiction, 1988**

**Go to Chapter 14 playlist example "Jane Says" Jane's Addiction, 1988**

Jane's Addiction made a substantial contribution to early 1990s alternative rock with their 1990 album, *Ritual de lo habitual*. It would be their final album before their initial breakup in 1991. The music has been praised for its originality and cited as a major influence on countless alternative rock and metal bands that would emerge in the 1990s and beyond. *Ritual de lo habitual* is not a concept album but it is divided into two parts: tracks 1–5 are unrelated rock songs and tracks 6–9 are reflective pieces in which Farrell pays tribute to a friend who died of a heroin overdose in 1987, as well as his own mother's suicide that occurred when he was a child. Among the songs on the first half of the album are the hits "Stop!" and "Been Caught Stealing." The video for the latter was a major hit on MTV.

**Go to Chapter 14 playlist example "Stop!" Jane's Addiction, 1990**

**Go to Chapter 14 playlist example "Been Caught Stealing" Jane's Addiction, 1990**

"Three Days" is a reflective epic which deals with death and redemption.

**Go to Chapter 14 playlist example "Three Days" Jane's Addiction, 1990**

Jane's Addiction disbanded in 1991. During the recording of *Ritual de lo habitual*, the band realized that they were imploding. Navarro's heroin use had progressed to such a point that he claims to have very little memory of recording the album. Farrell organized the Lollapalooza festival as a farewell tour for Jane's Addiction. The festival would become one of the biggest annual tours of the decade and include an astonishingly diverse range of musicians, though it would be criticized by many for its eventual overcommercialization. It ran from 1991–1997 and from 2003 to the present day and has grown into an international event. Jane's Addiction reformed in 1997 and continues to record and tour.

## Green Day

The popularity of the band **Green Day** speaks to the enduring impact of punk rock elements in the mid-1990s and beyond. The band was formed in 1986 by singer/guitarist **Billie Joe Armstrong** (b. 1972) and bassist **Mike Dirnt** (b. 1972) near Berkeley, California. Drummer **Tré Cool** (b. 1972) was recruited in 1990. Following several modestly successful independent label releases and international tours, Green Day signed with Reprise Records and entered the studio with producer Rob Cavallo to record what would be their commercial breakthrough album, *Dookie* (1994).

Videos from the album's singles, as well as performances on the 1994 Lollapalooza tour and Woodstock '94, which was seen by millions on pay-per-view TV, propelled the band to superstardom. *Dookie* won a Grammy in 1995 for Best Alternative Album. The music is rooted in punk, though with a modern nineties polish and production that would be credited with igniting an alternative style known as **pop punk**. Lyric themes reflect an updated nineties relationship to punk values, addressing subjects such as pot smoking, anxiety, sexuality, masturbation, self-loathing, and apathy. The song "Basket Case" deals with several of these subjects. It was the album's biggest hit single; and the video, shot in an abandoned mental institution, was enormously popular on MTV. It was nominated for nine Video Music Awards, though it did not win any. *Dookie* has sold more than 20 million copies worldwide.

**Go to Chapter 14 playlist example "Basket Case" Green Day, 1994**

"Welcome to Paradise" is emblematic of 1990s pop-punk.

**Go to Chapter 14 playlist example "Welcome to Paradise" Green Day, 1994**

1995 saw the release of *Insomniac*, a somewhat darker, less melodic album which some critics viewed as a reaction by the band to the success of *Dookie*. Other critics denounced the album, pointing out that the band had failed to achieve any substantial artistic growth aside from a "palpable degeneration in their sense of humor." Although the album was not as successful as its predecessor, it still sold more than 3 million copies worldwide and peaked at number two on the US album chart. The singles "Geek Stink Breath" and "Jaded" are fairly representative of the album as a whole; simple, short structures with punk energy and pop polish.

**Go to Chapter 14 playlist example "Geek Stink Breath" Green Day, 1995**

**Go to Chapter 14 playlist example "Jaded" Green Day, 1995**

Image 14.1: Green Day in 2013

Following a brief hiatus, the band returned in 1997 with the album *Nimrod*. Perhaps in reaction to the criticism of *Insomniac*, *Nimrod* presented a more experimental approach that included elements of folk rock, surf rock, and an acoustic ballad called "Good Riddance (Time of Your Life)." The song became an enormous hit for Green Day and was featured as accompanying music in several major network TV shows including the series finale of the 1990s hit sitcom *Seinfeld*.

**Go to Chapter 14 playlist example "Good Riddance (Time of Your Life)" Green Day, 1997**

The song "Last Ride In" is a surf rock–flavored instrumental:

**Go to Chapter 14 playlist example "Last Ride In" Green Day, 1997**

Green Day has experienced massive success in the new millennium and continue to record and tour. Their impact and influence, in spite of much criticism from punk insiders, has significantly shaped post-nineties alternative rock and modern pop punk.

## The Smashing Pumpkins

Formed in 1988 in Chicago, the lineup of **The Smashing Pumpkins** through most of the 1990s consisted of guitarist/singer **Billy Corgan** (b. 1967), drummer **Jimmy Chamberlin** (b. 1964), guitarist **James Iha** (b. 1968), and bassist **D'arcy Wretzky** (b. 1968). The band gained recognition in the Chicago alternative music scene in 1989 and 1990 through live performance and the release of several singles. In 1990, they signed with Caroline Records, a subsidiary of major label Virgin Records, and entered the studio with producer Butch Vig to record their debut album.

*Gish* was released in 1991. Tensions in the band would arise early as principal songwriter Corgan and Vig felt it best for Corgan himself to record most of the guitar and bass parts in order to achieve their vision for the record, which was fairly grandiose in comparison with their alternative rock contemporaries. The thick, heavily overdubbed production style that would become a hallmark for the band as the decade progressed was more of a throwback to 1970s arena bands like Queen and Journey. In terms of musical style, structure, and lyric content, the album fit in quite well with the music of its time. It featured many of the characteristic, moody dynamic changes ranging between hard rocking and delicate moments as well as the personal, introspective lyrics associated with alternative rock in the early 1990s. *Gish* was modestly successful, although many critics noted the potential of The Smashing Pumpkins calling them the next Jane's Addiction. The song "Rhinoceros" lends insight to the album's character and production:

**Go to Chapter 14 playlist example "Rhinoceros" Corgan, 1991**

Touring for *Gish* placed more of a strain on the band as Chamberlin began drinking heavily and using narcotics, Corgan entered a state of deep depression, and Iha and Wretzky—who had been romantically involved—went through a breakup. Members would state in later interviews that it was miraculous that the band stayed together.

Apparently realizing The Smashing Pumpkins' commercial potential in the wake of the grunge and alternative explosion of 1991, Virgin Records officially rostered the band and put them back in the recording studio with Vig and a much larger budget. The resulting album, *Siamese Dream*, was recorded over a four month period in late 1992 and early 1993. As with *Gish*, Vig and Corgan saw fit to have Corgan record nearly all of the guitar and bass parts, deepening resentment within the group. Chamberlin's drug and alcohol use escalated as well. That the album was an enormous success—debuting at number ten in the album charts, being almost universally praised by critics, and eventually exceeding sales of 4 million copies—did little to ease pressures within the band. Corgan's depression worsened. He would later state that he had begun "planning his suicide." In spite of all of the internal difficulties in its making, the album is frequently held up as one of the best recordings of the decade. The singles "Disarm" and "Today" received massive amounts of airplay on radio and their accompanying videos were heavily rotated on MTV. The band toured extensively and were part of Lollapalooza '94.

**Go to Chapter 14 playlist example "Disarm" Corgan, 1993**

**Go to Chapter 14 playlist example "Today" Corgan, 1993**

Like many of their contemporaries in the alternative scene, The Smashing Pumpkins were accused of "selling out;" and—in keeping with the character of the times—much of the criticism came from other successful alternative musicians and industry professionals. Corgan addressed this kind of infighting in the song "Cherub Rock." Its first verse:

*Freak out and give in*

*Doesn't matter what you believe in*

*Stay cool and be somebody's fool this year*

*'Cause they know*

*Who is righteous, what is bold so I'm told*

**Go to Chapter 14 playlist example "Cherub Rock" Corgan, 1993**

Corgan entered a phase of intense creativity between 1994 and 1995, writing more than fifty songs. He had conceived the band's most ambitious project to date, what he described as "*The Wall* for Generation X." Opting to change producers so as to reduce the possibility of becoming stagnant, The Smashing Pumpkins hired Alan Moulder and Mark "Flood" Ellis to work on the project. Their vision became more about capturing the live band and, as a result, the recording process was much more inclusive to Iha and Wretzky; it included much more of their input on arrangements and structure. The resulting album, *Mellon Collie and the Infinite Sadness*, is a sprawling collection of twenty-eight related songs connected to the emotion of sorrow. The album produced five hit singles (which all crossed over to the top 40 charts), topped charts all over the world, and sold more than 10 million copies.

The instrumentation is slightly more varied on *Mellon Collie* and includes keyboards, strings, and orchestral arrangements.

**Go to Chapter 14 playlist example "Tonight, Tonight" Corgan, 1995**

"Bullet with Butterfly Wings" won a Grammy in 1997 for Best Hard Rock Performance.

**Go to Chapter 14 playlist example "Bullet with Butterfly Wings" Corgan, 1995**

The rest of the decade marked dramatic changes in the band's sound as they shifted to a more electronic-based approach as well as a decline in their popularity as the musical landscape shifted away from alternative rock as the mainstream. Nevertheless, The Smashing Pumpkins are considered to be among the most representative and influential alternative rock bands of the decade. Their music videos, introduced in the dying days of MTV as a primarily music video station, have been hailed as some of the most artistically poignant videos ever made. The band continues to record and tour.

Image 14.2: Billy Corgan circa 2011

Nine Inch Nails

**Nine Inch Nails** is the brainchild of **Trent Reznor** (b. 1965). A talented multi-instrumentalist, vocalist, songwriter, producer, and engineer, Reznor began his musical life as a child, learning several instruments before graduating from his rural Pennsylvania high school. An early job in a recording studio as an assistant allowed Reznor access to the facilities during off-hours. He began making demos of his original music and looking for musicians with whom to form a band and share his artistic vision. Having no luck in his search, he decided to finish the demos by performing all of the parts himself—with the exception of the drums, for which he used a drum machine. The resulting recording landed Reznor a contract with the indie label, TVT Records.

Nine Inch Nails's first studio album, *Pretty Hate Machine*, came in late 1989, coproduced with Reznor by Mark "Flood" Ellis and Adrian Sherwood. The album features the angst-ridden, self-exploratory lyric style of alternative rock, wrapped in catchy, mechanically precise riffs and easy-to-grasp verse/chorus forms. Reznor hired musicians to perform the songs live, although the live renditions were usually more aggressive than the studio versions. The album's singles and promotional videos received a fairly heavy amount of airplay and, along with touring, brought the band a considerable following. Nine Inch Nails was part of Lollapalooza '91 and *Pretty Hate Machine* would go on to sell more than 3 million copies in the United States alone.

**Go to Chapter 14 playlist example "Head Like a Hole" Reznor, 1989**

Disputes with TVT would lead Nine Inch Nails to sign with Interscope Records, a subsidiary of Geffen and Universal Music Group. An EP called *Broken* followed in 1992. This recording features a much heavier sound inspired in Reznor by the aggressive energy of his touring group and by his apparent distaste in being labeled as synthpop after *Pretty Hate Machine*. Lyrically, the album deals variously in themes of self-destruction, anger, and control, as well as social critique with songs like "Happiness in Slavery," an attack on government and corporate oppression. A video was produced that depicts a naked man strapped to a machine that first brings him to ecstasy, then tortures him and finally kills him. It was banned by MTV. The outro of the song:

*I don't know what I am I don't know where I've been*

*Human junk just words and so much skin*

*Stick my hands through the cage of this endless routine*

*Just some flesh caught in this big broken machine*

**Go to Chapter 14 playlist example "Happiness in Slavery" Reznor, 1992**

Image 14.3: Trent Reznor performing on the Self Destruct tour circa 1994

Nine Inch Nails' greatest commercial success—and arguably their greatest artistic achievement of the decade—would come in 1994 with the album *The Downward Spiral*. It is a concept album that follows its protagonist through a twisted series of events into his own madness and suicide. The lyrics are richly laden with metaphor, allowing for various interpretations; although they overtly deal with themes of religion, violence, drugs, disease, and death. Musically, the album breaks from traditional forms and employs elements of metal, techno, rock, and electronica. *The Downward Spiral*'s unique sound spawned many imitators. Live shows for the album's Self Destruct tour were steeped in theatrics. There were moments of semi-feigned violence played out by band members that often resulted in actual injuries. The album is widely regarded as one of the most important recordings of the decade.

>  Go to Chapter 14 playlist example "March of the Pigs" Reznor, 1994

>  Go to Chapter 14 playlist example "Closer" Reznor, 1994

>  Go to Chapter 14 playlist example "Hurt" Reznor, 1994

Nine Inch Nails would not release another album until late 1999. The much anticipated album did not perform as well as its predecessor, although it still displayed Reznor's visionary approach to music, rock, and recorded sound. Trent Reznor has exerted a massive influence on modern music, be it rock, alternative, or electronica. His lyrics have tackled issues ranging from greed to fame to lust to addiction and more. As the only official member of Nine Inch Nails, he has toured and collaborated with many significant artists and has garnered glowing praise from a multigenerational group of musicians and critics. In 1997 he appeared on *Time* magazine's list of the year's most influential people. Nine Inch Nails have released eight studio albums to date, won two Grammy Awards, and have sold more than 20 million records worldwide.

## The Alternative Movement and Third Wave Feminism

As the so-called Second Wave Feminist Movement—which began in the 1960s with organized social efforts such as the National Organization for Women (NOW), the National Black Feminist Organization (NBFO), and legislative efforts such as the proposed Equal Rights Amendment— evolved, music and popular culture, most notably beginning in the 1970s, expanded its boundaries to give voice to the cause of gender equality. As we have seen, popular musicians like Carole King, Helen Reddy, Roberta Flack, Joni Mitchell, and others wrote music and lyrics that became anthems of feminine empowerment and helped shift the entrenched patriarchal values of the music and entertainment industries toward a more equitable standard. In the 1980s, musicians like Madonna, Whitney Houston, Cyndi Lauper, Tina Turner, Janet Jackson, and many others gave women a powerful presence in mainstream pop rock music.

In the late 1980s and early 1990s, perceived failures of Second Wave Feminism, such as the lack of focus on women of color and the notion of "post-feminism"—the implication that gender equality had been fully achieved—helped to ignite the so-called Third Wave of feminism. Likewise, the many successes of the Second Wave—such as policies for women in the workplace, equal access to education, funding for women's studies programs, access to contraception, and so forth—fueled Third Wave Feminism.

In music, the expression of women's concerns was evident, in part, in factions like **Riot grrrl**, an underground feminist punk rock movement with origins in and deep connections to the Seattle alternative music scene, as well as visible mainstream events like **Rock for Choice**, a series of benefit concerts supporting the pro-choice movement; and **Lilith Fair**, a highly successful charity concert tour which began in 1997 and featured all-female acts.

Many female alternative musicians associated with Third Wave Feminism were involved in a revival of the singer-songwriter styles of the 1970s and, in some cases, a rekindling of blues and/or folk elements. Like grunge and alternative metal and rock, much of the music of these female alternative rock musicians found its way into the mainstream. Nevertheless, the perception of these musicians representing alternative styles was retained through much of the 1990s.

## Tracy Chapman

With a career that began in the late 1980s, singer/songwriter/guitarist **Tracy Chapman** (b. 1964) represents a reawakening of acoustic-based blues and folk rock as it appeared in the context of 1990s alternative music. Chapman began her career as a busker and coffeehouse musician while she was a college student in Cambridge, Massachusetts. The father of a schoolmate who operated a music publishing company took an interest in Chapman and helped her to secure a recording contract with Elektra Records in 1988. Her self-titled debut album included her first hit single, "Fast Car," which gained massive attention following Chapman's performance of the song at the televised Nelson Mandela 70th Birthday Tribute concert. Touring and radio airplay of the song resulted in its peaking at number six on the *Billboard* Hot 100 chart. The song deals with social inequity through vivid storytelling.

**Go to Chapter 14 playlist example "Fast Car" Chapman, 1988**

Chapman's follow-up album, *Crossroads*, was also commercially successful and offered more of her folk rock stylings. Her third album, 1992's *Matters of the Heart*, marked a shift that placed Chapman comparatively in the realm of alternative rock, though it would prove to be the least commercially successful of her early efforts. Songs like "Woman's Work" made Chapman a champion among Third Wave Feminists. Chapman's characteristic concern with social issues was evident in songs like "Dreaming on a World" and "So."

Image 14.4: Tracy Chapman performs at the Human Rights Now concert in 1988

**Go to Chapter 14 playlist example "Woman's Work" Chapman, 1992**

**Go to Chapter 14 playlist example "Dreaming on a World" Chapman, 1992**

**Go to Chapter 14 playlist example "So" Chapman, 1992**

Tracy Chapman's 1995 album, *New Beginning*, saw a sharp upturn in her commercial presence and garnered Chapman a Grammy Award for Best Rock Song in 1997 for "Give Me One Reason," a deeply bluesy song with a powerful feminine perspective on love. *New Beginning* went on to sell nearly 4 million copies.

**Go to Chapter 14 playlist example "Give Me One Reason" Chapman, 1995**

The song "The Rape of the World" is a thoughtful ballad about environmental catastrophe brought on by humankind in the name of industrialism and war. The second verse:

*You've seen her stripped mined*

*You've heard of bombs exploded underground*

*You know the sun shines*

*Hotter than ever before*

**Go to Chapter 14 playlist example "The Rape of the World" Chapman, 1995**

Tracy Chapman is widely known for her socially and politically charged lyrics. Beyond her lyrics, she is noted for her participation as a performer in major charitable concert events and her work with underprivileged minorities, AIDS charities, and other humanitarian causes.

## Alanis Morissette

Canadian-born singer/songwriter **Alanis Morissette** (b. 1974) began her music career as a budding Canadian pop star with her first album scoring major hits in Canada and prompting the Canadian music press to compare her to American pop stars like Debbie Gibson and Tiffany. Her second album was less successful as she began a shift toward a more ballad-driven, introspective style. When her two-record contract with MCA Canada expired, Morissette moved from Canada to Los Angeles where she signed a new deal with Maverick Records and met producer/songwriter Glen Ballard (b. 1953), with whom she cowrote her next album, *Jagged Little Pill*.

Released in 1995, *Jagged Little Pill* became a surprise success when its lead single "You Oughta Know" began appearing on KROQ-FM, a popular Los Angeles modern rock radio station. The song was heavily requested and attracted a great deal of attention for its bitter, explicit lyrics and alternative rock character. The song's video soon began to gain a great deal of attention on MTV as well.

**Go to Chapter 14 playlist example "You Oughta Know" Morissette/Ballard, 1995**

Other singles from the album soon became hits. The post-grunge sound of Ballard's music and the angry but empowering feminine stance of Morissette's lyrics received widespread critical acclaim. Some compared the album to Carole King's 1970s masterpiece, *Tapestry*, while others hailed Morissette's quirky delivery of universally relatable emotions. The album won five Grammy Awards, topped charts worldwide, and went on to sell more than 33 million copies.

**Go to Chapter 14 playlist example "Hand in My Pocket" Morissette/Ballard, 1995**

**Go to Chapter 14 playlist example "Ironic" Morissette/Ballard, 1995**

**Go to Chapter 14 playlist example "All I Really Want" Morissette/Ballard, 1995**

Alanis Morissette has released eight studio albums to date and has become a pop culture icon. Her recordings have been enormously successful, although she has yet to match the astounding success of *Jagged Little Pill*.

## Natalie Merchant

Natalie Merchant (b. 1963) began her musical career as the singer for the 1980s alternative rock band, 10,000 Maniacs. She left the band in 1993 to pursue a solo career. Her self-produced debut album, *Tigerlily*, was released in 1995 and spawned three hit singles, "Carnival," "Wonder," and "Jealousy." Merchant toured heavily to promote the album which would eventually sell more than 5 million copies. Her presence on alternative and college radio was extensive.

**Go to Chapter 14 playlist example "Carnival" Merchant, 1995**

**Go to Chapter 14 playlist example "Wonder" Merchant, 1995**

**Go to Chapter 14 playlist example "Jealousy" Merchant, 1995**

Merchant's 1998 follow-up album, *Ophelia*, was a particular favorite among Third Wave Feminists. The title track describes a historical progression of women throughout history who have dared to question the values of a patriarchal society and have, at times, paid dearly for doing so. Merchant performed as part of Lilith Fair in its debut season and several of *Ophelia*'s videos were heavily rotated on MTV's sister station, VH1. Musically, the album marked an expansion from the sparse, alternative rock textures of *Tigerlily* to include more richly orchestrated moments and featured a complement of more than thirty guest musicians. *Ophelia* would go on to sell more than 1 million copies in its first year alone.

**Go to Chapter 14 playlist example "Ophelia" Merchant, 1998**

**Go to Chapter 14 playlist example "Kind & Generous" Merchant, 1998**

## Tori Amos

A *bona fide* child prodigy, pianist/singer/songwriter **Tori Amos's** (b. 1963) musical career began at the age of five when she was the youngest person ever to be accepted to the prestigious Peabody Institute in Baltimore. By age eleven, she was expelled for "musical insubordination." Young, talented, and rebellious, she made her breakthrough into the world of alternative rock in 1992 with her debut solo album, *Little Earthquakes*. The album is a soul-baring account of her personal struggles and explores an assortment of powerful and disturbing subjects ranging from guilt to rape and sexual alienation.

**Go to Chapter 14 playlist example "Me and a Gun" Amos, 1992**

**Go to Chapter 14 playlist example "Winter" Amos, 1992**

**Go to Chapter 14 playlist example "Crucify" Amos, 1992**

The album that would deeply endear Amos to Third Wave Feminists was her third studio recording, 1996's *Boys for Pele*. The album explores women's roles in patriarchal religion and in personal relationships through obscurely poetic language, and with a decidedly feminist perspective. Amos described the album as "chronicling a woman's self-discovery in a male-dominated world." The song "Talula" conceptualizes the ideal woman and her fear of losing herself in a relationship. The first verse:

*Ran into the henchman who severed Anne Boleyn*

*He did it right quickly a merciful man*

*She said that one plus one is two*

*But Henry said that it was three so it was, here I am*

**Go to Chapter 14 playlist example "Talula" Amos, 1996**

**Go to Chapter 14 playlist example "Professional Widow" Amos, 1996**

**Go to Chapter 14 playlist example "Caught a Lite Sneeze" Amos, 1996**

As a survivor of sexual assault, Tori Amos has been a longtime supporter, spokesperson, and fundraiser for the Rape, Abuse & Incest National Network (RAINN), a help line established in 1994 to connect rape and other sexual assault victims with help in their area.

Image 14.6: Tori Amos in concert in 2005

## Britpop

As a subgenre of pop and alternative rock that grew in the United Kingdom in the mid-1990s and spread to the United States in the latter half of the decade, **Britpop** presented another kind of alternative musical and cultural movement. Originally born as a reaction to American grunge and alternative rock, Britpop developed its own references to British music and culture by forming musical connections between British rock, glam, psychedelia, and punk of the past, and lyrics that addressed the immediate concerns of 1990s British working-class youth culture. Far from another British Invasion, several Britpop bands had a noteworthy presence in the late 1990s alternative music scene in the United States. Among the most significant of these were Oasis and Radiohead.

### Oasis

**Oasis** was formed in 1991 in Manchester, England, by singer **Liam Gallagher** (b. 1972), guitarists **Noel Gallagher** (b. 1967) and **Paul Arthurs** (b. 1965), bassist **Paul McGuigan** (b. 1971), and drummer **Tony McCarroll** (b. 1971). Their debut album, *Definitely Maybe* came in 1994 on the independent label Creation Records. Having prereleased three of the album's singles, which had each become hits, the album would set a record for the fastest-selling debut in UK history at the time of its release. Additionally, the album reached number fifty-eight on the *Billboard* album chart and sold more than 1 million copies in the United States in its first year. The album's lyric tone was warmly noted by critics for its marked departure from the bleak, fatalistic lyric style of American grunge and alternative bands. The album has been credited with sparking a renewed interest in British guitar bands in the mid-1990s.

> Go to Chapter 14 playlist example "Supersonic" Noel Gallagher, 1994
>
> Go to Chapter 14 playlist example "Shakermaker" Noel Gallagher, 1994
>
> Go to Chapter 14 playlist example "Live Forever" Noel Gallagher, 1994

1995 saw the release of *(What's the Story) Morning Glory?* and a new drummer, **Alan White** (b. 1972) replacing Tony McCarroll. A marked stylistic shift from straightforward guitar rock to one that placed a heavy emphasis on greater variety in instrumentation, ballads, and big, catchy choruses launched Oasis to global superstar status. Critics initially panned the album for being too derivative of existing classic British and American rock as well as its more pop-oriented sound, though it has since come to be seen as a seminal work of the era, demonstrating the universal appeal that transformed the band from a well-known indie act to an international rock sensation.

> Go to Chapter 14 playlist example "Don't Look Back in Anger" Noel Gallagher, 1995
>
> Go to Chapter 14 playlist example "Wonderwall" Noel Gallagher, 1995
>
> Go to Chapter 14 playlist example "Cast No Shadow" Noel Gallagher, 1995

Oasis reached their greatest heights of popularity around 1996. Their 1997 studio effort, *Be Here Now*, sold quickly in the first weeks but sales soon tapered off as many came to see the album as an overblown, uninspired work. The band themselves, as well as their producer, Owen Morris, blame the album's apparent lack of inspiration on too much drug use, infighting between the Gallagher brothers, and a general sense of complacency. The band continues to record and tour and has undergone numerous lineup changes. Although Oasis would never match their mid–late 1990s success, they have nonetheless served as a major source of inspiration for many modern rock acts including Coldplay, Arctic Monkeys, Maroon 5, and Ryan Adams.

## Radiohead

Called out as "Nirvana-Lite" by critics and with slow sales following the release of their February 1993 debut album, *Pablo Honey*, the British band **Radiohead** seemed to be going nowhere. Singer/guitarist **Thom Yorke** (b. 1968), guitarist/keyboardist **Jonny Greenwood** (b. 1971), bassist **Colin Greenwood** (b. 1969), guitarist **Ed O'Brien** (b. 1968), and drummer **Phil Selway** (b. 1967) would soon find success through the unlikely source of Israeli radio. The album single "Creep" became a hit in Tel Aviv and the band was invited to play there. Shortly after, the song was picked up by radio stations on the west coast of the United States. Ensuing rotation of the song's video on MTV prompted further interest in the band as they embarked on a North American tour in June 1993. By the end of the year, Radiohead had played more than 150 concerts around the world and album sales were brisk. In spite of its poor early reviews, *Pablo Honey* has since come to be seen as one of the best albums of the decade as well as one of the strongest debut rock albums of all time.

> **Go to Chapter 14 playlist example "Creep" Radiohead/Albert Hammond/Mike Hazelwood, 1993**
>
> **Go to Chapter 14 playlist example "Anyone Can Play Guitar" Radiohead, 1993**
>
> **Go to Chapter 14 playlist example "Stop Whispering" Radiohead, 1993**

Seeking to avoid the pitfalls of pop fame and being pigeonholed by the press, Radiohead aimed for a harder edge and greater sonic depth than they had achieved with their debut. An experimental yet successful EP and several short tours would fill the interim until the spring of 1995 when they released their second studio album, *The Bends*. Musically, the album marks a strong shift towards thicker textures, richer harmonies and a deeply classic British rock sound. Lyrically, themes began to move away from earlier personal subjects to a more socially oriented style, a trend toward which the band would continue. Critics consistently hold *The Bends* up as one of the greatest albums of all time. The British publication the *Observer* named it as one of their 50

Albums That Changed Music and *Virgin Media* ranked it number two on their list of the Top 1000 Albums of All Time.

**Go to Chapter 14 playlist example "High and Dry" Radiohead, 1995**

**Go to Chapter 14 playlist example "Fake Plastic Trees" Radiohead, 1995**

**Go to Chapter 14 playlist example "Just" Radiohead, 1995**

Radiohead's art/prog rock tour de force of the 1990s would come in 1997 with *OK Computer*. The band experimented with ambient electronic sounds, avant garde elements, and nonstandard formal structures to create a work many would compare to *The Dark Side of the Moon* and other 1970s art rock masterpieces. Yorke himself admitted his amazement that people actually understood the record's musical content. Lyrically, Yorke said he was trying to express the rapid pace of life in the 1990s and drew some of his inspiration from the writings of Noam Chomsky. *OK Computer* earned Radiohead a Grammy Award for Best Alternative Album. The singles "Paranoid Android," "Karma Police," and "Climbing Up the Walls" offer a reasonable cross-section of the album's material.

**Go to Chapter 14 playlist example "Paranoid Android" Radiohead, 1997**

**Go to Chapter 14 playlist example "Karma Police" Radiohead, 1997**

**Go to Chapter 14 playlist example "Climbing Up the Walls" Radiohead, 1997**

Image 14.7: Radiohead at Coachella 2004

Radiohead would make a dramatic stylistic shift once again with their 2000 album, *Kid A*, to a more instrumentally diverse, electronic-based sound and a relatively minimalist approach to texture.

Their post-2000 impact has been significant in many ways, as have their creative online marketing techniques (in one instance they allowed record buyers to name their own price). They have had a substantial influence on electronic music of the twenty-first century and have released new music as recently as 2012.

## Rock at the End of the 1990s

Artists, critics, fans, and commentators have declared the death of rock at several junctures since its earliest beginnings. Rock was certainly not "dead" at the end of the 1990s but it most assuredly was no longer "King of the Hill." Deena Weinstein notes that:

> Rock was not dying at all, but it was being displaced as the new century began. Rock became peripheral to its mediators, its fans and even its artists. Rock itself, the music that was the result of the sets of exchanges between those three social actors, was pushed out of the center of mainstream culture. Other musical styles, from rap and country to R&B and teen pop, took center stage. (p. 269)

A variety of factors were at work as the new millennium dawned. The primacy of MTV as a central source for new rock had long passed; numerous, sometimes meaningless sub-classifications had fragmented rock into a thousand smaller pieces; cultural values had changed; and digital technology and the Internet profoundly altered the way people encountered and purchased (or didn't purchase) music. In the conclusion, we will briefly discuss rock's presence after 2000 and explore the question of rock's lasting musical and cultural validity.

### Suggested Chapter Related Activities

- Listen for and define the polycultural/polystylistic elements of pop-punk. What is gained or lost in the fusion?
- What are your general observations of '90s alternative rock?

### Suggested Discussion Topics

- Both Second and Third Wave Feminism had their unofficial musical spokespeople. Who represents this in modern feminism? How does the culture and expression of feminist ideals relate to popular music and how does it compare/contrast with Second and Third Wave?
- Compare/contrast the meaning of the term "alternative" as it is understood today with its understood meaning in the 1990s.
- It has been said that we are in the era of "Post-Irony." Discuss what this means and its implications to rock specifically and popular music in general.

- Each generation is viewed historically, in part, by its popular culture. How do you feel that your generation will be defined in that regard? Have you ever actually considered what forces shape popular culture and your individual role in that process?

- If you were stranded in the desert with only a canteen full of water, it would be quite precious and you would treasure every drop. On the other hand, if you had a tanker truck full of water, it would not be so cherished and closely guarded. If we use the analogy of music to water and the Internet to the tanker truck, could we speculate that the ubiquity and ease of accessibility of music in the digital age diminishes its value? In other words, instant, nearly total access to any song you want to hear at any time was not always a reality. Does this encourage us to take music for granted?

- Looking back to your initial response at the beginning of the semester on how you felt about David Byrne's and Gene Simmons' claims that rock is dead, compare your viewpoint now after having taken the course.

## Image Credits

# Conclusion: Rock Music and Culture in the Twenty-First Century

As I stated in the opening paragraph of this book, rock music is deeply and indelibly cemented in our cultural consciousness. Rock music continues to excite a multigenerational fan base and classic bands of the era still have the power to fill stadiums, headline major festivals, and form the basis for radio and internet programming. As your understanding of the revolutionary history of rock has increased throughout the course of the semester, you have gained a sense of the variety of musical and cultural factors that have built our enduring relationship with rock music. That said, the height of musical innovation in rock is long past and it seems as likely that much, if not all of the culturally revolutionary energy that rock generated is spent—or at least dormant. It's a simple fact that the music which was once was viewed as dangerous and hedonistic is now used to help sell things like pet food and pickup trucks, to segue between the segments of a morning news broadcast, as filler music in films, and many other painfully banal things. Likewise, that rock has become a fairly normalized field of research and study in universities is also a sign of its popular decline; leading popular styles have historically never been taken seriously in academia. This is not to say that there are not great *new* rock bands, it's simply that what these bands are doing no longer holds the same consequence—musically or culturally—as it once did. There are a multitude of factors contributing to this, some of them relatively simple, like changing tastes and trends; and others are vastly more complex, such as digital technology and Internet commerce, two forces that have defined the course of popular music and culture thus far in the twenty-first century. Another significant and highly nuanced element is the cultural climate, the general set of cultural values held by youth in the digital age; Millennial youth culture embraces a different worldview than did the Baby Boomers or the Gen Xers. It is not my intention here to thoroughly analyze these factors, but I will offer some parting bullet-point observations as food for thought and potentially for wider classroom discussions.

## Digital Technology and Internet Commerce

- The cultural revolution of the late twentieth century held music as a central feature. The revolution of the twenty-first century—at least so far—has been centered on digital technology. Music is no longer central but is bumped along in the wake of the larger digital movement. Put another way, the symbiotic relationship that once existed between music and technology has become lopsided in favor of technology. Two decades of mainstream digital technology have had a massive impact on music in *every* imaginable way. Its creation, dissemination, consumption, shelf life, promotion, and performance have not simply been altered in the twenty-first century, but essentially remade.

- Even from the days of multitrack recording and other improved studio techniques, making records has always involved a bit of "smoke and mirrors." We know that as early as the mid-1960s, artists like The Beach Boys and The Beatles were using the studio as a tool in the creative process and as a means of "enhancing reality." Still, music had to be *performed* in the studio *by musicians*. The studio technology of our time allows for such advanced manipulation of sound that the focus of the recording process today is on what can be digitally *assembled*, regardless of what a musician can actually perform with an instrument or the voice. This is not a value judgment; it is simply the industry standard. Popular music is often described as having a "cut and paste" or "plastic" quality to it. Much of it is quite literally assembled with cut-and-paste technology, perfectly aligned to rhythmic grids and cleaned up with digital tools like auto-tune.

- On one hand, the Internet has opened many windows of opportunity for artists to expose their music in places they could have never otherwise reached. On the other hand, "free" music on the Internet, arguably the worst thing that has ever happened to the music business, has created an entire generation of people who possess no ethical compass to guide their understanding of the meaning and value of intellectual/artistic property. In other words, "sneaking under the fence" is no longer understood as a wrongful act; we live in an era where outright theft of digital music is perfectly acceptable behavior. A number of my students have never paid for any of the music they carry around with them; and worse, most don't seem to understand that this will inevitably choke off their supply.

- In countless interactions with students, I have heard them voice their dissatisfaction with what they see as a vapid, insignificant popular music culture; the future legacy of their generation is not unfolding in the way many would wish. The missing piece of the puzzle here is *active participation* in music culture. In a capitalistic society, this equates to *financial* participation. In other words, if one is not spending money on music, one has no say in defining what is popular or what will endure. Another driver in modern popular music is the sense of disposability with new material. Rapid and voluminous access to music seems to have created a "flavor-of-the-minute" mentality. The creation of future classics is derailed by the almost addictive need for constant "freshness" and variety, real or imagined.

- The promotion of new popular music in the twenty-first century bears many similarities to the pre-British Invasion early 1960s, when teen idols were manufactured by the corporate entertainment industry in hopes of scoring a big hit. Wildly popular shows like *American Idol* and *The Voice* are clear evidence of this. These performances place the emphasis squarely on the individual rather than an ensemble. Some have described this approach as little more than a "glorified karaoke" performance. Many live concerts, too, have lowered the bar for the actual performance of music; laptops and light shows often supplant live bands, particularly in styles like electronic dance music (EDM), but often in popular hip-hop and other contemporary dance styles as well. Granted, live DJs have been entertaining people since the disco era, but DJs performing in arenas or at major festivals is a relatively new phenomenon.

## Modern Cultural Values

What might be termed "neo-modernism," the rekindling of an abiding faith in science and technology to provide all of the answers to the world's problems, seems to be the dominant mindset of our time and of youth culture most particularly. As ever, obsequious, unquestioning faith in social forces and the powers that be can lead to absurdity and contradiction.

- Seemingly innocuous technological devices, particularly smartphones, which are designed to improve our lives, have become potential threats both socially and physically. These devices have played a substantial role in shaping a more self-absorbed and increasingly distracted, sometimes deeply troubled culture. It is a common sight in restaurants, malls, and other public places to see groups of people "hanging out" together, yet each utterly absorbed in his or her own device. Many find this kind of self-inflicted isolation somewhat disturbing. Moreover, distracted driving and other behaviors centered on technological devices create dangerous and even deadly situations. It is ironic that Steve Jobs, a noted practitioner of Zen meditation, an activity calculated to bring one deeply into the present moment, has helped to create technology that removes people so far from their own "now" that they might run over a bicyclist while driving and texting or walk off of a cliff while taking a selfie.

- Cultural conformity is also greatly influenced by modern technology. Youth culture is drawn to what is "trending" on the Internet and many young people are completely preoccupied with their online personae to the point of personal detriment. In addition to this, online bullying has become a serious issue in recent times. Stories abound of teenagers taking their own lives as a response to being bullied and harassed on social media. Perhaps the modern "rebel" is the one who puts down the phone and disavows herself of the pressures and entanglements of her Internet persona, opting for a *neo-postmodernist* view.

- Modern youth culture worships fame, beauty, wealth, and power in a way that far outstrips even the most excessive attitudes of the 1980s; these things have become ends unto themselves. Mass media, particularly reality TV, has created the bizarre phenomenon of "fame for its own sake." A glaring example of this is the Kardashian family. For these obnoxiously ubiquitous figures, *attention* is the currency of success; not attention for actually *doing anything*, mind you, just simply attention.

- In stark contrast to this blatant "look at me" mentality is the brand of prudish conservatism witnessed in the criticism of stars like Miley Cyrus. Her 2013 MTV Video Music Awards performance with Robin Thicke drew heavy fire for its lewdness, and Cyrus has been vilified for her open use and glorification of marijuana. By comparison, her behavior—on and offstage—holds little shock value next to some of the things that 1980s stars like Madonna pulled off, and the endorsement of pot is laughable by comparison to the overt drug use and excessive behavior of countless rock era artists. As one who grew up in the 1970s and 1980s I am forced to wonder what all the fuss is about.

- People who are now of college age, sadly, have been reared on a mix of ultraconservative (neocon) politics through eight long years of the Bush/Cheney administration and the many failed promises of the Obama administration. The average student has also been conditioned and desensitized to constant war, violence, rampant government corruption, social control, surveillance/police presence, and runaway corporate capitalism through a nonstop barrage of images, videos, news stories, and vitriolic commentary. Ironically, in the same era that the United States has had its first black president, racism and bigotry have reared their ugly heads in a way not witnessed since before the rock era began.

- In recent times, there have been only two visible movements toward major social change, the Occupy Movement, which was swiftly crushed by an excessively violent police response, and the Black Lives Matter movement, which is still unfolding at the time of this writing. If history does indeed repeat itself, it would seem we are in ripe times for a cultural/social revolution. We may soon witness—or even personally participate in—massive counterculture movements akin to the 1960s. Whether or not this is possible, and whether music will play any role, remains to be seen.

# Bibliography and Reading List

AllMusic. "Prog-Rock." Last modified 2016. http://www.allmusic.com/subgenre/prog-rock-ma0000002798.

Assante, Ernesto. *Rock: The Artists, Instruments, Myths and History of 50 Years of Youth Music*. Vercelli, Italy: White Star, 2007.

Brown, Charles T. *The Art of Rock and Roll*. Englewood Cliffs, NJ: Simon & Schuster, 1992.

Brown, Peter, and Steven Gaines. *The Love You Make: An Insider's Story of The Beatles*. New York: New American Library, 2002.

Burgess, Richard James. *The Art of Music Production: The Theory and Practice*. New York: Oxford University Press, 2013.

Campbell, Michael, and James Brody. *Rock and Roll: An Introduction*. Belmont, CA: Schirmer/Cengage Learning, 2008.

Christe, Ian. *Sound of the Beast: The Complete Headbanging History of Heavy Metal*. New York: HarperCollins, 2004.

Contributors. "Album-Oriented Rock." *wow*. n.d. http://www.wow.com/wiki/Album-oriented_rock.

Covach, John, and Andrew Flory. *What's That Sound: An Introduction to Rock and Its History*. New York: Norton, 2012.

Crawford, Ruth, and Larry Hamberlin. *America's Music*. New York: Norton, 2013.

Crowe, Jerry. "'Pet Sounds Sessions:' Body of Influence Put in a Box," *Los Angeles Times*, November 1, 1997.

Eddy, Chuck, ed., *Rock and Roll Always Forgets: A Quarter Century of Music Criticism*. Durham, NC: Duke University Press, 2011.

Everett, Walter. *The Beatles as Musicians: The Quarry Men Through "Rubber Soul"* (New York: Oxford University Press, 1999.)

————. *The Beatles as Musicians: "Revolver" Through the "Anthology"* (New York: Oxford University Press, 1999.)

Everett, Walter, ed., *Expression in Pop-Rock Music: Critical and Analytical Essays*. New York: Routledge, 2008.

Friedlander, Paul. *Rock and Roll: A Social History*. Boulder, CO: Westview Press, 1996.

Gould, Jonathan. *Can't Buy Me Love: The Beatles, Britain and America*. New York: Random House, 2008.

Graham, Dan. *Rock/Music Writings*. New York: Primary Information, 2009.

Hale, Grace Elizabeth. *A Nation of Outsiders: How the White Middle Class Fell in Love with Rebellion in Postwar America*. New York: Oxford University Press, 2011.

Hertsgaard, Mark. *A Day in the Life: The Music and Artistry of the Beatles*. New York: Delacorte Press, 1995.

Hibbard, Don J., and Carol Kaleialoha. *The Role of Rock*. Englewood Cliffs, NJ: Prentice Hall International, 1983.

Kim, Ben. "Raw Material: Lost Youth, a Tourist in Teenage Wasteland." *New City*, November 11, 1993, 13.

MacDonald, Ian. *Revolution in the Head: The Beatles' Records and the Sixties*. 2nd ed. London: Pimlico/Random House, 2005.

Martin, George, and Jeremy Hornsby. *All You Need Is Ears: The Inside Personal Story of the Genius Who Created the Beatles*. New York: Macmillan, 1994.

Moore, Allan F. *Rock: The Primary Text*. Burlington, VT: Ashgate, 2001.

Orman, John. *The Politics of Rock Music*. Chicago: Nelson-Hall, 1984.

Pattie, David. *Rock Music in Performance*. New York: Palgrave Macmillan, 2007.

Peddie, Ian, ed., *The Resisting Muse: Popular Music and Social Protest*. Burlington, VT: Ashgate, 2006.

Rock and Roll Hall of Fame. "Chuck Berry Biography." n.d. https://rockhall.com/inductees/chuck-berry/bio.

————. "Fats Domino Biography." n.d. https://rockhall.com/inductees/fats-domino/bio.

Schloss, Joseph G., Larry Starr, and Christopher Waterman. *Rock: Music, Culture and Business*. New York: Oxford University Press, 2012.

Sheff, David. "The 'Playboy' Interviews with John Lennon and Yoko Ono." *Playboy*, 1981, 129.

Sklar, Rick. *Rocking America: An Insider's Story*. New York: St. Martin's Press, 1984.

Starr, Larry, and Christopher Waterman. *American Popular Music*. New York: Oxford University Press, 2010.

Stephenson, Ken. *What to Listen for in Rock: A Stylistic Analysis*. New Haven, CT: Yale University Press, 2002.

Waksman, Steve. *This Ain't the Summer of Love: Conflict and Crossover in Heavy Metal and Punk*. Berkeley: University of California Press, 2009.

Wallach, Jeremy, Harris M. Berger, and Paul D. Greene, eds., *Metal Rules the Globe: Heavy Metal Music Around the World*. Durham, NC: Duke University Press, 2011.

Walser, Robert. *Running with the Devil: Power, Gender and Madness in Heavy Metal Music*. Hanover, NH: University Press of New England, 1993.

Weinstein, Deena. *Rock'n America: A Social and Cultural History*. Toronto: University of Toronto Press, 2015.

CPSIA information can be obtained
at www.ICGtesting.com
Printed in the USA
LVHW061828170822
726115LV00003B/18

2 370009 415807